# BUDDHIST ART
IN
# SOUTH-EAST ASIA
## The Indian Influence on the Art of Thailand

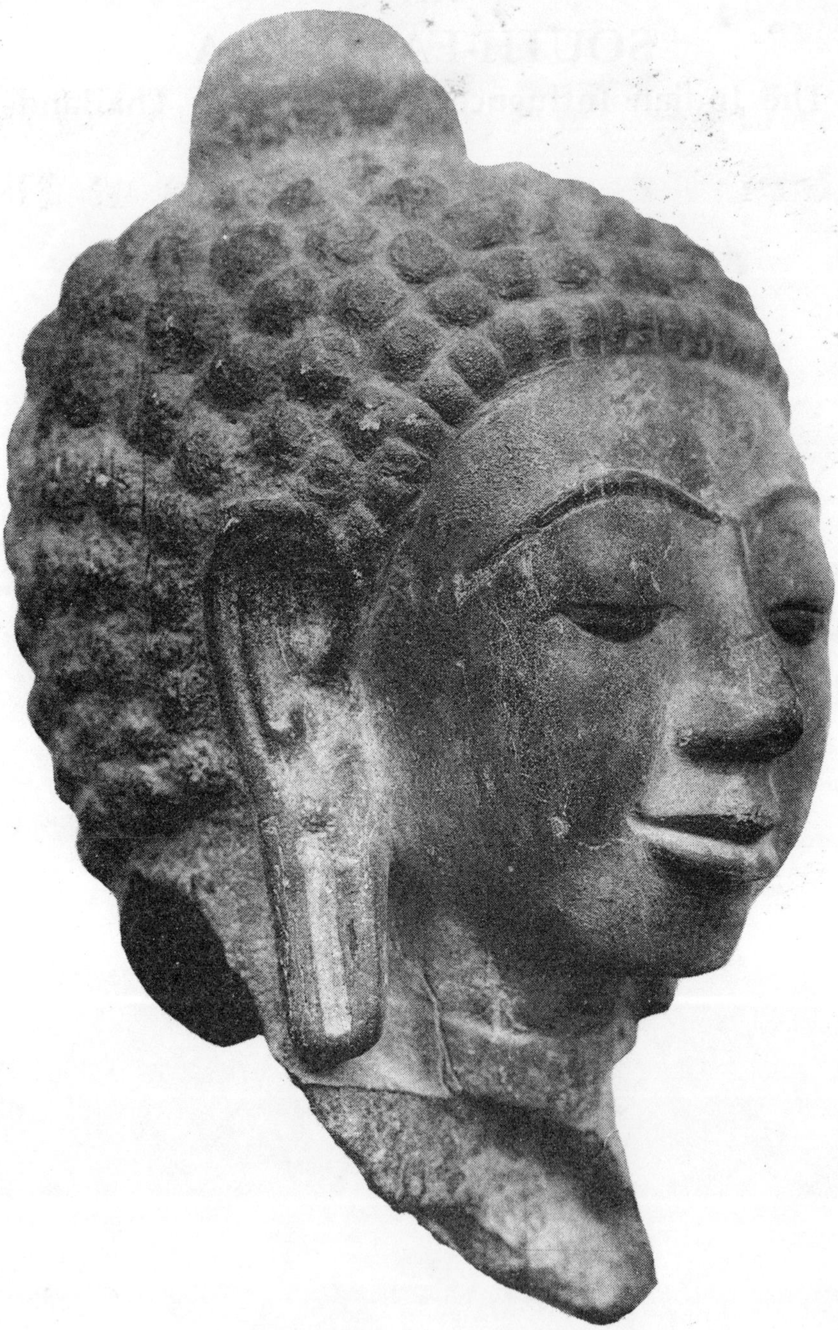

Limestone Head of Buddha, from Lopburi.
Môn-Gupta type. *Author's Collection.*

# BUDDHIST ART
# IN
# SOUTH-EAST ASIA
## The Indian Influence on the Art of Thailand

By

REGINALD LE MAY

ARYAN BOOKS INTERNATIONAL
NEW DELHI

BUDDHIST ART IN SOUTH-EAST ASIA
The Indian Influence on the Art of Thailand

ISBN 81-7305-260-3

First published in 1938
under the title
*A Concise History of Buddhist Art in Siam*



Reprinted in **2004** by :
**ARYAN BOOKS INTERNATIONAL**
Pooja Apts., 4B, Ansari Road, Darya Ganj, New Delhi-2
Tel.: 23287589, 23255799; Fax: 91-11-23270385; E-mail : aryanbooks@vsnl.com

Printed in India at Print Perfect, New Delhi

# FOREWORD

There are few of those who are interested in the cultural history of the Middle and Far East who will not give a warm welcome to this latest book of Dr le May, which furnishes us for the first time with a connected and comprehensive account of the art of Siam, and has many sidelights also to throw on the intimately connected arts of India, Burma, Cambodia and other neighbouring countries. The subjects of Siamese art and Siamese history have received attention from not a few distinguished writers, and to these Dr le May tenders full acknowledgement, those to whom he is specially indebted being the French savants, Pelliot, de Lajonquière, Parmentier, Claeys and, above all, Cœdès, of whose brilliant labours it would be difficult to speak in overstrained praise. But with all the valuable help afforded by these scholars in connexion with different phases of the subject, the task before Dr le May has been unusually complex and difficult: for, on the one hand, most of the history of Siam is still so wrapped in obscurity that it is impossible to trace with any degree of accuracy the racial and dynastic changes which have left their impress on the national culture; on the other, the art of Siam was for so long dependent for its inspiration on outside countries, that it seldom exhibits a markedly original and distinctive character of its own, and its historian, therefore, has more often than not to seek for the solution of his problems elsewhere than in Siam itself.

This dependence on foreign, and particularly on Indian, teaching is, of course, useful to the historian, in that it provides him with a variety of chronological data which would otherwise be lacking; but when, as in Siam, the various streams of foreign influence overlap one another or operate concurrently in different parts of the country, the difficulty of tracing out their several courses seems at times well nigh insuperable. That out of all this complexity Dr le May has succeeded in putting together a reasoned and convincing account of Siamese art over a period of some 1500 years is an achievement for which everyone labouring in the field of Indian and Indonesian studies will be sincerely grateful; and their gratitude to him will be all the greater because of the eminently sane and temperate language in which he expresses himself. The cause of Indian art, as is well known, has suffered much from the hysterical outpourings of some of its critics, and it is a relief, therefore, to find in Dr le May a writer of restrained and well-balanced judgment, who, like Dr Coomaraswamy (whom he quotes with just approval), can express his admiration for a work of art without going into ecstasies over its supposed cosmic or transcendental qualities.

In a pioneer work such as this, particularly in one covering so large a field, there must necessarily be many points inviting controversy; indeed, there are several relating to Indian art and architecture on which I myself hope elsewhere to offer some remarks; and doubtless there are others connected with Burmese, Cambodian and Javanese archaeology which may provoke discussion among specialists in those fields. As time goes on, too, we may be sure that exploration among the ruined cities and temples of Siam, which has hardly yet begun, will throw new light on many problems of her history and art. But whatever fresh discoveries the future may bring forth, and however much the story of Siamese art may be elaborated, we can rest assured that the foundations of that story have been well and truly laid by Dr le May, and that no material disturbance of them is ever likely to be needed.

May I add that, though I have devoted a lifetime to the study of Indian art, the reading of this book has helped me to realize more than ever its amazingly vital and flexible character. Whatever may be thought of the relative merits of Greek and Indian art—a subject on which the author has something to say in the first chapter of this book—it must be admitted that they had this much, at least, in common: that they could adapt themselves to suit the needs of every country, race and religion with which they came into contact. To know Indian art in India alone, is to know but half its story. To apprehend it to the full, we must follow it, in the wake of Buddhism, to Central Asia, China and Japan; we must watch it assuming new forms and breaking into new beauties as it spreads over Tibet and Burma and Siam; we must gaze in awe at the unexampled grandeur of its creations in Cambodia and Java. In each of these countries Indian art encounters a different racial genius, a different local environment, and under their modifying influence it takes on a different garb. Therefore the art of each and every one of these countries is complementary to the rest and a knowledge of each, such as this book provides, is indispensable to our understanding of the whole.

JOHN MARSHALL

# PREFACE

THE aim of the present volume is to give a connected history of the different forms of Buddhist Art which have flourished in Siam from the early years of the Christian era up to the end of the sixteenth century.

The only works known to me which have hitherto been published dealing specifically with this subject are two: the first in English entitled *Sculpture in Siam* by Herr Alfred Salmony, formerly Director of the Far Eastern Museum at Cologne, and the second in French entitled *Les Collections Archéologiques du Musée National de Bangkok* by Professor Georges Cœdès, formerly Secretary-General of the Royal Institute of Siam and now Director of the Ecole Française d'Extrême-Orient at Hanoi, French Indo-China. The first of these works, *Sculpture in Siam*, appeared in 1925, and, although no doubt praiseworthy as a first brief attempt to shed some light on a little known subject, has unfortunately, owing to an insufficiency of data, confused the problems at issue, which are exceedingly complex; on the other hand, Professor Cœdès' volume on the Siamese National Museum, although only a monograph, has been of inestimable value in indicating the lines most profitable for research, and I owe him a debt of gratitude which I have acknowledged with pleasure in the work itself.

Now, I am no "jargonneur" and those who look in this work for the jargon of many modern writers on art will be disappointed. But I am profoundly interested in all forms of art, and I set myself the task of trying to explain this one phase of Eastern art in simple language, because, after twenty-five years' residence in the East, I believe that no one, whether Western or Eastern, can have any true knowledge of the basis of Art itself until he has absorbed the underlying concepts of Eastern art. This is perhaps "a hard saying", but I am convinced that it is true, and the urge to write this work has been reinforced, since my return to Europe in 1933, by the widespread ignorance of, and indifference to, Eastern art which I have found among many of the established artists in England to-day.

Fortunately, there are signs of an awakening among the younger generation of artists to the importance of studying Eastern art forms, without attempting to imitate them slavishly, and this has encouraged me to persevere in a task which might otherwise have appeared hopeless.

As the origins of all the forms of Buddhist Art found in Siam are to be sought in India (and Ceylon), it is essential to obtain a thorough knowledge of Indian Buddhist art as a groundwork for study, and I have thought it best, therefore, to divide my bibliography of works consulted, which runs to some hundred and seventy-five in number, into two main categories, namely (*a*) GENERAL, in which are listed all those works dealing with Indian and Sinhalese art which I consider suitable for study, and (*b*) SPECIAL, which contains those works actually bearing directly on art forms found in Siam. Where any doubt has arisen as to the category in which a volume should be included, I have placed it in the second. To these two lists a third has been added, giving the names of the principal Journals dealing with Far Eastern Art. Naturally I do not claim that the bibliography is complete, but I hope that no serious omission has been made from the second, or Special, list given.

The text of this volume is accompanied by 80 plates, containing 208 photographs, selected to illustrate the different phases through which the art forms in Siam have passed, and containing examples from India, Ceylon, Burma and Cambodia for purposes of comparison.

Two maps are also attached, the first designed to show the relations and sea-routes between India and the Indo-Chinese Peninsula, and the second showing Siam and the adjoining countries. Every place mentioned in this work is included in one or other of these two maps.

The question of the transliteration of Siamese words and names has been for many years, and still is, a controversial one, and until a suitable system has been evolved and universally accepted, I have thought it best to use as phonetic a system as possible. For the transliteration of Chinese names I have used the Wade system, and I am greatly indebted to Professor Ellis H. Minns, Litt.D., F.S.A., Disney Professor of Archaeology in the University of Cambridge, not only for his invaluable help in this regard but also for much useful criticism of the body of the work.

My thanks are also due to the Master and Fellows of Pembroke College, Cambridge, for receiving me as a member of their ancient and renowned college, and for making my stay in Cambridge such a happy one.

I should also like to express my warm thanks to Mr E. J. Thomas, Under-Librarian of the University Library at Cambridge, and the chief authority on Buddhism in England, for allowing me access at all times to his vast stores of knowledge of Indian life and thought. Both he, and Dr Perceval Yetts, O.B.E., Professor of Chinese Art at the Courtauld Institute, London, to whom I am also much indebted, have examined the whole work thoroughly and made a number of valuable criticisms and suggestions. I must also not omit to mention Prof. G. H. Luce of Rangoon University both for the interest he has shown in this work and for the help he has given me concerning ancient Burmese history.

The illustrations contained in this volume have been drawn from a variety of sources, and I wish to offer my grateful thanks to the following authorities,

Societies, Journals, and individual owners for their courtesy in granting me permission to publish them:

The Siam Society, Bangkok: Figs. 1, 2, 3, 6, 68, 69, 70, 167, 168, 196, 197.

The Royal Institute, Bangkok: Figs. 4, 13, 14, 17, 18, 21, 22, 25, 27, 31 (A) and (B), 32, 34, 39, 40, 43, 44, 45, 48, 49, 50, 51, 52, 53, 64, 65, 85, 92, 112, 115, 117, 118, 129, 130, 131, 144, 145.

The Director of the École Française d'Extrême-Orient, Hanoi: Figs. 5, 59, 60, 61, 62, 66, 108, 152, 160.

The Trustees of the British Museum: Figs. 15, 16, 110, 121, 124.

The Director of the Pnompenh Museum, Cambodia: Figs. 19, 20, 46, 47, 80, 88.

Major Erik Seidenfaden: Figs. 23 (A) and (B), 36, 37, 38, 102, 159, 161, 162, 194, 195.

*The Burlington Magazine*: Figs. 125, 149, 155, 188.

The India Society (*Indian Art and Letters*): Figs. 29, 30, 114, 147, 157, 171, 183.

*The Burlington Magazine* and the India Society (combined): Figs. 24, 77, 81, 175, 200.

Dr H. G. Quaritch Wales: Figs. 41, 42.

Mr H. Foster Pegg: Figs. 96, 98, 135, 136, 138.

Rev. Kenneth E. Wells: Figs. 101, 103, 104, 105.

Mr E. W. Hutchinson: Figs. 106, 107, 119, 123, 126, 153.

The Secretary of State for India: Figs. 111, 116, 120.

Mr Gunnar Seidenfaden: Figs. 127, 128, 154.

Mr S. Paranavitana (Colombo Museum): Figs. 132, 133, 134.

Dr A. K. Coomaraswamy: Figs. 139, 140.

Mr K. de B. Codrington: Fig. 63.

Messrs R. Lenz and Co., Bangkok: Figs. 71, 72, 73.

The Director of the Victoria and Albert Museum, South Kensington: Figs. 84, 204, 205.

Professor Georges Cœdès: Figs. 169, 170, 187, 203.

Rt. Hon. Lord Lee of Fareham: Fig. 174.

Messrs E. W. Heffer and Sons, Cambridge: Figs. 158, 163, 164, 165.

The remaining illustrations, with the exception of those taken from the book published by the late Nai Hong Navanagruha of Bangkok (which I have acknowledged in the text), were supplied by myself. All the photographic reproductions required were executed by Messrs Kidd and Baker of Cambridge.

Finally I must express my keen sense of obligation to Sir John Marshall, Kt., C.I.E., Litt.D., F.B.A., F.S.A., late Director of the Archaeological Survey of India, first, for his kindness in writing a Foreword to this volume; secondly, for his help in transliterating Sanskrit names, and, thirdly, for certain valuable criticisms. I have fortunately no need to labour insistence on his suitability for the task, and I have reason to hope that, whatever my own shortcomings may be, with him as my sponsor, this work will be assured of a welcome in all Eastern art circles.

REGINALD LE MAY

CAMBRIDGE
*September*, 1937

# CONTENTS


LIMESTONE HEAD OF BUDDHA (Môn Type) *frontispiece*

FOREWORD, by SIR JOHN MARSHALL, Kt., C.I.E., Litt.D., F.B.A., F.S.A. *page* vii

PREFACE ix

LIST OF ILLUSTRATIONS xv

*Chapter* I Introductory 1

II The Different Schools of Art in Siam 13

III The Dvāravatī (Môn-Indian) Period in Siam 21

IV The Kingdom of Çrīvijaya and the Indo-Javanese School 35

V Funan, and the Khmer Period in Siam 50

VI The Khmer Period in Siam (continued) 67

VII The Origins of the Tai and Relations with Burma 82

VIII Further Relations with Burma and India, and the Rise of the Chiengsen School 97

IX The Rise of the Tai in Siam and the Origin of the Suk'ōt'ai School 109

X The Suk'ōt'ai School 120

XI The Schools of U-T'ong, Lopburi (Tai) and Ayudhya 135

BIBLIOGRAPHY: A. General 151

B. Special 152

C. List of Journals dealing with Far Eastern Art 155

INDEX 157

TWO MAPS: (1) showing relations and sea-routes between India and the Indo-Chinese Peninsula

(2) showing Siam and the adjoining countries

# LIST OF ILLUSTRATIONS

FIG.

1. Excavations at Pong Tük. Steps of Sanctuary.
2. Excavations at Pong Tük. Plinth of Sanctuary.
3. Bronze Buddha (standing), Amarāvatī type. From Pong Tük. (Nat. Mus. Bangkok.)
4. Bronze Buddha (standing), Amarāvatī type. From North-east Siam. (Nat. Mus. Bangkok.)
5. Bronze Buddha (standing), Amarāvatī type. From Dong Dūang, Annam. (Ecole Française.)
6. Bronze Buddha (standing), Gupta style but locally made. From Pong Tük. (Nat. Mus. Bangkok.)
7. Bronze Buddha (seated with halo), origin unknown (? North-east India). Found in Siam. (Priv. Coll. Bangkok.)
8. Bronze Buddha (seated), origin unknown (? Ceylon). Found in Siam. (Priv. Coll. Bangkok.)
9. Bronze Buddha (seated), origin unknown (? Kāngra, India). Found in Siam. (Priv. Coll. Bangkok.)
10. Bronze Buddha (seated), origin unknown. Found in Siam. (Priv. Coll. Bangkok.)
11. Bronze Buddha (seated), origin unknown. Found in Siam. (Priv. Coll. Bangkok.)
12. Bronze Buddha (seated), origin unknown (probably Pagān). Found in Siam. (Priv. Coll. Bangkok.)
13. Bronze Buddha (seated in "European" fashion, with halo, on throne decorated with figures), origin unknown. Found in Siam. (Nat. Mus. Bangkok.)
14. Bronze Buddha (seated cross-legged on lotus-throne with halo and attendants), origin unknown (? North-east India). Found in Siam. (Nat. Mus. Bangkok.)
15. Stone Buddha (seated in "European" fashion, with halo), Gupta type. From India. (Brit. Mus.)
16. Stone Buddha (standing, with halo), Gupta type. From India. (Brit. Mus.)
17. Stone Buddha (standing), Dvāravatī-Gupta (Môn) type. Outside Temple of Benchamabopit, Bangkok.
18. Stone Buddha (standing), Dvāravatī-Gupta (Môn) type. Outside Temple of Benchamabopit, Bangkok.
19. Stone Buddha (standing), pre-Angkor type. From Angkor Borei, South Cambodia. (Pnompenh Mus.)
20. Stone Buddha (seated), pre-Angkor type. From Angkor Borei, South Cambodia. (Pnompenh Mus.)
21. Stone Wheel of the Law, Dvāravatī (Môn) type. From P'rapatom. (Nat. Mus. Bangkok.)
22. Stone Deer (representing the Buddha), Dvāravatī (Môn) type. From P'rapatom. (Nat. Mus. Bangkok.)

23 (A). *Stūpa* at P'rapatom, 380 feet high, as restored by King Mongkut.
23 (B). *Stūpa* at P'rapatom, 380 feet high, as seen at the present day.
24. Stone Head of the Buddha, Dvāravatī (Môn) type. From P'rapatom. (Author's Coll.)
25. Stone Buddha (standing), Dvāravatī (Môn) type. (Nat. Mus. Bangkok.)
26 (A). Stone Head of Buddha, Dvāravatī (Môn) type. Front view. (Author's Coll.)
26 (B). Stone Head of Buddha, Dvāravatī (Môn) type. Side view. (Author's Coll.)
27. Stone *Stela*, depicting Miracle of Srāvastī, Dvāravatī (Môn) type. (Nat. Mus. Bangkok.)
28. Stone *Stela*, depicting Buddha with disciples on Rāhu, Dvāravatī (Môn) type. (Priv. Coll. Bangkok.)
29. Stone Head of Buddha, Dvāravatī (Môn) type. (Author's Coll.)
30. Stucco Mask of Buddha, Dvāravatī (Môn) type. From P'rapatom. (Author's Coll.)
31 (A). Terra-cotta Head of Buddha, Dvāravatī (Môn) type. From P'rapatom. Front view. (Nat. Mus. Bangkok.)
31 (B). Terra-cotta Head of Buddha, Dvāravatī (Môn) type. From P'rapatom. Side view. (Nat. Mus. Bangkok.)
32. Stone Slab, depicting the Buddha under seven heads of Nāga King, Dvāravatī (Môn) type. (Nat. Mus. Bangkok.)
33. Bronze Buddha (standing), Dvāravatī (Môn) type. (Priv. Coll. Bangkok.)
34. Bronze Buddha (seated cross-legged), Dvāravatī (Môn) type. From North-east Siam. (Nat. Mus. Bangkok.)
35. Bronze Buddha (seated), late Dvāravatī (Môn) type. (Author's Coll.)
36. Temple of Na P'ra Tāt, in Javanese style, at Jaya, South Siam.
37. *Bōt* (Consecrated Hall) of Temple of Na P'ra Tāt, in Tai style, at Nakon Srītammarāt, South Siam.
38. *Stūpa*, in Sinhalese style, of Temple of Na P'ra Tāt at Nakon Srītammarāt, South Siam.
39. Stone Viṣnu (standing), pre-Khmer type. From South Siam. (Nat. Mus. Bangkok.)
40. Bronze Head and Torso of Lokeçvara, Pāla style. From Jaya, South Siam. (Nat. Mus. Bangkok.)
41. Three stone Deities, two male and one female, Pallavan style, *in situ* near Takuapā, South Siam.
42. Female Deity (right figure in No. 41).
43. Stone Lokeçvara, possibly from Buddh Gayā, Pāla type. From South Siam. (Nat. Mus. Bangkok.)
44. Bronze Lokeçvara (standing), Pāla style. From South Siam. (Nat. Mus. Bangkok.)
45. Bronze Buddha, seated on Nāga King, Môn-Khmer type. (Nat. Mus. Bangkok.)
46. Stone Hari-Hara (Viṣnu and Çiva in one), standing, pre-Angkor type. From Cambodia. (Pnompenh Mus.)
47. Stone Hari-Hara, standing, with arch-frame, pre-Angkor type. From Cambodia. (Pnompenh Mus.)

48. Stone Viṣnu, standing, pre-Khmer type. From Vieng Sra, South Siam. (Nat. Mus. Bangkok.)
49. Stone Ardhanari (Çiva and Umā in one), seated, pre-Khmer type. From North-east Siam. (Nat. Mus. Bangkok.)
50. Stone Head and Torso of Yakṣi, pre-Khmer type. From Çrīdeb, North-east Siam. (Nat. Mus. Bangkok.)
51. Stone Viṣnu, standing, pre-Khmer type. From Çrīdeb, North-east Siam. (Nat. Mus. Bangkok.)
52. Stone Torso of Deity, pre-Khmer type. From Çrīdeb, North-east Siam. (Nat. Mus. Bangkok.)
53. Stone Inscription (in Sanskrit), fifth to sixth century A.D. From Çrīdeb, North-east Siam. (Nat. Mus. Bangkok.)
54. Buddha, with an Apsaras above on each side and devotees below. Carving on Brick at Tāt Panom, North-east Siam.
55. Elephant with Rider. Carving on Brick at Tāt Panom, North-east Siam.
56. Horse, galloping, with Rider. Carving on Brick at Tāt Panom, North-east Siam.
57. Elephant with Rider. Carving on Brick at Tāt Panom, North-east Siam.
58. Men, with umbrellas, in Procession. Carving on Brick at Tāt Panom, North-east Siam.
59. The Temple of Angkor, aerial view.
60. Sanctuary (one of three) at Banteai Srei, Cambodia, tenth century A.D., as now restored.
61. Stone Pediment at Banteai Srei.
62. Stone Pediment at Banteai Srei, depicting fight between two Asuras for the Apsaras, Tillottamā.
63. Brick Sanctuary at Kharod, Central Provinces, India, late Gupta type.
64. Stone Buddha (seated), Khmer type. From Pimai, North-east Siam. (Nat. Mus. Bangkok.)
65. Stone Buddha (seated), Khmer type. From Lopburi, Central Siam. (Nat. Mus. Bangkok.)
66. Two Stone Heads of Buddha, Khmer type. From Angkor, Cambodia, eleventh century. (École Française.)
67. Bronze Buddha (seated), Môn-Khmer type. From Lopburi. (Priv. Coll. Bangkok.)
68. Stone *Stela*, depicting woman with attendants, Khmer type. From Panom Rung, North-east Siam.
69. Ruins of Khmer Temple (or Palace) at Panom Rung. Exterior view.
70. Ruins of Khmer Temple (or Palace) at Panom Rung. Interior view.
71. Stone Lintel, depicting Buddha with attendants. Over doorway of Khmer Sanctuary at Pimai, North-east Siam.
72. Stone Lintel, depicting Mahāyānist Deity. Over doorway of Khmer Sanctuary at Pimai, North-east Siam.
73. Stone Carving, showing details of decoration. At Khmer Temple of Pimai, North-east Siam.
74. Khmer Sanctuary in Temple of Mahā-Tāt at Lopburi, Central Siam.

75. Khmer Temple of P'ra Prāng Sām Yôt at Lopburi, Central Siam.
76. Stone Buddha (seated on Nāga King), Khmer type with lacquer Tai face superimposed, in Temple of P'ra Prāng Sām Yôt, Lopburi.
77. Stone Buddha (seated on Nāga King), Khmer type with lacquer Tai face superimposed. (Author's Coll.)
78. Stone Buddha (seated on Nāga King), Khmer type with lacquer Tai face superimposed. Back view. (Author's Coll.)
79. Stone Buddha (seated), Khmer type, *in situ* at Temple of Mahā-Tāt, Lopburi, Central Siam.
80. Stone Buddha (seated), Khmer type. From Angkor (Bayon), Cambodia. (Pnompenh Mus.)
81. Stone Head of Buddha, Khmer type. From Lopburi. (Author's Coll.)
82. Stone Head of Bodhisattva, Khmer type. From Lopburi. (Author's Coll.)
83. Stone Head of Buddha, Khmer type. From Lopburi. (Author's Coll.)
84. Stone Head of Buddha, Khmer type. From Lopburi. (V. and A. Mus.)
85. Bronze Buddha (standing), late Khmer type. Outside Temple of Benchamabopit, Bangkok.
86. Bronze Buddha (seated on Nāga King), Khmer type. From Lopburi. (Author's Coll.)
87. Bronze Buddha (seated), Khmer type. (Author's Coll.)
88. Bronze Buddha (seated on Nāga King), Khmer type. From Angkor. (Pnompenh Mus.)
89. Bronze Buddha (standing), Khmer type. From Lopburi. (Priv. Coll. Bangkok.)
90. Bronze Buddha (standing), Khmer type. From Lopburi. (Priv. Coll. Bangkok.)
91. Bronze Buddha (standing), Khmer type. From Lopburi. (Priv. Coll. Bangkok.)
92. Bronze Head and Torso of Woman, Khmer type. Provenance unknown. (Nat. Mus. Bangkok.)
93. Temple of Çulamāni, Pitsanulōk, Khmer type. Southern Entrance.
94. Temple of Çulamāni, Pitsanulōk, Khmer type. Eastern Entrance.
95. Temple of Mahā-Tāt at Sawank'alōk, Tai-Khmer type. Sanctuary Tower.
96. Temple of Mahā-Tāt at Sawank'alōk, Tai type. Ruins of *Vihāra*.
97. Temple of Mahā-Tāt at Sawank'alōk, Môn *Stūpa*, Eastern face.
98. Temple of Mahā-Tāt at Sawank'alōk, Stone Gateway, Khmer type.
99. Stone Pillar, with stucco decoration, at Temple of Mahā-Tāt, Sawank'alōk.
100. Stone Buddha (seated on Nāga King) in niche at Temple of Mahā-Tāt, Sawank'alōk.
101. Chinese Temple at Müang Hai, north-west of Chiengrung, Yunnan.
102. Tai Temple of P'ra Sing at Chiengmai, North Siam.
103. Tai Temple near Müang Hai, west of Chiengrung, Yunnan.
104. Tai-Burmese Temple at Chiengtung, Southern Shan States.
105. *Sālā*, or resting-place, at Müang Yong, Southern Shan States.
106. Temple of Sī Liem, at Wieng Kŭm-Kām near Chiengmai.
107. The Great *Stūpa* at Lamp'ūn, Tai type.
108. Temple of Kŭkŭt, near Lamp'ūn.

109. Temple of Kŭkŭt, Lamp'ūn; details of Buddha images in niches.
110. Stone Buddha (seated on lotus-throne). From Buddh Gayā, Bihar. Pāla type. (Brit. Mus.)
111. Bronze Buddha (seated on lotus-throne). From Pagān, Burma. Pāla style.
112. Bronze Buddha (seated on lotus-throne), Tai (Chiengsen) type, Pāla style. (Nat. Mus. Bangkok.)
113. Bronze Buddha (seated on lotus-throne), Tai (Chiengsen) type, Pāla style. (Author's Coll.)
114. Bronze Head of Buddha, Tai (Chiengsen) type, Pāla style. (Author's Coll.)
115. Bronze Head of Buddha, Tai (Chiengsen) type, Pāla style. (Nat. Mus. Bangkok.)
116. Bronze Buddha (seated). From Pagān, Burma. Pāla style.
117. Bronze Buddha (seated), Tai (Chiengsen) type, Pāla style. In Temple of Benchamabopit, Bangkok.
118. Bronze Buddha (seated), Tai (Chiengsen) type, Pāla style. In Temple of Benchamabopit, Bangkok.
119. Stone Buddha (standing, with Elephant and Ānanda). Pāla type. From Buddh Gayā, Bihar. Now at Chiengmai.
120. Stone Buddha (standing, with two Elephants and two Disciples). Pāla type. From Buddh Gayā, Bihar. (Ind. Mus. Calcutta.)
121 Stone Buddha (seated on lotus-throne), decorated style. Pāla type. From Buddh Gayā, Bihar. (Brit. Mus.)
122. Bronze Buddha (seated on lotus-throne), Pāla decorated style, Tai (Lü) type. From North Siam. (Priv. Coll. Bangkok.)
123. Lacquered Earthen Buddha, Pāla decorated style, Tai type. From North Siam.
124. Stone *Stela*, depicting Pari-Nirvāna of Buddha, with disciples mourning below. Pāla type. From Buddh Gayā, Bihar. (Brit. Mus.)
125. Stone Head of Buddhist Saint, Tai (Ayudhya) type. From Cave near Chiengrai, North Siam. (Author's Coll.)
126. Temple of Chiengmān, in Chiengmai. Pagān style.
127. Temple of Chet Yôt (Seven Spires), near Chiengmai. Pagān style.
128. Buddha, in Brick and Stucco, Tai type, on exterior of Temple of Chet Yôt, Chiengmai.
129. Bronze Buddha (seated), Tai (Suk'ōt'ai) type. (Nat. Mus. Bangkok.)
130. Bronze Buddha (walking), Tai (Suk'ōt'ai) type. In Temple of Benchamabopit, Bangkok.
131. Bronze Buddha (seated), P'ra Sihing, Tai (Suk'ōt'ai) type. (Nat. Mus. Bangkok.)
132. Bronze Buddha (seated); Sinhalese type. (Colombo Mus.)
133. Stone Buddha (seated), at Anurādhapura, Ceylon.
134. Rock-hewn Buddha (seated), at Galvihāra, Polonnāruwa, Ceylon.
135. Ruins of Temple of Mahā-Tāt at old Suk'ōt'ai.
136. Stone and stucco Buddha, with Scene of Pari-Nirvāna above, Tai type. At Temple of Mahā-Tāt, old Suk'ōt'ai.
137. Ruins of Temple of Çri Chŭm at old Suk'ōt'ai.
138. Façade of Temple of Çri Chŭm at old Suk'ōt'ai.

139. Stone Carving with Inscription (Devadharma Jātaka), Tai type. At Temple of Çri Chŭm, old Suk'ōt'ai.
140. Wall painting in Cave (Apsaras with attendant) at Sigiriya, Ceylon, fifth century.
141. Temple of Chāng Lôm (Elephant-surrounded) at old Sawank'alōk.
142. Stone Buddha (seated on Nāga King), Tai (Suk'ōt'ai) type. At Temple of P'rajedi Chet Teo (Seven Rows of *Stūpas*) at old Sawank'alōk.
143. Bronze Head of Buddha, found at Temple of Chāng Lôm, old Sawank'alōk. Tai-Khmer type. (Author's Coll.)
144. Bronze Buddha (seated), Tai (Suk'ōt'ai) type. (Nat. Mus. Bangkok.)
145. Bronze Head of Buddha, Tai (Suk'ōt'ai) type. (Nat. Mus. Bangkok.)
146. Bronze Buddha, Tai (Suk'ōt'ai) type, in Temple of Mahā-Tāt, Pitsanulōk.
147. Bronze Head of Buddha, Tai (Suk'ōt'ai) type. (Author's Coll.)
148. Bronze Head of Buddha, Tai (Suk'ōt'ai) type (modified). (Author's Coll.)
149. Bronze Buddha (walking), Tai (Suk'ōt'ai) type. (Author's Coll.)
150. Votive Tablet (probably Tin), showing Walking Buddha, Tai (Suk'ōt'ai) type. (Author's Coll.)
151. Bronze model of *Stūpa* (with Ivory Spire), Tai (Suk'ōt'ai) type (probably of Temple of Chāng Lôm). (Author's Coll.)
152. Temple of P'ra Yün (the Standing Buddha) at Lamp'ūn.
153. Temple of Sirikŭt, near Chiengmai.
154. *Stūpa* with Buddha in ruins of the Royal Temple at Chiengsen.
155. Silver Buddha (seated), late Tai (Chiengsen) type, dug up at Chiengsen. (Author's Coll.)
156. Bronze Head of Buddha, Tai (Chiengsen-Suk'ōt'ai) type. (Author's Coll.)
157. Bronze Head of Buddha, Tai (Chiengsen-Suk'ōt'ai) type. (Author's Coll.)
158. Tai Temple at Nān.
159. *Stūpa* of Tai Temple of Cha Heng at Nān.
160. Bronze Buddha (seated), Tai (Chiengsen-Suk'ōt'ai) type. At Chiengmai.
161. Four Brick and Stucco Buddhas (seated back to back), Tai type. In Temple at Nān.
162. Carved Teak Door, facing one of the four Buddhas in Temple at Nān.
163. Tai Temple at Lampāng Lūang. General view.
164. Tai Temple at Lampāng Lūang. Front of *Vihāra*.
165. Tai Temple at Lampāng Lūang. Side view of *Vihāra*, with *Stūpa* behind.
166. Group of Buddhist Priests and Acolytes in North Siam.
167. The "Emerald" Buddha, Tai (Chiengsen) type. In the Royal Temple at Bangkok.
168. Bronze Buddha (seated), Tai (early Ayudhya) type, in imitation of Khmer. In Temple of Benchamabopit, Bangkok.
169. Stone Buddha (seated), Tai (early Ayudhya) type, in imitation of Khmer. In Temple on K'ao T'ammamūn, Supanburi district.
170. Bronze Buddha (seated), Tai (U-T'ong) type. (Nat. Mus. Bangkok.)
171. Bronze Head of Buddha. Khmer-Tai. First U-T'ong type. (Author's Coll.)
172. Bronze Head of Buddha. Khmer-Tai. First U-T'ong type. (Author's Coll.)

173. Bronze Head of Buddha. Khmer-Tai, with flame-top. Second U-T'ong type. (Author's Coll.)
174. Bronze Head of Buddha. Khmer-Tai, with flame-top. Second U-T'ong type. (Lord Lee of Fareham Coll.)
175. Bronze Head of Buddha. Khmer-Tai, with flame-top (missing). Second U-T'ong type. (Author's Coll.)
176. Bronze Head of Buddha. Khmer-Tai, with flame-top (missing). Second U-T'ong type. Deep-set features. (Author's Coll.).
177. Bronze Head of Buddha. Khmer-Tai. Second U-T'ong type. Peculiar flame-top. (Author's Coll.)
178. Bronze Head of Buddha. Tai-Khmer. Third U-T'ong type. (Author's Coll.)
179. Gilt Bronze Head of Buddha. Tai-Khmer. Third U-T'ong type. (Author's Coll.)
180. Bronze Head of Buddha. Tai. Fourth U-T'ong type. (Author's Coll.)
181. Bronze Head of Buddha. Tai. Fourth U-T'ong type. (Author's Coll.)
182. Bronze Head of Buddha. Tai. Fourth U-T'ong type. (Author's Coll.)
183. Bronze Head of Buddha. Tai. Fourth U-T'ong type. (Author's Coll.)
184. Bronze Head of Buddha. Tai. Fourth U-T'ong type. (Author's Coll.)
185. Bronze Buddha (walking). Tai. Fourth U-T'ong type. (Author's Coll.)
186. Stone Head of Buddha. Tai (Lopburi) type. Khmer influence. (Author's Coll.)
187. Stone Head of Buddha. Tai (Lopburi) type. Suk'ōt'ai influence. (Nat. Mus. Bangkok.)
188. Stone Head of Buddha. Tai (Lopburi) type. Later style. (Priv. Coll. London.)
189. Stone Head of Buddha. Tai (Lopburi) type. Last style. (Author's Coll.)
190. Ruins of Temple of Çrī Sarap'et at Ayudhya.
191. Great Bronze Buddha. Tai (Ayudhya) type, near ruins of Çrī Sarap'et at Ayudhya.
192. Ruined Brick and Stucco *Stūpa*. Tai (Ayudhya) type, near Temple of Mahā-Tāt at Lopburi.
193. Ruined Brick and Stucco *Stūpas*. Tai (imitation Khmer) type, at Lopburi.
194. Row of Disciples in Stucco. Tai (Ayudhya) type, on ruined brick *Stūpa* at Lopburi.
195. Ruined *Stūpa*. Tai (imitation Khmer) type, at Temple of Nakon Kosā T'ibodi, Lopburi.
196. Bronze Buddha (standing). Tai (Ayudhya) type. In Temple of Benchamabopit, Bangkok.
197. Bronze Buddha (standing). Tai (Ayudhya) type. In Temple of Benchamabopit, Bangkok.
198. Bronze Buddha (standing). Tai (Ayudhya) type. (Author's Coll.)
199. Gilt Bronze Head of Buddha. Tai (Ayudhya) type. (Author's Coll.)
200. Bronze Head of Buddha. Tai (Ayudhya) type. (Author's Coll.)
201. Bronze Head of Buddha. Tai (late Ayudhya) type. (Author's Coll.)
202. Wooden Head (lacquered) of Buddha. Tai (late Ayudhya) type. (Author's Coll.)
203. Bronze Çiva (standing). Tai (Ayudhya) type. From Kampengp'et. (Nat. Mus. Bangkok).
204. Bronze Çiva (standing). Tai (Ayudhya) type. (V. and A. Mus.)
205. Bronze Head and Torso of (?) Viṣnu. Tai (Ayudhya) type. (V. and A. Mus.)

"The extensive and long-continued emigration from India to the Far East—including Pegu, Siam and Cambodia on the mainland, with Java, Sumatra, Bali and Borneo among the islands of the Malay Archipelago—. . . and the consequent establishment of Indian institutions and art in the countries named constitute one of the darkest mysteries of history.

"The reality of the debt due to India by those distant lands is attested abundantly by material remains, . . . by Chinese history and by numerous traditions preserved in India, Pegu, Siam and the Archipelago. But when the attempt is made to transmute vague, conflicting traditions and imperfectly known archaeological facts into orderly history, the difficulties in the way of success appear to be largely insurmountable."

VINCENT SMITH, *History of Fine Arts in India and Ceylon* (1911), p. 259.

# Chapter I

## INTRODUCTORY

BEFORE we can appreciate the beauties of an alien art, it is essential to understand wherein it differs from our own. Fundamentally no doubt all mankind is one, but each branch of the human race has evolved its own system of culture and its own modes of expression, due, in the first place, to its geographical situation and, secondly, to its own inherent strength, whether it can be influenced by exterior forces brought to bear upon it or whether it is strong enough to resist them. And here we are faced with an apparent paradox, for the practical, strong, dominating race may be the most receptive of culture from outside, while the politically weak may be the most resistant to it.

England, the world power, has influenced nobody in the world of art except in the territories which it has colonised: on the contrary it owes its own chief architectural glories to France, its furniture and gardens largely to Italy, while Holland, France, and Italy have all profoundly affected its sculpture and painting. China, on the other hand, which from an early period has been overrun and politically conquered by alien races—Huns, Tartars, Manchus and the like—has never failed to absorb them all, and to turn them culturally into good Chinese citizens, so strong is the inherent force of its culture. In India, while Persian (Achaemenid) and quasi-Hellenistic influences both made a strong attack upon the native art in its infancy and certainly left their mark upon it for a time, yet in the end these foreign influences were thrown off and a purely Indian art appeared, whether Hindu, Buddhist or Jain. India, indeed, once it recovered its independence of outlook about the second century of the Christian era, began to exercise a profound cultural influence on its neighbours to the east and south—Burma, Siam, Cambodia, Java and Ceylon all falling beneath its sway. And this, as far as one may judge, almost entirely as a result of trading and peaceful penetration by missionaries and others, and not by force of arms.

Indian religious art and culture seem naturally to have exercised an extraordinary fascination over the indigenous peoples of all these territories, no doubt owing to the attractions offered by Buddhism and Hinduism, while Chinese art, not bearing any particular religious message, apparently made but little impression, in spite of the fact that the Chinese, too, sailed the southern seas in search of trade from very early times.

Vincent Smith, in the extract quoted in the preface to this work, imagines that the difficulties of tracing the history of Indian influence in south-eastern Asia are largely insurmountable. That was written in 1911. The object of this volume, written a quarter of a century later, is to try and fill the gap as far as one country is concerned, and to present a picture of all the different influences from India, and Ceylon, which have played their part in what is now the Kingdom of Siam in the building up of a national Siamese art.

For reasons as yet unexplained, perhaps too deep for explanation, from the dawn of European history, at least from the time of the beginnings of Greek art more than 2500 years ago, the mental conceptions underlying Western and Eastern art seem to have been as the poles apart. Whereas the European, whether Greek or Roman, was content to cling to the earth in his desire to give expression to his aesthetic tastes, and to lavish all his skill on representations of the animal and plant kingdoms, the aim of the Eastern was to reach out after something unattainable, to try and define something beyond and above himself. Although no doubt in ancient India secular art was not lacking among the general population, yet the highest forms of religious art which have remained above ground for our admiration appear to me to possess a spirituality not to be found in Western art.

This seems to me to be the great inherent difference between Eastern and Western art. In the matter of technique, too, a most important difference is seen. In the Eastern artist (whether Chinese, Indian, or Egyptian) there is an innate feeling for economy of line in delineating his subject. The Western artist, with his intense individualism, wishes the spectator to see the form, or the scene, exactly as he sees it, down to the very last detail, but the Eastern artist is content, in his simplicity, to give just the very essentials of the subject-matter and to leave it to the spectator to fill in the background and all inessential details from the resources of his own imagination and experience. A perfect example of this economy of line, which will explain my meaning better than any words to the true artistic eye, may be seen in a Chinese plate of Ting ware of the Sung period, now in the possession of Sir Percival David.[1] The scene incised on the plate is that of "Two ducks in a lotus-pond", and the whole picture is accomplished in about two dozen sure strokes of the engraving tool: but the essentials of the scene are there and nothing but the spectator's imagination is needed to fill in the background. It is, indeed, one of the most finished works of art that I know and can never be forgotten by anyone who has seen it with his "inner" eye. The truth is that the Chinese

[1] Hobson and Hetherington, *Art of the Chinese Potter*, Pl. XLVII. Ernest Benn, London, 1923.

artist has realised that no two pairs of eyes ever "see" the same picture, and that the artist's chief aim should be to give full rein to the spectator's own imagination.

These ingredients, a spiritual aim and economy of line, combined with an intense feeling for form, make up the reason why the highest forms of Eastern art are to me so immeasurably more satisfying than their compeers of the West. If only the youthful artist of Europe will take these lessons to heart—a spiritual aim, economy of line, coupled with true simplicity and sincerity of heart—what may the future not produce?

It is only because I believe he is striving to do so that I feel the urge to write these words. Why is that great artist, Holbein, so completely satisfying? Because he, too, whether consciously or unconsciously, adopted the Eastern precept of "economy of line", and because, if one looks at those wonderful portraits of John Fisher or Thomas More, one sees a simplicity, a sincerity and a spirituality which appeal direct to the heart and the mind.

Chinese art has in some respects maintained its simplicity and serenity almost up to the present day, but the later forms of Hindu and Siamese art are entirely decadent, grossly overladen with ornament and, indeed, running riot in an orgy of decoration. I am, however, writing of the earlier periods, up to the fourteenth and fifteenth centuries A.D., and I do not propose to treat of Siamese art after the year 1600, there being little of interest or artistic value after that date, unless we except the temple architecture of Bangkok which, in spite of its lavish and somewhat garish decoration, has in it much to be admired.

An account of my own "conversion" in the matter of Eastern art may be useful to record, especially as I have reason to believe that the modern European artist is coming more and more to realise the truth of what I am about to say. Having been brought up from my youth to admire classical Greek art, I found, when first I went to the East, little or nothing of beauty in Siamese or Indian sculptural art. The general treatment in Eastern art is nearly always symbolical, "natural form" being of little account, while in classical Greek art it is just this "natural form" of the human body that the student is taught to study and that the critic is taught, as a European, to admire. But during a residence of twenty-five years in the East and a constant study of Indian, Sinhalese, Chinese, Cambodian, Siamese, Japanese and Javanese art, I gradually and imperceptibly found myself, so to speak, changing front—and I think now that I know the reason why. It is just the spiritual appeal in Eastern art, to which something universal and deep within one responds, and which is lacking in all Greek art except the very earliest. So that now, when I gaze at the Elgin Marbles, for instance, or the sculptures from the altar of Pergamum, although I can and do admire the perfection of the human form portrayed, still I come away with part of me unsatisfied. I see the beauty of the form, but it is a physical beauty of a particular European type, and there it ends. There is nothing universal in its appeal, and it touches none of the deeper chords of one's nature. But when I gaze at the finest examples of Eastern art (for example, at the pottery Lohan of the T'ang Dynasty in the Chinese Exhibition or the similar figure in the British Museum), I find that my spirit is satisfied as well as my more superficial senses. My inner eye sees beyond the form, as it is intended to do, and I experience something more than the sensation of enjoying the sight of physical beauty or, in the case mentioned, of an example of the highest form of the potter's art. It is true that the best examples of Byzantine and also of early Mediaeval European art also satisfy the spirit, but they again owe their inspiration to Eastern forms.

On the subject of "treatment" Coomaraswamy has written words which must surely give the clue to any student wishing to understand the significance of form in Eastern art:

> It cannot be too clearly understood that the mere representation of nature is never the aim of Indian art.[1] Probably no truly Indian sculpture has been wrought from a living model, or any religious painting copied from the life. Possibly no Hindu artist of the old schools ever drew from nature at all. His store of memory pictures, his power of visualisation and his imagination were for his purpose finer means: for he desired to suggest the Idea behind sensuous appearance, not to give the detail of the seeming reality, that was in truth but *māyā*, illusion....To mistake the *māyā* for reality were error indeed. "Men of no understanding think of Me, the unmanifest, as having manifestation, knowing not My higher being to be changeless, supreme" (*Bhagavad Gita*, VII, 24).[2]

In one sense Eastern art has an advantage over its Western sister in that it is nearly always devoted to religious ends and may therefore be expected to show an attempt to inspire religious feelings, but the same criticism as I have made above would apply with almost equal force to a comparison between Eastern and Renaissance religious art. There is, in my eyes, very little spiritual appeal in the figures of our Lord and of the Madonna that adorn Western churches, in spite of an obvious attempt to endow them with such, and I wonder how many of the artistic souls who admire them are filled with any spiritual inspiration. Indeed, with few exceptions, although they may be works of great artistic merit, these figures fill my spirit with neither devotion nor peace of mind, nor do they give my inner vision any sense of glory. In some cases I feel something almost akin to

[1] The same applies to Siamese art.

[2] A. K. Coomaraswamy, *The Aims of Indian Art*, p. 4. Essex House Press, Broad-Campden, 1908.

repulsion, in others the reaction is more physically satisfying than is intended. As an example of my meaning, I personally love the subject of Lippo Lippi's Madonna, Lucrezia Buti, but not, alas, for the reason I ought to do so. I love her for the same reason as that which induced him to carry her off from a nunnery.

Those pictures which inspire in me the most religious feeling are the earliest, and they again are Byzantine or Eastern in origin. The reason for this is not easy to explain. It is not that I lean more towards Buddhism than towards Christianity, for I do not. No, if it is to be explained at all, I think the difference lies in this. The Buddhist artist painted his picture or fashioned his image to represent a Being far more exalted than himself purely for religious edification and not as a conscious work of art, while the Western artist was chosen to adorn the churches of Italy, France, Germany and England because he was an expert painter or sculptor and *not* because he was a man of ardent spiritual feeling who happened to be a skilled artist. I am told that in ancient days in Siam many of the images of the Buddha were made by the priests themselves within closed walls, so that no profane or curious, prying eyes should watch or disturb them at their work. If they happened to be skilful in the art, their images would naturally be of a high artistic order; if they were not skilful, as would probably be the case in many provincial centres, the result would be mediocre or even poor, artistically. But what counted was the spiritual atmosphere in which the image was created, and not the degree of skill that went to its making.

The European, on the other hand, is averse from symbolism and a purely spiritual appeal. He cannot forget that "God created man in his own image", and he prefers to see his own manly form portrayed in all its glory.

However heretical this confession may seem to some, I am not ashamed to admit it, because it gives, I believe, the clue to the fundamental difference between the Eastern and Western outlook, and it is only by an appreciation of what the Eastern mind is striving to convey that the Western mind can come into harmonious contact with it. The late E. B. Havell, who was artistic to his finger-tips, strove to preach the same gospel, but he was too fanatical and too bitter in his attacks on what he considered Western Philistinism ever to make much impression upon his hard-headed fellow-countrymen. If one is to bring about an understanding between East and West, it is, first of all, necessary to eradicate from Western minds the feeling, if it still exists, that there is something inherently "heathenish" or unnatural in Eastern religious art.

One has to realise that there are other peoples in the world who have not the same modes of thought as oneself, and to try and understand what is the fundamental basis of their thoughts. It is a trite saying, "tout comprendre, c'est tout pardonner", but it is true nevertheless, and it is my belief that human ideals all over the world are in essence the same, only that different people approach them by different roads and by different forms of conveyance. I therefore wish to plead for an open, tolerant spirit and for a genuine desire to understand the meaning of what is to us an alien form of art.

The arts of Siam, and sculpture in particular, are only known in England from the objects, either quite modern or of fairly recent origin, brought by travellers, and these in most cases, as might be expected, have been indiscriminately chosen and are decadent in style. The result of this has been that our museums present a very inadequate idea of the sculptural art that has been produced on Siamese soil, though in truth Siam is one of the most attractive and fascinating countries for the student of art history. Cultural influences have invaded it through the centuries from north, south, east and west, and there is still a wide field open for research. Archaeological exploration is in its infancy and it is only within the last few years that Siam herself has begun to show a real active interest in her own arts and crafts. Early in the present century H.R.H. Prince Damrong, who was then Minister of the Interior, began to form tentative collections of sculpture and other objects of Siam's ancient civilisations within his own Ministry, and to encourage Governors of Provinces to do the same in their respective spheres, but it was not until 1924 that King Rama VI (Vajiravudh) instituted an Archaeological Service, and not until 1926 that his successor, King Prajadhipok, established a National Museum with Prince Damrong at its head, thereby giving a great impulse in Siam to the study of the arts and crafts of the country. This Museum, which is already one of the richest of its kind in the Far East, is housed in the former Palace of the Second King, which was built soon after the founding of the city of Bangkok in 1782 and constitutes a perfect example of a Royal Siamese Palace before European influence insinuated itself into Bangkok. It contains a separate chapel and more than a dozen halls and audience-chambers, and forms a most fitting site for a National Museum.

In architecture the Tai (Siamese) have been more eclectic than in any other form of art, and have borrowed from India, China, Cambodia, Ceylon and Burma at one time or another. Of the earliest forms of architecture erected in Siam, of the period a thousand years before the Tai people came into it, nothing is known, as there is nothing standing above ground on which to form an idea as to its style. Khmer (Cambodian) temples and ruins are still to be seen in certain districts of Siam, and demonstrate by their beauty of style and setting the heights to which those master-builders could rise, even in the provinces. The earliest Tai forms in Central Siam seem to have largely followed the Khmer style, but later forms show a certain Chinese influence in the roofing, with an Indian influence in the decoration. The "carpet" roofs of Bangkok, in all shades of blue, green, red and yellow, are one of its most distinctive and beautiful features. The exterior columns of these later temples nearly always incline slightly inwards from the base upwards, and this style has been followed in the gilt-lacquer cabinets kept in most monasteries as receptacles for the Buddhist Scriptures, forming a very distinctive and artistic feature in both cases.

The *stūpa*, or memorial pagoda, as erected in Siam, is of two kinds, either the blunted *p'ra-prāng*, a debased form of the Khmer *çikhara* or sanctuary-tower, or a *p'ra-jedi*, a sharply pointed bell-shaped memorial in the Sinhalese or Burmese style, whose origin clearly lies in Northern India.

The architectural and decorative features of the temples of Bangkok, i.e. of the late eighteenth and nineteenth centuries, have been fully described and illustrated by Karl Döhring in his *Buddhistische Tempelanlagen in Siam* in three volumes, published by Walter de Gruyter in Berlin in 1920.

In the past a good deal of attention has been paid to the arts of Siam by German, and more particularly French explorers, scholars and archaeologists, and one is always sure of a welcome for Siamese art in France and Germany. Of the writers who have contributed to our knowledge of Siam mention may be made among the German, of Bastian (1867), Carl Bock (1884), Voretzsch (1906), Döhring (1920), and Salmony (1925); and, among the French, of Henri Mouhot (1864), Francis Garnier (1873), the *Mission Pavie* (1892–1902), Lefèvre-Pontalis (1897–1910), Aymonier (1903–6), Fournereau (1903), Pelliot (1904), as well as, more recently, Lunet de Lajonquière, Parmentier, Claeys, and above all Georges Cœdès, who from 1917 to 1929 was Chief Secretary of the National Library and Museum at Bangkok. But, with the exception of W. A. Graham, who has written the standard reference work on Siam (latest edition 1924), England shows a complete blank in all pertaining to the arts of Siam. Colonel Gerini, although he wrote in English, was an Italian. In the present work I am under a great debt of obligation to the French scholars, to Pelliot, de Lajonquière, Parmentier, Claeys, and in particular to Cœdès, which I take great pleasure in thus acknowledging, but unfortunately I have to make one exception.

In 1897 and again in 1909 Lefèvre-Pontalis, who came as French Minister to Siam shortly before the War, was responsible for an historical summary of early political movements in Siam in the French Journal, *Toung Pao*, under the heading "L'Invasion Thaie en Indo-Chine",[1] an event which he placed in the first centuries of the Christian era. His chief sources of information seem to have been the local legendary histories and, as a scientific record, it is almost valueless. Not only so, but the "fantaisies" contained therein have led other scholars and students woefully astray and have caused a serious misapprehension of the history of the country.

To show what ramifications the publication of such "evidence" may have, I have only to mention that Graham appears to have been seriously influenced by Lefèvre-Pontalis in his romantic chapters on the history of Siam, Salmony has based thereon his whole theory of the evolution of sculpture in Siam, while Coomaraswamy in his *History of Indian and Indonesian Art* has in his turn taken Salmony as his guide on the sculptural art of Siam. In addition, O. C. Gangoly, in his study of Siamese Buddhist Images, and E. A. Voretzsch in his article on Indian Art in Siam, both in the Indian Journal *Rūpam*, have been led astray by the same will-o'-the-wisp.

I cannot deal with the works of Lefèvre-Pontalis or Graham in this volume, but I must refer to Salmony, since, apart from the admirable volume by Cœdès devoted to the National Museum of Bangkok,[2] which is, however, in French, the only specialised work in English on the subject under discussion is a volume entitled *Sculpture in Siam*, by Alfred Salmony, published by Ernest Benn in 1925.[3]

At that time Salmony was Assistant Director in the Museum for Far Eastern Art in Cologne and was evidently genuinely interested in the arts of Siam, but unfortunately, as far as I am aware, he had no first-hand knowledge of Siam or its history, while the material at his disposal for study was meagre in quantity and, taken as a whole, not of a particularly high quality. Moreover, a glance at the bibliography at the end of his work will show how little of real value was apparently available for the purposes of study of such an intricate problem as the one he undertook to solve, seemingly in rather a light-hearted fashion.

I have no space to discuss throughout in detail this work, which has not lightened the labour of its successors, but I must point out two cardinal errors which appear in it and which I have no doubt are due to the statements of Lefèvre-Pontalis.

[1] P. Lefèvre-Pontalis, "L'Invasion Thaie en Indo-Chine", *Toung Pao* (1897), pp. 53–78; and vol. x, 2nd series (1909), pp. 495–512.

[2] G. Cœdès, "Le Musée National de Bangkok", *Ars Asiatica* (vol. XII). G. Van Oest, Paris, 1928.

[3] A. Salmony, *Sculpture in Siam*. Ernest Benn, London, 1925.

In the first place Salmony postulates the existence of Tai (Siamese) sculpture at Sawank'alōk and Suk'ōt'ai in North-central Siam in the eighth and ninth centuries A.D. (Pls. 9, 10, 11, 12 A, B, and 13 A), and again in the tenth and eleventh centuries (Pls. 13 B, 14, 15 A, B, 16 A, B, 17 and 18). In chapter IV of his work he begins by stating that "the twin cities of Sawank'alōk (which he translates as 'Sangha-Land') and Suk'ōt'ai (as 'Dayspring of Good Fortune') exert an influence at some distance from the sea, and both serve as capitals to an empire to which Suk'ōt'ai has given its name". This is true of a certain period though, incidentally, Sawank'alōk is the phonetic way in which the Siamese pronounce the Sanskrit *svarga-lōka* ("The Heavenly Region", or, as we should say, "Paradise"), while Suk'ōt'ai means "The happiness of the Tai or 'the free'".[1] But Salmony goes on to say that "the great migration,[2] which makes the fortunes of Siam full of changes for a thousand years, must be dated as early as the first centuries of our era". And further on: "Politically, from the seventh and eighth centuries the Tai fall more or less under the sway of their neighbours to the eastward. Subjugation by Cambodia follows as early as the seventh century."

As far as I know, there is no evidence, historical, epigraphical, architectural or sculptural, which can warrant either the first or the two latter statements. The history of Siam in the first millennium of the Christian era is still very obscure, but, even if there were isolated Tai settlements in Central Siam at that early date, it is practically certain that they were not producing sculpture of the types shown in the plates above mentioned. What evidence there is goes to show that, before the annexation of the valley of the lower Menam to the Khmer dominions at the end of the tenth century A.D., this part of the country was peopled by the Môn or Talaing race from Lower Burma, or at least that this race exercised a dominating part in the religious, and presumably therefore political, life of the kingdom. And this influence extended, as early as the eighth century A.D., as far north as Lamp'ūn, 17 miles from Chiengmai in the north of Siam.

The Tai race, it is believed, comes from the Chinese provinces of Szechuan, Yunnan, Kweichow and Kwang Si, south of the Yangtsze Kiang, and at one time were in occupation of a kingdom there called by the Chinese Nan-Chao, or "the Southern Lord", until the country was finally conquered by the Mongols under Kublai Khan in the middle of the thirteenth century. No doubt bands of

[1] Lefèvre-Pontalis finds that Suk'ot'ai means *sroc-tai* or "the Land of the Tai" (*Toung Pao* (1897), p. 74). Why, I do not know, when the meaning is clear.

[2] I.e. of the Tai race.

Tai had been penetrating into Burma (the land of the now extinct Pyu), the Shan States and the *Sip-song Panna* (a no-man's land to the north-east of Siam) for many centuries past, but, according to the *Pongsāwadān Yōnaka* (the standard Siamese history of the North of Siam),[1] the first Tai settlement of any importance to be made in Siam itself is recorded as taking place about the year A.D. 860, when a strong Tai prince named Brahma crossed the Mekōng and founded a principality at Chai Prakā in the district of Chiengrai, in the furthest north of Siam.

Now the historical aborigines of Siam were a race called Lawā, and the resulting fusion of Tai and Lawā (together with Môn) is clearly seen to-day in the racial characteristics of the modern Lao, or northern Siamese, who have never received any immixture of Khmer blood and are consequently to be clearly distinguished from those of their southern brethren who have. So far from there being people of the Tai race occupying a position of importance at Sawank'alōk or Suk'ōt'ai in the seventh century, it may be recorded that the earliest Tai inscription from that centre is dated 1214 of the *Mahā-Sakarāt*, or A.D. 1292.

In this connection it is interesting to note that Harvey in his *History of Burma*[2] says that the Shans, who are a kindred race to the Siamese (the Shans being called *Tai Yai* or "Great Tai", and the Siamese, *Tai Noi* or "Little Tai"), did not enter the plains of Burma until the twelfth century. This coincides in a remarkable manner with the history of the Tai in Siam.

Secondly, Salmony lays it down that subjugation by Cambodia follows as early as the seventh century, and that from this time "the Tai fall more or less under the sway of their neighbours to the eastward".

As the rise of the Khmer race to sovereignty in the delta of the Mekōng does not *begin* until towards the close of the sixth century,[3] and their eventual capital at Angkor was not established until the beginning of the ninth century, it seems scarcely likely that their power could have reached the heart of Siam during the seventh and eighth centuries, even if the Tai had been there to submit to it.

Parmentier says that the Khmer kingdom was formerly a vassal state of the ancient Hinduised kingdom of Funan until the second half of the seventh century, when she broke the power of Funan and became mistress of the whole country. Even so, until the eighth century Cambodia (Chên-la, as it was called by the Chinese) was split into two kingdoms.[4]

1 P'ya Prajakich Korachakr (Jêm Bunnag), *Pongsāwădān Yōnaka* (in Siamese). Bangkok, 1907.

2 G. E. Harvey, *History of Burma*, p. 4. Longmans, Green and Co. London, 1925.

3 P. Pelliot, "Le Founan", *B.E.F.E.O.* vol. III, pp. 248–303.

4 H. Parmentier, "History of Khmer Architecture", *Eastern Art*, vol. III (1931), pp. 141–79, Philadelphia.

It can be shown from inscriptions[1] found that, as the Khmer empire expanded northwards from the eighth century onwards, settlements were founded on the Siamese side of the Mekōng, on the Korāt plateau in North-eastern Siam; and at Tāt Panom, halfway between the towns of Nakon Panom and Mukdahān on the Siamese side of the Mekōng, may be seen what is possibly one of their earliest efforts in sculptured brick, to which I shall refer again later. But it is impossible to accept the statement that the Khmer became masters of Sawank'alōk and Suk'ōt'ai in the seventh or eighth century, much less that they conquered the Tai in doing so. Indeed, it is more than probable that the Khmer did not reach Sawank'alōk until the twelfth century.

It is stated in the *Jinakalamālini*,[2] a reliable history of the North of Siam written by a Buddhist monk in 1516, that at the end of the tenth century A.D. a chieftain from Nakon Srītammarāt in the Malay Peninsula captured the city of Lavō (Lopburi), while its master was contending against another foe from Haripūnjaya (Lamp'ūn) in the north of Siam. The son of this conquering chieftain is said to have usurped the throne of Cambodia itself and to have founded a new Khmer dynasty. He may be identified with Sūryavarman I who is the first king known from Khmer inscriptions found at Lopburi, which date from the early eleventh century (1022–5). Lopburi then became part of the Khmer dominions, and it is from this time that the Khmer began to exercise sovereignty over Central Siam, the conquests of Sūryavarman II in the twelfth century carrying the Khmer flag as far north as Sawank'alōk and Suk'ōt'ai. Attacks were also made by the Khmer of Lavō on Haripūnjaya during this latter century, but do not appear to have been successful.

The name of the King of Lavō who was conquered by Sūryavarman's father is given as Ucchitta-Cakkavatti, but his race is uncertain at present. What is becoming increasingly clear, however, from the archaeological finds made in recent years, is that the people inhabiting the Lopburi region and Lower-central Siam, before the coming of the Khmer, were of the Môn race following the Buddhist religion of the Hīnayāna school.

It would appear from his work that Salmony knew nothing of this period of pre-Khmer art in Siam, for he does not mention it, and he places the magnificent head shown on his plates (nos. 21 and 22) at the beginning of the Khmer domination, whereas it is a singularly beautiful example of Môn or pre-Khmer sculpture.

[1] H. Parmentier, "Cartes de l'Empire Khmer", *B.E.F.E.O.* vol. xvi, pt 3 (1916–17), p. 69.
[2] G. Cœdès, "Documents sur l'Histoire Politique et Religieuse du Laos Occidental", *B.E.F.E.O.* vol. xxv, pt. 1 (1925), pp. 18, 23–4.

I have had, very reluctantly, to make these references to Salmony's work, because the whole subject of Indian influence in Siam is most complicated, and it is essential that a clear view should be obtained of the sequence of the peoples who have impressed their civilisation upon the territory of Siam. For instance, there was a strong tradition formerly in Siamese circles that the town of Haripūnjaya, the modern Lamp'ūn, in the north of Siam was founded by a Khmer princess from Lopburi in the seventh century, but it is certain, from evidence found in Lamp'ūn itself by Cœdès, that this princess, Chām T'ewī, was Môn and not Khmer. It is naturally obvious now that she could not have been Khmer as the latter did not arrive at Lopburi until the beginning of the eleventh century, but it shows how easily local opinions, founded on no actual evidence but on purely traditional suppositions, gradually come to be accepted as facts and are thereafter not easily displaced. In my work on the Coinage of Siam[1] I have referred to another, and to me particularly disastrous, example of how easily and quickly traditions are formed.

This is why Salmony's book on *Sculpture in Siam* gives rise to so much misgiving. It is perfectly true that he had not at his disposal much of the evidence which has been forthcoming during the last ten years, but my friendly quarrel with him is that he has assumed as facts suppositions for which there is no historical or archaeological *evidence*, and, without stopping to consider their intrinsic value, has built up round them his whole theory of the evolution of sculptural art in Siam. We have seen the ramifications that the publication of such theories can have, and to me, in England at least, falls the difficult task of attempting to tear down this fanciful structure and of building a new one. I do not claim to be able to indicate the nature of every link that goes to form the whole, much less to have solved all the problems involved; all that this modest work can claim to do is to reduce the many complex and intricate problems to some kind of order, and to give the structure a somewhat more substantial foundation.

If I can show in main outline the different schools of art which have penetrated Siam and left their impress upon that attractive country, I shall be well satisfied.

Finally, I can say that, with very few exceptions, I have personally examined every object from Siam shown in the illustrations given, and have visited every site and temple in Siam and Cambodia mentioned in these pages.

[1] Reginald le May, *The Coinage of Siam*, pp. 24–5. Siam Society, Bangkok, 1932.

# Chapter II

## THE DIFFERENT SCHOOLS OF ART IN SIAM

FOR a clear understanding of the racial movements which have given rise to all its various schools of art, we must take a good look at a map of Siam. It will be seen that the country is divided naturally into four parts.

First, there is the north of Siam, which comprises the modern Circle of Bayab—a province larger than Ireland—and which I have described at length in *An Asian Arcady*.[1] Secondly, there is Central Siam, which is formed by the valley of the Menam. Thirdly, there is North-eastern Siam, which forms a large plateau about 800 feet high; and, fourthly, there is the Siamese portion of the Malay Peninsula.

Now, as Siam is 1020 miles long and 500 miles broad at its greatest width, and is situated in the midst of countries whose peoples have been drawn from many different races, it follows that these four widely separated divisions have been influenced by varying types of civilisation flowing into them, according to the form of culture in which each of the immigrant races was nurtured.

The north of Siam was colonised by the Môn people of Central Siam from the eighth century onwards and was also influenced by tne Indian culture and religion which penetrated the Shan States and Upper Burma at a later date. Strangely enough, although the home of the Tai race is in Western Yunnan, south of the Yangtsze Kiang in China, there is little evidence of early cultural Chinese influence (if we except that of language) in the north of Siam. The temple architecture with its sloping carpet-like roofs, which is such a feature of Siamese cities to-day and which may show some Chinese influence, seems to be comparatively late in point of period. Even in the thirteenth century northern temples were still being built in the style of Pagān.

Central Siam was first of all influenced from the west, namely by the Môn of Lower Burma (and apparently at an even earlier date from Amarāvatī in India direct), then from the east, namely by the Khmer of Cambodia, and lastly by the Tai of the north-central region of Sawank'alōk and Suk'ōt'ai.

North-eastern Siam appears at a very early period to have formed part of the Hinduised kingdom of Funan, a kingdom whose centre was in Cambodia

[1] Reginald le May, *An Asian Arcady*. Heffer, Cambridge, 1926.

before the rise of the Khmer, or at any rate to have been culturally under its aegis; secondly, to have fallen thoroughly under the sway of the Khmer empire, and finally to have succumbed to the Tai.

Southern Siam, on the other hand, being open to direct immigration, seems to have been directly influenced by India itself perhaps as early as the first century A.D., then by a wave of Pallavan culture from its south-eastern seaboard which resulted in the rise of the Hinduised kingdom of Çrīvijaya in the sixth or seventh century, and lastly by another wave in the eighth to ninth centuries from the central-eastern seaports of Kalinga and Bengal. Pure Tai influence does not appear until the close of the thirteenth century, by which time a definite religious influence had been introduced from Ceylon.

If we study the physical map of Siam carefully, it is easy to see how the limits of these movements were determined.

Northern Siam is a combination of mountain, stream and jungle, with valleys between, and the foothills come down as far south as Utaradit (lat. $17\frac{1}{2}°$ N., long. 100° E.) before the plains begin. It forms naturally a self-contained unit of territory.

Central Siam comprises the fertile valley of the Menam Chao P'ya and the lower reaches of its tributaries, the Me Ping, the Me Yōm, the Me Wang and the Me Săk. It stretches from Utaradit in the north, past Lopburi to Bangkok at the head of the Gulf of Siam, and thence to Petchaburi in the south. On the west it is bounded by the range of hills which divides Siam from Burma, through which entries are effected by the famous Three Pagodas pass and also by a more northern route via Kawkareik and Myawadi; and on the east it is closed by the dense feverish forest of Dong P'ya Fai ("the Forest of the Lord of Fire") and the walls of the Korāt plateau.

North-eastern Siam is, like the North, a self-contained unit, with the Menam valley to the west, the Mekōng to the north and east, and the Dang Rek range of hills to the south.

Finally, Southern or Peninsular Siam comprises two-thirds of the length of the Malay Peninsula, and may be said to begin about the region of the now well-known seaside resort, Hua Hin, just north of lat. 12° N., opposite to Mergui on the Burma side.

From this brief geographical survey it will be realised how complicated, and at the same time how interesting is the study of artistic remains found on Siamese soil. One conclusion from the study of the sculpture found is, however, clear and may be stated at once. All the sculptural influence brought to bear upon the peoples inhabiting Siam in historic times has come, either directly or indirectly, from India.

The arts of Funan and of the Khmer empire may be considered as more or less homogeneous, but in Siam there has been an infusion of so many different elements and peoples that, as far as can be judged at present, we have no less than nine different schools or periods of art with which to deal. These schools are as follows:

Pure Indian, i.e. brought from India itself—up to the fifth century A.D.
Môn-Indian (Gupta)—fifth to tenth centuries A.D.
Hindu-Javanese—seventh to twelfth centuries A.D.
Khmer, and Môn-Khmer transition—tenth to thirteenth centuries A.D.
Tai (Chiengsen)—eleventh to fourteenth centuries A.D.
Tai (Suk'ōt'ai)—thirteenth to fourteenth centuries A.D.
Khmer-Tai transition (U-T'ong)—thirteenth to fourteenth centuries A.D.
Tai (Lopburi)—fifteenth to seventeenth centuries A.D.
Tai (Ayudhya)—fourteenth to seventeenth centuries A.D.

If we do not confine ourselves to purely Buddhist art, we may even add another school, namely that of Funan, of which a number of important Brāhmanic sculptures have been discovered in Southern, Eastern and North-eastern Siam. These lie rather outside the scope of the present study, but still it is felt that the work would not be complete without some reference to them, and further details and illustrations of the art of Funan will be found in the chapter dealing with the Khmer period in Siam.

It will be convenient to consider the above schools in the order given.

## PURE INDIAN

The most ancient objects found in or on Siamese soil came to light in August 1927 at a village called Pong Tük, about 10 miles along the road to Kānburi from the station of Ban Pong, where the railway from Bangkok turns south for the Peninsula and Penang.

The attention of the Royal Institute having been drawn to the site, excavations were undertaken both in a banana garden and on the land of a villager near by, with the result that the plinth of a temple sanctuary, with the steps leading up to it, and the bases of several other buildings were unearthed. The illustrations show (i) the outline of the base of the sanctuary, which is oblong with projecting bays in the centre of both sides, and (ii) the steps leading up to it on the south-eastern face. The temple is just over 80 feet long and 47 feet broad (Figs. 1 and 2). The material used was mostly laterite, but in some places brick, but except for some fragments of broken pillars and stucco decoration, similar to those found at P'rapatom, no clue has yet been afforded as to the nature of the superstructures. It has been found possible, however, to propose some dates for the period of their use from the objects found in conjunction with the buildings.[1] The earliest of these is, curious to relate, a Graeco-Roman lamp of Pompeian style, in the form of a bird's body with the erect palmette tail and head of Silenus on the cover-flap, possibly left by some unknown Greek or Roman trader as a relic of the days when China and Ta-Tsin, as the Eastern Roman empire was called, first came into contact with each other. Cœdès considers the lamp as of Mediterranean make and not an Eastern copy, and places it in the first century A.D.

The next earliest object is undoubtedly a small bronze statue of the Buddha in the Amarāvatī style ascribed by Cœdès to the second century A.D. (Fig. 3), not of such fine execution as the similar statue found by Prince Damrong at Korāt in North-eastern Siam and now in the National Museum (Fig. 4), but still of pleasing appearance and showing the so-called Greek influence in the folds of the drapery.[2] These images I believe to be of Indian make, and Fig. 4 may be compared with an equally beautiful and much larger image of the Buddha found as far east as Dong Dūang in Annam (Fig. 5). In addition to the lamp and the image from Amarāvatī, several small bronze images of possibly local make, showing the Gupta style with stiff drapery and conventional treatment of the body, have been brought to light, which cannot be much later than the sixth century A.D. (Fig. 6).[3] As no Khmer or Tai images or objects have been found on the site, it may be concluded that a centre of Buddhist worship existed at Pong Tük from early in the Christian era up to the sixth or seventh century at least. There is nothing surprising in this, as Pong Tük is on the Meklong river, only one day's journey distant from both the important early centre of P'rapatom to the east and Kānburi to the west. Kānburi itself is an old town on the route to the famous Three Pagodas pass leading to Burma and in particular to the port of Martaban, which at latitude $16\frac{1}{2}°$ N. is in a direct line with the ancient Indian centre of Amarāvatī.

As regards the style of the plinth of the sanctuary found in the banana garden, Cœdès says that it is similar to the early type of platform found at Anurādhapura in Ceylon, which, according to Hocart, also owes its earliest Buddhist buildings

[1] G. Cœdès, "Excavations at Pong Tük", *J.S.S.* vol. XXI, pt. 3 (1928), pp. 195–209.

[2] *Ibid.* Pls. 17 and 18. Sir John Marshall considers Fig. 3 as not earlier than the fifth century A.D.

[3] *Ibid.* Pl. 16 (right).

to the great centre of Amarāvatī.[1] So it may be that Pong Tük and Anurādhapura were subject to a common influence. Votive tablets of the Buddh Gayā style, possibly of later origin but undeniably of Indian make, and pottery jars of a type hitherto unknown in Siam also formed part of the spoils of Pong Tük, which may now be seen in the National Museum at Bangkok.

In October 1927, shortly after the discoveries at Pong Tük, a Siamese friend of mine, the late Nai Hong Navanugraha, who was much interested in Buddhist iconography, privately published, as an act of merit on his birthday, a small but most interesting book,[2] illustrating nearly 100 images of the Buddha to be found in private collections among the royalty and nobility of Bangkok, thereby giving the student a glimpse of hitherto unattainable material for study. A careful survey of this book shows that a certain number of the images do not appear to be of local manufacture, but to possess Indian or possibly in some cases Sinhalese characteristics. It is not easy to judge definitely from photographs, but all these images have the appearance of being of an early date and I am including six of them in this work as examples found in Siam which merit further investigation as to their origin (Figs. 7–12). Fig. 8 may be Sinhalese; Fig. 9 has affinities with the well-known sixth-century image from Fatehpur, Kāngra;[3] and Fig. 12 reminds one of a Nālandā-Burmese type. The other three bear no resemblance to any type known to me. To these I join yet two other rather more elaborate images, both in the National Museum, which have been discovered on Siamese soil, but which also do not appear to be of local origin (Figs. 13 and 14). It will be observed that both these latter images have a large nimbus round the head (as has Fig. 7) and that the decoration is most elaborate. It is more than possible that both are Mahāyānist figures, but I can offer no definite opinion as to their original provenance.[4] It remains to be seen whether any of them can be identified as belonging to well-defined Indian or Sinhalese schools. It only remains to state that the images shown above have been found not only in Lower-central Siam, but also as far away as the province of Udorn on the North-east plateau; and yet, as far as I am aware, similar images have very seldom, if ever,

[1] A. M. Hocart, *Ceylon Journal of Science* (G) (1924–7), Archaeological Summary, p. 95.

[2] Nai Hong Navanugraha, *Bronze Images of the Buddha*. Bangkok, 1927.

[3] A. K. Coomaraswamy, *History of Indian and Indonesian Art*, Pl. XLIII, fig. 163. Edward Goldston, London. It is interesting to note that Coomaraswamy observes the "ajouré" pedestal of this image to be closely related to one found at Supanburi in Siam.

[4] Fig. 13 was found on the bank of the river Menam at Intaburi (north-west of Lopburi). Fig. 14 came from the district of Mahāsārakām in the centre of North-eastern Siam. Cf. *Ancient Monuments in Siam* (in Siamese) by Luang Boribal, Pls. 7 and 18 (both left).

been found in the north of Siam as represented by the modern province of Bayab.

These discoveries and objects indicate clearly that there must have been immigrants from India into Siam at a very early date, possibly even from before the Christian era. We have the statement, reasonably well authenticated, that Açoka himself sent missionaries into the "Land of Gold" as well as to Kashmir and Ceylon, and there is little doubt in my own mind that a memory of this "Land of Gold" still lingers in the Siamese town of Supanburi or Suvarnapuri (the City of Gold) and the ancient U-T'ong ("the Source of Gold"),[1] both early cities north-west of Bangkok. There were no images of Buddha made in Açoka's time, but Açoka claimed that both the Cholas in the south and the Andhras of Telingāna on the east coast had accepted Buddhism as their religion;[2] and we know that Amarāvatī at the mouth of the Kistna river was an important centre in the second and third centuries A.D. for the dissemination of Buddhism. It seems probable, therefore, that there was from that time at least an infiltration of Indian colonists into Siam from Telingāna and Kalinga on the east coast, whether they came as missionaries of the Faith, or simply (and more probably) as traders and brought their own objects of worship with them to what must naturally have seemed to them an uncivilised and barbarous land.

Regarding the matter broadly, it seems to me that we have three different routes to consider for this immigration into Siam. These routes may have been in use simultaneously or at different periods, according to the preponderating influence in India itself, and they were certainly used to bring into Siam very different styles of Indian art.

It looks as if the earliest immigrants came from the region of Amarāvatī and landed probably at the port of Martaban: and thence travelled south, through the Three Pagodas pass, into South-central Siam.

In the days of the Gupta emperors, who had their capital at Pātaliputra (the modern Patna), it is more than likely that missionaries and traders coming eastward would use the ancient port of Tāmralipti (Tamluk) on the Hugli river, now a good many miles from where modern Calcutta stands but then much nearer the sea. These emigrants would make equally for Martaban, unless they were bound for Akyab and Arakan on the west coast of Burma, since Thatôn was the ancient seat of the Môn civilisation in Lower Burma, and Martaban was an equally useful port either for Siam or for that country. For a long time past Martaban,

[1] E. Aymonier, *Le Cambodge*, vol. III, pp. 349–50. E. Leroux, Paris, 1904.

[2] *Cambridge History of India*, vol. I, pp. 597–9.

or rather Moulmein, has been the starting-point of the overland caravan route from Lower Burma to Chiengmai in Northern Siam, via Kawkareik and Raheng, but evidently the early Indian traders did not venture thus far, or, if they did, they have left no traces behind them in the north.

Thirdly, in Pallava times, we have the southern route from Kānchī (Conjeeveram) either straight across to Mergui and Tenasserim or, as seems more likely, slightly southwards to Takuapā and Puket Island (Junk Ceylon) in the Siamese portion of the Malay Peninsula. In a stimulating little book on the *Early History of Ceylon*,[1] G. C. Mendis relates how in the sixth and seventh centuries the Pallavas, especially under Narasinhavarman (A.D. 635–8), gradually became the dominant power in Southern India and the Deccan: and how much they did for the advancement of religion, architecture and sculpture. Mendis claims that the history of stone architecture in Southern India begins with the Pallavas, and that their sculpture out of rocks was executed with remarkable skill.

In the tenth century the power in Southern India passed to the Cholas, but there must have been a strong emigration from Southern India to the Malay Archipelago in the earlier Pallava times, to account for the rise there of the Hinduised kingdom of Çrīvijaya and for the Brāhmanic sculpture found in those regions. Moreover, the presence of beautiful Buddhist sculpture in the heart of the Malay Peninsula, of the Mahāyānist School, has to be explained.

Quaritch Wales, who has recently been on a voyage of exploration to the Malay Peninsula for the precise object of studying routes of Indian colonisation, has stated his case very clearly for considering the region of Jaya (lat. 9° N., long. 99° E.) as that from which the dissemination of Indian culture took place to Java and Sumatra in the eighth and ninth centuries, as well as to Cambodia and Funan at a much earlier date.[2] Naturally his views cannot be accepted off-hand, but they certainly merit every consideration. Further and fuller investigation will, it is to be hoped, shed more light upon this highly important and interesting question. I will discuss it more fully when dealing with the art of Çrīvijaya.

There is, of course, a fourth route to consider, the entire sea-route round the island of Singapore and up the gulf of Siam to where Bangkok now stands. Chinese junks were certainly trading with India as early as the fifth century A.D., as witness Fa Hsien's account of his travels, and it is possible that a certain number of the hardier Indian immigrants may have chosen this all sea-route,

[1] G. C. Mendis, *Early History of Ceylon*, pp. 48–9. Y.M.C.A. Publishing House, Calcutta, 1935.

[2] H. G. Quaritch Wales, "A newly-explored Route of Ancient Indian Cultural Expansion", *I.A.L.* vol. IX (1), 1935.

but in all probability the bulk of them would land at the nearest point available, rather than brave the elements in the cruel China Sea and its equally cruel offspring, the Gulf of Siam.

Up to the present no inscriptions of the earliest, or, if we may call it so, Amarāvatī period have been discovered in Siam, and, apart from the finding of early Indian images, we are left guessing as to the conditions surrounding their arrival. All we can say for certain is that Buddhism of the Amarāvatī School had made its way into Lower-central Siam from India, probably some time during the first three centuries of the Christian era.

If we are now permitted, however, to pass over a century or two, we come to a period of Buddhist art in Siam which was certainly of local production and for the dating of which there is some archaeological evidence.

# Chapter III

## THE DVĀRAVATĪ (MÔN-INDIAN) PERIOD IN SIAM

FROM the architectural and sculptural remains that have been brought to light during recent years, scanty as they are, it can be said with some confidence that during the second half of the first millennium of the Christian era, and probably for some part of the first half, the dominating people inhabiting Central Siam were of the Môn race, practising the Buddhist religion of the Hīnayāna School. The sculpture which they have left behind is of a definite style, and is for the most part in a particular material which enables it to be readily recognised. It is entirely of a religious character.

In 1929 Cœdès published his work on the early inscriptions of Siam, dealing with those connected with Dvāravatī, Çrīvijaya and Lavō (Lopburi).[1] He had already published the volume dealing with the later Tai inscriptions (Part I) in 1924. In Part II he summed up all the archaeological evidence available regarding the early history of Siam, and I freely acknowledge my indebtedness to him in the survey contained in the present work.

In the city of Lopburi, 80 miles due north of Bangkok, which was formerly known as Lavō and is certainly one of the oldest sites in Central Siam, the most ancient monuments standing above ground do not carry us back beyond the Khmer period, that is, before the year A.D. 1000. But in the temple of Mahā-Tāt, which is in the heart of the city, and in the surrounding neighbourhood standing images of the Buddha have been discovered which are certainly of neither Khmer nor Tai workmanship and apparently belong to an earlier period of art.

One of these statues bears an inscription in Sanskrit, analogous to that seen on the most ancient inscriptions found in Cambodia, which date from a period anterior to the establishment of Angkor as the capital at the beginning of the ninth century A.D.

Another statue bears a mutilated inscription in characters equally ancient and perhaps containing words in the Môn language. There has also been found at Lopburi an octagonal pillar with a carved cubical capital, which has definitely a Môn inscription of a peculiarly archaic type. This pillar, which is now in the National Museum, is identical with several others found during the restoration

[1] G. Cœdès, *Recueil des Inscriptions du Siam* (Part II). In Siamese and French. Royal Institute, Bangkok, 1929.

of the famous temple at P'rapatom. In addition to these, there is a Hermit's Cave in the Ngu hills near Rājaburi, which bears an inscription containing Môn words.

A cursory examination of these images and sculptures from Lopburi and P'rapatom shows that they must belong to a school, distinct both from the classical Khmer and from the Indo-Javanese School of Çrīvijaya; and at the same time that they are in no way connected with Tai sculpture.

The chief features of this school of sculpture, as found in Siam, are as follows: the spiral curls of the hair and their abnormal size, the elliptical form of the face, the prominent, bulging upper eye-lids, the lightly outlined eye-brows in the form of a swallow springing from the top of the nose-bridge, and the modelling of the torso, where the limbs appear from under the robe like a nude, sexless body under a fine diaphanous cloth. The general appearance of these statues is very similar to that of Indian statues of the Gupta period, especially to those from Sārnāth and the cave temples of Ajantā, but on the whole those locally made in Siam are more simple and austere in form. In his volume on the National Museum at Bangkok[1] Cœdès gives a large number of references in support of this kinship. For my purpose I think it sufficient to show two of these references, namely, the large standing image and the seated figure, both of the Gupta period of about the fifth century, now in the British Museum (Figs. 15 and 16). If these are compared in general outline with the two best preserved Môn images (Figs. 17 and 18), both found at Lopburi, which are now in niches adorning the exterior of Wat Benchamabopit in Bangkok, a beautiful temple built by the late King Chulalongkorn early in this century, it will, I think, be conceded that the relationship admits of no doubt.

The material from which the figures found in Siam are carved is never sandstone, the medium almost exclusively used during the Khmer period, but a slate-blue, hard limestone which is found in the hills situated to the east of Lopburi and to the south-west of Rājaburi.

None of the statues found in Siam bears a date, but various signs which they exhibit will allow of them being attributed to an early period, not far removed from that of their Indian prototypes.

The statues of the Buddha which have been found, chiefly at Lopburi and P'rapatom but also at Ayudhya and elsewhere in Central Siam, and which are included under the term given to them of "pre-Khmer", may be divided into two general types:

(A) The Buddha *standing* with his right hand raised making either the gesture

[1] G. Cœdès, "Le Musée National de Bangkok", *Ars Asiatica*, vol. XII (p. 21, n. 3). Paris, 1928.

of Dispelling Fear, or that of Bestowing Favours, or occasionally with both hands raised in that of Instruction or Argumentation. Of statues of this type there are three in the local museum at Lopburi, four in the Ayudhya museum, and several others at P'rapatom, besides the colossal figure now in the Bangkok museum, of which both forearms are unfortunately missing.

(B) The Buddha *seated* in the so-called "European" fashion, either turning with his two hands the "Wheel of the Law", or else making with his right hand the gesture of Instruction, while his left hand rests in the lap. The best specimens known of this type are the Great Image preserved in the temple at P'rapatom and another formerly in Wat Mahā-Tāt at Ayudhya but now resting in a small sanctuary attached to Wat P'ra Meru (also at Ayudhyā). This latter image has been most unskilfully repaired.

According to Cœdès the first of these two types (i.e. the Standing Buddha), which can represent either the heavenly Buddha, Dipankara, or the earthly Buddha, Gautama, enjoyed a great popularity in the islands of Southern Asia, particularly in Java and Ceylon. The figure with both hands raised is known in Siam as "the Buddha Calming the Ocean": while that with only one hand raised is called "the Buddha forbidding his relations".

The statues of the Buddha sitting in the European fashion, which is a position very rare if not unknown in Khmer iconography, are a realisation in the round of images on early bas-reliefs representing either the first sermon at Sārnāth (of which there is one at P'rapatom) or the Great Miracle of Srāvastī[1] (of which there is one in the National Museum). The characteristic motifs of the throne on which the Buddha is seated are identical in both types of the seated Buddha. Both the statues and the bas-reliefs are akin in style to certain large rectangular votive tablets found at P'rapatom, Rājaburi and in the Malay Peninsula, all of which represent the Great Miracle at Srāvastī, and also to the great rock image of the Hermit's Cave in the Ngu hills near Rājaburi. Both types (A) and (B) appear constantly in the Indian statuary of the Gupta period, as seen from the two images illustrated here, and are also to be seen among the rock sculptures decorating the entrance to the cave temples at Ajantā.

Now the palaeography of the characters in the well-known Buddhist formula YE DHAMMA, etc., inscribed on the votive tablets, as well as that on the rock

[1] The Great Miracle of Srāvastī took place at the repeated invitation of King Prasenajit in order to confound the sceptics. The Lord Buddha caused countless images of himself to appear all around him, in the midst of which he enunciated the Law, to the accompaniment of a violent storm. Cf. A. Foucher, "Le Grand Miracle de Sravasti", *J.A.* (1909), pp. 9–10.

image of the Hermit's Cave, point to a period at least as early as that of the inscribed Buddhas from Lopburi. Also, it is not without interest that the sculptor of the rock image calls himself *Samādhi-Gupta*. At least one other inscription has been found in the Indo-Chinese Peninsula, in which the suffix *Gupta* is used. This was found some time ago in the Malay state of Kedah and refers to a certain *Buddha-Gupta*, who was captain of a ship from the country of Raktamrittika. It is considered to date from the fifth century A.D., a time when the Gupta dynasty was actually the ruling power in India.

From the evidence given above Cœdès concludes that the Buddhist images of pre-Khmer style found in the region of Lower-central Siam, round the head of the Gulf of Siam, must date *at the latest* from the sixth and seventh centuries. I myself do not feel that we can as yet come to such a definite conclusion. If colonists could and did come from India in the days of Amarāvatī, then there is no reason why their successors should not follow them in the times of the Gupta emperors, though possibly from the port of Tāmralipti. The sculpture found is to me clear proof that they did. There may, indeed, have been a continuous stream of immigrants from the second century onwards. It is possible, or even probable, therefore, that the Gupta style of image was *introduced* even as early as the fourth or fifth century, but the Khmer did not enter upon their rule of this part of the kingdom until the end of the tenth century, and it seems that we must give a range of something like five hundred years to this pre-Khmer art. Naturally, Gupta influence had ceased to come into Siam long before the tenth century, but the style may have been continued locally for several centuries after the original inspiration had ceased to influence the art, gradually becoming more and more debased. I think this degeneration can already be detected from the material at our disposal to-day. Although, then, we may perhaps attribute the *best* of the type to the sixth or seventh centuries at the latest, I cannot put that limit to the duration of the style.

It was during these centuries that the Chinese pilgrims Hsüan-Tsang (or Chuang) and I-Ching, as well as the texts of other writers, make mention in this part of the Indo-Chinese Peninsula, between Çrīksetra, the ancient name for Burma (Prome), and Içanapura (Khmer-Land), of the kingdom of T'o-lo-po-ti, a name which Cœdès has restored as Dvāravatī.[1] This latter name is one of those

[1] It is interesting to note that the Rev. E. J. Eitel, in *Chinese Buddhism* (Hongkong and Shanghai, 1870), restores T'o-lo-po-ti as "Dvāra-pāti", i.e. "Lord of the Gate". But E. J. Thomas considers that Dvāravatī is the more likely, as this is the name of the chief place of worship of Viṣnu in his avatar of Krishna in Kathiawar: it is known to-day under the name of Dwārkā.

forming part of the official designation of the old capital of Siam, Ayudhya, which was founded as the capital in A.D. 1350 by the Prince of U-T'ong. But that city was built on the site of a much older one, and was no doubt the successor of a much more ancient capital in the region of Supanburi where the ancient U-T'ong was situated; and, following the immemorial custom, it had to incorporate in its own name that which preceded it, just as the present capital, Bangkok, in its full title, contains the name of Ayudhya. We are justified then in regarding the statues and inscriptions found in Lower-central Siam as the products of a kingdom called Dvāravatī situated between modern Burma and Cambodia. Of this country all that can be said at present is that its predominating people were of the Môn race under the influence of an Indian civilisation, that it practised the Buddhist faith and that its sculpture was based on Gupta models. Of its history we know nothing.

The Buddhist statuary of Dvāravatī is very similar to the primitive sculpture found in Cambodia, of which some magnificent specimens have been recently discovered near Angkor Borei in Southern Cambodia.[1] I show here illustrations of two such images now in the museum at Pnompenh (Figs. 19 and 20). It is not at all impossible that this style of Buddhist art was brought to ancient Cambodia, or Funan as it then was, through the intermediary of Dvāravatī. From Pelliot's account of the history of Funan[2] it is not likely that this state was in direct contact with India, but rather that it received its Indian character through the Hinduised states of the Malay Peninsula and, as far as Gupta art is concerned, from the Môn State of Dvāravatī in particular. Apparently in some French circles this art (of Funan) has received the name of "Greco-Khmer", but, as Cœdès agrees, it is a complete misnomer, since it is clearly a transmigration of a Gupta spirit into a Funan body, and the feeling is to my eyes entirely Eastern. And here I may say, without further delay, that I am entirely on the side of Coomaraswamy in denying the Greek origin of the Indian Buddha, as so confidently asserted by Foucher in his monumental works on the Gandhāra School.[3] It is not for me to call in question Foucher's powers and qualities as an archaeologist, but I do suggest that his "European" sense of racial superiority seems, temporarily at least, to have been too strong and to have mastered his sense of artistic perception. It may be, of course, admitted that quasi-Greek influence

[1] G. Groslier, "Note sur la Sculpture Khmère ancienne", *Études Asiatiques*, Pls. 22 A, 33. Paris, 1925.

[2] P. Pelliot, "Le Founan", *B.E.F.E.O.* vol. III, pp. 290–1.

[3] A. K. Coomaraswamy, "The Indian Origin of the Buddha Image", *Art Bulletin*, vol. IX, no. 4. New York University, 1927.

crept into Indian art during the Kushān period in the treatment of drapery and so forth, but such details are incidental and neither add to, nor subtract from, the living spirit which the sculpture breathes. During the Gupta period such foreign influences as had been imbibed were completely thrown off, and one has only to glance at the famous seated Buddha from Sārnāth to recognise its pure Indian origin. Besides, it is clear that the earliest images of the Buddha (or Boddhisattva) from Mathurā, even if only contemporary and not anterior in point of time, are completely independent of the Gandhāra School, which, though it certainly produced some fine examples, is on the whole representative of a dead and not a living art.

In addition to the evidence already set forth, certain other symbols of the Buddhist Faith belonging to this period have also been discovered, chiefly at P'rapatom; the temple there I will discuss more fully in a moment. These symbols are: (1) the Wheel of the Law, elaborately decorated and supported in some cases by caryatids (an unusual form), and (2) the Deer; both in the same material as the images of the Buddha, namely, a hard bluish limestone. I show examples of both types from specimens in the National Museum (Figs. 21 and 22). It is not to be supposed that these symbols date from a time in the pre-Christian era before images of the Buddha were made and are contemporary with Bharhut and Sānchī in India; but they must, I think, be attributed to a reasonably early date, say the fifth or sixth century at the latest. They are probably of the same period as, and some of them possibly are prior to, the earliest images of the Dvāravatī period. I see it constantly asserted that these symbols of the Buddha, as well as certain attitudes in which he is depicted, such as "Turning the Wheel of the Law", are always to be attributed to the Mahāyāna School of Buddhism, but a great authority on Buddhism has warned me against the loose acceptance of attachment of styles to one particular form of Buddhism. Fig. 21 is just under 3 feet in height; Fig. 22 is 11 inches high and 16·4 inches long.

The enormous image of the Buddha now set up in the great temple at P'rapatom, already mentioned, was found in a marshy swamp near the town. It is portrayed as sitting in the "European" fashion, turning the "Wheel of the Law", and is cut in five sections, which fit into sockets, from a light-coloured quartz. This image, which from the material used must also be ascribed to an early date, possibly fifth century, is of the same racial type as those which I am illustrating. There must naturally still be great difficulty in dating these statues, as we do not yet know the precise limits of duration of the Môn kingdom of Dvāravatī. All that can be said at present is that none are probably earlier than the fifth century or later than the middle of the tenth century, at the end of which the Khmer took possession of Central Siam.

I have already said that there are no buildings of the Dvāravatī period above ground to-day in Siam, but this volume would not be complete without some description of the famous temple at P'rapatom, which stands on one of the most ancient temple sites in this country, if one may judge from the statuary and other ancient material found in its neighbourhood.

The city of P'rapatom lies about 30 miles due west of Bangkok, and is now an important station on the southern railway line. The temple, which is approached from the railway station by an avenue of trees, consists of a vast circular *p'ra-jedi* or *stūpa* with four *vihāra* grouped round it, and a terraced platform.[1] Seidenfaden gives the height of the *stūpa* as 115 metres (or 374 feet), while Karl Döhring states it to be 118 metres (or 383 feet).[2] Thus it is roughly 50 feet higher than the famous Shwe Dagon pagoda in Rangoon, whose present height is given by Harvey as 327 feet.[3] According to Seidenfaden, the original form of the *stūpa*, as erected by the Môn, was that of a Sinhalese *dagoba*, which was later transformed by the Khmer into a *çikhara* or Cambodian tower. The ruins of this tower were apparently still standing in the nineteenth century, though completely overgrown with jungle, and in 1860 King Mongkut decided to restore it in the form of a *p'ra-jedi*, as seen in the accompanying illustration (Fig. 23 A and B). He built four new *vihāra* to replace the old ones, as well as the present circular gallery which completely encloses the *stūpa*. He also placed models of the original monuments in the enclosed grounds. The entire work was not completed till the end of the reign of King Chulalongkorn, who covered the dome with the orange, glazed Chinese tiles which now add so much to its beauty. The first illustration shows the temple as rebuilt by King Mongkut but before the glazed tiles were added. The model of the former *çikhara* is seen to the left.

According to the local tradition, two thousand years ago there existed on the site of the present city of P'rapatom a very ancient and flourishing city called Chaisiri or Sirichai, which was visited by Açoka's missionaries, Sona and Uttara. This is not very likely, as the present town is low-lying and the land around it was probably in early days not very fertile, consisting only of salty swamps. There are, however, the ruins of an old fortified city, Kampeng Sen, which is now entirely

[1] E. Seidenfaden, *Guide to Nakon Patom*, Siam State Railways, 1929 (from which the details of the temple are taken). P'rapatom is the same as Nakon Patom (Nagara Patama).

[2] K. Döhring, *Buddhistische Tempelanlagen in Siam* (3 vols.), vol. II, Pl. XIV. W. de Gruyter and Co. Berlin, 1920.

[3] G. E. Harvey, *History of Burma*, p. 260. Longmans, 1925.

deserted, lying some few miles to the north-east of P'rapatom on a plateau, and here the debris of ancient *stūpa* have been found, as well as Indian symbolic coins similar to those illustrated on Pl. I of my *Coinage of Siam*. But there may well have been a sanctuary at P'rapatom, lying on a kind of island and serving as a beacon for Indian immigrant settlers.

During the course of the restorations carried out in the past fifty years a large number of ancient images and other objects have been brought to light, including burnt-clay tablets bearing the well-known Buddhist *credo*, written in the Pāli language and in the Grantha script, statues of the Buddha, of both Môn and Khmer origin, in all stages of repair, some singularly well preserved, others defaced almost beyond recognition, as well as many heads and other objects in stucco, both Buddhist and Brāhman, and stone Wheels of the Law. King Vajiravudh some years ago set up in the porch facing north a great image of the Buddha found among the ruins of Sawank'alōk and possibly dating back to the time of King Rām K'amheng, the first Tai King of Siam. The image has been very largely restored, but the head, hands and feet are of the original stone. It stands about 25 feet high. In the western *vihāra* there is a reclining gilt image of the Buddha, depicting the Mahāpari-Nirvāna, which is fully 30 feet in length. This is, however, in the later Siamese style. Finally, there is also to be seen the magnificent image of the Buddha in the Gupta style to which I have already referred. Altogether, P'rapatom has been of extreme value to the archaeologist in piecing together the fragments forming the mosaic of Siam's early civilisations, and there is little doubt that more systematic digging in the neighbourhood would yield important results.

The illustrations shown of the Dvāravatī (or Môn-Indian) school will, it is hoped, give an adequate representation of the various styles and types found in Siam during that long period of five centuries or more.

Fig. 24, a little head of the Buddha (5 inches high without stand) in the rare quartz material, is to me singularly attractive, and has a charm all its own, with its boy-like features and its slightly snub nose. I once tested this head by asking an educated Siamese friend, but one who was not particularly interested in sculpture, whether it reminded him of anybody whom he knew. He said at once: "No, but it is very like a Môn." This I have always considered to be a valuable confirmation of the racial type portrayed, coming as it did from an intelligent but disinterested source.

It has been suggested to me that this quartz was probably not carved in the ordinary way with a chisel because of its tendency to chip, but was "rubbed" with special filing instruments after it had been roughly cut to shape, just as jade is "rubbed" to-day after being prepared with ruby dust. Certainly it must have been a very difficult material to handle, and it is not surprising that we find it giving way to a slate-blue limestone, which is found in the hills of Rājaburi and Kānburi, to the west of P'rapatom.

Next, Fig. 25 shows a large figure of the Buddha, 10 feet high or more, which has been cut in two pieces out of blue limestone. It is now in the National Museum. Both forearms and hands are missing, but it would appear that they were originally both raised in the attitude of Argumentation which is often known in Siam as "Calming the Ocean". Here we have the thick, heavy spiral curls covering both the head and the *uṣnīṣa*, the "swallow" type of eyebrows in one continuous line, and the body seen as though sexless under a thin diaphanous robe, all of which features are so characteristic of the Dvāravatī School. The pedestal is roughly carved, but obviously represents an expanded lotus-flower. There seems little doubt that this style of statue must be ascribed to a Gupta prototype. The calm and blessed dignity are worthy of its origin.

Here will be an appropriate place for introducing an interesting but somewhat puzzling problem. The figure just referred to is of Môn origin, as produced in Siam. Now the Môn people came from the land of Rahmanadeça, which is the ancient Indian name given to Lower Burma. When the Môn, who are linguistically allied to the Khmer, first settled in Lower Burma is not known, nor yet when they first received the teaching of the Buddhist Hīnayāna School, though it is popularly supposed that the *Chula-Sakarāt* or "Little Era", which begins in A.D. 638, as opposed to the *Mahā-Sakarāt* or "Great Era" of A.D. 78, dates from the introduction of Hīnayāna Buddhism into Burma. In his work on *Brahminical Gods in Burma*, Nihar Ranjan Ray states that the earliest Buddhist objects found in Burma come from Maunggan near Hmawza (old Prome), the ancient Pyu capital of Burma, and consist of two gold plates, some fragments of a stone inscription, and twenty gold leaves of MS. The gold plates are inscribed with Pali texts and, according to Finot, are in an archaic script like the Kadamba script of the fifth century A.D. (Southern Indian of the Canara-Telegu type).[1] The stone inscription and the gold leaves also bear inscriptions in the Pali language and are in the same script as the above. Ray concludes from this that Hīnayāna Buddhism must have been known in Burma from the fifth or sixth century, at a time when there was a great Hīnayāna movement in India, centred at Conjeeveram (the ancient Kānchīpuram) on the Madras coast.

[1] Nihar Ranjan Ray, *Brahminical Gods in Burma*, pp. 3–4. University of Calcutta, 1932.

But apparently the earliest images found in Burma, also at Hmawza, are of the Brāhmanic gods, Viṣnu, Ganeça, and Brahmā, dating from the sixth or seventh century; and the fact remains that no *Môn* images of the Buddha have been found hitherto in Burma, contemporaneous with, and similar to, those created by their brother-Môn which are coming to light nowadays in Siam.

I hardly know how to account for this curious fact. It would appear as if one were justified in drawing the conclusion that the Môn in Siam had no connection, political or religious, with their brethren in Burma, and yet, even as late as the eleventh century, when a severe epidemic of cholera broke out in Lamp'ūn (Haripūnjaya) in Northern Siam, the entire surviving population fled back to Thatôn, just north of Moulmein, the ancient Môn capital, apparently as if to their homeland.[1] Unless and until therefore fresh archaeological finds in the region round Thatôn disprove it, it looks as if Hīnayāna Buddhism must have come to Siam and taken a firm hold there some time before it gained solid ground among the Môn of Lower Burma. And yet Gupta art must surely have come via the port of Tāmralipti in Bengal to Martaban in Burma in order to reach Siam, and Thatôn is thence much the nearer at hand. The subject has become more complicated since the finds by Duroiselle of undoubted Gupta-like images of the Buddha at Hmawza (that is, among the Pyu), but a thorough investigation of Lower Burma from Thatôn southwards is necessary to shed light upon this puzzling problem.

Fig. 26, which is 10 inches high, shows a most attractive head of the Dvāravatī School in blue limestone, the work of a Môn sculptor imbued with Indian feeling. Here the *uṣnīṣa* is not covered with the spiral curls but rises abruptly from the centre of the head, but otherwise the features are identical with Figs. 24 and 25, and one sees clearly the fine sensitive nose, which is a marked characteristic of this school, and the fleeting smile which plays upon the lips. It is a face of ageless wisdom, which has known everything, seen everything, suffered everything. This is a masterpiece of modelling, and peculiarly "modern" in its treatment.

Fig. 27 is a large stone slab, about 3 feet in height, and originally gilded, showing the famous Miracle of Srāvastī, and is now in the National Museum. The Buddha is seated in "European" fashion on the lotus throne with the right hand raised in the gesture of Dispelling Fear while the left hand rests in the lap. The two chief attendants have large fly-whisks, and to be especially noted is the huge pair of buffalo-horns which form a canopy over the Buddha's head. The physiognomy of the attendants is obviously Môn, but, except for the two quaint

[1] G. Cœdès, "Documents", *B.E.F.E.O.* vol. xxv, pt. 1 (1925), p. 23.

figures in the lower right-hand corner (the meaning of which scene is obscure), the treatment is conventional.

Fig. 28 is a *stela*, about a foot high, in blue limestone usually associated with P'rapatom, which, according to modern Siamese interpretation, represents the Buddha with two attendants standing upon Rāhu, brother of the sun and moon, who chases them continually because they stole his patrimony and causes their eclipse by swallowing them. Rāhu, in Indian mythology, is an Asurinda, or King of Asuras (Demons). The danger which Rāhu can cause is still ever present to-day in the minds of the peasant population of Siam, and as soon as there is any sign of an eclipse taking place, the whole village will turn out and, with noise of gongs and drums, do their utmost to chase Rāhu away and turn him from his fell purpose. I can testify to this, because I have heard it myself.[1] In the opinion of E. J. Thomas, however, the figure portrayed under the Buddha was not, in Môn times, necessarily Rāhu. It might be one of many evil spirits who harassed the Buddha in his hermitage. The execution of this sculpture is rather rough and not of the same quality as that of the previous ones shown. It may be of a later date.

Fig. 29, 8 inches high, shows another head of the Buddha in blue limestone, which is of interest, because it has the features much more sharply cut than is usual. But there is the same lightly indicated "swallow" form of eyebrows, the same fine, delicate nose, and the same heavy eyelids.

Fig. 30 is a mask in stucco, 6 inches high, which is also closely associated with P'rapatom, as these masks have been found there in some quantity but nowhere else to my knowledge. There is no back to the head, and it was evidently intended to be stuck onto a wall or to a plaque for hanging on the wall. The specimen shown is in unusually good preservation, most of those discovered being badly damaged through falling from their places. All the characteristic features are prominent and we may attribute this type of mask roughly to the seventh or eighth century. Whether moulded or cut, it is a wonderful piece of modelling.

Fig. 31 is a terra-cotta head of Buddha partially damaged, now in the National Museum, which was discovered not long ago at P'rapatom. It is clearly of the same period, and is of a rare beauty; indeed, it is in my eyes the work of a creative genius. Prince Damrong, the founder of the National Museum, has declared this head, damaged as it is, to be the finest work of art in the Museum, and there is much to be said for the contention. As is so often the case with works of true genius, it is impossible to express adequately in words the feelings which this little head inspires. It must be seen.

[1] Reginald le May, *An Asian Arcady*, pp. 175–7. Heffer, Cambridge, 1926.

Fig. 32 is a slab of bluish limestone, about 3 feet in height including the socket, now in the National Museum, which shows the Buddha seated cross-legged in the attitude of *samādhi* or "meditation", under the seven heads of the Nāga king, and with a small *stūpa*-crown model on either side. This is the only instance so far known in the Dvāravatī period of the Buddha sitting under the Nāga king, but it is interesting to note that as early as A.D. 484, when Kaundinya Jayavarman, King of Funan, sent Nāgasena, the Indian priest, to the Emperor of China asking for help against the kingdom of Lin-I or Champā, he promised, if his request were granted, to send the emperor, among other things, "an image in gold (sculptured) with the seat of the king of the dragons".[1] In his petition Kaundinya expresses the hope that Buddhism is flourishing in China, and there can be little doubt that the reference here is to an image of the Buddha seated under the protection of the Nāga king, a form which found so much favour at a later date among the Khmer successors of Funan. As Kaundinya's request for troops was "laid on the table", his conditional gift presumably never materialised!

The features of this image, the spiral curls and the treatment of the robe clearly stamp it as of Môn creation, but I am inclined to agree with Cœdès that it may be "tardive"[2] or considerably later than the figures already shown. It was found at Prachinburi, about 60 miles E.N.E. of Bangkok.

From an artistic point of view, I find the stone sculpture of Dvāravatī, especially the earlier images, entirely satisfying, though possibly to other Western eyes the treatment of the torso, indeed of the whole body, may appear too stiff and conventional. It is, of course, of a static quality, but what is particularly noticeable in this early sculpture, to my austere taste, is the purity and economy of line, and the absence of all unnecessary decoration: moreover, it breathes the very spirit of Buddhism.

Early bronze figures of the pre-Khmer or Dvāravatī period are, as a rule, not particularly interesting. Usually they are small and of crude manufacture, but Cœdès shows one rather larger than usual (16·5 inches high).[3] It is a standing figure with both hands raised in the gesture of Instruction, but it has little value as a work of art, and indeed it is clear that the art of creating bronze images was in a very elementary stage during most of this period. Fig. 33 shows a typical example, from Nai Hong's book. This raises an interesting point for discussion, namely why a people should be able to produce such astonishingly fine sculpture

[1] P. Pelliot, "Le Founan", *B.E.F.E.O.* vol. III, p. 259.
[2] G. Cœdès, "Le Musée National de Bangkok", *Ars Asiatica*, vol. XII (1928), Pl. VI (right).
[3] *Ibid.* Pl. IV.

in a stone as hard as the blue limestone, or in terra-cotta and stucco, and yet not be able to create anything approaching it in bronze. The same question arises with Khmer sculpture, as will be seen later, though not to the same degree. If I were to ask a Siamese this question, I am almost certain of the answer that I should receive. He would say, in his terse language, *mai keui*, meaning thereby that the Môn and Khmer sculptors were "not accustomed" to work in bronze, which in any case was probably rare in those early days. But, after all, they had to make themselves "accustomed" to working in the rough stone, and one would have thought that, if they could reach a high degree of perfection in the one, they could equally well in the course of centuries have done so in the other. It may be that the very rarity, and consequent expense, of bronze prevented them from obtaining the same amount of practice in this art, and I am inclined to think that herein lies the probable explanation.

Stone was there ready to hand in many parts of the kingdom, to be had for the quarrying, but although there is plenty of tin in Southern Siam and a certain amount of copper to the east of Bangkok (not being worked now), it is possible that both minerals were very scarce in Dvāravatī days and only to be had in very small quantities.

Figs. 34 and 35 show two small images of the Buddha in black bronze which I think may be attributed to the Dvāravatī period. At any rate, they are certainly pre-Khmer. Fig. 34, which is 4½ inches high (without stand), shows a most curious and unusual formation of the legs and robe. It is difficult to make out where the one begins and the other ends. Cœdès shows this figure on Pl. V of his work on the National Museum, where he states that it comes from the district of Udorn in the north-east of Siam. Note the exaggerated size of the hand (the left one is missing). This feature is common to nearly all the bronze figures of this early period.

Fig. 35, which is 6½ inches high (with stand), shows the height to which the art of the sculptor could on occasion rise. It is doubtless of a later period than Fig. 34 and may even be of the ninth century, but it is as beautiful a piece of modelling as one could wish to find. The poise of the body, the proportions, and the set of the limbs are perfect.

One interesting point to be noticed here, from the purely sculptural aspect, is how the legs, though resting on one another, are drawn inwards, to form a curve in the centre, and how both the soles of the feet are uppermost. This feature persists through the Khmer period in Siam, but disappears with the Tai or Siamese, who made the image either sitting definitely cross-legged with both soles uppermost or with one leg upon the other in a perfectly straight line. The position of the arms and hands is also very characteristic and provides another interesting link with the Khmer sculpture which follows the Môn in Siam.

The foregoing illustrations are representative of Buddhist sculpture of the Hīnayāna school produced in Siam before the advent of the Khmer. Many of the objects shown must have been contemporaneous with the sculpture produced in the Mahāyānist kingdom which flourished in the Peninsular portion of Siam between the seventh and twelfth centuries, and which I propose to discuss next. It is probable that the two schools of sculpture overlapped in the region south of Petchaburi. Of architectural remains of the Dvāravatī period there is practically nothing known except, as I have mentioned already, the plinth or base of a temple at Pong Tük and a few fragments of limestone work found at P'rapatom. No doubt more systematic digging would bring to light yet other remains of the early history of Siam, but that is for the future, and in the meantime I cannot go further without paying a high tribute of both affection and admiration for what Prince Damrong and Cœdès have already done for archaeological work in Siam, and without expressing the fervent hope that the new Government will not permit matters to rest where they are at present, but push energetically forward with the archaeological survey of Siam.

# Chapter IV

## THE KINGDOM OF ÇRĪVIJAYA AND THE INDO-JAVANESE SCHOOL

It is only within recent years that the existence of a hitherto unsuspected Hinduised kingdom in the Southern or Peninsular part of Siam has been revealed. A certain amount of sculpture, of both Buddhist and Brāhmanic images, has at times been discovered in the Malay Peninsula, but there was no solid basis on which to found any theory regarding their origin, and in the past it has been assumed that most of these sculptures were imported by colonists and traders from India direct.

It is only natural, however, that the Malay Peninsula, which was known even in Ptolemy's time as the Golden Chersonese, should have been one of the first territories of the Far East to attract colonisation from India, lying as it does "just across the sea" from the eastern seaboard of that sub-continent, and we already find an early indirect reference to it in the Chinese annals of the sixth century A.D. According to the History of Liang, among the vassal States of Funan was one called Lang-Ya-Hsiu, identified by Groneveldt as Tenasserim, which sent an embassy to China in A.D. 515 and reported that "Our people say that the kingdom was founded more than 400 years ago" (i.e. in the first century A.D. and presumably from India).[1] There is reason to believe that the Chinese themselves came to the Malay Peninsula at a very early date to work the tin mines, and it is even possible that the Phoenicians came, too, though this latter theory depends upon the identification of hoards of small flat silver or billon coins, blank on the one side and with a sunk incuse square on the other, which have been excavated not only in Siamese Malaya but also in Borneo and the Dutch Islands.[2] The earliest coins known to me with an incuse square are the coins of Lydia in the sixth century B.C., which based its coinage on the Phoenician standard. However this may be—it is more than probable that Indian colonists began to appear in the Peninsula as early as the beginning of the Christian era if not before. Aymonier indeed, in his enthusiasm, ascribes the arrival of the earliest immigrants to the

[1] L. Finot, *B.E.F.E.O.* vol. XII, no. 8, pp. 1–4 (p. 3).

[2] Reginald le May, *The Coinage of Siam*, Pl. XXXII, no. 8. Siam Society, Bangkok, 1932. I am indebted to Mr J. Allan, Keeper of Coins at the British Museum, for the information regarding the finding of these coins in Borneo and the Dutch Islands.

sixth century B.C. He also quotes Herodotus as affirming that the extreme point of the African continent had been seen by Phoenician adventurers about six centuries before our era.[1]

According to the History of Liang, Funan itself received its Hinduised art and culture from the state of P'an-P'an, which is now generally agreed to have been situated in the region of Nakon Srīt'ammarāt and the Bay of Bandon, and that there was a definite cultural link between Funan, Dvāravatī and the States of the Malay Peninsula is shown by the fact that Buddhist statuary derived from a Gupta prototype is found in all three centres, even as far south as the modern province of Kedah. Such finds, however, in the Malay Peninsula have been isolated, and we still have no correlated data on which to form any definite theory regarding the cultural or administrative history of this territory before the seventh century A.D. On its history subsequent to this date, light, if fitful, now begins to be shed.

In his monograph, published in 1918,[2] Cœdès put forward his evidence for the assumption that at least from the seventh to the twelfth century A.D., Southern Siam and the Malay Peninsula, from the region of Jaya on the Bay of Bandon southwards, formed part, or was under the political control, of the Sumatran kingdom of Palembang (Çrīvijaya), which was a highly Hinduised State, practising Buddhism of the Mahāyānist school, and which, according to the Chinese pilgrim, I-Ching (A.D. 671–2 and 685–9), had even by the seventh century reached a high degree of culture. Çrīvijaya was known in Chinese as Shih-li-fo-shih.

Some years ago two stone inscriptions were brought to light, belonging to the seventh and eighth centuries respectively, the one in the district of Kota Kapur on the west side of the island of Banka (lat. 2½° S., long. 105° E.) off the south-east coast of Sumatra, half-way between Singapore and Batavia, an island which is famous for its tin production, and the other at Vieng Sra (lat. 9° N., long. 99° E.), an ancient site near Jaya on the Bay of Bandon in the Peninsular part of Siam.

The inscription from Banka, which is dated M.S. 608 = A.D. 686, is in an archaic kind of Malay, while that from Vieng Sra, which is dated M.S. 697 = A.D. 775, is in Sanskrit. The Banka inscription was originally published by Kern in the Bijdragen for 1913 (Deel 67, p. 393), while the Vieng Sra inscription was published and analysed by Finot in the *Bulletin de la Commission Archéologique de l'Indo-Chine* for 1910, p. 153, from a rubbing brought to France by Lunet de Lajonquière.

[1] E. Aymonier, *Le Cambodge*, vol. III, pp. 348–9. Leroux, Paris, 1904.

[2] G. Cœdès, "Le Royaume de Çrivijaya", *B.E.F.E.O.* vol. XVIII, no. 6 (1918), pp. 1–36.

Cœdès analysed these two inscriptions afresh and, as a result of his detailed examination, affirmed that in both there was a clear reference to "the King of Çrīvijaya", rather contrary to the sense derived from them by Kern and Finot respectively.

The script on the Vieng Sra tablet, especially on the second face, is similar to that used in Javanese inscriptions of the same period, and this tablet contains the title "Çri-Mahārāja", which is never seen in Khmer epigraphy but, according to the Chinese annals, was a title borne by vassal kings of the Palembang kingdom in Sumatra. The annals record the first embassy to the Court of China from Çrīvijaya in A.D. 670, and similar embassies are recorded right up to the fourteenth century.[1]

Thus, according to Cœdès, there is clear evidence of a Hinduised kingdom of Çrīvijaya, ranging at least from the island of Banka to the Bay of Bandon, in existence in the Malay Peninsula in the seventh century, confirming the testimony of the Chinese pilgrim, I-Ching.

Further references, presumably to this same State, are made in the epigraphy of the Chola dynasty of Southern India. In the twenty-first year of the reign of Rāja-rāja I (A.D. 1006) mention is made of the gift of a village to the Buddhist temple at Negapatam, begun by Çulamāni-Varman, and finished by his son, Maravi-jayottunga-Varman, who is called King of Katāha and Çrīvisaya and is said to belong to the family of the King of the Mountains. In the Vieng Sra tablet it is also stated that the "Çrī-Mahārāja" belongs to the family of the King of the Mountains, and there is thus established a clear connection between Çrīvisaya and Çrīvijaya. The two kings mentioned above can also be identified from the annals of the Sung Dynasty, which relate the coming of two embassies in 1003 and 1008 respectively, and in which "Çulamāni-Varman" is rendered as "Chu-lo-wu-ni-fo-ma", and "Maravi" as "Ma-lo-pi".[2]

In the next reign of Rajendra-Chola (A.D. 1012–42) the country of Katāha plays an important part, and in two inscriptions of A.D. 1024 and 1030 the story is told of a warlike expedition "over the rolling sea", and a list is given of the countries conquered, of which the first is Çrīvijaya, the prosperous, and the last Kadāra (or Katāha). Other places mentioned are Ma Nakkavara (the Nicobar Islands), Old Malaiyur, and Ilangaçoga, identified with Lankasuka in the south of the modern province of Kedah which itself is identical with the old Katāha or Kadāra.

[1] G. Cœdès, *Recueil des Inscriptions du Siam*, Part II, p. 5 (French). Bangkok, 1929.
[2] G. Cœdès, "Le Royaume de Çrivijaya", *B.E.F.E.O.* vol. XVIII, no. 6 (1918), p. 7.

One of the successors of Rajendra-Chola claims in 1068 to have conquered Kadāra again and to have handed it back to its king, presumably because he could not hope to hold and govern it from such a distance. But some years later the tables are turned, and the embassy from San-fo-ch'i (the name given by the Chinese to this State at that period) to China then claimed that Chola was vassal to them. This is clear from a problem which arose in A.D. 1106 at the Court of China as to whether the embassy from the King of Pagān in Burma (Kyanzittha), "who was sovereign of a large kingdom", was to be treated (as the Emperor had directed) in the same way as that from Chola, which was stated to be only a vassal of San-fo-ch'i.

It is not yet agreed whether the Chinese names, San-fo-ch'i and Shih-li-fo-shih, refer to one and the same kingdom, but the analogy of the latter with Çrīvijaya is corroborated by Cham epigraphy. At the end of the tenth century the Chinese called the capital of Champā "Fo-shih" and it is known for certain that the Cham capital at that time, at Bin Dinh on the east coast of Annam (lat. 14° N., long. 109° E.), was called "Vijaya".

Cœdès thus claims that the inscriptions just described all refer to a kingdom of Çrīvijaya, which held political sway from the seventh and eighth centuries A.D., on both sides of the Malay Peninsula, as far north as the Bay of Bandon, and in his work on the National Museum he makes the significant remark: "One now understands why the Wat P'ra Tāt at Jaya, as Parmentier has very justly observed, represents exactly the type of the most beautiful buildings depicted on the bas-reliefs of Borobodur, which correspond precisely as to date with the Sumatran influence on Indo-Javanese art."[1]

Cœdès has placed the capital of this kingdom of Çrīvijaya at Palembang in Sumatra, and this has hitherto been generally accepted, although I myself have always considered the evidence for this belief as rather slender and have kept an open mind on the subject. Now, Quaritch Wales has come forward to combat this view and, in a lecture given at the Royal Geographical Society in June 1935, stated that, as a result of his investigations on the spot, while admitting the existence of a State, Çrīvijaya, in the seventh century in South-eastern Sumatra, he has come to the conclusion that this State was supplanted in the eighth century by a powerful kingdom called Jāvaka (referred to as Zābag by the Arabs) under a Mahāyānist Dynasty of Sailendras, who had their capital at a place called Jaya in the Siamese portion of the Malay Peninsula, on the Bay of Bandon. Further, he supplements this conclusion by the theory that it was from Jaya, and *not* from

[1] G. Cœdès, "Le Musée National de Bangkok", *Ars Asiatica*, vol. XII, p. 25. Paris, 1928. Author's translation.

Palembang, that the wonderful sculptors of Borobodur and elsewhere in Java drew their inspiration.[1]

Wales' theory is based mainly on an interesting study of the inscriptions and other relevant data made by R. C. Majumdar,[2] who claims that the Sailendras must have wrested the Bandon region from Çrīvijaya towards the close of the eighth century and have established their authority over Java about the same time, thus bringing the greater part of Malaysia under the control of one political unit for the first time.

The introduction of a new kind of script (Nagarī) as well as of a new type of culture (Mahāyāna Buddhism), and the adoption of the name Kalinga for Malaysia may also be attributed to this Sailendra empire. Majumdar does not commit himself so fully as Wales as regards the site of the Sailendra capital, but holds the view that it was either in the Malay Peninsula or in Java, and says that for the present the question must be left open. Krom has put forward the hypothesis that, while Java no doubt came under the sphere of influence of Çrīvijaya, sooner or later it came to form a separate State under a member of the same dynasty which ruled over Çrīvijaya.[3] Majumdar is not inclined to concur in this, and is of the opinion that at the end of the eighth century Malaysia, including the Peninsula, Sumatra and Java, formed one integral kingdom ruled over by the same Sailendra king, though by the close of the ninth century the Sailendras had lost their authority over Java.

To make his position clear, Majumdar has summarised the evidence from which his conclusions are drawn, as follows:[4]

1. The Malay Peninsula, at least the Ligor region, formed part of the realm of Çrīvijaya round about A.D. 775.

2. Shortly after this a king of the Sailendras is found reigning in the same locality, of a different dynasty from that of Çrīvijaya.

3. By A.D. 782 the Sailendra dynasty had established its authority over Java.

4. A powerful kingdom, with its capital in the Ligor region, is known to the Arabs in 844–8 under the name of Zābag. Its king is always styled "Mahārāja".

5. The Nālandā copper-plate of Devapāla's thirty-ninth year (= A.D. 850) refers

[1] H. G. Quaritch Wales, "A newly-explored Route of Ancient Indian Cultural Expansion", *I.A.L.* vol. IX, no. 1 (1935), pp. 1–31.

[2] R. C. Majumdar, "The Sailendra Empire", *J.G.I.S.* vol. I, no. 1 (1934), pp. 11–27.

[3] N. J. Krom, *Hindoe-Javaansche Geschiednis*, pp. 138–40.

[4] R. C. Majumdar, "Les Rois Sailendra de Suvarnadvipa", *B.E.F.E.O.* vol. XXXIII, pt. 1, pp. 121 *et seq.*

to three generations of Sailendras, the first called King of Javabhūmi, and the third King of Suvarnadvīpa.

6. At first the name, Zābag, only referred to the Ligor region, but finally included the Malay Peninsula and the Archipelago, and was referred to as either Javabhūmi or Suvarnadvīpa by the Indians, and as San-fo-ch'i by the Chinese.

7. In the eleventh century, although they had lost Java, the Sailendras were still ruling over Sumatra and the Malay Peninsula.

It may also be added that in later times, up to the thirteenth century, this realm, at least that part in the Malay Peninsula, was referred to as Jāvaka, whose king, Chandrabhanu, twice invaded Ceylon, in 1236 and 1256, but was defeated on both occasions.[1]

From the evidence available, it is not yet possible to come to a definite decision on these important questions, but Wales and Majumdar have certainly put forward a case for full consideration. According to Wales, Jaya showed signs of having at one time possessed a city of considerable dimensions, while at Palembang there are no signs of any extensive ruins. Jaya is also in the direct line of communication with the south of India, much more so than Palembang in Sumatra, and is, in fact, a much better and more natural centre for the diffusion of Indian art and culture eastwards than the latter could possibly be. We have already seen that the kingdom of Funan received its Hinduised culture from the State of P'an P'an in the centre of the Malay Peninsula, a culture which was completed by the second Kaundinya about the end of the fourth century, thus showing that an Indian culture had already been established in the Malay Peninsula at that early date.[2] Further, it is agreed by all that the finds of sculpture in the region of Jaya are more numerous and more important than any discovered in the region of Palembang, and are as near, if not nearer, to Indian prototypes than Sumatran or Javanese models. Finally, Parmentier's comparison of the temple of Jaya with the most beautiful buildings seen on the bas-reliefs at Borobodur is a highly significant fact in any consideration of the origin of the latter's architecture and sculpture.

Fig. 36 shows the part of the temple of Na P'ra Tāt at Jaya referred to by Parmentier. It has been obviously restored, several times indeed, but the fact is still not disguised that it is akin to the Javanese (Tjandi) style of the seventh or eighth century. For comparison two other temple-buildings from the south are included. Fig. 37 illustrates the *Bōt* or consecrated chapel of Wat Na P'ra

[1] R. C. Majumdar, "The Decline and Fall of the Sailendra Empire", *J.G.I.S.* vol. II, no. 1, pp. 18–21.

[2] P. Pelliot, "Deux Itinéraires de Chine en Inde", *B.E.F.E.O.* vol. IV, p. 229.

Tāt at Nakon Srītammarāt, in the Siamese style and showing one of the earliest forms of the carpet-roof now so common throughout the country. Fig. 38 is a photograph of the *stūpa* in the same temple, with minor *stūpas* in the exterior courtyard. It is probably of the eleventh to twelfth century and is in the style of a Sinhalese *dagoba*, with its bell-shaped dome. This is important as indicative of the Sinhalese influence which was brought to the Peninsula after the Pāla influence had begun to wane and which ushered into Siam a new wave of Buddhism of the Hīnayāna school. This aspect of the problem will be dealt with later when discussing the changes that took place on the arrival to power of the first Tai king of Central Siam at the expense of the Khmer in the second half of the thirteenth century.

In his reply to Majumdar, Cœdès obviously leaves the matter open for further consideration. On one point he now agrees to a certain extent, namely that the Sailendras were separated from Çrīvijaya sometime before the eleventh century.[1] There we must leave the problem for the present until further exploration leads us to form a more definite conclusion.

We must not forget, however, that the Hinduised kingdom of Çrīvijaya, or Zābag, or Jāvaka, had no monopoly of the sculpture or inscriptions found in the Malay Peninsula. In contradistinction to the Mahāyānist figures of the Sailendra period, statues of the Buddha of the Gupta type as well as numerous Brāhmanic figures have also been found, which may well be of an earlier period. Also two inscriptions are known, one in the temple of Mahā-Tāt at Nakon Srītammarāt (Ligor) written in archaic Sanskrit of possibly the fifth or sixth century, and another in the temple of Maheyang in the same city written in a Sanskrit of a kind used in Cambodia in the seventh and eighth centuries.[2]

The Buddha statues of the Gupta type are akin to those of Dvāravatī, but the Brāhmanic figures are peculiar to themselves, as will be seen from Fig. 39. This has no direct relevance to the subject-matter of this work, but is shown as an interesting example of the type of Brāhmanic image found. It is a standing image of Viṣnu in limestone, now in the Siamese National Museum, and is 27 inches high. It is of rather clumsy make, but the head-dress, the ears and the decoration are astonishing in the peculiar heaviness of their style. It had originally four arms, of which the posterior left is broken off, the anterior left holds the conch-shell, the posterior right rests upon a heavy club, while the anterior

[1] G. Cœdès, "On the origin of the Sailendras of Indonesia", *J.G.I.S.* vol. 1, no. 2, p. 64. He is replying to Wales in the *J.R.A.S.* (Malayan Branch) and does not accept his theories *in toto*.

[2] G. Cœdès, *Recueil des Inscriptions du Siam*, Part II, Pl. XXI (Inscrips. 28 and 27), pp. 9 and 51–5.

right holds the discus. Similar statues to this one can still be seen *in situ* at Nakon Srītammarāt (Ligor).

Brāhmanic statues of two male and one female deities (Figs. 41 and 42) can still also be seen at the spot where they were abandoned, now protected by a huge tree which has grown over them, near the bank of the Takuapā river just south of Takuapā harbour (lat. 9° N., long. 98·5° E.), almost opposite the hill of P'ra Narai.

Of the Mahāyānist or Indo-Malaysian type of Buddhist sculpture, associated with the Kingdom of Çrīvijaya or Jāvaka, three characteristic examples, Figs. 40, 43, and 44, are illustrated: and anyone acquainted with the Buddhist statuary of the eighth century in Java will at once recognise their mutual affinity.

Fig. 40, which is in black bronze (or *samrit* as it is called by the Siamese), is one of the most beautiful objects in the National Museum. It is 27 inches high as it stands now and probably represents the Bodhisattva, Lokeçvara (or Avalokiteçvara as known in North-eastern Asia). It was discovered by Prince Damrong at Wat P'ra Tāt at Jaya, but unfortunately the crown and the lower half of the body are missing. The beauty of the features and the proportions of the modelling bespeak a very high state of development in the art of sculpture. In his work on the National Museum, Cœdès attributes this figure to the ninth or tenth century, and I incline to think that the earlier century may be the more likely. It seems to me to be close to a true Indian prototype of the Pāla period, and, unless there was a continous influx of new inspiration from India, I cannot think that local art of the tenth century could have produced such a masterpiece. One interesting feature is the cord running from the left shoulder down the body and reaching below the waist. This is part of the sacred thread of the "twice-born", of which the remainder on the back of the figure is invisible. It has no connection with the similar thread hanging over the right shoulder. I cannot find an exact analogy to this figure in Pāla sculpture, but there are certain resemblances, for instance, in Stella Kramrisch's "Pala and Sena Sculpture", to her No. 8 (ascribed to early ninth century A.D.) as to the torso, and to her No. 13 (end of ninth century) as to decoration.[1]

Fig. 43 is again an image of the Bodhisattva, Lokeçvara, in grey-black stone, also in the National Museum. It is a fine piece of modelling, especially the face and the torso, and is clearly akin to Pāla sculpture of the same period. The sacred thread is seen falling down to the waist. There is an interesting analogy to this figure in the volume devoted by Cunningham to the Mahā-Bodhi, the

[1] Stella Kramrisch, "Pala and Sena Sculpture", *Rūpam*, no. 40 (Oct. 1929).

Great Buddhist Temple at Buddh Gayā in India.[1] Plate XXVI (1) in that book shows a stone slab depicting the Buddha in the centre, with a figure on either side of him. Cunningham took this to represent the *Tri-Ratana* or Trinity of the Buddhist Faith, viz., the Buddha, the Law and the Order, of which the figure now under discussion (to the right of the Buddha) represented the Order. He stated that this was the only example of the Buddhist Trinity that he had ever seen in sculpture. But actually this figure, though inferior in execution, is identical not only in style but also in almost every detail with that found in the Malay Peninsula, and is clearly an image of Lokeçvara, as witnessed by the lotus-flower above the shoulder and by the lotus again acting as a footstool to his right foot. Cunningham thought the inscription on the slab to be as late as the twelfth century A.D., but it is difficult to assign such a late date to the figure illustrated, which seems to belong to the ninth century.

In her monograph on "Pala and Sena Sculpture",[2] Stella Kramrisch does not show any figure exactly similar to that illustrated, but her No. 28, a six-armed Lokeçvara in stone from Nālandā in South Bihar, attributed to the early ninth century, resembles it slightly, while her No. 44, which may be of later date as it is more ornate in style, is certainly analogous. No. 10, a Buddha of the time of Surapāla I (A.D. 820–30), is also rather similar in the style of its architectural details in the background. R. D. Banerji, in his *Eastern Indian School of Mediaeval Sculpture*, gives an almost identical figure on Pl. XIV (*a*), which he describes, however, as that of Manjuṣri.[3] On the evidence of all these figures I am inclined to think that the image illustrated may have been brought from India itself.

Fig. 44 is also a figure of Lokeçvara in black bronze from the National Museum, this time in a standing posture. Here the treatment is more conventional and the general effect is not quite so pleasing as that of Fig. 40. The upper half of the figure is clearly of a higher artistic order than the lower. Once more we see the lotus, now held in the left hand; the original and attractive form of the crown, and the jewelled ornaments on the neck and arms, as well as the streamers, like strands of hair, falling on both shoulders as in Fig. 40. This figure may be a little later in date than the latter, but cannot be far removed from it in point of time. Apparently there is no sacred thread of the "twice-born" shown on this image, since the scarf or fold of the robe across the body is seen on both the previous

[1] Sir A. Cunningham, *Maha-Bodhi, or the Great Buddhist Stupa at Buddhagaya*, p. 55. Allen and Co., London, 1892.

[2] Stella Kramrisch, "Pala and Sena Sculpture", *Rūpam*, no. 40 (Oct. 1929).

[3] R. D. Banerji, *The Eastern Indian School of Mediaeval Sculpture*. A.S.I. Delhi, 1933.

figures in addition to the thread. No. 13 in "Pala and Sena Sculpture" has much in common with this figure.

The discovery of these large bronze images in the Peninsula gives rise to an interesting thought. In Central and North-eastern Siam, during the first millennium of the Christian era, all the bronze images known are of comparatively small dimensions and of a rather rough execution, thus showing both the scarcity of metal and the inability to treat it effectively. Here in the south of Siam we have not only an abundance of metal but a highly developed technique in the sculptural art. The first may be due to the plentifulness of tin in the Malay Peninsula, as opposed to Siam proper, and the second can only be accounted for by the advent of a race from India still in the full vigour of its power and possessed of a fully developed artistic style.

Cœdès' summing-up in his volume on the National Museum is worth repeating here. He says:

> The archaeology (and I will add, the art) of the Peninsula presents interesting problems which the evidence at present available is not enough to resolve. It is only from about the seventh century that the sovereignty of Çrivijaya [or, as it may now be, of Zābag or Jāvaka] began to be exercised over the petty States of the Peninsula which were already strongly Indianised. One of these States at least, Tambralinga [i.e. the region of Jaya-Nakon Srītammarāt], existed as early as the second century A.D. It is not to be wondered at, therefore, that recent research in ancient Vieng Sra near Jaya and its neighbourhood has led to the discovery of Brahmin and Buddhist sculpture representing a variety of types. Some of these are very near to pure Indian prototypes, others by their complicated head-dresses recall the sculptures of Kanheri and Aurangabad [in North-western Hyderabad] of the sixth and seventh centuries, though not without some resemblance in feature to the statuary of Dvāravatī; others again are not without an analogy to certain Cham images. This rather unexpected affinity between the art of Champā and that of the Malay Peninsula is found again in the architecture, as witness the Temple of Wat Keo at Jaya, whose resemblance to the Cham monuments of the "cubic" period is undeniable.[1]

As regards the stone Brāhmanic figures, such as those seen at the foot of P'ra Narai hill at Takuapā, I am inclined to agree with Wales that they are fairly close to the Pallavan style of Southern India and may be dated approximately in the seventh or eighth century, though it is clear that they were made locally, as they are in a slaty schist exactly similar to the stone employed in building the temple of Tung Tük on the island in Takuapā harbour.[2]

[1] G. Cœdès, "Le Musée National de Bangkok", *Ars Asiatica* (G. Van Oest), vol. XII, pp. 25–6. Paris, 1928. Author's translation.

[2] H. G. Quaritch Wales, "A newly-explored Route, etc.", *I.A.L.* vol. IX, no. 1, pp. 14–15.

For prototypes in India of Pallava images reference may be made particularly to Jouveau-Dubreuil's *Pallava Antiquities*, vol. II, Pls. 6, 7 and 8, showing Dvārapālas, Çiva, Viṣnu and Brahmā in the Pallava temple at Tiruttani, and to the same author's *Archéologie du Sud de L'Inde*, Pls. XXI B, XXXV B, and XLIII B. showing Pallava figures attributed by him to the seventh or eighth century A.D.: also to Stella Kramrisch's *Indian Sculpture*, Pl. XXVII, no. 73, showing two royal figures of the seventh century from the Dharmarāja Ratha at Māmallapuram.

But the important question that still requires an answer is—Where did the Mahāyānist Sailendras who spread their art and culture throughout the whole of Malaysia originate in India?

Wales offers no views on this point, but Majumdar suggests that they came from the country of Kalinga on the west coast of the Bay of Bengal, whose celebrated port, Paloura,[1] was from time immemorial (according to him) the port of embarkation for the Far East. This is an over-statement in view of the importance, for a similar purpose, of Tāmralipti, Amarāvatī (Bezwada) and Conjeeveram (Kānchī) at different periods of Indian history. Yet we may pass it over because of two other important factors which help to shed light on the problem, namely, the introduction of the Nagarī character in writing and of the name, Kalinga, to the Malay Peninsula, a name still given to the Indian immigrants who are brought to the Colony as indentured labour in the rubber plantations.

Majumdar states that in the sixth and seventh centuries Kalinga was under the control of the Ganga and Sailodbhara dynasties, while in the interior, in the Vindhya region, there was also a dynasty of Saila. The names of the Ganga kings all end in Mahārāja or Mahādhirāja (as in the inscription of Ligor), and Majumdar considers that these dynasties may be considered as the origin of the name Sailendra.[2] The Ganga family was widely spread through India, but the chief dynasties were of Kalinga and Mysore, which was their original home. Kāmārnava was king of the "Tri Kalinga" in the second half of the eighth century, and Majumdar affirms that it is from this country that the Môn of Lower Burma obtained their name of "Talaing". It is usually accepted that the name "Talaing" comes from Telingāna which ran with Kalinga on the eastern seaboard of India, and one would only be inclined to agree with Majumdar if Telingāna itself is a corruption of Tri Kalinga. The latter further suggests that

[1] This ancient port was at the mouth of the river Ganges.

[2] R. C. Majumdar, "Les Rois Sailendra de Suvarnadvipa", *B.E.F.E.O.* vol. XXXIII, pt. I, pp. 140–1.

Tri Kalinga conquered Lower Burma in the eighth century, and that their authority gradually spread from this point southwards over the whole of the Malay Peninsula. Przyluski, in discussing the *Sailendra-vamsa*, says that the source of this Mahāyānist influence must be sought in Northern India and principally among the Pālas of Bengal.[1] If the countries of Suvarnadvīpa and Javabhūmi, referred to in it, are synonymous with the Sailendra Empire in Malaysia (as seems very probable), then colour is certainly lent to the above suggestion by the Nālandā copper-plate inscription of the thirty-ninth year of Devapāla, which records the grant of five villages by Devapāla at the request of the illustrious Bālaputradeva, King of Suvarnadvīpa, and also significantly states that this king had built a monastery at Nālandā itself.[2]

E. J. Thomas, the great authority on Buddhism, informs me that Sailendra is a name for the Himalaya Mountains, and that the Ganges river is called "the daughter of Sailendra", which would certainly account for the Ganga Dynasty taking the name of Sailendra. He also suggests the possibility that disturbances in Eastern India and their defeat by another power in their own land may have driven the Sailendras to found a new empire overseas in the Far East.

Unfortunately the second volume of the *Cambridge History of India*, which would embrace the period from the first century of the Christian era up to the time of the arrival of the Arabs and Turks, still remains unpublished, and our knowledge of the history of Northern India during that period is still fragmentary. Jouveau-Dubreuil, in his valuable *Ancient History of the Deccan*,[3] makes an attempt to unravel the complexities of all the dynasties reigning in that region and of their conquests north and south. According to him, the Gangas were the rulers over Mysore and Kalinga in the sixth century, but at the beginning of the seventh a new power had arisen, and Pulakesin II, King of the Chalukyas, overthrew the Gangas, both in Mysore and Kalinga, and established a new dynasty. He became master of the Deccan and created a new kingdom of the Eastern Chalukyas. He also defeated the Pallavas of the south.

French, in his little volume on the *Art of the Pal Empire*[4], places the first of the Pāla kings of Bengal, Gopāla, in the middle or second half of the eighth century. This would leave, unless some other conqueror intervened, a period of roughly a century and a half for the rule of the Chalukyas over the Eastern sea-

[1] J. Przyluski, "The Sailendravamsa", *J.G.I.S.* vol. II, no. I, p. 35.

[2] R. C. Majumdar, "The Sailendra Empire", *J.G.I.S.* vol. I, no. I, p. 14.

[3] G. Jouveau-Dubreuil, *Ancient History of the Deccan.* Pondicherry, 1920.

[4] J. C. French, *Art of the Pal Empire.* Oxford University Press, London, 1928.

board of India, and, if Majumdar is correct in his surmise that the Ganga-Sailendras were responsible for the colonisation of the Malay Peninsula, their defeat by the Chalukyas may well be responsible for the expulsion of their power from India and their expansion overseas. Or it may be that the Chalukyas, after their conquest of Kalinga, were themselves the originators of this urge to colonise and spread their culture in the Far East. Until further evidence is forthcoming, we cannot arrive at more than a tentative conclusion, especially as some of the Mahāyānist figures found in Malaya, though they cannot as yet be exactly matched in India itself, do bear a resemblance, especially in their decorative motives, to the early images of Pāla sculpture.[1]

In his work on the National Museum, Cœdès makes the following remarks in this regard. After referring to the connection between the earliest images of the Buddha from the north of Siam and those of the Pāla period of Bengal, he says:

> A curious fact, which may be noted in passing, is that of all the images of Buddha found on Siamese soil it is precisely those from the neighbourhood of Ligor [Nakon Srītammarāt], i.e. from the region farthest from Chiengsen, which show the strongest resemblance to those from the extreme north of Siam. We find there the same position of the legs (in *Vajrasana*), the same development of the breast, the same treatment of the scarf as well as of the hair and the *uṣṇīṣa*. These resemblances are easily explained by a common origin. Ancient images of the Buddha are unfortunately very rare in the Malay Peninsula, where by antithesis figures of Lokeçvara are fairly plentiful, but an examination of the votive tablets found in the caves of the Peninsula clearly shows that the type of Buddha depicted is closely allied to the Magadhan type of the Pāla period. It is not therefore surprising to find at Ligor, at the beginning of the Tai occupation, images recalling those of Chiengsen in many details.[2]

This would seem to confirm the view expressed by Przyluski, and on the whole I am inclined to think that the source of the Mahāyānist art found in Malaya, at any rate after the close of the eighth century, is probably to be found among the Pālas of Bengal.

Fig. 45, the last one shown whose provenance is from the Peninsula, presents another interesting example of the problems awaiting solution. Here we see a beautiful image of the Buddha of the Hīnayāna school seated on the king of the Nāgas. It is about 4 feet in height and is fashioned in black bronze (*samrit*) which has been gilded. It is reported to have come from Wat Hua Wiang at Jaya and,

[1] R. D. Banerji, *The Eastern Indian School of Mediaeval Sculpture*. A.S.I. Pl. XXXIV (*a*). Delhi, 1933.

[2] G. Cœdès, "Le Musée National de Bangkok", *Ars Asiatica* (G. Van Oest), vol. XII, p. 31. Paris, 1928. Author's translation.

for some years during the present century, remained set up in a small *sālā* in front of the new temple of Benchamabopit built by King Chulalongkorn in Bangkok. It is now housed in the National Museum.

The form and execution of the Nāga king obviously points to a Khmer origin, but the statue itself, which is detachable from its seat, has no Khmer feature about it. From a cursory examination it might appear doubtful whether the two parts were cast at one and the same time. On the base of the Nāga, which forms part with the whole statue, is an inscription in pure Cambodian, similar in language and orthography to old Khmer inscriptions. But the *script* is quite different and is nearly analogous to that of the Kawi inscriptions of Java. It reads as follows:

> In 1105, year of the Hare (Rabbit), by order of the Kamraten An Maharajaçrimat, etc., etc., etc., on the 3rd day of the waxing moon of Jyestha, Wednesday, the Mahasenapati, Galanai, who governs the country of Grahi, invited Mraten Çri Nano to make this statue. The weight of the *samrit* is one *bhara*, two *tula*, and the value of the gold used for decoration is ten *tamling*. Erected for the faithful to venerate and worship.[1]

Now the era is undoubtedly the *Mahā-Sakarāt*, and the year 1105 = A.D. 1183. During the twelfth century the Khmer were masters of Central Siam, but Cœdès states that there is no such king known in Khmer annals as the one named in the inscription, and that, as already shown, the title "Mahārāja" was not used by Khmer royalty. But the Sung annals of China mention, among the States bordering on Cambodia, the country of Chia-lo-hsi (Kia-lo-hi) to the south; and Chao-ju-kua, writing in A.D. 1225, says that Chia-lo-hsi was a tributary of San-fo-ch'i. It seems reasonable, therefore, to assume that Chia-lo-hsi and Grahi are one and the same country, and that Grahi is to be found in the region of Jaya and Nakon Srītammarāt, where the statue under discussion was discovered.

The use of the Khmer language in the inscription shows that Khmer influence, if not political sovereignty, was strong in the Malay Peninsula at this time; and this may have some bearing on the fact, already mentioned, that, after a prince had come from this southern region at the end of the tenth century A.D. and captured Lopburi, his son went on to capture Angkor itself and make himself ruler of the whole Khmer empire, under the style of Sūryavarman I.

But the fact remains that the statue on the Nāga king is certainly not Khmer, nor yet, I think, of true Peninsular origin. It is, to my mind, closely akin to Fig. 35 which is a late product of Môn or Dvāravatī art. I need only point to

[1] G. Cœdès, *Recueil des Inscriptions du Siam* (Part II), pp. 45–7. Royal Institute, Bangkok, 1929.

the set of the legs which are drawn inwards, to the way in which the arms and hands are placed, the heavy fold of the robe, and the type of features with the oval face, the "swallow" form of eyebrow and the sensitive nose, to show at once the affinity between these two figures.

The tantalising question remains: if the statue and the Nāga are not of the same period, which of them is the earlier? Cœdès seems to incline to the view that the image of the Buddha is of later date than the Nāga, but I do not feel at all sure about this. If the image is, as I believe, of Môn origin, however late, one would expect it to be anterior to A.D. 1183. On the other hand, if the original statue (of Khmer type) were broken or lost, it would be a singular occurrence if an antique Môn image were found to fit the stand exactly, as the image in question obviously does. Altogether, the problem is a nice one, especially as the ruler of Grahi invited Mraten Çrī Nano to make "this image". For iconographical reasons I myself feel reasonably certain that the image of the Buddha is not of later date than the Nāga seat, and I suggest then that the two figures are contemporaneous, and that it was an "artist" still under Môn influence who modelled the image, while it was only a "craftsman", under Khmer influence, who manufactured the Nāga king. This would, according to Hodson of Cambridge, be in keeping with Indian traditions, and presents to me the most reasonable solution of the problem.

If this explanation is the correct one, it would tend to show that Môn sculptural influence was still exercising its sway as late as A.D. 1183.

From the historical point of view it remains to add that towards the end of the thirteenth century the first Tai kingdom in Siam under Rām K'amheng claimed dominion over the Malay Peninsula as far south as Nakon Srītammarāt, as witnessed by the stone inscription of Suk'ōt'ai dated M.S. 1214=A.D. 1292, and that this conquest was simultaneous with the Javanese campaigns against Malaya and Sumatra which lasted from 1275 to 1293. These two attacks, coming at the same time, put an end to the sovereignty of Çrīvijaya or Jāvaka over the Malay Peninsula.

# Chapter V

## FUNAN AND THE KHMER PERIOD IN SIAM

By the "Khmer period in Siam" in Siamese archaeological circles is generally understood the period of Khmer dominion over Central Siam, i.e. the valley of the Menam, with its chief centre at Lopburi, or Lavō as it was then called: and Khmer sculpture found on Siamese soil is generally attributed to "The School of Lopburi". But the Khmer dominions once embraced almost the whole of North-eastern Siam, and especially the valley of the Mūn river, and in any survey of Khmer art in Siam, we have to take both regions into consideration.

At a later date the tables were turned with a vengeance, and, when the Tai had finally smashed the Khmer power in the middle of the fifteenth century, Cambodia became a vassal state of Siam. Right up to modern times Angkor itself was in Siamese territory until it was ceded to France as lately as 1907.

This is why Siamese and Cambodian customs, dress, music and dancing are to-day so much akin, in spite of the fact that the two languages, which are allied in script,[1] have remained separate in speech. Indeed, though I have been able to converse freely in Siamese with old Siamese-born residents of Angkor, who were bilingual, I could scarcely understand a word of the Cambodian tongue.

The rise of the Khmer empire took place at the expense of the old Kingdom of Funan, the heart of which occupied modern Cambodia and Cochin-China, and which lasted, roughly, from early in the third to the end of the sixth century A.D. Practically all we know of Funan is due to the researches of Pelliot who unearthed and translated a large number of references to this State in the early Chinese annals.[2]

Funan was completely Hinduised by the end of the fourth century, and statues of the Buddha as well as splendid stone statues of Viṣnu and other Brāhmanic gods have been found in Cambodia and Cochin-China, and even as far north as Çrīdeb in the valley of the Pā-săk river in North-eastern Siam, which possibly belong to the art of this early kingdom and which are probably not later in date

[1] Cf. the stone inscription of the first Siamese King, Rām K'amheng of Suk'ōt'ai, dated A.D. 1292, from which it has been proved that the Siamese script is based on a cursive form of Khmer script.

C. B. Bradley, *J.S.S.* vol. x, pt. 1; L. Finot, *B.E.F.E.O.* vol. xvii, pt. 5, pp. 10–29 (p. 14); Cœdès and Burnay, *J.S.S.* vol. xxi, pt. 2, p. 88.

[2] P. Pelliot, "Le Founan", *B.E.F.E.O.* vol. iii, pp. 248–303.

than the fifth or sixth century A.D. To call this statuary provincial would be to underrate it completely. It shows a breadth of conception and execution which is only given to master-sculptors and is certainly as fine as anything found on Indian soil.

I have already referred to the images of the Buddha found in Cambodia relating to this period in my chapter on the Dvāravatī (Môn-Indian) period in Siam. For the sake of completeness I am including a number of examples of Brāhmanic gods, which may also be included in the art of Funan, found both in Cambodia and in the territory of Siam.

First I give illustrations of two magnificent images of Hari-Hara[1] (Figs. 46 and 47), both from the southern part of Funan and now in the Museum at Pnompenh, which it would be difficult to match, by any standards of form and virility, in India itself. They are both incomplete, and Fig. 47 has been partially restored, but they are clearly expressions of a mature art, at once highly localised and yet showing no sign of provincialism. They are greater than life-size.

For comparison with them I show examples of three Brāhmanic gods found on Siamese soil. Fig. 48 is a similar statue, 4 feet 10 inches high, in sandstone, which is said to have come from Vieng Sra, an ancient city of Peninsular Siam, in the province of Surāshtradhāni. It was, however, first found and recorded by de Lajonquière in the Museum at Ayudhya. It has the same cylindrical head-dress as that seen in Fig. 46 from Pnompenh, which head-dress is so characteristic of early Pallava sculpture, but, in place of a loin-cloth, wears a nether garment hardly distinguishable from the *dhoviti* worn by the modern Hindu. It wears a more provincial aspect than its brother statue from Cambodia, but there are still a virility and a movement about the form which bespeak a high degree of skill and artistry. Two of the arms are missing. Similar statues have been found as far west as Takuapā.[2]

Fig. 49 is an image of Ardhanari, who symbolises Çiva and his wife Umā united in one form. It is in sandstone, 2 feet 4 inches in height. The ears and the head-dress, according to Cœdès, are very near to their Indian prototypes, and indeed the figure is an extremely rare one for Further India. Its provenance is unknown, and it was found in the Ayudhya Museum by de Lajonquière, but it undoubtedly belongs to the period of pre-Khmer art and may be confidently ascribed to the Funan period of ascendancy.

Fig. 50 shows an inspired image of a Yakṣi in sandstone, 2 feet 4 inches in height. It was found in a remote district of Siam at Çrīdeb, in the province of

[1] Viṣnu and Çiva combined in one.

[2] Cf. H. G. Quaritch Wales, "A newly-explored Route", *I.A.L.* vol. IX, no. 1, Pl. II, fig. 1.

Petchabūn in North-eastern Siam in the valley of the Pā-săk river, round about lat. 17° N. and long. 101° E., where other relics of an early Indian civilisation have also been discovered.[1] It is akin to the beautiful Yakṣa figure in the Stoclet collection, and the hair is dressed in a form similar to that of a Yakṣa found at Koh Ker, an ancient city of Cambodia. It is one of the most beautiful works of art to be seen in the National Museum at Bangkok. All three images are illustrated in Cœdès' volume on that Museum.

In a recent short monograph Cœdès has published illustrations of further Brāhmanic images, together with a fragmentary stone inscription in Sanskrit, sent down to the National Museum within the last few years by the District Authorities of Çrīdeb.[2] One of these figures, together with a torso and the fragmentary inscription, is reproduced here (Figs. 51, 52 and 53). The writing itself is beautiful in character but unfortunately the inscription does not give any connected sense; from its palaeography Finot places it in the fifth or sixth century A.D., and Cœdès states that in his eyes "such a period does not appear too remote for sculptures which recall so closely the Indian canon of the Gupta period". I agree with him when he says that what especially differentiates these Brāhmanic statues from the Khmer or even pre-Khmer Buddhist art in Cambodia is the triple curve of the body; I would not, however, associate these figures with Gupta art. They may be contemporary with it, but I have a feeling that the origin of all these early stone figures of Viṣnu and other Brāhmanic gods found in Siam must be sought in Central and Southern India, among the Pallavas, Chalukyas and Pandiyas. They are, to my eyes, the undoubted forerunners of those swaying, lissome, sinuous figures of the Chola period in the south, and pure Gupta art is too austere to introduce such sensuous feeling into its creations. Cœdès also doubts whether the kingdom of Funan ever extended so far towards the north-west, and hints at the possibility of another Hinduised State in this region. This may quite well be the case, as will be seen from a discussion on this point entered into later on.

Very little is known about the architecture of Funan, but a short reference to it will be found in Parmentier's "History of Khmer Architecture", from the few remnants which still exist on French territory.[3]

[1] H. G. Quaritch Wales has recently delivered a lecture on a visit paid by him and his wife to Çrīdeb.

[2] G. Cœdès, "Notes sur quelques sculptures provenant de Çrideb (Siam)", *Mélanges Linossier*. Musée Guimet, Paris. No date.

[3] H. Parmentier, "History of Khmer Architecture", *Eastern Art*, vol. III (1931), p. 143. Philadelphia.

Funan was in the habit, like all the other States of South-eastern Asia, of sending embassies with tribute to the Court of China, but in the Sui-shu (History of the Sui, A.D. 589–618) two new states, Ch'ih-t'u and Chên-la, are mentioned for the first time as following this admirable custom.[1] In the Chinese annals it is stated that Chên-la, from which the first embassy came to China in A.D. 616–17, lay south-west of Champā (which occupied then the coast of Annam) and was originally a vassal state of Funan. The dynastic name of the King was Kshatriya and the personal name Chitrasena. This king is said to have conquered Funan, and his son, Içanasena, who succeeded him, lived at Içanapura. It is clear from this that Chên-la represents the Khmer kingdom. It must, however, be borne in mind that, when Chên-la first conquered Funan, it was split up into two parts, Chên-la of the Water (i.e. the Great Lake and the lower reaches of the Mekōng), and Chên-la of the Earth (i.e. the Lao States to the west of Annam). It was not until the eighth century that the northern part obtained control over the whole of Cambodia.[2]

To turn now to the Khmer dominion over Siam.

The limits of time set to this dominion in the valley of the Menam Chao P'ya, or Central Siam, can now be more or less accurately fixed, within a few decades of years. For reliable evidence of its beginnings we have the facts related in the reputable *Jinakalamālini* from Chiengmai,[3] referred to in chapter I, which correspond with the evidence adduced from the stone inscription of the Khmer king, Sūryavarman I, from Lopburi, dated A.D. 1022–5; and, for its close, we have inscriptions from Suk'ōt'ai and Kampengp'et, which prove conclusively that some time towards the middle of the thirteenth century the Khmer viceroy had been superseded politically in that region by the father of the famous King Rām K'amheng (the so-called P'ra Rūang, or Father of the Tai), who set up the first Tai kingdom at Sawank'alōk-Suk'ōt'ai.

From the inscription referred to above it is clear that at the beginning of the eleventh century both schools of Buddhism (Mahāyāna and Hīnayāna) were being practised at Lopburi, and Brahmins practising *yoga* are also mentioned.

During most of the Khmer period the kings distributed their favours equally among Buddhists and Brāhmans, and Çaivism seems to have been at times the official form of religion. The same remarks apply to the earlier kingdom of Funan,

[1] P. Pelliot, "Le Founan", *B.E.F.E.O.* vol. III, p. 272.

[2] H. Parmentier, "History of Khmer Architecture", *Eastern Art*, vol. III (1931), p. 141. Philadelphia.

[3] G. Cœdès, "Documents", *B.E.F.E.O.* vol. XXV (1925), pp. 1–200.

and this is why one finds images both of the Buddha and of Brāhmanic deities of the same period side by side.

Sūryavarman I appears to have been an active and energetic king, as one would imagine from his feat of capturing the throne of Cambodia in A.D. 1002. An inscription in Sanskrit verse, undated, has been discovered at Prah K'an in the province of Kompong Suay 40 miles due east of Angkor, in which the author, having done homage to the Buddha, extols the valour of the King which, he states, can be imagined from the manner in which he wrested the kingdom from its previous ruler.[1] Although Sūryavarman I is described as being born of the Sun and possessing the grace of Viṣnu, it is likely that he was a Buddhist by faith as his posthumous name was Nirvānapada. Like all modern Kings of Siam, he probably kept Brāhmans at his Court.

Other inscriptions of Sūryavarman I have been found at P'ra Vihāra, the Mountain Temple, and in his own Palace at Angkor T'om. This last is dated M.S. 933=A.D. 1011, nine years after his accession, and records on eight different *stelae* the solemn oath of fealty which had to be sworn by all the Governors of the kingdom, of whom about four hundred are mentioned by name.[2] This demonstrates the wide extent of the empire at that period, but at the same time it gives rise to an uneasy suspicion that Sūryavarman I did not at first feel too sure of his seat on the throne, as may well have been the case. He seems, however, to have established himself firmly in the end, as he ruled till A.D. 1049, a length of reign, 47 years, equalled by few, if any, other kings of Cambodia.

Sūryavarman I is thus clearly fixed. But what of his father, the Chief of Nakon Srītammarāt, who captured the city of Lavō (Lopburi) from its former ruler, and his kingdom as well? Of what nationality was he? And of what religion? By all accounts he should have been a Malayanised Chief under the King of Çrīvijaya, practising the Mahāyānist form of Buddhism, and his son should have been the same. But here we find the son, after conquering Cambodia, introducing Cambodian forms of architecture and art into Siam. It is just as if an Italian prince, having first conquered France and then England, introduced English art into France! Altogether it is rather puzzling, but it looks as if by the tenth century the Malay Peninsula had been subjected to a considerable amount of Khmer influence, even if still vassal to Çrīvijaya. And this hypothesis is much strengthened by the image of the Buddha on the Khmer form of the Nāga king, with its Khmer inscription, which we discussed previously under Fig. 45.

[1] L. Finot, "L'Inscription de Prah Khan", *B.E.F.E.O.* vol. IV, pp. 672–5.

[2] E. Aymonier, *Le Cambodge*, vol. III, p. 140. Leroux, Paris, 1904.

In North-eastern Siam the problem of the duration of Khmer rule is of a different order. From a study of the six interesting maps prepared by Parmentier,[1] one can follow the gradual expansion of the Khmer empire as shown by the stone inscriptions found in various centres; Parmentier marks the place of discovery of each on his maps. Further research may, and doubtless will amplify these maps in detail, but is not likely to alter the general outline or trend of political affairs.

A résumé of the facts determined by the inscriptions gives the following results.

From the second half of the sixth century A.D., down to the reign of Jayavarman II, who came to the throne in A.D. 802, practically all the inscriptions found are in the southern and eastern portions of Cambodia and Cochin-China.[2] There are, however, a few scattered about above lat. 14° N., namely in the regions of Korāt and Surin in Siam, at Vat P'ū on the Mekōng just south of Bassac, and one as far north as Chan Nakon at the junction of the Mekōng and Mūn rivers: and, though these show that the Khmer had at an early date penetrated the Korāt plateau, the great bulk of the inscriptions found indicate that, when the Khmer of Chên-la had overthrown the kingdom of Funan, they naturally confined their main attentions at first to the centre of that kingdom which, as described above, occupied most of modern Cambodia and Cochin-China, the capital being in the region between Pnompenh and Chaudoc to the south of it.

In the early years of the ninth century A.D. Jayavarman II established the supremacy of the north over the south and was the first king to remove the capital to Angkor in the north-western region of the Great Lake. Towards the end of that century the great Yaçovarman built the original city of Angkor T'om and also, it is said, the temple of P'ra Vihāra on the Dangrek range of hills, 2300 feet above sea-level.[3] Early in the tenth century Jayavarman IV temporarily removed the capital to Koh Ker, just south of P'ra Vihāra. Of this period inscriptions are still fairly frequent in the south, but hitherto no inscriptions at all have been found in North-eastern Siam, only one place being marked on the map, viz. P'amniep which is near Chantaburi in south-eastern Siam.

Pelliot conjectures that Ch'ih-t'u may have been situated in the basin of the Menam Chao P'ya, but the Chinese annals state that Ch'ih-t'u was another branch

[1] H. Parmentier, "Cartes de l'Empire Khmer", *B.E.F.E.O.* vol. XVI, pt. 3 (1916–17), pp. 69–73.

[2] There are certain grounds for the belief that in the eighth century the Khmer kingdom came under the sovereignty of Java, and that it was Jayavarman II who threw off this yoke.

[3] Judging from its decorative motives, I think this temple must be of later date.

of Funan and, as I have just referred to the fact that Brāhmanic figures, similar in style to those found in Cambodia, have also been unearthed in the valley of the Pā-săk river, round about lat. 17° N., long. 101° E. (though none have been found in the valley of the Menam), I am inclined to think that Ch'ih-t'u is more likely to refer to the Pā-săk region than to the valley of the Menam, especially if we bear in mind the kingdom of Dvāravatī which the Chinese referred to about this period as T'o-lo-po-ti.

Here may be interposed a rather singular fact. Although all the States of South-eastern Asia were colonised from India and drew from that sub-continent their religious and cultural inspiration, they all considered themselves as tributary to China and sent embassies with tribute regularly to that Court: and this, in spite of the fact that China never attempted any military conquests over them, except in the case of Tonkin which was adjacent to Chinese territory, or tried to dominate them by force. In fact, on the one occasion, already referred to in another connection, when the King of Funan, Kaundinya Jayavarman, sent an embassy to China in A.D. 484, asking the Emperor to send him troops to assist in punishing the usurping king of Champā, whom he described as "a miserable criminal", the request was laid on the table and brought forth no concrete response.[1]

The most feasible explanation of this acknowledgement of the Chinese Emperor as overlord seems to lie in the respective geographical positions of India and China. India was far away across the blue sea and required months of arduous travel to reach, while China was close at hand. Evidently also the fame and splendour of the "Son of Heaven" had already imposed itself firmly on the then known far-eastern world.

The capital of the Kingdom of Funan was situated between Pnompenh and Chaudoc to the south of it, and the earliest Khmer kings, after conquering Funan, established themselves at Vyadhapura, or Angkor Borei, which is in the same region, about lat. 11° N., long. 105° E.[2] According to a Sanskrit inscription from Vat Prei Vier in Cambodia, dated A.D. 665, Kaundinya Jayavarman of Funan died in A.D. 514. His eldest son, who was born of a concubine, killed the legitimate heir, his half-brother by a Queen, and reigned as Rūdṛavarman. In A.D. 539 he offered the Emperor of China a hair of the Buddha 12 feet long, and the Emperor sent the priest Yun Pao or T'an Pao to fetch it. This is the last King of Funan to be mentioned in the Chinese annals, but apparently an embassy still came from

[1] P. Pelliot, "Le Founan", *B.E.F.E.O.* vol. III, pp. 258–9.

[2] *Ibid.* pp. 288–90.

Funan as late as the first half of the seventh century, after which the name disappears altogether.[1]

In early Khmer inscriptions found in Cambodia, of which the earliest is dated A.D. 624, mention is first made of two kings, Çrutavarman and his son, Çreṣthavarman, who had their capital at Çreṣthapura. These two are not yet traceable as having existed, but after an unknown period of time there appears a reigning family, whose names are given as follows:

1. Rūdravarman—*c.* A.D. 550.
2. Bhavavarman—between A.D. 550–600. } Brothers
3. Mahendravarman (Chitrasena)—early seventh century. } Brothers
4. Içanavarman (son of 3)—A.D. 616–17.
5. Jayavarman—A.D. 665.

An interesting problem is involved in the name of Rūdravarman, as to whether he is the same personage as the last Rūdravarman of Funan. Their dates are roughly similar, and Pelliot inclines to the view that they were one and the same person. It is, indeed, more than likely that they are identical.

The Chinese annals quote Chitrasena (Mahendravarman, after his accession) as the conqueror of Funan, but Pelliot thinks it was probably his elder brother, Bhavavarman, who performed this feat in the second half of the sixth century, and this is the view generally accepted now. Inscriptions describe him as ruling from Stung Treng on the Mekōng (lat. 13½° N., long. 106° E.) to Battambang in the south-west (lat. 13° N., long. 103° E.), and as far south as the present province of Treang (Cochin China). The father of Bhavavarman and Chitrasena was Viravarman, but it is known that he did not reign. Texts which celebrate the successes of Bhavavarman attach him to the race of the Sun, but are silent about his predecessors. It is also not clear whether Bhavavarman was related to Rūdravarman. Perhaps the former was a vassal ruling in the north—for there were then two parts of the kingdom—and on the death of Rūdravarman seized the major throne.[2] We do not know for certain, but, whoever was the founder, it may be confidently accepted that the beginnings of the Khmer Empire date from the second half of the sixth century A.D.

During the period between A.D. 950 and 1000 inscriptions become of much less frequent occurrence in the south, while a certain number appear north of the Mūn river on the north-eastern plateau, even as far north as Sakon Nakon

[1] P. Pelliot, "Le Founan", *B.E.F.E.O.* vol. III, pp. 294–5.

[2] *Ibid.* pp. 300–2.

(lat. 17° N., long. 104° E.); but it is not till the reign of the usurper, Sūryavarman I, early in the eleventh century that we find Khmer inscriptions at Panom Wan near Korāt, at Panom Rung between Angkor and Korāt, and at Lopburi in Central Siam.

Khmer inscriptions of the twelfth and thirteenth centuries are found in North-eastern Siam, but in Southern Cambodia they become practically non-existent. Parmentier remarks that at one period, at the beginning of the thirteenth century, the Khmer seem to have completely given up the practice of inscribing their deeds and victories, or the foundation of monasteries, on stone, at a time when the Empire was probably at its highest point of development. But, at the risk of differing from an old friend, I would suggest that the course of affairs in Siam seems to give rather an opposite indication, namely, that by the thirteenth century the power of the Khmer was definitely on the wane, that there were no more conquests and victories to record, and that even institutions of piety and devotion had lost their savour in Khmer eyes.

It has already been mentioned that the Khmer were ousted from North-central Siam by the Tai in the middle of the thirteenth century. Their shadowy rule may have persisted in the Lopburi and North-eastern regions for some little time longer, but by A.D. 1350 the Tai had established themselves firmly at Ayudhya, and the wars which took place between Siam and Cambodia during the succeeding century finally resulted in the complete overthrow of the Khmer Empire and the sack of Angkor by the Tai in A.D. 1431. Thereafter the Khmer withdrew their capital to a new site at Lōvek, a little north-west of the modern capital of Pnompenh, and the Empire gradually sank into insignificance and decay.

But from its early beginnings about A.D. 550, the Khmer Empire had a continuous run of nearly nine hundred years—about as long a run as any other empire of the world has had in historic times—and during that time made its power felt throughout the whole of South-eastern Asia. What is most to my liking is that it produced a succession of kings who were not only mighty warriors but also magnificent builders as well—who have left behind them a striking testimony to their powers of conception in the remarkable series of monuments still remaining, if alas mostly in ruin, to-day.

Is it merely a coincidence that that European race, which is perhaps most fitted by taste and inclination for the purpose, has now found itself in a position to care for and, wherever possible, to restore those beautiful monuments? Whether coincidence or not, it is a most providential chance that has enabled the French to carry out the wonderful work which they are performing in French Indo-China.

When I say that Lunet de Lajonquière, in his *Inventaire Descriptif des Monuments du Cambodge*,[1] had already in 1911 recorded the existence of no less than 887 monuments, as well as 235 stone inscriptions, some idea will be gained both of the magnitude of the task awaiting the French archaeologists as well as of the building capacity of the ancient Khmer.

Of the total given above, 111 monuments and 22 inscriptions of Khmer origin have been found in North-eastern Siam, spread as follows among the three Siamese Provinces of Udorn, Isān, and Korāt:

| | Monuments | Inscriptions |
|---|---|---|
| Udorn | 4 | 1 |
| Isān | 46 | 11 |
| Korāt | 61 | 10 |
| | 111 | 22 |

To this number Seidenfaden has added another 89 monuments and 15 inscriptions in his "Complément à L'Inventaire des Monuments du Cambodge",[2] published in 1922. This makes a grand total for North-eastern Siam of 200 monuments or archaeological remains and 37 inscriptions.

De Lajonquière was of the opinion that the Khmer civilisation did not extend beyond the valley of the Mūn river and its principal tributary, the Lam Chi, but Seidenfaden asserts that, from his investigations, the Khmer dominions stretched much farther afield, and covered practically the whole of North-eastern Siam with the exception, perhaps, of the north-west portion of Udorn. Maspero placed the capital of Chên-la (as the Chinese called Funan's vassal state) at Pāk Hin Būn on the Mekōng (lat. $17\frac{1}{2}°$ N., long. $104\frac{1}{2}°$ E.), but Seidenfaden states that no Khmer ruins are to be found there, and that the capital was probably at Tāk'ek (opposite Nakon Panom) slightly to the south, where there are the remains of a large city still to be seen.

Actually, the most northern Khmer ruins have been found at Say Fon on the Mekōng, near Nongkai south of Vieng Chan, but there is also a temple called Tāt Panom, half-way between the towns of Nakon Panom (Siamese), opposite to Tāk'ek (French), and Mukdahān (Siamese), opposite to Savannaket (French),

[1] Lunet de Lajonquière, *Inventaire Descriptif des Monuments du Cambodge* (3 vols.). Paris, 1902–7–11.

[2] E. Seidenfaden, "Complément", *B.E.F.E.O.* vol. XXII (1922), pp. 55–99.

which is and has long been an object of great veneration and pilgrimage by the Tai, and which merits attention here.

Aymonier makes scant mention of it and records little but the name and site. He points out that *Tāt* or *Dhatu* is Sanskrit, and *Panom* is Khmer = *Bnam*, or Hill. He adds, however, that the pagoda is a massive pyramid built of *brick*, 10 metres broad at the base and 45 metres high, covered with "moulures" and "arabesques".[1]

Lunet de Lajonquière gives a more detailed account.[2] He gives a good description of the site and temple, and then adds: "We thought we recognised in the lower part of the edifice works in *brick* arranged in squares like those of a sanctuary orientated in regular fashion, which showed traces of a Cambodian hand. The sculpture on the brick to be seen there, although not of any remarkable finish, inclines to support this conjecture, for nowhere else have the Lao, who scarcely ever use any other form of ornamentation than stucco, employed this style. This original part of the work has been altered by restorations and successive retouches which have entirely modified the entire superstructure."

In the course of an extensive tour of the North-east in January-February 1929 I visited Tāt Panom and made an inspection of the temple. The whole *stūpa* was being whitewashed and was surrounded by scaffolding which made access very difficult and photography almost impossible. However, when I found that the base of the *stūpa*—which fortunately had not been whitewashed at the time of my visit—was constructed of large rectangular red bricks, and that their surface was covered with spirited carving, I determined to bring away some photographic record, if this were at all possible. The results, as will be seen, are not good, but they are sufficiently clear to show the nature of the carving, part of which at least to my eye is undeniably of Khmer handiwork (Figs. 55, 56, 57 and 58), but the other part is much more Indian in type (Fig. 54).

The scenes depicted on this sculptured brick in a progressive series are as remarkable in execution as they are lively in composition. They are "alive" to an unusual degree, even for early Khmer work. First, we have the Buddha himself seated in the attitude of "Turning the Wheel of the Law" or "Preaching the First Sermon", attended by an *apsaras* on each side above and devotees below. The Buddha appears to be seated on a lotus-throne, but it is hard to see whether his legs are crossed or not—probably not. This sculpture is undoubtedly a link with the Amarāvatī school. Next follow scenes of animal and court life

[1] Aymonier, *Le Cambodge*, vol. II, p. 144.

[2] Lunet de Lajonquière, *Inventaire Descriptif des Monuments du Cambodge*, vol. II, p. 99.

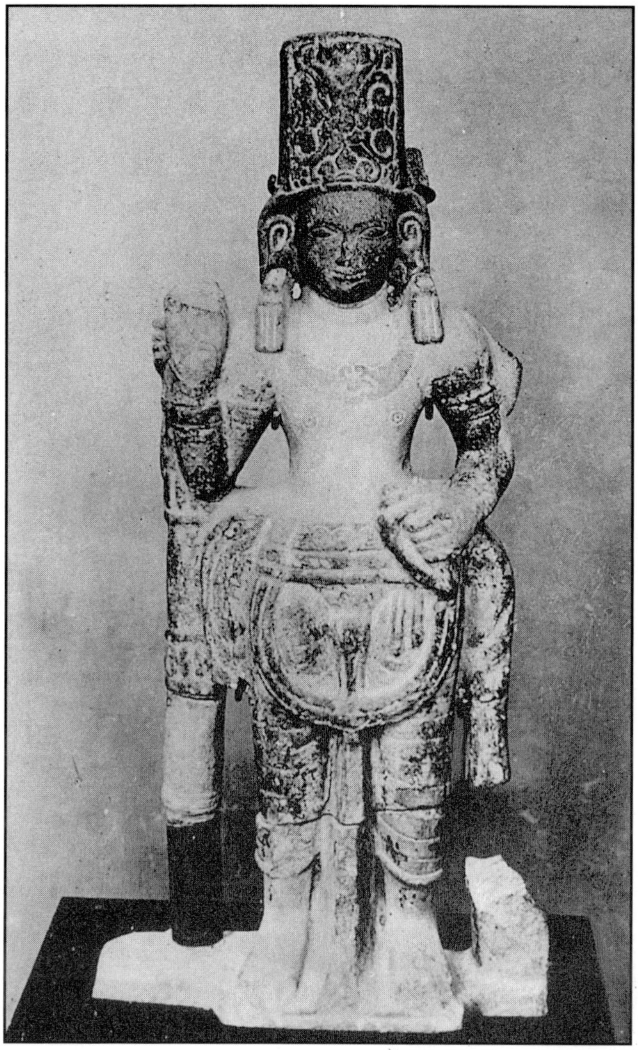

39. Stone Viṣnu, from South Siam. Pre-Khmer type.

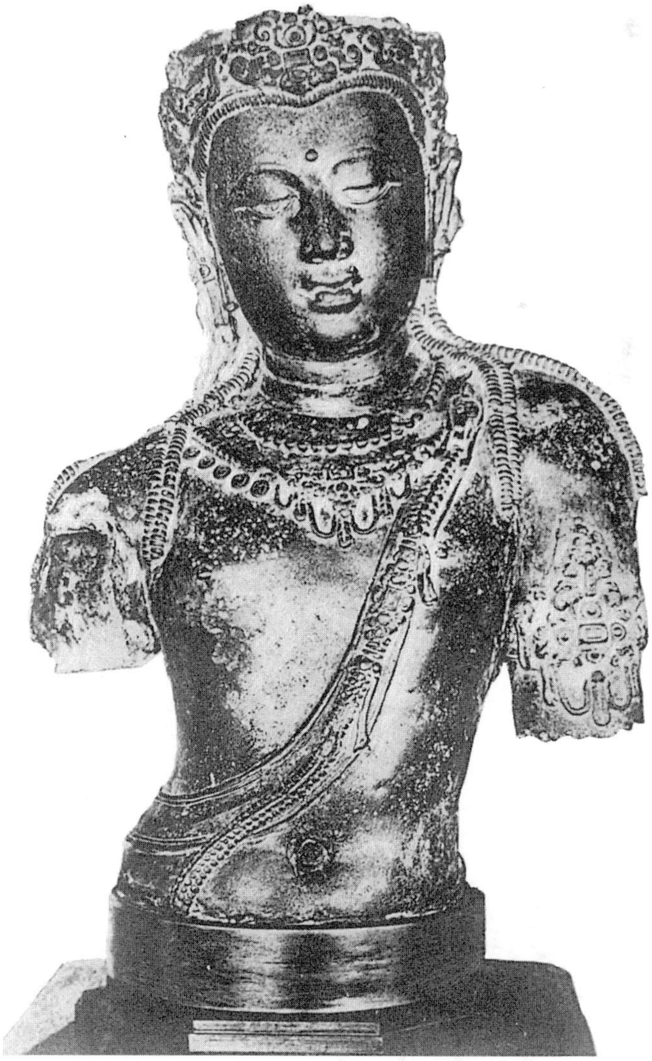

40. Bronze Head and Torso of Lokeçvara, from Jaya. Pāla style.

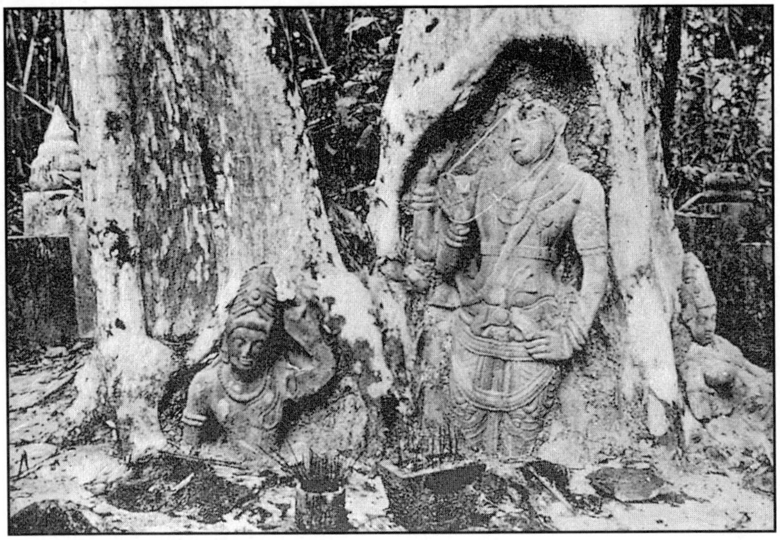

41. Three stone Deities, two male and one female, *in situ* near Takuapā. Pallava style.

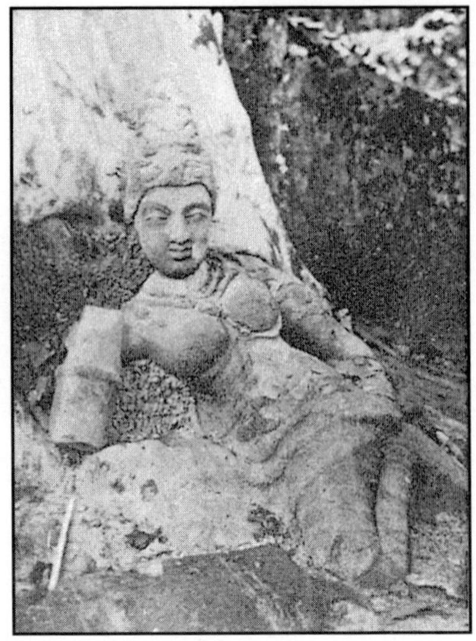

42. Female figure seen on right in No. 41.

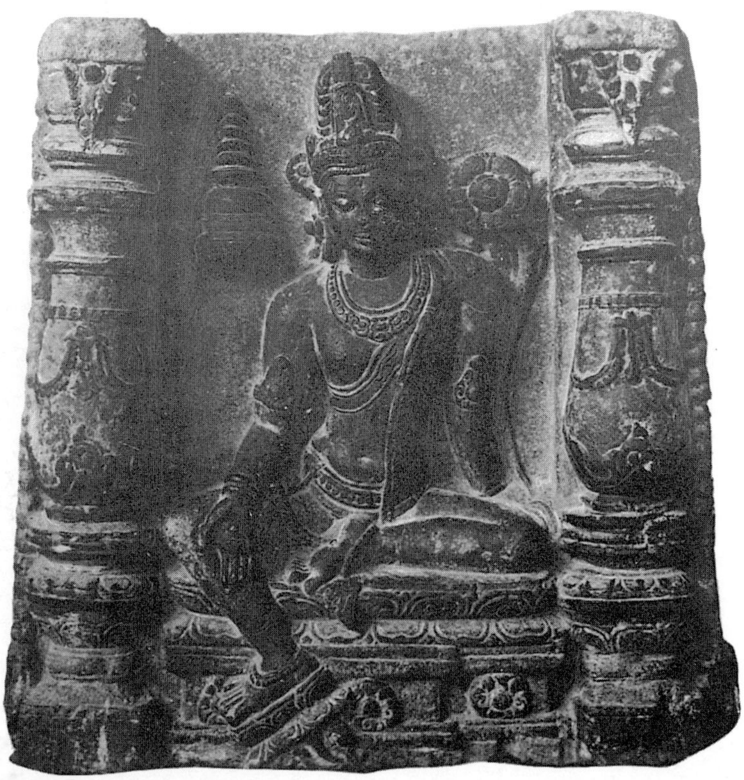

43. Stone Lokeçvara, from South Siam. Pāla type (possibly from Buddh Gayā).

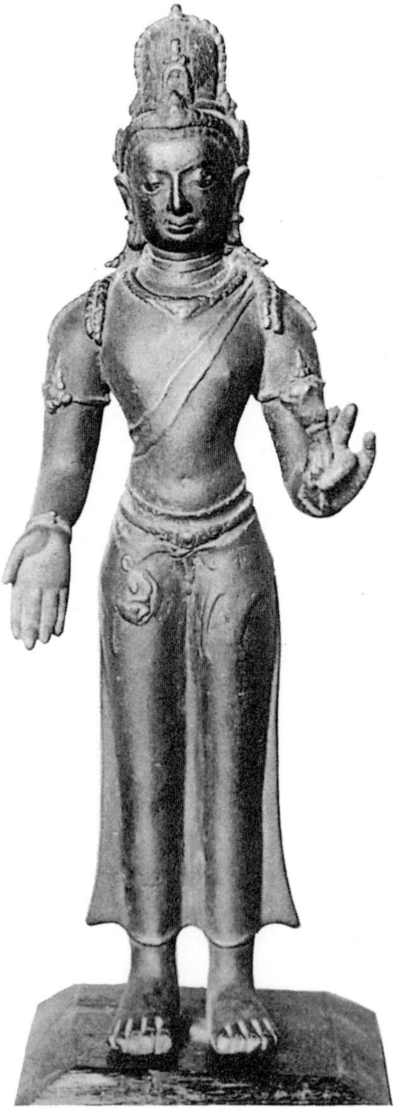

44. Bronze Lokeçvara, from South Siam. Pāla style.

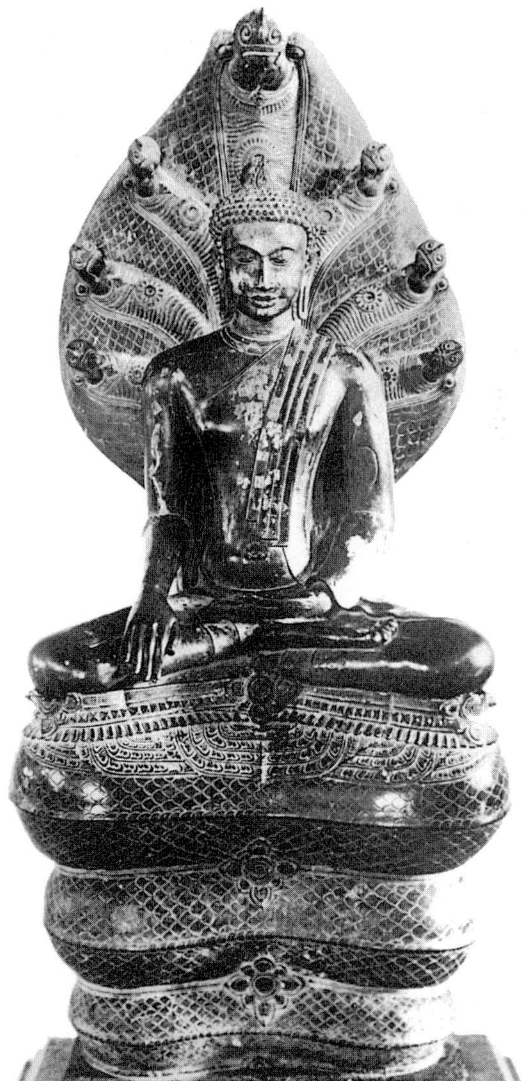

45. Bronze Buddha seated on Nāga King. Image of Môn, but Nagā King of Khmer, type.

46. Stone Hari-Hara (Viṣnu and Çiva in one) from Cambodia. Pre-Angkor type.

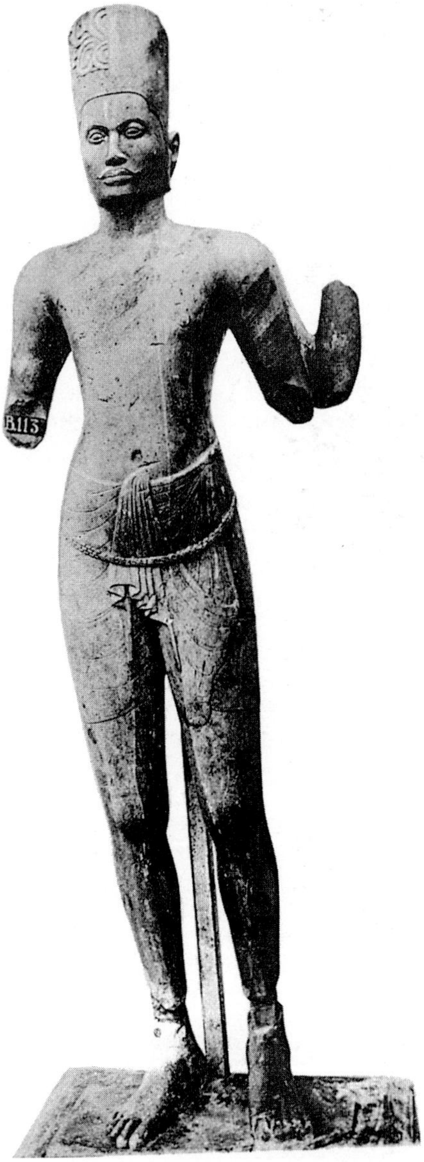

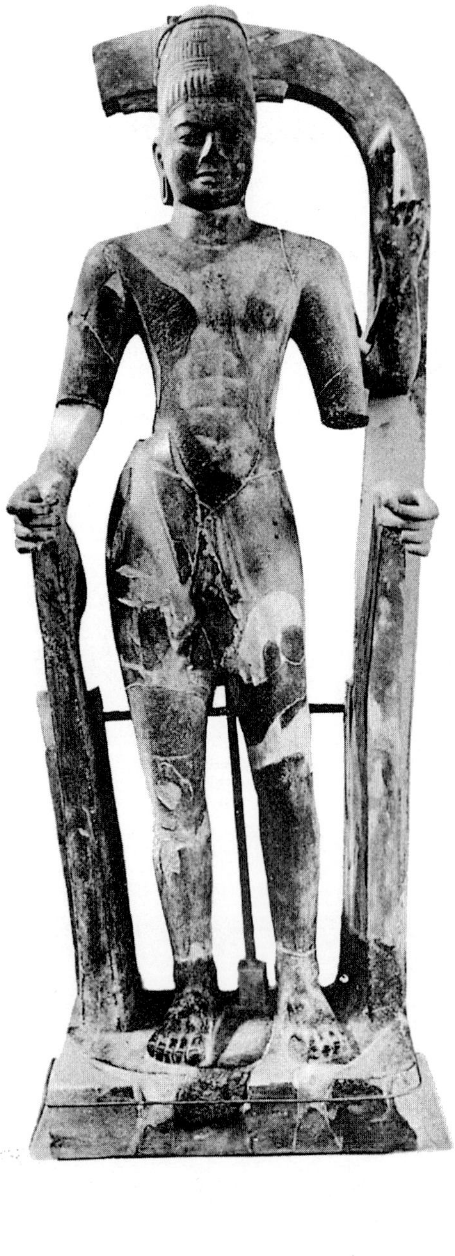

47. Stone Hari-Hara from Cambodia. Pre-Angkor type.

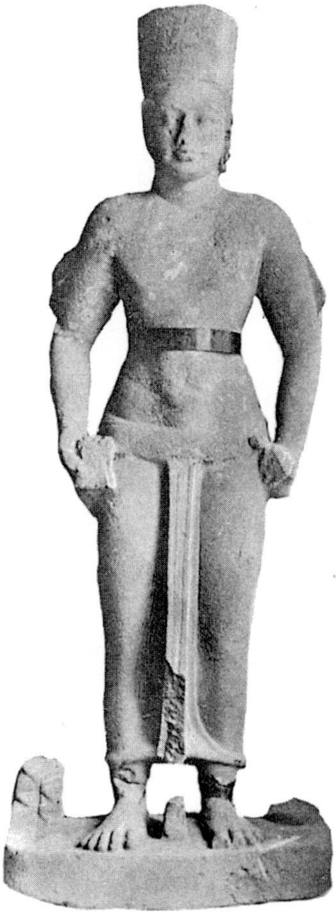

48. Stone Viṣnu from Vieng Sra. Pre-Khmer type.

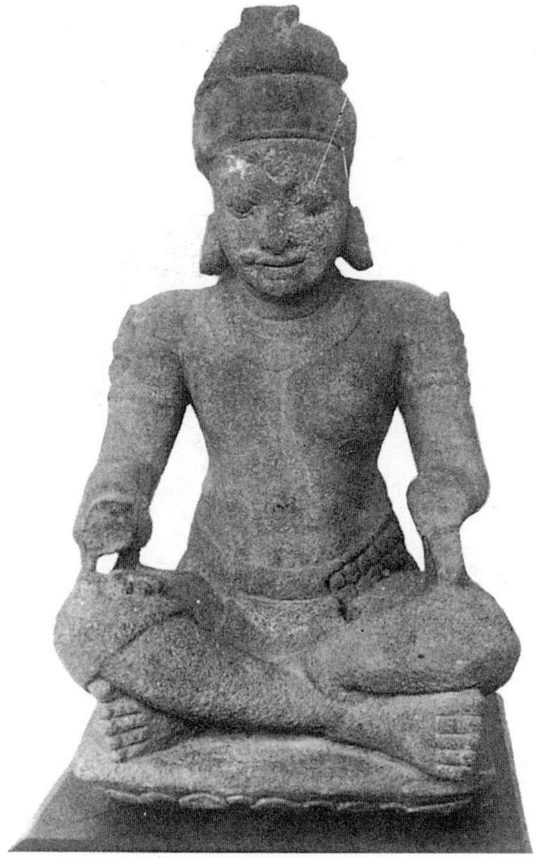

49. Stone Ardhanari (Çiva and Umā in one) from North-east Siam. Pre-Khmer type.

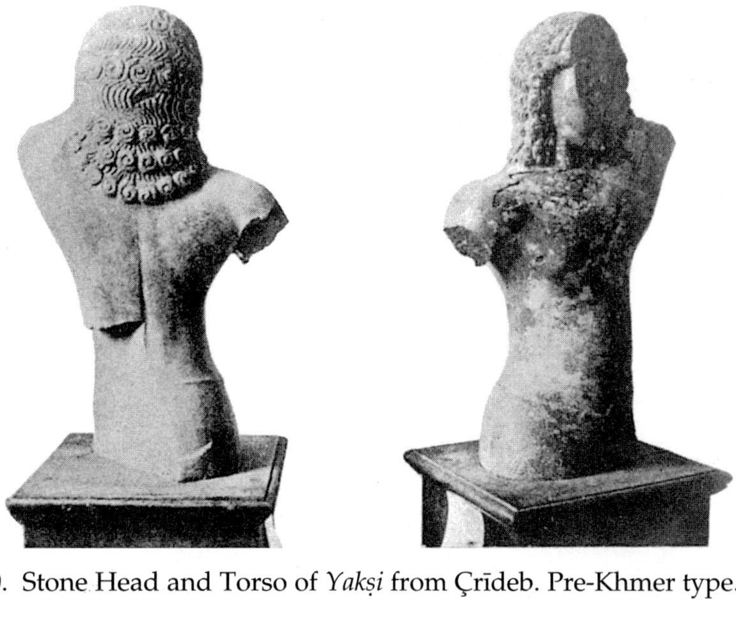

50. Stone Head and Torso of *Yakṣi* from Çrīdeb. Pre-Khmer type.

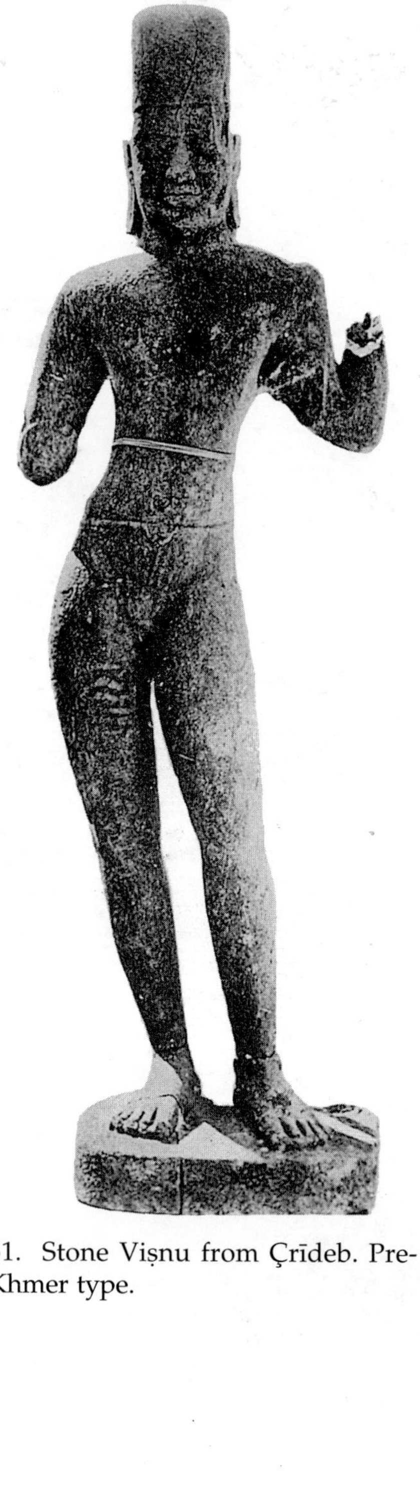

51. Stone Viṣṇu from Çrīdeb. Pre-Khmer type.

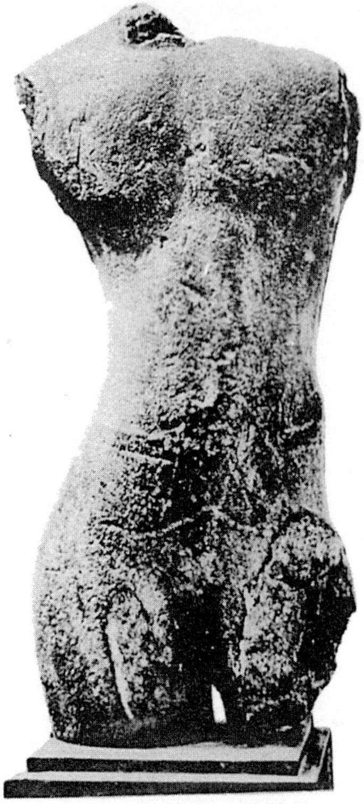

52. Stone Torso of Deity from Çrīdeb. Pre-Khmer type.

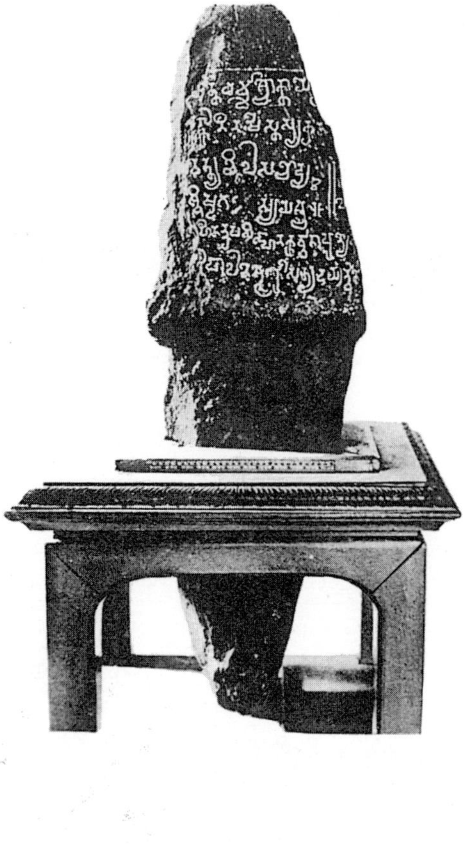

53. Stone Inscription (in Sanskrit). Fragment from Çrīdeb. Fifth to sixth century A.D.

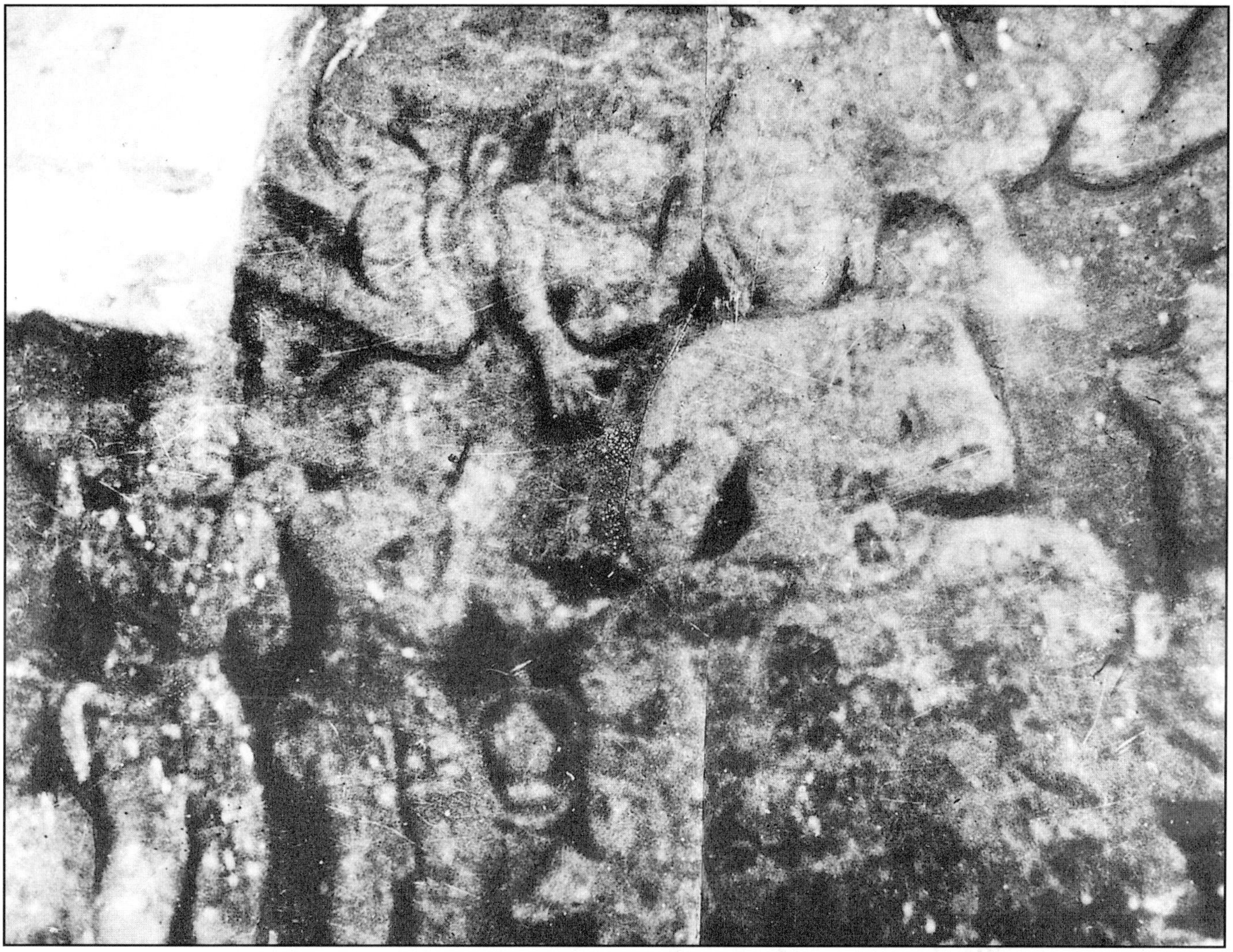

54. Buddha, preaching, with an *Apsaras* above on each side and devotees below. Carving on Brick Base of *Stūpa* at Tāt Panom. Funan, or early Khmer type.

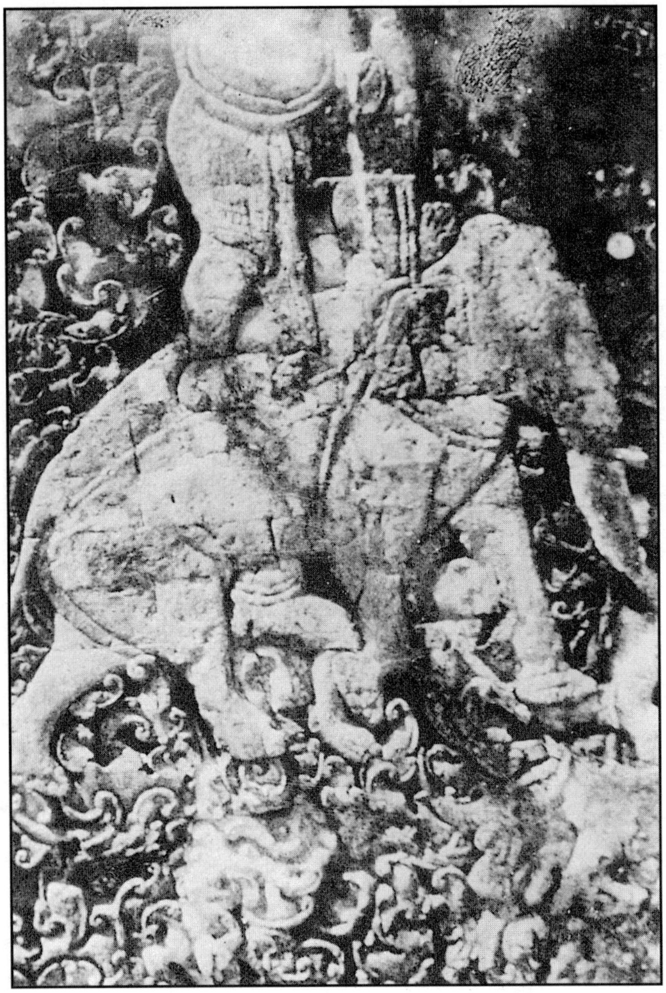

55. Elephant, with rider. Carving on Brick at Tāt Panom. Early Khmer type.

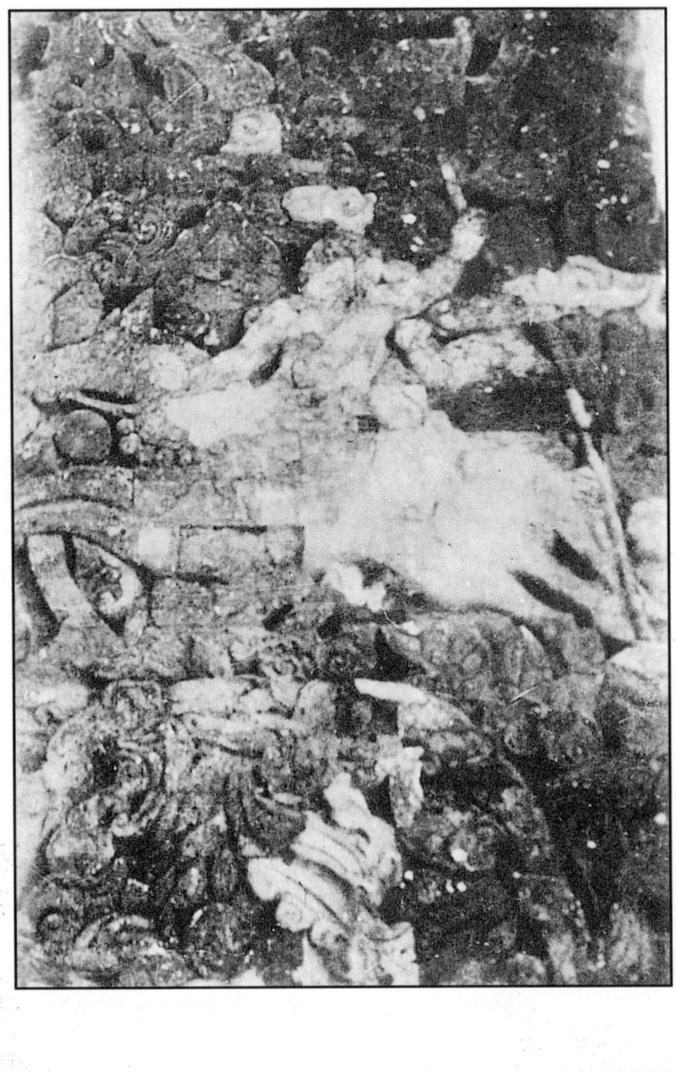

56. Galloping Horse, with their rider. Carving on Brick at Tāt Panom. Early Khmer type.

that may be by a different hand but show a vigour and a sense of proportion which would do credit to any artist. Look at the two elephants. In the one, how urgently vehement is the animal's tread as he strides along with his rider standing on his back in his eagerness to advance—and in the other, how measured and stately is his tread, with the rider now seated as if in some royal procession. Look again at the horseman with left arm raised and his steed with legs outstretched galloping along at the fullest speed.[1] In the last scene of the procession notice the figure in the foreground with his hair in a "bun" behind his head and also the last figure of all, in the top right-hand corner, who looks for all the world like a wealthy self-satisfied Chinese merchant. Notice also the intricate carving of the leafy detail in which the scenes are set. Whoever were the authors of this wonderful sculpture, this is no "primitive" art—the detail alone would rule out such a suggestion—but an art which is clearly in the vigour of its prime.

In the absence of other similar sculptures which could be put alongside for comparison, it is difficult to ascribe a date to this frieze, but we know that the earliest buildings in the Khmer period were built of brick and not of sandstone, and I am left wondering whether we have not at Tāt Panom some of the earliest Khmer sculptures still in existence. On the other hand, the Buddhist figures at the beginning of the series show a clear relationship to early Indian forms, and I suggest that the whole frieze of sculpture may be attributed to an early date, the sixth or seventh century A.D., at the latest, and perhaps belongs to the time when the capital of Chên-la was at Tāk'ek. What is remarkable is to find a Buddhist structure at this early date in the heart of Khmer-land, as has been pointed out by Prince Damrong.[2]

Now, it is true that part of Cambodia with the ancient capital of Angkor remained in Siamese territory until the year 1907, but I cannot undertake in this work to show the full glories of Khmer architecture and sculpture, first, because it is clearly outside its scope, and secondly, because I have not the space at my command. But I will show an aerial view of that great masterpiece of Khmer architectural art, the Temple of Angkor (Fig. 59), built between A.D. 1110 and 1160, which will give a clear idea of the heights to which Khmer constructional skill could rise.

[1] This is the only example of "the flying gallop" known to me in Siam, but it has of course been known in China from Han times at least. A friend of mine, W. Grant Keith, of Baldock, Herts., has a beautiful specimen in wood-carving which is possibly of the T'ang period. Cf. S. Reinach, *La Représentation du Galop dans l'art ancien et moderne*. Leroux, Paris, 1925.

[2] H.R.H. Prince Damrong, "History of Siam prior to the Ayudhya period", *J.S.S.* vol. XIII, pt. 2, pp. 11–12 (reprint).

Some of my readers may have seen the model shown at the French Colonial Exhibition in 1931. There could be seen the nature of the building, but here you see it in its own beautiful, leafy setting—one of the greatest, if not *the* greatest work of man still standing. I do not propose to describe the temple here, but, to give an indication of the size, the inner gallery between the towers, which are seen at the four corners, is a square of half a mile in circumference, each side being one furlong; and the whole of the back wall of this gallery is carved in low bas-relief.

I will also show a series of three photographs (Figs. 60, 61 and 62) taken of a temple in miniature at Banteai Srei, about 12 miles south-east of Angkor, which has been completely restored.

The sculptures belong to the latter half of the tenth century (the temple was built in A.D. 969 by Jayavarman V), when Khmer art was clearly reaching its apogee and shortly before the arrival of the purely classical style. The temple comprises a group of three sanctuaries and two libraries, all finely decorated, with curious *gopūras* opening into the first courtyard. The buildings are of laterite and have fine angular gables at the roof-ends.[1] The small sanctuary (Fig. 60) is a gem of architecture, and for delicacy of detail in the tracery the pediment to the lower right (Fig. 61) is scarcely to be excelled. But, for sheer exquisite beauty of conception and for sculptural skill in composition and execution, the scene portrayed in the pediment shown in Fig. 62 will always remain in my eyes the most perfect example of its kind. The story appears to be "The Eternal Triangle", which the spectators below regard with pity and compassionate mercy, but which the two little *Devas*, dancing a "pas de deux" above, obviously look upon with devilish, or should it be angelic, glee. Actually it illustrates the history of the *Apsaras*, *Tillottamā*, who was created by the gods solely to cause the mutual destruction of two brother-*Asuras*, Sunda and Upasunda, who were sowing havoc throughout the world. Each claims her as his bride, and they fight for her to the death. The figures below are Brāhman Rishis, recognised by their "chignons", and the dancing figures above are *Devas*.[2]

I must not dwell longer upon Khmer architecture and art in Cambodia itself, but, for the study and right understanding of Khmer art and architecture in Siam, it is important that the geographical and historical facts related above should be borne in mind. I think, however, that this is an opportune place to

[1] H. Parmentier, "History of Khmer Architecture", *Eastern Art*, vol. III (1931), p. 171. Philadelphia.

[2] G. Cœdès, "Études Cambodgiennes", *B.E.F.E.O.* vol. XXXII, p. 81.

broach a subject which is at once very puzzling, but, by that same token, very dear to the hearts of all scholars and antiquaries interested in the arts of Further India.

In an inspiring article published in French in *Études Asiatiques* in 1925,[1] and later in English in *Rūpam* in January 1929,[2] Parmentier seeks to discover "the common origin of Hindu architecture in India and the Far East". He is of the opinion that the connection is a consequence of religious dependence rather than the result of an examination of the forms. At the most he feels that there is an undefined family likeness about them, but by no means any direct relationship, although vague points of resemblance seem to establish their filiation with the monuments built in the Deccan by the Pallavas, whose relations with the countries of the Far East are an historical fact. He adds that the origin of the *çikhara*, or sanctuary-tower, has remained a mystery hitherto, and he concludes his analysis by claiming that the main forms of Indian architecture (wherever found) have their sole origin in one of the first edifices of the ancient Buddhist world, namely, the venerable *sanghārāma* of wood of the most ancient communities. This type of building, which naturally perished in a short period of time, was taken and copied wherever Buddhism spread, and this architecture, imported at various stages of its evolution, was developed more or less independently in each country in accordance with the varying conditions obtaining there. Parmentier also states that, if we set aside that of the Pallavas, there is no other architecture in India which could serve as an origin, as the other constructed monuments are all more or less of a later date. Nevertheless, he has a strong feeling that this origin should be sought for in India itself.

One aspect of the question which obviously puzzles him is that Cham architecture, presumably the earliest in Indo-China showing Indian influence, i.e. the earliest still standing, does not afford us any evidence of its art until the seventh century, when at that period it suddenly appears constituted in its most perfect form (in just the same way as the art of Java a century later). Now I am not competent, nor do I wish, to controvert my old friend's theory of origin on general grounds, but I wish to make a suggestion in regard to the *çikhara*, which seems to me likely to provide a fruitful source of further enquiry. These square towers, fascinating to the eye, which form sanctuaries in conjunction with a *mandapa* (or ante-hall), are familiar features of both Cham and Khmer art. While studying the early reports of the Archaeological Survey of India, I happened to come across an interesting description of a visit paid to the Central Provinces by

[1] H. Parmentier, *Études Asiatiques*, vol. II (1925), pp. 199–241.

[2] H. Parmentier, *Rūpam*, no. 37 (Jan. 1929), pp. 32–53.

J. D. Beglar, an assistant of the Archaeological Survey, in 1873–4.[1] The two places of the greatest interest from my point of view which he visited are Sirpur and Kharod. Sirpur (lat. 21·2° N., long. 82° E.) is now a small village on the right bank of the Mahānadī river, 37 miles east by north of Raipur (Rayapura) town in Raipur district of the Central Provinces, but is reported to have been once upon a time a large and thriving town. Kharod (lat. 21·8° N., long. 82·7° E.) is three miles north-west of Seori-Narayan on the Mahānadī river in the Bilaspur district of the Central Provinces.

According to Beglar nearly all the sculpture from Sirpur had been removed to Raipur, and much of it was to be seen in the courtyard of the Brahmin Dudhadhari Math temple there. Beglar reported this sculpture to be Buddhist and Jain as well as Brāhmanic in form and style. At Sirpur itself he found the remains of ten temples all on cell foundations and of brick picked with stone, mostly Vaishnava in form, but one dedicated to Indra, in which Viṣnu and Buddha were both represented, and also three other temples partially destroyed but still standing, one of which is the Lakṣmana temple illustrated by Coomaraswamy[2] and by Codrington.[3] The buildings are of brick and the sculptures and construction of most of the Sirpur temples are similar to those of the Indra temple just mentioned, and characteristic of them is the fact that the roofs of the sanctuaries are formed of successively projecting courses of bricks till the latter nearly meet. There is no second roof between the floor of the sanctum and the pyramidal tower roof (as is usual in a stone structure).[4] The Lakṣmana temple is built in the same manner as the others and rises from a terrace six feet high above the ground. It contains a sanctum ten feet square, an *antarāla*, and a *mahāmandapa*, both now roofless and in ruin. The sanctum was roofed as described above, but how the other parts were roofed is not certain. Beglar goes on to say: "Externally the temple depended for ornament on cut brick, and the designs appear to have been executed after the bricks were put in position.[5] The sunk false-panelled doorways with deep, delicate mouldings, and the sunshade over the doorway are features deserving of attention, betraying unmistakably a wooden as well as an un-Indian origin; and the thin pillars with bell-capitals point also to a wooden Persepolitan type. At the corners we have the usual tier on tier of

[1] "Report on a Tour in the Central Provinces, 1873–74", *A.S.I.A.R.* vol. VII (1878), pp. 167 *et seq.*

[2] A. K. Coomaraswamy, *History of Indian and Indonesian Art*, Pl. LI. E. Goldston, London, 1927.

[3] K. de B. Codrington, *Ancient India*, Pl. XLIV C. Ernest Benn, London, 1926.

[4] J. D. Beglar, *A.S.I.A.R.* vol. VII (1878), pp. 185, 187, 191.

[5] Cf. Temple of Tāt Panom in Siam.

*āmalakas* (fruit) separated by niched spaces, which bear a close resemblance to the trefoil arches of Kashmir."

Beglar states that the worship of Indra in North India ceased prior to the sixth century of the Vikrama era, and that some of the temple ruins which he examined cannot be later than the fifth century A.D. At Kharod he found the ruins of five temples appearing to consist of sanctuary cells with small projecting porticos, and one of these, illustrated by Codrington, is shown here (Fig. 63).[1]

Now it appears to me that we have been reading an almost exact description of a Khmer sanctuary tower, and indeed the sanctuary shrine at Kharod appears to be practically identical in form with, for instance, the temple of Mahā-Tāt, still to be seen at Lopburi in Siam (Fig. 74). In *Ancient India* Codrington does not discuss this temple in detail, and his only reference to the Sirpur temples is as follows: "The nearest thing existing to this structure (viz. the Gupta Viṣnu stone temple of the late fifth century at Deogarh, Lalitpur District, United Provinces) seems to be the Bhitargaon temple.[2] This is of burnt brick and is full of carved and moulded brick and terracotta panels. It probably dates from the middle of the fifth century. It is certainly earlier than the Sirpur brick temple [i.e. presumably the Lakṣmana] where many of the Gupta motives are preserved. There the chaitya-window has above it a lion's head with open mouth, the *sinha-mukham* of Southern India."[3] Cunningham describes the temple at Deogarh in *A.S.I.A.R.* vol. x (1874–5 and 1876–7), calling it a Gupta temple, and dates it between A.D. 600 and 700.

Codrington's Pl. XLVII, however, shows in A and C the entrance doorways of the Viṣnu temple at Kharod and of the Lakṣmana temple at Sirpur respectively, and an examination of these shows again the close affinity between them and Khmer sanctuary doorways, first, in the whole scheme of construction and most particularly in the door-jambs and lintels. Of especial interest, too, is Beglar's noteworthy reference to the fact that in one case he found the lintel, or architrave, of the sanctuary entrance sculptured at the outer extremities with two lions' heads, the bodies being attenuated and prolonged into wavy lines ending in a *makara's* head, the design accordingly showing a lion and a *makara* with a common wavy body.[4] These carved lintels ending in *makara* heads are a marked characteristic of Khmer art. Codrington assigns the temples at both

[1] K. de B. Codrington, *Ancient India*, Pl. XLII D.

[2] Described by Cunningham in *A.S.I.A.R.* vol. XI (1875–6 and 1877–8), pp. 40–6, as unique in Northern India.

[3] K. de B. Codrington, *Ancient India*, p. 62.

[4] *A.S.I.A.R.* vol. VII, p. 175.

Sirpur and Kharod to the eighth century, without giving any specific reason for doing so, but Beglar was of the sure opinion from the inscriptions found that the temples of Sirpur as a whole could not be dated later than the fifth century, although certain ones specified were clearly of a later period. In his Report for 1881–2 Sir A. Cunningham, whose pioneer work has never received the recognition that it deserves, describes briefly the inscriptions found at Sirpur, which contain the names of Chandragupta, Harshagupta, and Çivagupta, and says that he has no doubt that the temple (i.e. the Lakṣmana temple) belongs to the same period as the inscriptions, all of which give the name of Çivagupta, whose date he believes to be between A.D. 475 and 500. Cunningham also maintains that the carvings on the door-jambs are Gupta in style, as at Benares and Erān. He thus supports Beglar's theory.[1]

I am not in a position to judge between these two theories, but even if we assign these temples to a date mid-way between the two extremes and call them both late Gupta, there is no good reason why they should not have served as models for colonial construction overseas, and as Parmentier makes no mention either of Sirpur or Kharod in his search for a common origin, I feel that this district is sufficiently important to repay further examination, bearing in mind the aspect of *immediate* origins, at least, as regards the *çikhara* or sanctuary-tower. My own opinion is further strengthened by Coomaraswamy, who considers that the temple of Lakṣmana at Sirpur may perhaps be assigned to the reign of Harsha (606–47) and also remarks that the *cella* is decorated with false windows very like those of the Bayang tower (and, I may add, of many others) in Cambodia.[2] He illustrates several other analogous forms of tower, such as the Hacchimalligudi temple at Aihole, in stone of the sixth century (Pl. XXXVII, no. 153), the Mālegitti temple at Bādāmi, in stone of the early seventh century (Pl. LII, no. 187), and the Virupaksa temple at Pattadakal, mid-eighth century, the last two Chalukyan (early mediaeval).

[1] "Tour in Central Provinces", *A.S.I.A.R.* vol. XVII (1881–2), pp. 25–9.

[2] A. K. Coomaraswamy, *History of Indian and Indonesian Art*, p. 93.

# Chapter VI

## THE KHMER PERIOD IN SIAM (continued)

It has been shown that the Khmer began to penetrate the North-east of Siam at an early date, in the seventh and eighth centuries. Now, it is true that certain examples of Dvāravatī (Môn) images of the Buddha, usually small bronze figures, have also been found in North-eastern Siam, but it is not likely that the Khmer had the same forceful competition to meet there, in the artistic world, as they found later on at Lopburi. It will be interesting, therefore, at this point to show two images of the Buddha, both made in Siam and both products of Khmer art, the one from the Khmer garrison town of Pimai near Korāt and the other from Wat Mahā-Tāt at Lopburi (Figs. 64 and 65).

These two will, I think, exactly illustrate the differences which I wish to demonstrate. The features of the figure from Pimai have undoubtedly close affinities with those of typical eleventh-century images from Angkor itself, as will be seen from a reference to the two heads shown in Fig. 66. Let us take the Pimai image first (Fig. 64). Notice the slight downward tilt of the head itself, as well as the downward cast of the eyes; also the manner in which the hair is treated, and the *uṣnīṣa*. There is little doubt that the Pimai image is the work of a pure Khmer artist carrying on the traditions of the metropolis. According to Cœdès, it is also similar to a statue found at Bantei Chmar in the north-west of Cambodia. Now look at the Lopburi figure (Fig. 65). The *uṣnīṣa* and the hair treatment, which are entirely different from the Pimai figure, are characteristic of Khmer figures created in Central Siam. The eyebrows are slightly curved and the half-closed eyes look straight ahead. What is very noticeable is the broad fold of cloth hanging from the left shoulder; and this brings me to the main point of my contention which is that in Lopburi the artists were following in the Môn tradition of scuplture, and that Môn influence, which was absent at that time in Angkor, has, as one would expect, its part to play in fashioning the Khmer figures of Central Siam.

To buttress my contention and advance it one stage further, I now show a bronze image of the Buddha about 15 inches high which also comes from the Lopburi region (Fig. 67). At a casual glance this image might easily be ascribed to the Lopburi school of Khmer sculpture, and there is a noticeably strong Khmer influence in it. But actually it represents a perfect example of the transition from Môn to Khmer in Central Siam. The square head, the long, cruel mouth and the straight forehead are typically Khmer, but the treatment of the hair and *uṣṇīṣa*, the inward curve formed by the legs, the broad fold of the robe, and the peculiar raised fold of cloth showing round the waist are equally typical of late Môn sculpture. One has only to compare this image with Fig. 35, which is clearly *not* Khmer, to realise the affinity between the two.

In his work on the National Museum at Bangkok, Cœdès says that "even if certain images from Lopburi possess all the characteristics of statues originating from Cambodia itself, the greater number of those found show peculiar features which mark a period of decadence or, more precisely, of transition. It is from the school of Lopburi, rather than from the classic art of Cambodia, that Siamese art has borrowed a portion of its traditions".[1]

I accept this statement as regards the influence of the Khmer on the Tai who came later, but it does not give any weight to the transition period at the other end, or indicate how the Khmer themselves inherited the Môn traditions at Lopburi and thereby produced a sculpture which, while showing its Khmer origin, was yet different from the parent art in Cambodia itself. As for "decadence", it may be said that Khmer sculpture at Lopburi ranges from the sublime to the ridiculous. It has produced masterpieces of sculpture such as the grey sandstone head now in the South Kensington Museum (Fig. 84) and at the same time specimens of the crudest provincial art, such as may be seen to-day in the local Museum at Lopburi. This is not to be wondered at, seeing that Lopburi, after all, was only a provincial centre of Khmer rule.

An interesting point made by Cœdès deals with the proportions of the statues from Cambodia itself and those of a later date from Lopburi. Cambodian seated figures are cut, so to speak, to the square, that is to say, the width from one knee to another corresponds to the height of the figure, and this is the case in the two statues from Pimai and Lopburi just illustrated, both of which may be dated as pre-thirteenth century. In Khmer statues from Lopburi of a later date the width is appreciably less than the height.

A survey of all the sculptural art from Lopburi reveals the astonishing fact that the school of Lopburi, used in its broadest sense and not to denote the particular Khmer period, must have been in existence for over a thousand years, always changing in style with the predominating race but remaining unbroken until the seventeenth century. There cannot be many schools of art of which the same can be said, and the chief reason why the study of art in Siam is so

[1] G. Cœdès, "Le Musée National de Bangkok", *Ars Asiatica*, vol. XII, pp. 26–7. Paris, 1928. Author's translation.

fascinating is because one can follow therefrom all the racial changes that have taken place in that kingdom.

From the historical evidence given in the preceding chapter, it is obvious that Khmer monuments will be commoner in North-eastern than in Central Siam. This region took its place in the natural expansion of the Khmer Empire, and parts of it probably belonged to the ancient kingdom of Funan or its vassal State, Chên-la. Central Siam, on the other hand, was always an outlying Province.

In an interesting article on the Temple of K'ao Panom Rung,[1] which lies 42 miles south-east of Pimai, Seidenfaden discusses a strong local tradition of a Khmer king who left Angkor to found settlements elsewhere in his kingdom. He followed the course of the ancient highway, 140 miles long, which connected Angkor with Pimai, and of which the remains can still be traced to-day. Finot, in his "Dharmaçalas au Cambodge",[2] gives a plan of the road and states his opinion that the numerous rest-houses for pilgrims, still found (in ruins) along that road, were built by Jayavarman II who came to the throne in A.D. 802.

Now the oldest Khmer inscriptions in Siam are those written in Sanskrit found at T'am Pet T'ong (cave of the Golden Duck), 15 miles south of Nāng Rong near Panom Rung, at Pāk Mūn (mouth of the Mūn river), at T'am Prasāt near by, and at Surin, all dating from the time of Chitrasena (Mahendravarman) early in the seventh century. There are also others, in both Khmer and Sanskrit, dating from the seventh century, which have been found at Bān Hin K'oṇ, 8 miles south-east of Pāk Tung Chai, and at Bo Ika, just north-west of Sung Nern, all in the Korāt region.

Seidenfaden concludes, therefore, that the region south and west of Korāt already at that early period formed part of the Khmer kingdom: in which case it might possibly be Chitrasena who built the road between Angkor and Pimai. On the other hand, during the reign of Chitrasena Angkor was not yet the capital of ancient Cambodia and, unless it were already a military fort, there seems to be no good reason why he should choose Angkor as the starting-point for his road. On the whole, it seems more likely to have been Jayavarman II who constructed it and who is the King of the Panom Rung tradition, seeing that it was he who removed the capital to the north-western region of the Great Lake, and who was one of the most important kings in the whole of Khmer history. The probability is, then, that Chitrasena carried out certain military expeditions into the region

[1] E. Seidenfaden, "The Temple of Khao Panom Rung", *J.S.S.* vol. xxv, pt. 1 (1932), pp. 83–106.

[2] L. Finot, "Dharmaçalas au Cambodge", *B.E.F.E.O.* vol. xxv (1925), pp. 417–22.

of the Korāt plateau and left behind him stone inscriptions to commemorate those explorations, but that it was not until two centuries later that the task of bringing these outlying portions of the empire into close contact with the capital was completed.

Strange to tell, there appear to be no inscriptions of Jayavarman II himself in the region of Korāt and Pimai. The earliest inscriptions from the temple of Panom Wan, just north of Korāt, date from the eleventh century and continue up to A.D. 1187, while the only one found at Panom Rung dates from A.D. 1113.

There are still to-day remains of extensive Khmer temples at Pimai and Panom Wan near Korāt, and also at Panom Rung and Müang Tam on the road from Pimai to Angkor.

According to Parmentier, the temple of Pimai was built during the reign of Jayavarman V (968–1002), that of Panom Wan during the time of his successor, the usurper, Sūryavarman I (1002–49), and Panom Rung in that of Udayadityavarman (1049–65).[1]

Also, among many others, there are the remains of a truly magnificent temple at P'ra Vihāra on the summit of the Dangrek range of hills, 65 miles south of Srisaket, ascribed to Yaçovarman at the end of the ninth century. I have already published an illustrated description of this temple in *Indian Art and Letters*, vol. VIII (New Series), no. 2, issued in June 1935.

Now, as is known from the Lopburi inscription of 1022–5, Khmer kings appear at different times to have tolerated and even patronised all forms of Indian religion, whether Mahāyāna or Hīnayāna Buddhism, or Brāhmanism, or pure Yogism. They themselves sometimes inclined to the one, sometimes to the other, and in all probability Buddhism and Brāhmanism often flourished together, the people following the Buddhist Faith and the Royal Court surrounded by Brāhman rites and ceremonies.

The temples at P'ra Vihāra, Panom Rung and Müang Tam are clearly Brāhmanic in character. I saw no sign of any Buddhist figure at P'ra Vihāra, but at Panom Rung, in addition to much Brāhmanic sculpture, there is one peculiar scene portrayed on a large square *stela*, which is possibly of a Buddhist nature and recalls reliefs from Bharhut, Sānchī and Mathurā (Fig. 68). On the right is the figure of a woman, in typical Cambodian dress, i.e. nude as to the upper part of the body but with a folded skirt concealing the lower part, with her left arm raised and her left hand grasping, above her head, a tall stem ending in

[1] H. Parmentier, "History of Khmer Architecture", *Eastern Art*, vol. III, pp. 171–2. Philadelphia, 1931.

an animal's head. Her right hand rests on a pillar. It is difficult to imagine what this stem is intended to represent.[1] To her right are two figures of men. One, standing upright, is a Brāhman with a long beard who is holding some object, which is not distinguishable but is possibly a conch-shell, in both hands which are raised. The other figure, who is not bearded, is kneeling at her side and appears to be offering something in his folded hands.

Seidenfaden inclines to believe that this represents a figure of Queen Maya giving birth to the Buddha in the Lumbini garden;[2] but there is no sign of the child and, although the figure of the woman is strangely reminiscent of ancient Indian reliefs, I cannot see any particular reason for drawing this conclusion: the kneeling figure looks rather like a slave. In addition to Seidenfaden, both Aymonier[3] and Lunet de Lajonquière[4] have described the temple of Panom Rung, the latter's description being much fuller than the former's, as at Tāt Panom. A comparison of these two accounts is of interest, as it shows how difficult it is to accept the account of one author alone, however conscientious and careful he may be. According to Aymonier, the temple is built partly of red sandstone and partly of limestone. In the sculptures, which are of a good quality, "one sees neither gods nor men, but only rosettes, lianas and acanthus leaves". Also round about the temple may be seen much débris of ancient pottery. The temple was probably devoted to Buddhist worship and goes back to Sūryavarman I in the eleventh century A.D.: but also a Sanskrit *stela* of Sūryavarman II of the twelfth century came from Panom Rung.

Lunet de Lajonquière says that the building is situated on a hill, 500 feet above the surrounding plain. As regards its plan, although it is much in ruins now, still enough can be seen to show that, in execution and decoration, it is one of the most perfect of its kind. All the best means of Khmer ornamental art are employed there. He cannot understand Aymonier's remark that no gods or men are to be seen in the sculptures (and nor can I), since there are many lintels and other pieces which are decorated with figures of Brāhman gods. There is nothing to show that it was a Buddhist shrine; in fact all the evidence is against it, and the building is similar to many others in Cambodia which have nothing Buddhist about them. He concludes: "In spite of certain differences, this

[1] Sir John Marshall informs me that this *stela* is a copy of an early (probably Mālwā) relief of the first century (B.C.–A.D.), and that the stem is the lotus creeper of life and fortune (*Kalpalatā*). This relief is, therefore, of great interest.

[2] E. Seidenfaden, *J.S.S.* vol. xxv, pt. I (1932), pp. 99–100.

[3] Aymonier, *Le Cambodge*, vol. II, pp. 133–6.

[4] Lunet de Lajonquière, *Inventaire Descriptif des Monuments du Cambodge*, vol. II, pp. 203–4.

building presents the general characteristics of those which we have called 'Palaces', and it must be classed in this category. In this case the second palace is missing. There should have been one, and a more important one, on the other side of the causeway in front of the first." He strongly advocates reconstruction (Figs. 69 and 70). The temple at Pimai, on the other hand, appears to be Buddhist, though probably of the Mahāyānist order, judging from the carved lintels over the four doors of the main sanctuary, two of which are illustrated here (Figs. 71 and 72)..

This temple,[1] of which considerable remains are still standing, is enclosed within a rectangular wall, but it is not yet clear whether it served as a temple purely and simply or was designed as a guardian-fortress. Seidenfaden states, from reports given him by the late Siamese Lord Lieutenant of the Province, that there are the remains of a much larger enceinte near by, which the latter considered to have been the main town of Pimai in Khmer days. It will remain for future archaeological research to determine the character of this site, and whether perhaps the older site was the work of Jayavarman II in the ninth century.

Fig. 73 gives a clear indication of the type of moulding found at Pimai, which is admirably decorative, and I would draw particular attention to the "ball-flower", which is in general use there and which strongly resembles the ball-flower used in Gothic architecture in England of the Decorated period in the first half of the fourteenth century.[2] The only difference is that the globular flower has *four* petals at Pimai against three in England. A coincidence, no doubt, but a striking one. From Pimai to Lopburi is a distance of about 125 miles, or a little less than that from Angkor to Pimai. The road would pass through the present town of Korāt (Nakon Rājasīma), and debouch from the plateau on to the plains through a pass adjacent to the town of P'rabāt, which has been a centre of religious pilgrimage for many centuries past owing to the presence there of a famous "footprint" of the Buddha.

In Central Siam Lunet de Lajonquière only records eight monuments and six inscriptions of Khmer origin. Of these monuments two of the principal ones are situated at Lopburi. Another, Wat Mahā-Tāt, is at Sawank'alōk, and another, Wat Çulamāni, is at Pitsanulōk, but this latter is very largely a ruin to-day.

Lopburi, which was a centre of Môn culture from very early times and which was afterwards a summer residence of the Tai kings of Siam after the capital had been established at Ayudhya, was probably the seat of a Khmer Viceroy

[1] See *J.S.S.* vol. XVII, pt. I (1923).

[2] J. H. Parker, *A Concise Glossary of Architecture*, p. 28. Parker and Co., Oxford, 1913.

for Central Siam from the time of the accession of Sūryavarman I in 1002. It now wears a most venerable aspect, and its ancient sites are invested with all the charm of an old world city. It also possesses two rarities of the animal kingdom, said locally to be peculiar to itself, namely, a white squirrel and a blue chameleon. I can testify to their presence there as I have seen them both myself, though I cannot affirm that they are peculiar to Lopburi.

The two main Khmer temples still standing are Wat Mahā-Tāt and P'ra Prāng Sām Yôt (The Temple of the Three *Stūpas*). Both these temples have recently been restored by the Royal Institute of Siam and a considerable amount of sculpture has been discovered in the débris.

Wat Mahā-Tāt (Fig. 74) presents, to my eyes, a particularly imposing effect, and its affinity to the architecture of Angkor is obvious. It is on the usual plan of a sanctuary-tower with a *mandapa* attached, the whole in a walled enclosure, and it seems to carry the eye with it as it soars upward to heaven. All the images found here are of the Buddha, and there is little doubt that it was always intended for Buddhist worship. From the fact that Môn images of the Buddha of the Dvāravatī period have also been excavated here, it is almost certain that the Khmer temple was erected on the site of a more ancient one.

P'ra Prāng Sām Yôt (Fig. 75), which stands on rising ground, presents a more difficult problem. When I first visited it a good many years ago, the temple was full of sandstone images of the Buddha seated on the Nāga king (now mostly removed to the Lopburi museum), as seen in the illustration (Fig. 76) which was taken at the time *in situ*, thus showing that it must have been used for a long period as a Buddhist temple. But the design is certainly not Buddhist, and the three towers ranged alongside one another inevitably bring to the mind the Hindu Trinity of Brahmā, Çiva and Viṣnu. Non-Buddhist figures, too, have been found on the towers—bearded figures with their hands resting on clubs—which also points to an originally Brāhman construction. As far as I know, however, no images of Brāhmanic gods have ever been found on this site, and, whatever the original intention may have been, this temple may be looked upon as a Buddhist one for our purpose.

Claeys attributes the building of this temple to, probably, Tai "main d'œuvre".[1] I cannot understand this. It may be late in date and, if he simply means that Tai workmen were employed in erecting it, I have no wish to gainsay him since I do not know, but there is absolutely nothing Tai about the building itself—which is, indeed, quite foreign to Tai ideas. If one looks at the shape of the towers,

[1] J. Y. Claeys, "L'Archéologie du Siam", *B.E.F.E.O.* vol. XXXI (1931), p. 399.

at the figures of the *Rishis* on the door-jambs, at the figures on the antefixes, and at some of the faces moulded in stucco on the exterior (which recall contemporary grotesque Norman faces on some capitals of pillars in English cathedrals), to say nothing of the style of vaulting and framing of the doorways, one must surely admit that they are all typically Khmer and have nothing in common with Tai architecture.

Most of the images of the Buddha formerly in this temple are covered with black lacquer and gilt, though much of the lacquer and gilding has now disappeared. At one time I formed the opinion that these images must be Tai copies of Khmer originals, as the lacquer face in every figure is obviously Tai in form and expression. But, quite recently, since the removal of the images to the local museum, the lacquer has been removed from the faces of several images by the authorities, and, when once this with the cement filling had vanished, an easily recognisable Khmer face emerged from beneath, glad to see the light of day once more after wearing a mask for so many centuries! It seems, then, that at some later date, probably in the fifteenth century (from the style of the features), the Tai worshippers became dissatisfied with the Khmer presentment of the Founder of their common Faith and decided to transform him into a real Tai Buddha.

The lacquer is of an uncommon thickness and takes on a beautiful, high polish when carefully rubbed. Figs. 77 and 78 show both sides of an image of this type, 29 inches high, in which one can clearly see where the lacquer has broken off.

The folds, hood and tail of the Nāga are remarkably well executed, and there has been a good deal of discussion regarding the design which appears on the centre of the hood. It is thought by some to represent the Wheel of the Law, but I personally agree with those who look upon it as a stylised Lotus-flower, as often seen depicted on the open hand or foot-sole of the Buddha in Siam. The Lotus is perhaps the purest symbol of Buddhism.

The question of the different materials used by sculptors of different nationalities in Siam is of great interest. As has been shown, there are still extant early figures of the Buddha in a light-coloured quartz, but this material is obviously too liable to chip for general or extensive use, and as a rule the Môn sculptors worked in a bluish limestone which is quarried in the hills of Kānburi and Rājaburi, and which is a singularly attractive, though rather hard material for modelling. Apparently the Khmer tried their hand on the blue limestone, for I have seen several images, of Khmer inspiration, of this material in the Lopburi museum. But they are clumsy in make and some of them are unfinished; and it looks as if the Khmer in their turn found the limestone too hard and abandoned it at an early date for the softer sandstone, in the handling of which they showed such remarkable skill. I have also in my possession two Khmer heads carved out of rhyolite, but this is very exceptional. There is still a firm tradition in Lopburi, Korāt and elsewhere in the old Khmer regions of Siam that none of the sandstone figures of the Buddha were genuinely sculptured by the Khmer artists, but that they were all moulded out of crushed sandstone mixed with a sugary glue. One ancient official in Korāt assured me that he had actually seen it done, but a long time ago, and that the art was lost now. How this legend arose one cannot say, and it is, moreover, possible that attempts were made in the past to mould figures out of crushed sandstone. One has only to look, however, at the illustrations given, to rest content that the Khmer was also an accomplished sculptor.

Fig. 79 shows a large image of the Buddha in sandstone, still preserved *in situ* at Wat Mahā-Tāt, which is typical of the School of Lopburi.

Fig. 82 is the head of a Bodhisattva, 10½ inches high, with the Dhyani Buddha in front of the *uṣnīṣa*, in reddish sandstone; and Fig. 81 is that of a Buddha in the same material, both from the Lopburi region. Fig. 82 is an example of what may be called the classical style as found in Siam. The head is square and the forehead is straight. The jaw is square and firm. The eyebrows are almost straight, the nose is rather flattened, and the mouth is long with full lips. The eyes look downward and seem almost closed. The hair is no longer formed of spiral curls but seems like scales divided by partition lines. The whole gives the appearance of a strong, ruthless Being which, if satisfying artistically, is too human to fulfil the conditions necessary for the representation of a Buddha or a Bodhisattva. There is here little conception of an ideal. It is the portrait of some individual character. Fig. 81, 12 inches high, from which emanates a mysterious feeling of beauty as well as of dominant strength, is more akin to the Angkor type than is usually found at Lopburi. The face is more oval and the jaw not so pronounced. The eyes look down and seem almost closed, while the mouth is long and the lips are very full. For comparison I show a particularly fine image of the Buddha from Cambodia itself, now in the Pnompenh Museum (Fig. 80).

Fig. 83, 8 inches high, also in sandstone, is of rather an unusual type though of considerable artistic merit. It is certainly Khmer, but the face has a much more benign cast than in normal Khmer images. The mouth is smaller, the nose is more sensitive and the cheeks are fuller. It almost looks as if a suspicion of Tai feeling were creeping in.

Last is shown Fig. 84, 15½ inches high, now in the Victoria and Albert Museum, which is perhaps the most beautiful Khmer head ever found in Siam. For nobility of expression and sensitiveness in execution it would be hard to rival this figure either in Siam or Cambodia itself. All the essential features of Khmer sculptural art are present, but there is a delicacy and, at the same time, a strength about the face which is indefinable.

The question of treatment, from both an artistic and a religious point of view, is important. The Môn-Indian art of Siam was based on Gupta prototypes, and the sculptors of that school did succeed in evolving, in their images of the Buddha, their conception of the form of some ideal Being far superior to themselves, as did also the sculptors from Çrīvijaya in the Malay Peninsula. With the coming of the Khmer to Siam we see this abstract form giving way to a truly human form which we can judge by human standards, and this is probably why Khmer figures always make such a strong appeal to the Western mind with its intense individuality of expression and its close attachment to Mother Earth. Later, with the expulsion of the Khmer by the Tai, we see the human form once more displaced by symbolism and the abstract conception of an ideal Being: and there is, therefore, a much truer spiritual affinity between the Môn and Tai schools than there is between the Môn and Khmer, or the Khmer and the Tai.

The Khmer at Lopburi, though in most cases using their beloved sandstone for the creation of large images for temple worship, did not neglect bronze in the making of smaller images for private household use, and on the whole they reached a reasonably high standard in this respect, though in no way comparable with their execution in stone. Large bronze images of the Lopburi school are exceedingly rare (though occasionally good forgeries are met with), but there is one of exceptional size and quality now preserved in a niche behind the *bōt* of Wat Benchamabopit at Bangkok. Prince Damrong considers this image the finest example of its kind in Siam (Fig. 85). By some this figure is considered to show already some signs of Tai influence, and indeed it may, I think, be attributed to the end of the Khmer dominion over Central Siam. The smaller seated bronze figures are sometimes particularly pleasing and show a variety of decoration, especially in the stands and frames for the image, which is surprising. They are sufficiently rare and are much prized in Siam. I show two characteristic figures, one with the Buddha seated on the Nāga king, and the other a plain seated figure (Figs. 86 and 87), which are typical examples of their skill in bronze.

Fig. 86, which is 6 inches high (without the wooden stand which is modern), shows the Buddha seated in the attitude of *samādhi* or Meditation under the shade of the Nāga king. The features are typically Khmer, as are also the crown on the head, the jewelled collar round the neck, and the still existing portion of the

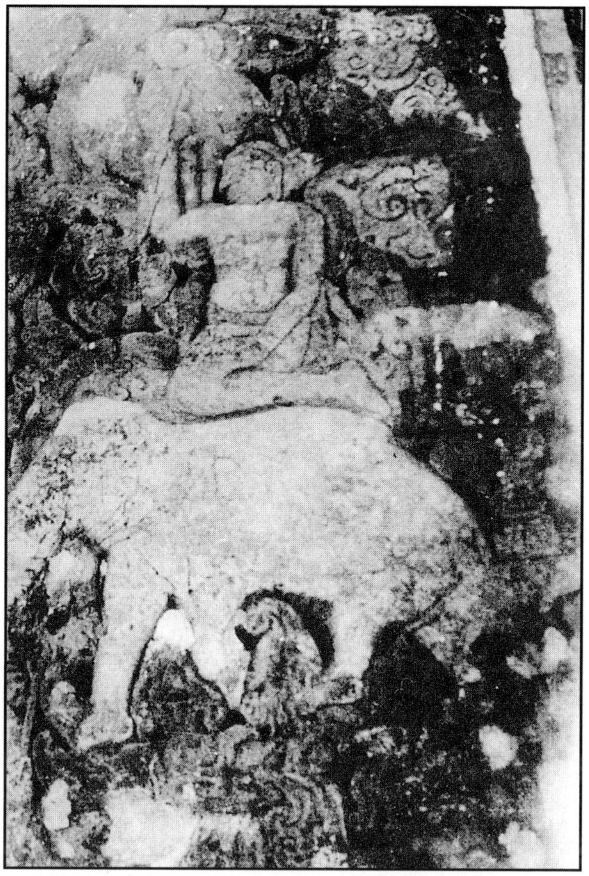

57. Elephant, with rider. Carving on Brick at Tāt Panom. Early Khmer type.

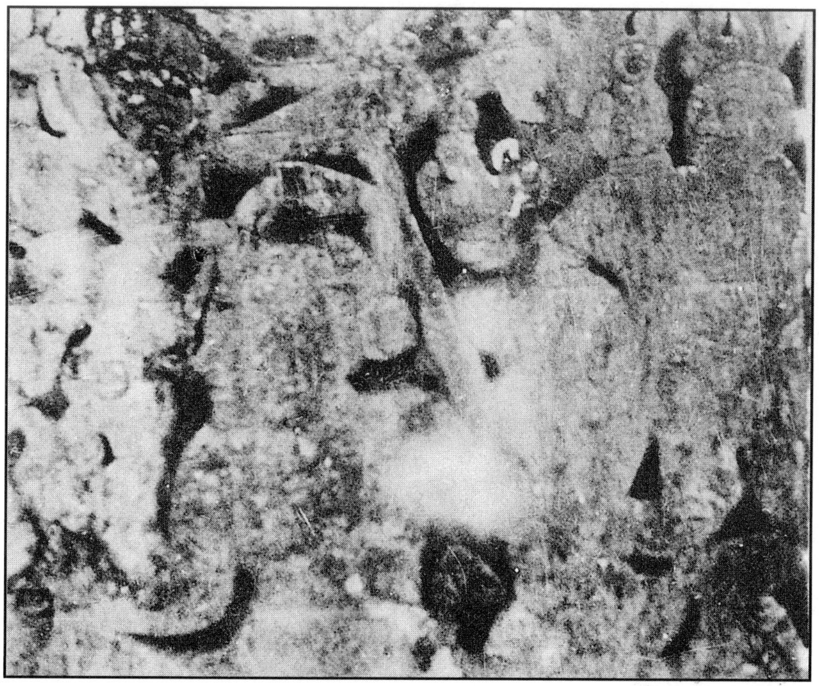

58. Men, with umbrellas, in Procession. Carving on Brick at Tāt Panom. Early Khmer type.

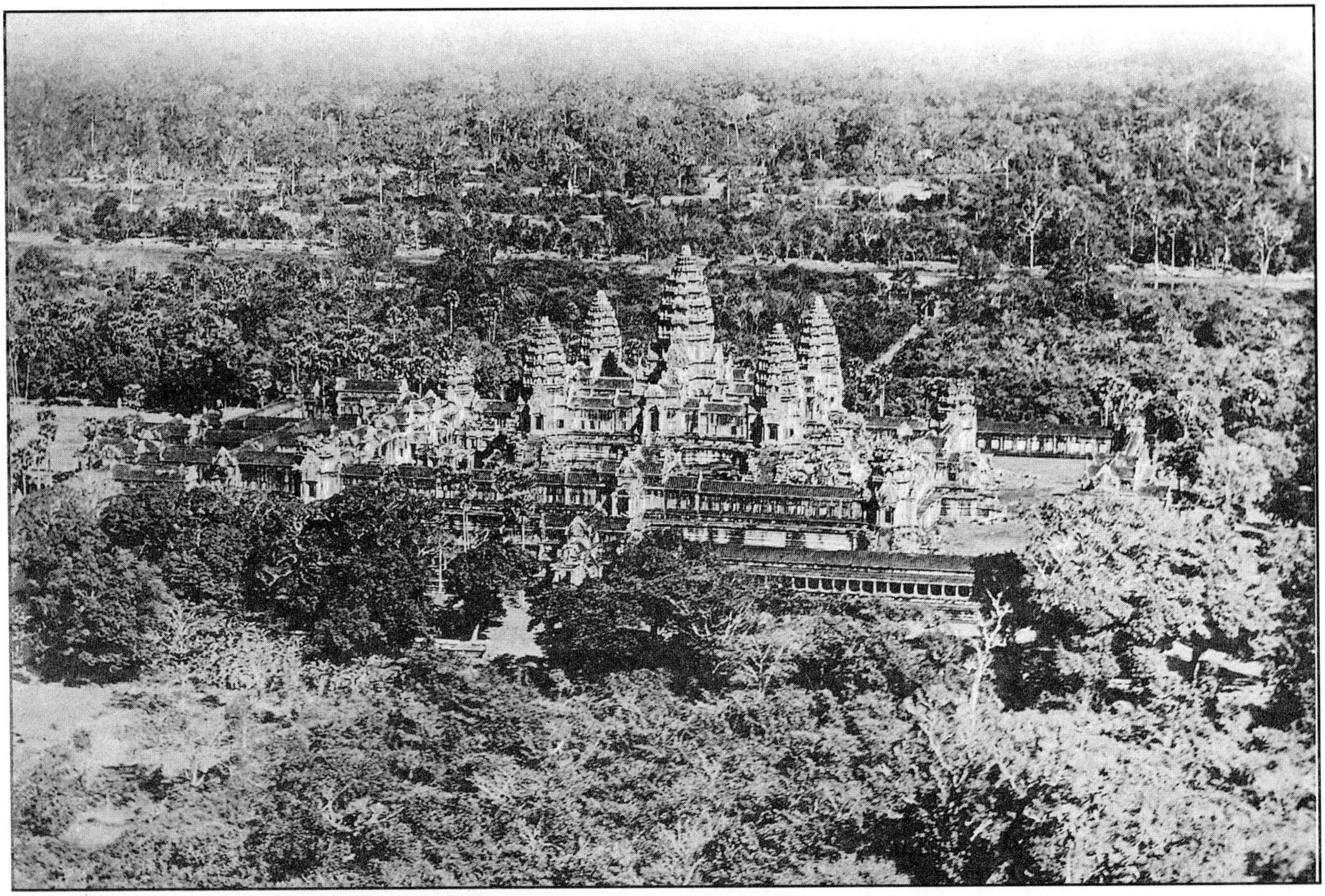

59. Aerial view of the Great Temple of Angkor.

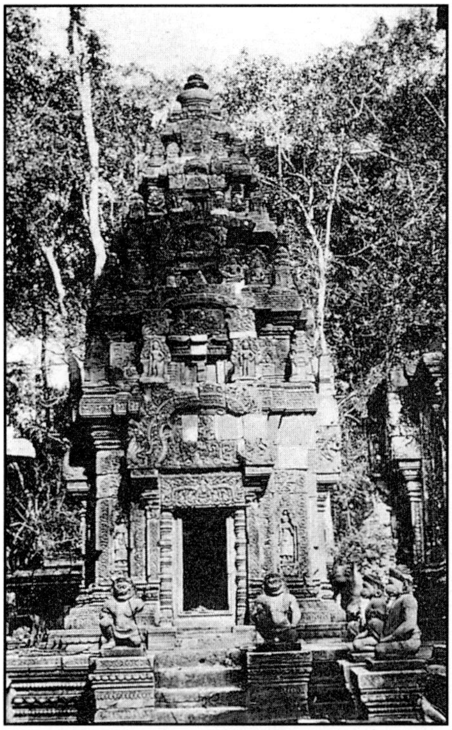

60. Stone Khmer Sanctuary at Banteai Srei, Cambodia, as now restored. Tenth century A.D.

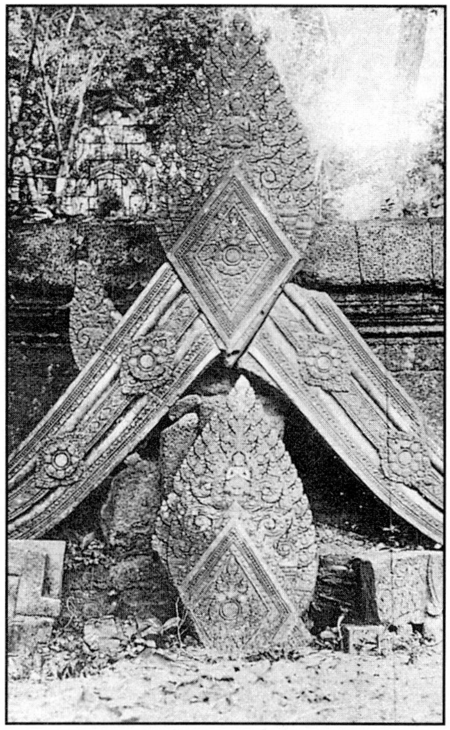

61. Stone Pediment at Banteai Srei.

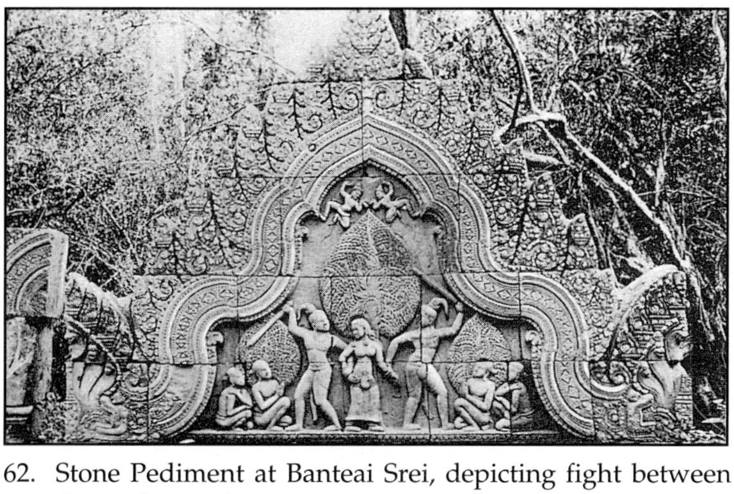

62. Stone Pediment at Banteai Srei, depicting fight between two *Asuras* for an *Apsaras*.

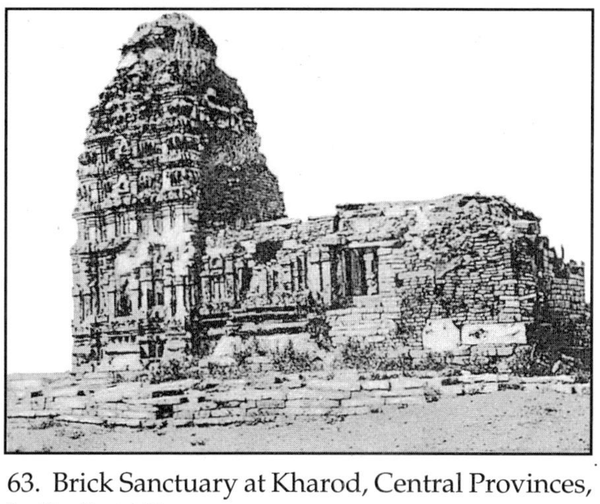

63. Brick Sanctuary at Kharod, Central Provinces, India. Late Gupta type.

64. Sandstone Buddha from Pimai. Khmer type.

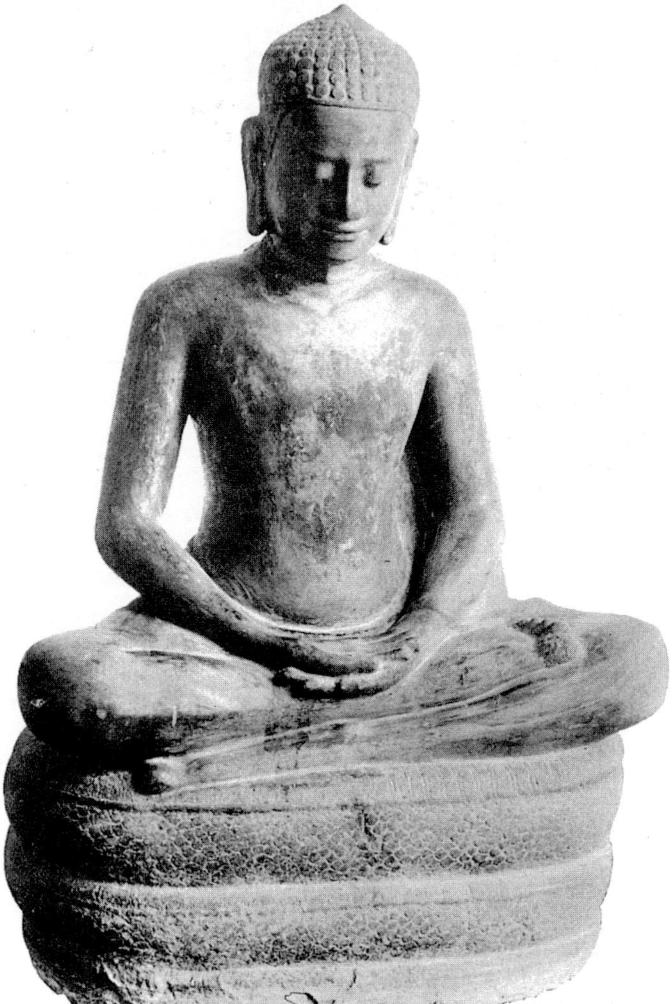

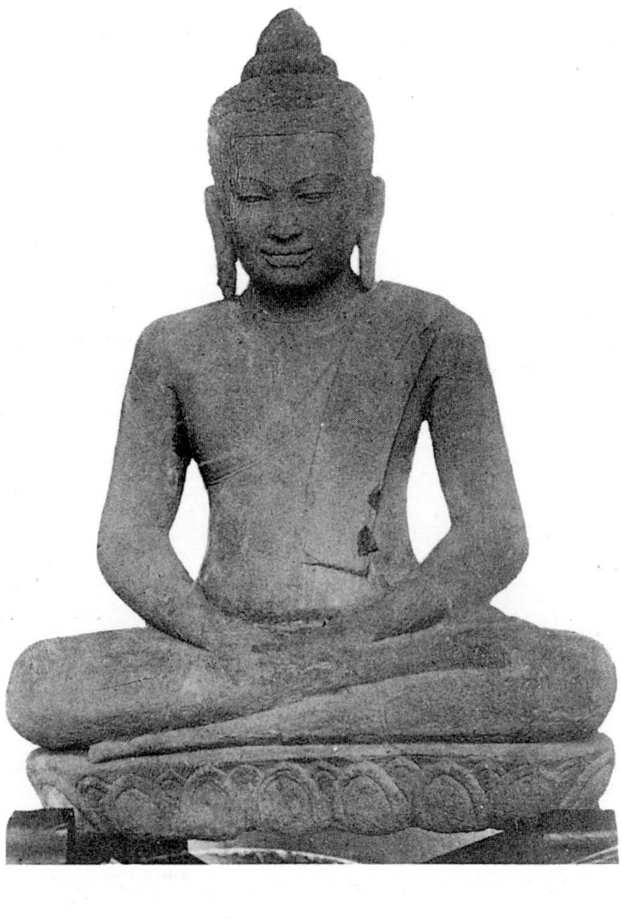

65. Sandstone Buddha from Lopburi. Khmer type.

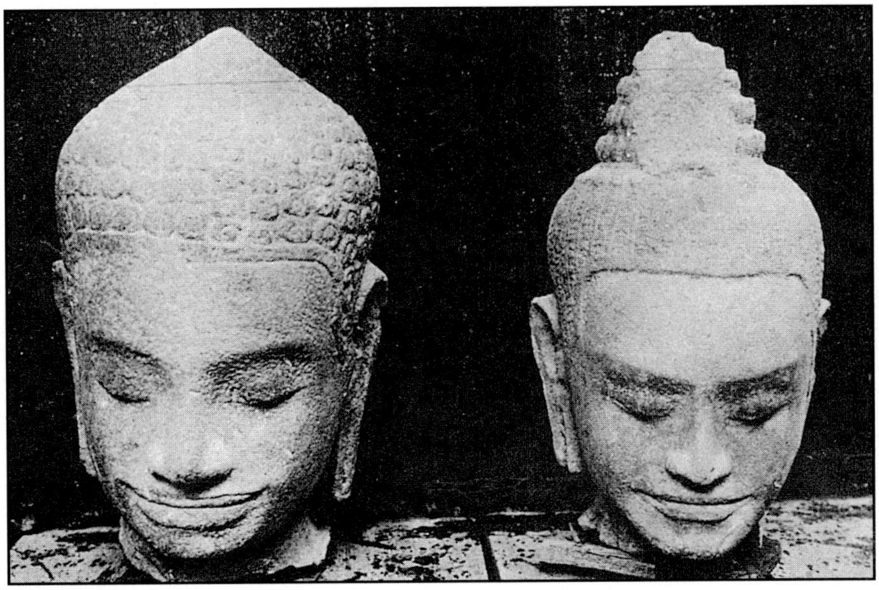

66. Two sandstone heads of Buddha from Cambodia. Khmer type, tenth to eleventh century A.D.

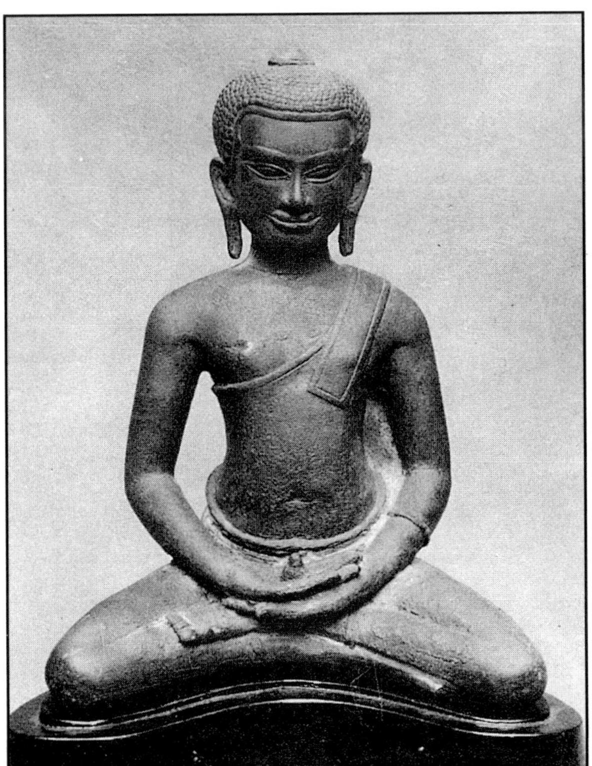

67. Bronze Buddha, from Lopburi. Môn-Khmer type.

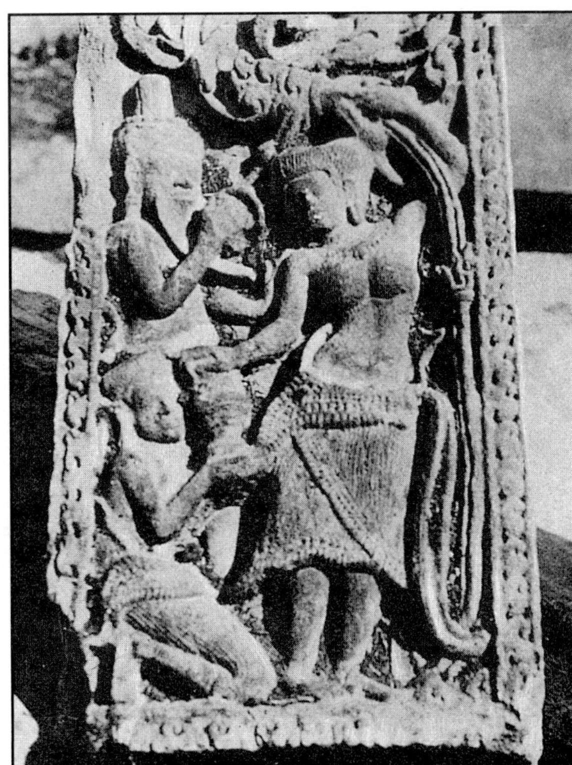

68. Stone Stela, depicting woman with attendants (? Queen Maya), at Panom Rung. Khmer type.

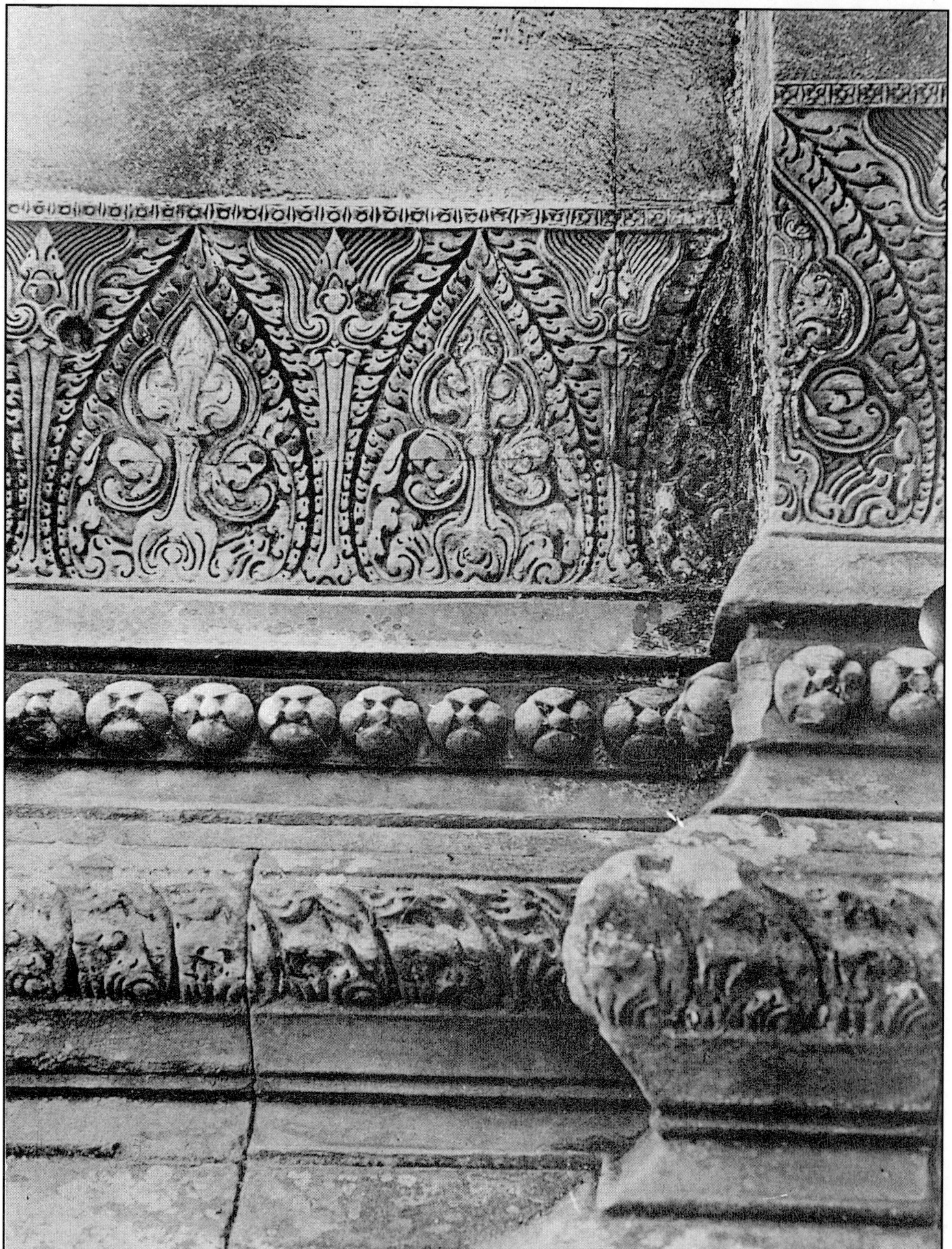

73. Sandstone carving, showing detail of decorative moulding on exterior of Khmer Temple at Pimai.

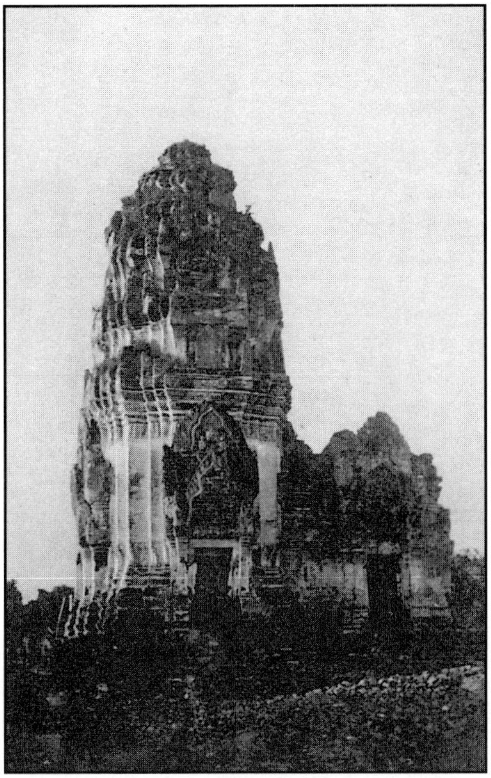

74. Khmer Sanctuary in Temple of Mahā-Tāt at Lopburi.

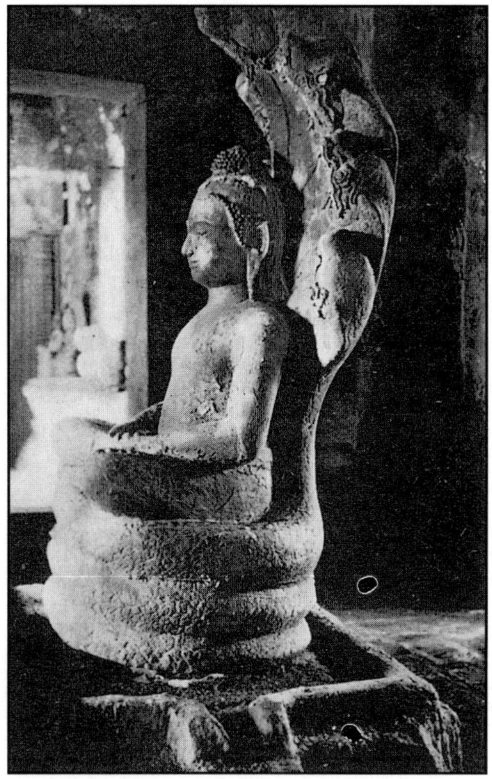

76. Khmer sandstone Buddha in Temple of P'ra Prāng Sām Yôt, Lopburi, with Tai lacquering.

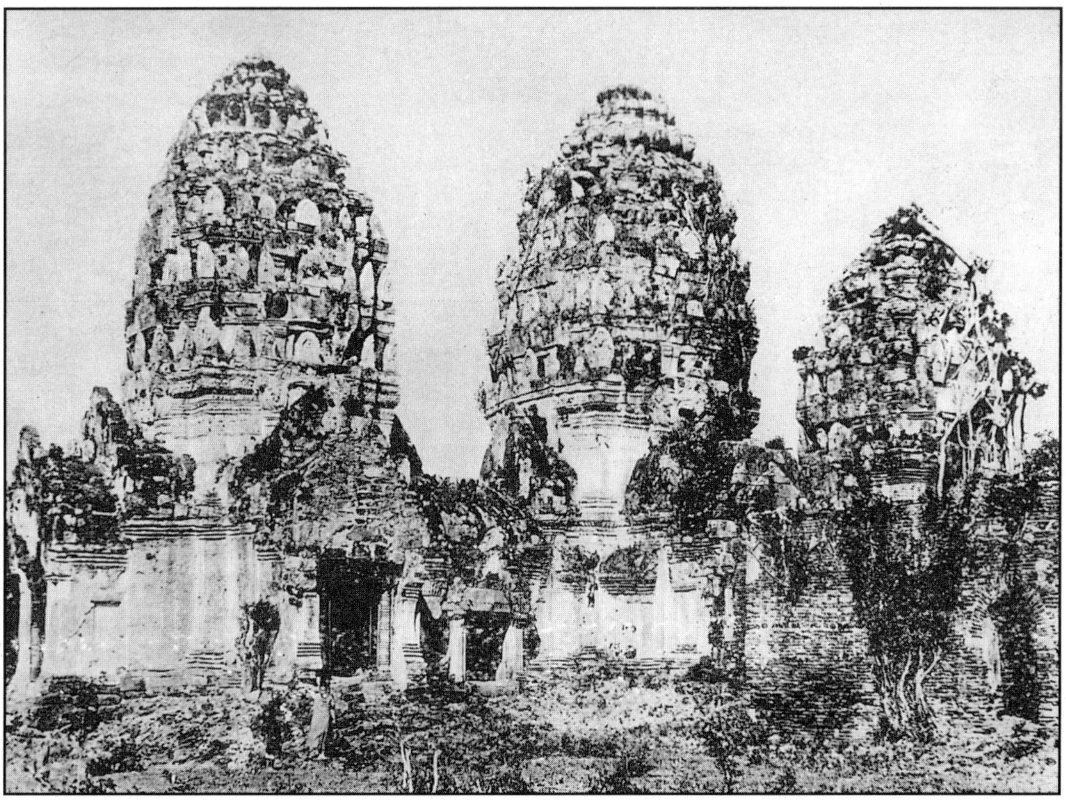

75. Khmer Temple of P'ra Prāng Sām Yôt at Lopburi.

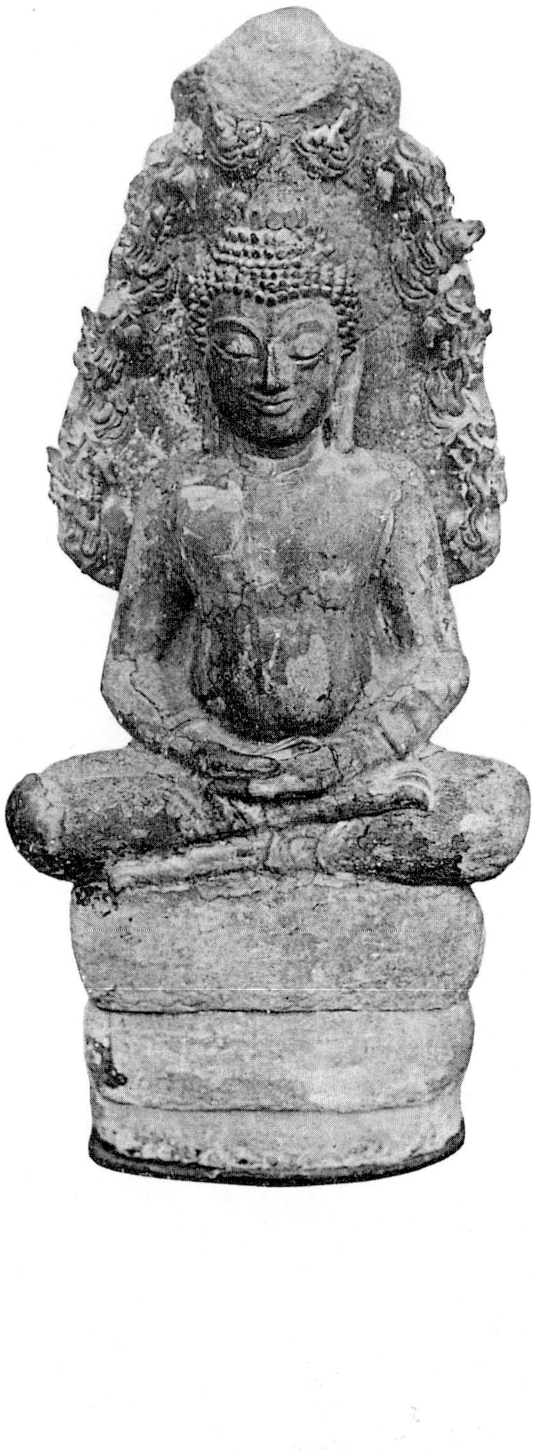

77. Sandstone Buddha from Lopburi. Khmer, with Tai lacquering.

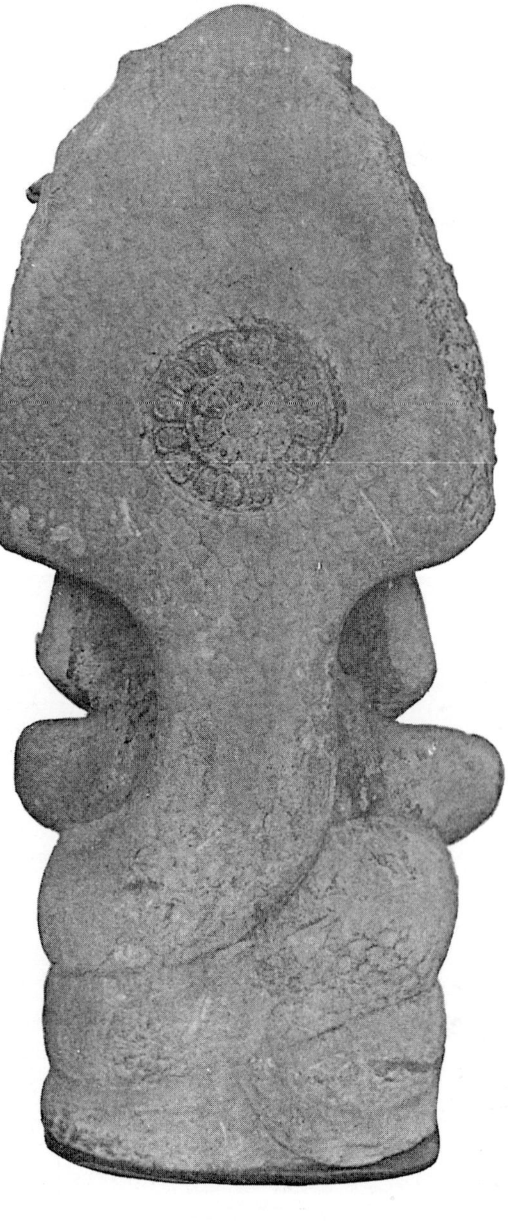

78. Reverse of Fig. 77.

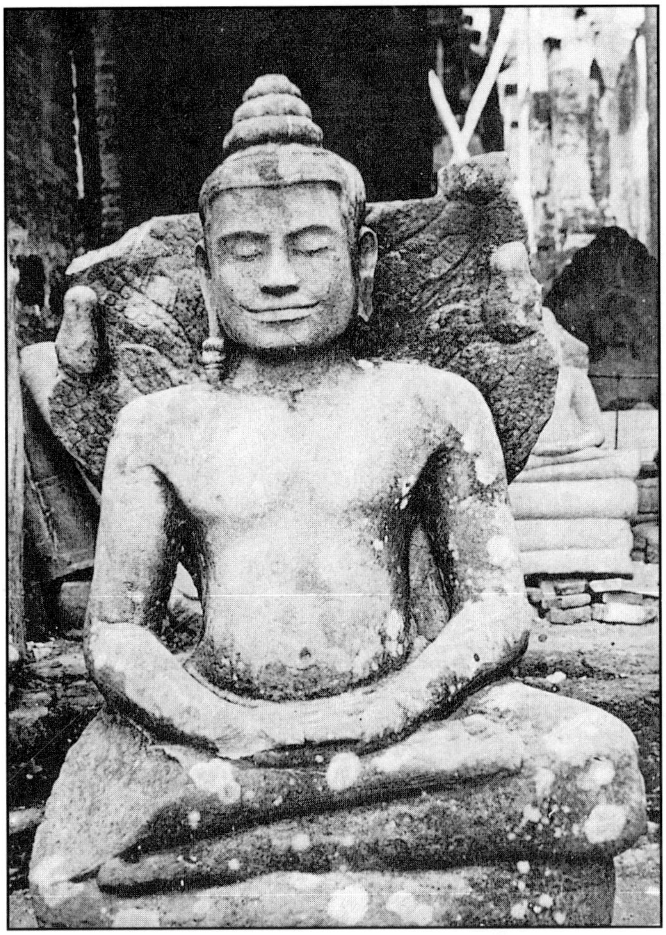

79. Sandstone Buddha, Khmer, *in situ* at Temple of Mahā-Tāt, Lopburi.

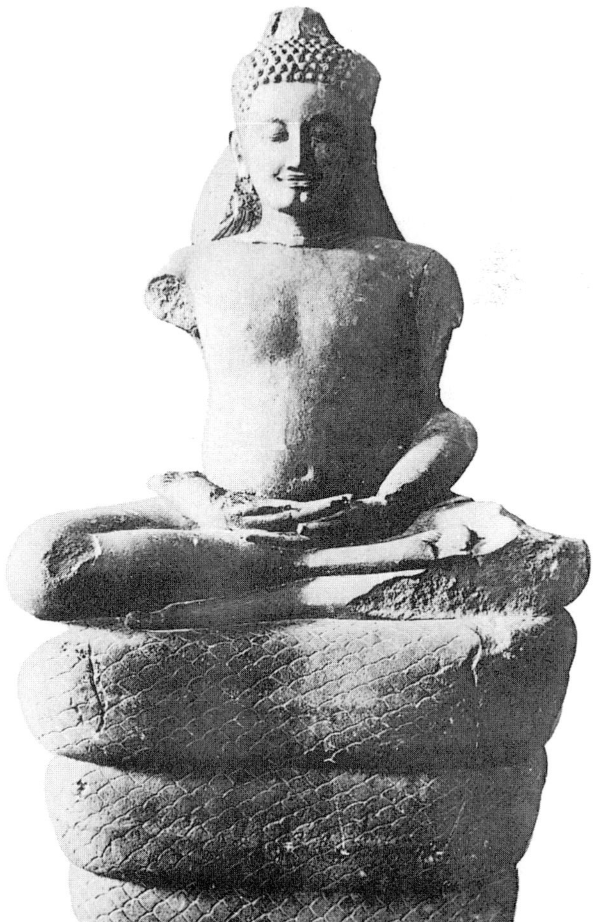

80. Sandstone Buddha, Khmer, from Angkor, Cambodia.

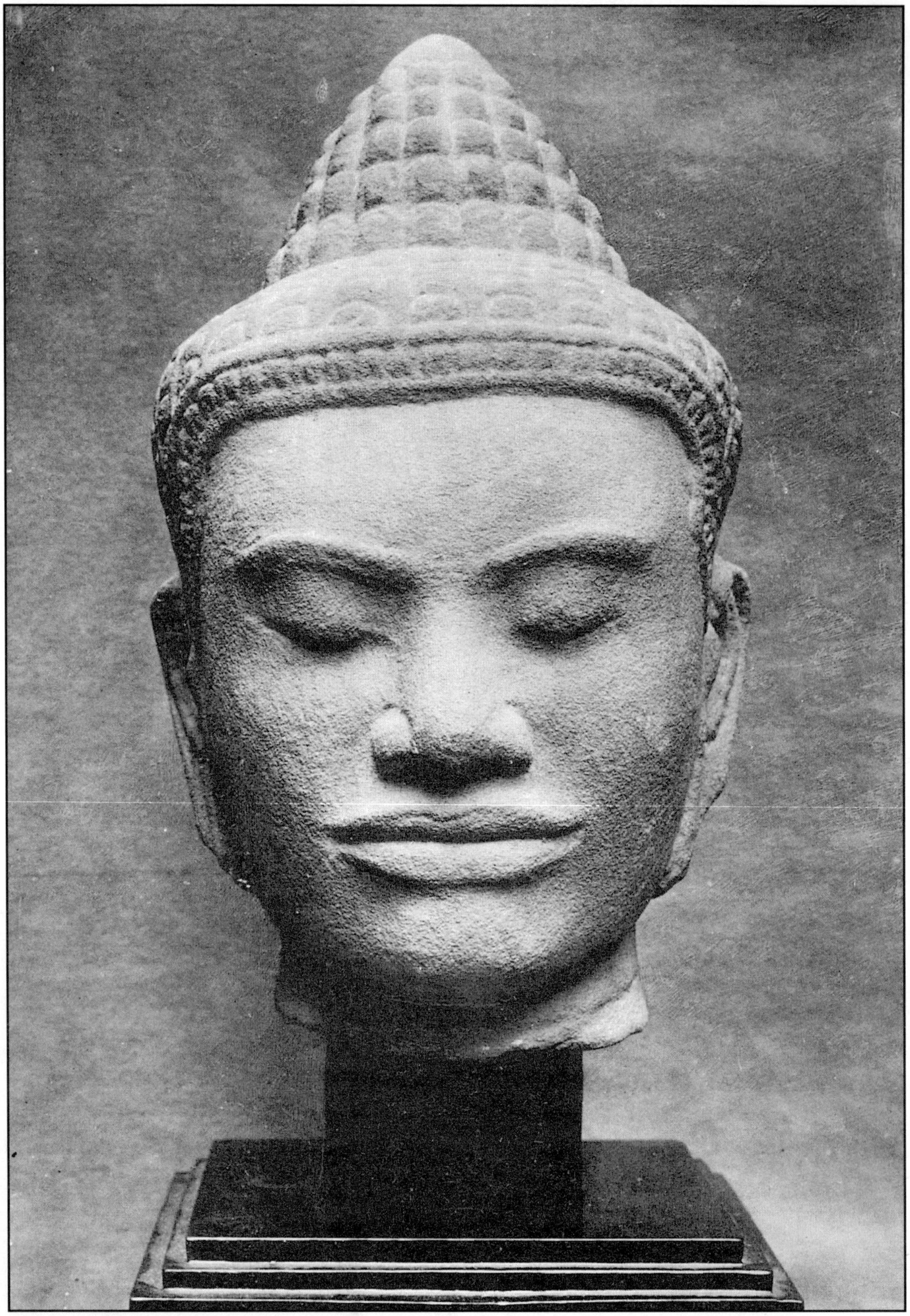

81. Sandstone Head of Buddha, Khmer, from Lopburi.

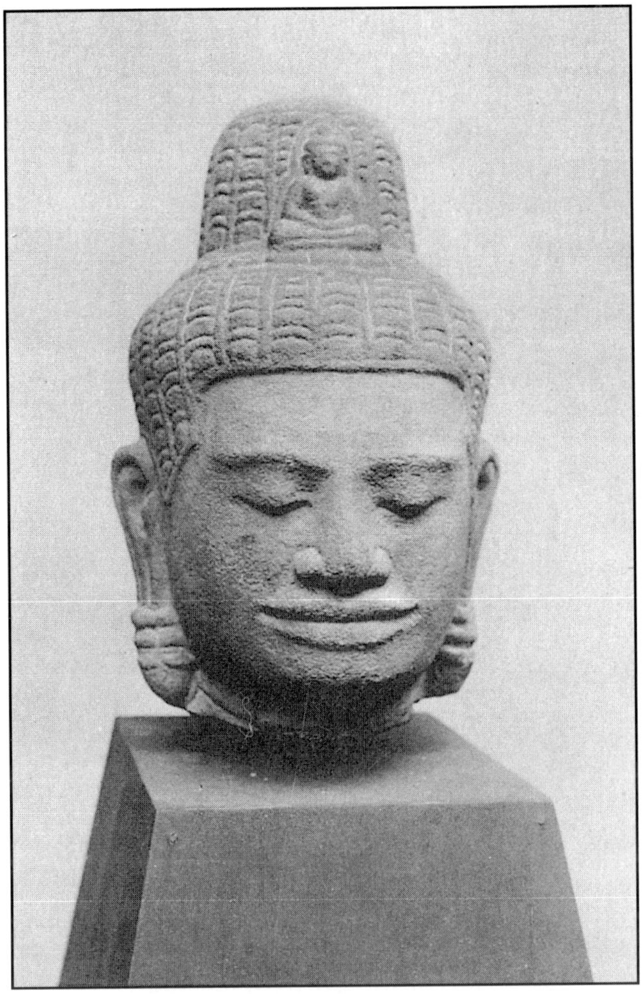

82. Sandstone Head of Bodhisattva, Khmer, from Lopburi.

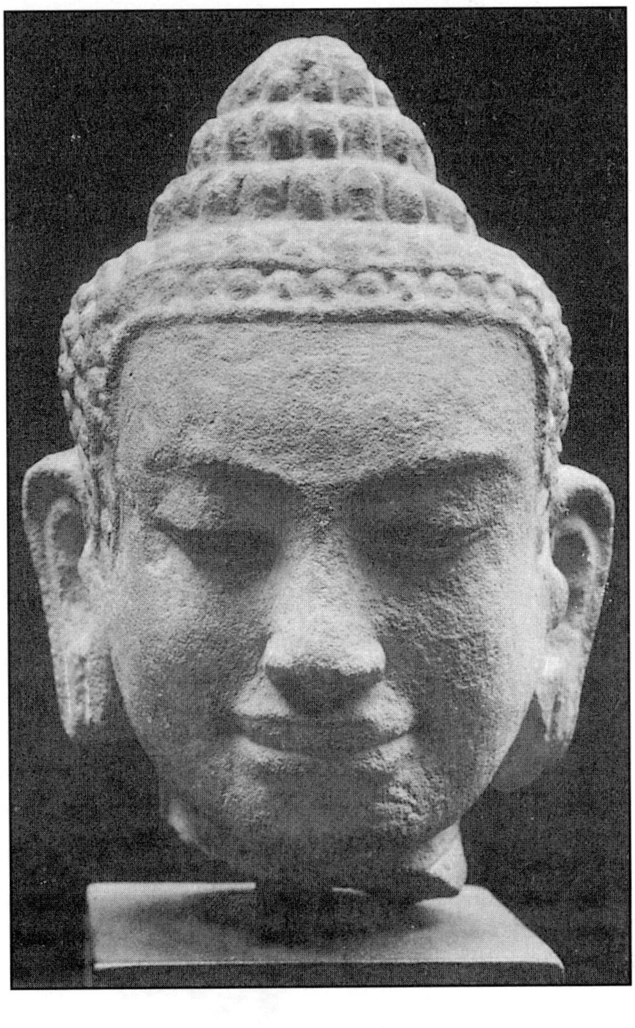

83. Sandstone Head of Buddha from Lopburi.
Khmer with Tai influence.

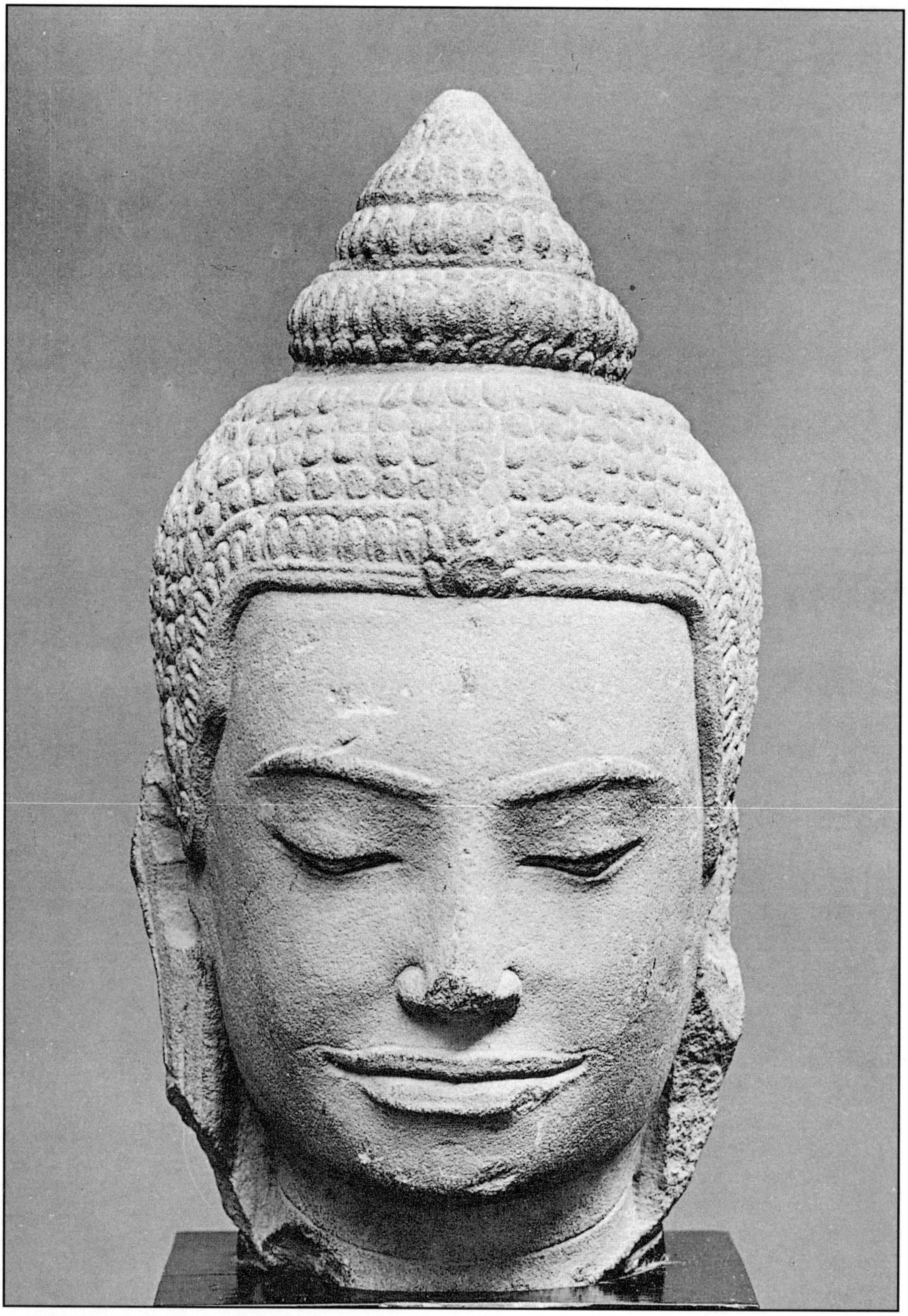

84. Sandstone Head of Buddha, Khmer, from Lopburi.

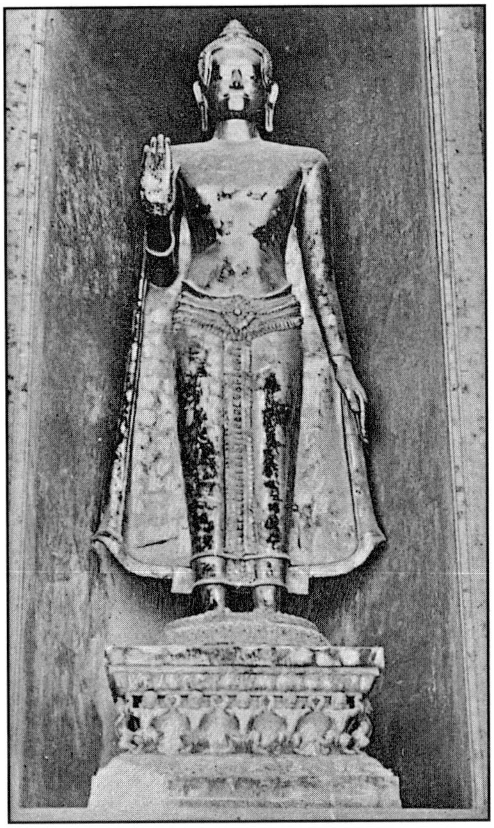

85. Bronze Buddha. Khmer. Outside Temple of Benchamabopit, Bangkok.

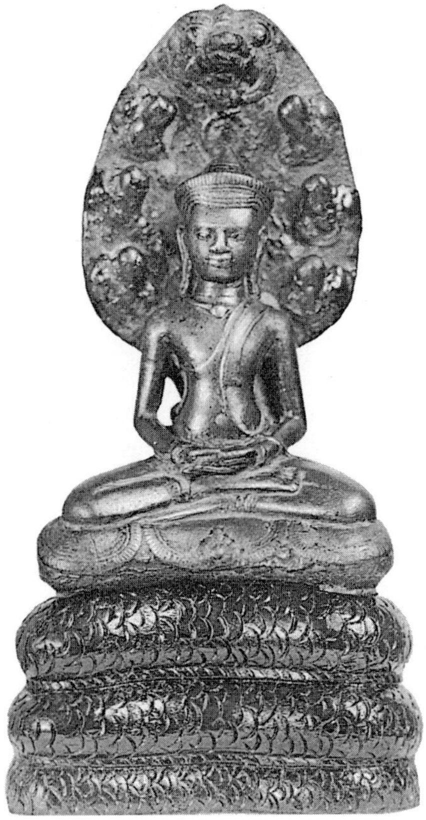

86. Bronze Buddha, seated on Nāga King. Khmer.

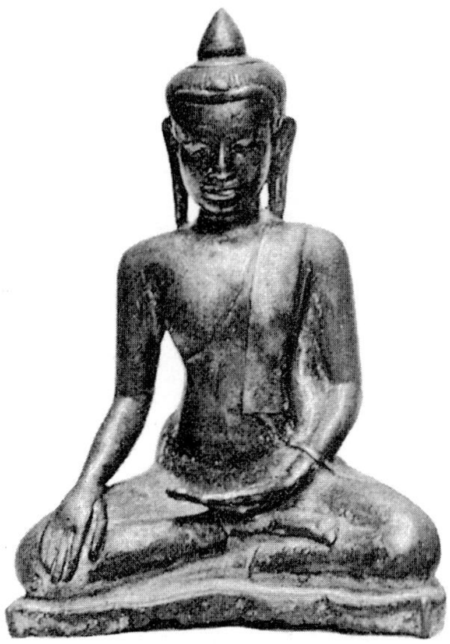

87. Bronze Buddha, Khmer.

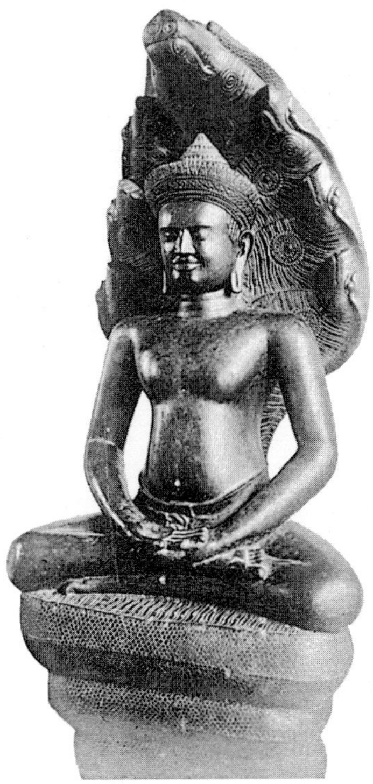

88. Bronze Buddha. Khmer. From Angkor.

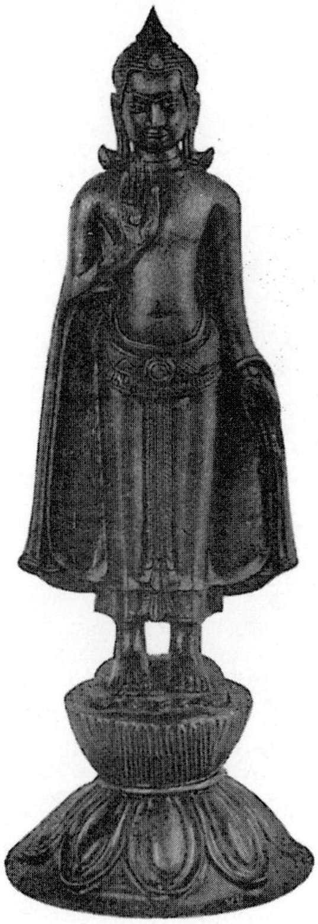

89. Bronze Buddha.
Khmer.

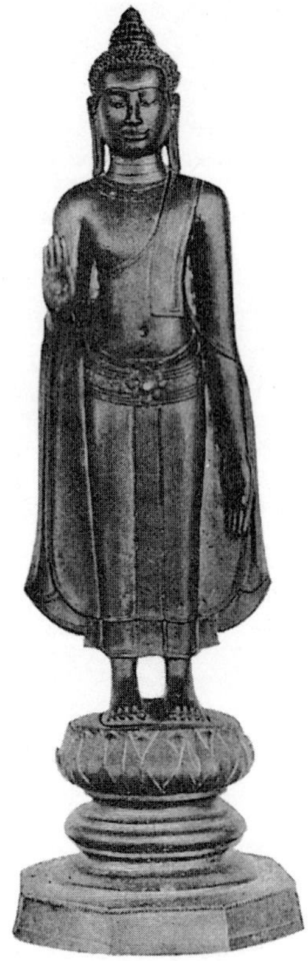

90. Bronze Buddha.
Khmer.

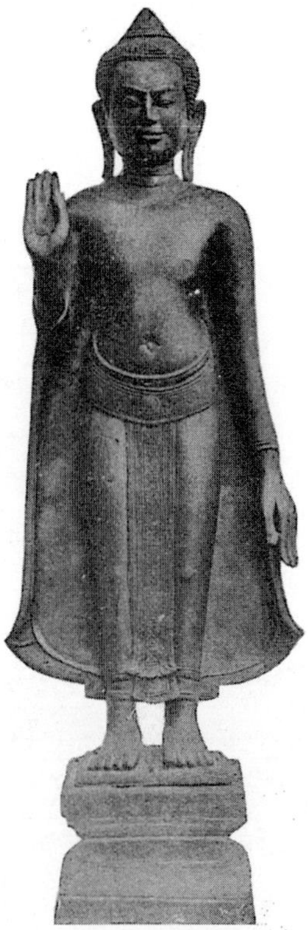

91. Bronze Buddha.
Khmer.

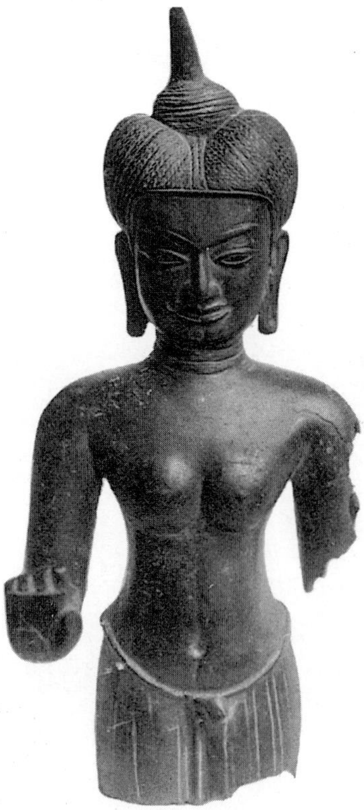

92. Bronze Young Woman.
Khmer.

original bronze seat. The ears touch the shoulders. But even here we still see the Môn influence in the treatment of the legs, which are drawn inwards forming a curve in the centre as in Fig. 35. The proportions are good, and the slender-waisted little figure wears a calm and dignified air.

Fig. 87, which is also 6 inches high, shows an even closer affinity to the Môn. The square head, the features and the head-dress, which is rather different from that in the preceding figure and has a jewel in front, are unmistakably Khmer, but the absence of all jewels on the body, the broad fold of the cloth, the set of the arms and hands, and the position of the legs betray a clear Môn influence. Notice particularly how the edge of the robe comes away from the broad fold and falls over the left arm exactly as in Fig. 35. But there is one feature which is noticeable in nearly all these small Khmer bronze images and which seems to be peculiar to them, namely, a very slight protuberance of the stomach. I have never remarked this feature in Môn images. As with the stone images, a large bronze seated figure of the Buddha under the Nāga king from Cambodia, now in the Pnompenh Museum, is shown for comparison with those from Siam (Fig. 88).

The standing images are not so interesting. They sometimes reach a height of 2–3 feet, but the treatment is usually much clumsier, especially in the hands and feet and lower part of the body which are modelled on purely conventional lines. Neither the Khmer nor the Tai seem to have worried themselves unduly about the treatment of hands and feet—to us essential features—but to have lavished all their care and art on the head and torso of the image. Considering the degree of skill which they bring to the modelling of this part of the body, it is hard to believe that they were incapable of showing equal skill in the treatment of the hands and feet, had they chosen to do so. Figs. 89, 90, 91, taken from Nai Hong's book, are good representative examples of standing figures of the Khmer school of Lopburi.

I will show one other figure (Fig. 92), purely out of curiosity, as it has obviously no connection with my subject: indeed, considering the duties enjoined by the Buddha on his disciples, it may be considered as out of place. This is the figure of an ordinary Cambodian young woman in her ancient dress, or undress. Its interest is twofold: first, it is the only such figure in bronze or stone known to me; and, secondly, it shows in a remarkable manner the ancient Khmer mode of "doing the hair". Presumably the spike at the top is a hair-pin!

The Khmer remained in possession of Central Siam for, roughly, three centuries, and during the course of that period penetrated as far north as Pitsanulōk and the region of Sawank'alōk-Suk'ōt'ai, where Khmer temple ruins are still to be seen. From a study of the remains there it would seem, however, that the Khmer never annexed what is now the North of Siam. As far as the historical evidence goes, this latter region was occupied from the ninth century onwards by Tai tribes, who took up their abode peacefully in the valleys between the ranges of hills without any violent disturbance of the aboriginal tribes of Lawā. During succeeding centuries these Tai settlements, growing stronger, gradually pressed farther and farther south, and I have no doubt that, during the Khmer occupation, there were considerable bodies of Tai living in the Sawank'alōk and Pitsanulōk areas. Probably they had reached as far south as Kampengp'et on the Me Ping, and some even to Lopburi. But it was not until the Mongol invasion of China had broken up the original home of the Tai in Nan Chao south of the Yangtsze-Kiang, and thereby caused an important further emigration of the Tai southwards, that the latter became powerful enough to contest dominion over Central Siam with the Khmer, as well as to establish a Tai dominion over the Lawā in the north. This fresh emigration, which pressed on the Tai already established in what are now the Shan States, happened to coincide with the waning power of the Khmer Empire which had already lasted for close on seven centuries and resulted in the establishment of the first Tai kingdom at Suk'ōt'ai and Sawank'alōk.

I propose, therefore, to conclude this chapter on the Khmer dominion over Siam by a short description of the principal Khmer temples at Piṭsanulōk, Suk'ōt'ai and Sawank'alōk.

The temple at Pitsanulōk, which is about five miles from the present modern town, goes by the name of Wat Çulamāni, and there is still a Siamese inscription *in situ* set up by King Narai in the seventeenth century, which states that a *vihāra*, or Assembly Hall, was added to it by King Trailōkanāth in the fifteenth century. The Khmer settlement was in the region surrounding it, and the site of the city has since been changed owing to the diversion of the river channel, as has happened at so many other places, including both Sawank'alōk and Suk'ōt'ai.

The temple sanctuary, which formerly measured 48 feet long by 24 feet wide, is largely a ruin, as will be seen from the accompanying illustrations (Figs. 93 and 94). But it is a singularly attractive ruin, as it is in miniature and was originally built on the same model as Wat Mahā-Tāt at Lopburi. In addition to the entrance on the east there are two other entrances, close at hand, on the north and south respectively, while the main part of the building, which lay behind and is now completely ruined, was in the form of a hexagon—which supported a tower.[1] The vestibule (with the three entrances) which is still standing, and which was connected with the nave by a passage, is about 28 feet high.

On the north and south there are six small *stūpas* all in ruin; on the east there are remains of a hall, possibly the one built by Trailōkanāth, and on the west are the ruins of a *bōt* (or consecrated chapel) surrounded by *sema* or plinths set up to mark the hallowed ground. But these I take to be all of later Tai construction. The temple was built of laterite blocks, covered with stucco. Claeys draws particular attention to the mouldings and decoration (a good deal of which still exists), of which the motifs, rather conventional and of the decadent period, appear to be copied from embroidery and bronze. The pillars and panels of the side walls have a dado with a hanging fringe in low relief, the decoration showing a marked resemblance to embroidery motifs. The style of the pediment, which has no tympanum, is closely analogous to the bronze frame for a Khmer image of the Buddha found in the Supanburi region to the west of Lopburi.

The finials at the end of the pediment are formed of four Nāga heads with a figure of Garuda in the centre. There is also a small indistinct personage standing above Garuda, which is probably a figure of Viṣnu. In any case the presence of Garuda seems to indicate that the temple was dedicated to Viṣnu. There are also some rather attractive figures of birds, probably intended to be *hamsa* birds, under the string-course on the plinth of the temple.

Altogether this temple presents an interesting example of Khmer architecture, possibly of the twelfth century, in one of the most outlying regions of its dominion.

At Suk'ōt'ai, as one walks along the famous P'ra Rūang Road paved with laterite blocks, and before one comes to the entrance to the old city, one will see to the left among the trees what is obviously a Khmer tower. This is all that remains of a series of three towers running north and south, now known by the name of Wat P'ra Pai Lūang. The temple is built of laterite with stucco decoration somewhat similar to that of Wat Çulamāni. The pediment here has a tympanum which shows a figure of the Buddha seated on a throne in the attitude of *Paryankānasa*. Below him are six persons seated in an attitude of prayer, with one knee raised. Against this, on the axial piece to the south, above the tympanum of the false door, is an image of Indra on his three-headed elephant.

Claeys thinks this temple was originally built for Brāhman worship, and from its form of three towers I should incline to agree with him—but in this case it is hard to account for the presence of the Buddha, unless this image is a later addition.

[1] Claeys gives an excellent drawing of it in his "L'Archéologie du Siam", *B.E.F.E.O.* vol. XXXI (1931), p. 406.

South-west of Wat Mahā-Tāt in old Suk'ōt'ai is another Khmer temple, Wat Sisawai, built, like P'ra Prāng Sām Yôt at Lopburi, with three towers running east to west, but with the principal entrance on the south. It is built of laterite below and brick above, covered with stucco decoration, and Claeys again attributes this structure to Siamese "main d'œuvre". He pays a tribute to the harmony and rhythm of the building and the satisfaction derived from the contrast presented by blocks of bare stone alternating with richly framed pediments and finely sculptured pieces.

It would serve no useful purpose to discuss this question of Siamese and Khmer "workmanship" at any length here, until Claeys has given a fuller explanation of exactly what he means by "main d'œuvre", and also of his reasons for attributing the construction of these three-towered temples to Siamese handiwork, when the form of the tower in particular seems to denote pure Khmer and not Tai feeling.

At Sawank'alōk there is the famous temple of Mahā-Tāt, which has a *prāng* tower of Khmer form, though, if Claeys had attributed this tower to Siamese "main d'œuvre", I should not have been surprised, as it looks to me to be entirely Tai in feeling, and not Khmer: and I feel almost certain that the former Khmer tower (if any) must have been reconstructed by the Siamese (Figs. 95 and 96).

I have given a full account of the lay-out of Wat Mahā-Tāt in the *Journal of the Siam Society*, vol. XIX, pt. 2 (1925), and shall not describe it here again in detail, especially as the majority of the buildings are obviously Siamese in origin. But there are certain features which deserve mention.

To the west of the main tower there is a *stūpa* of a construction most unusual in Siam (Fig. 97). The base is octagonal in shape, each face measuring 16 yards in length, giving a circumference of about 130 yards. The height is between 45 and 50 feet, and the summit is reached by a steep, narrow stairway going up the eastern face to a chamber with four openings, one towards each of the cardinal points.

The *stūpa*, which is built of laterite blocks and has no ornamentation whatever, is composed of a series of terraces leading up to the chamber above, which is surmounted by a pinnacle. This building, as far as I know, has no counterpart in Siam and in style somewhat resembles the great *stūpa* at Borobodur in Java. King Vajiravudh thought it might be of Môn construction as it resembles the style of Môn pagodas, and to belong to the period round about A.D. 1360, a time when the Môn form of Buddhism was in the ascendant at Suk'ōt'ai-Sawank'alōk. At this time the grandson of the famous Rām K'amheng, King Lü Tai, found his spiritual mentors in Môn priests from Pegu.[1] Duroiselle says that *stūpas* octagonal in form and plan may be seen in different parts of Burma, notably at Pegu, the most beautiful being the famous Sule Pagoda in the heart of Rangoon. He adds that the octagonal form of *stūpa* seems also to have been common in Old Prome.[2] He thus confirms the view of King Vajiravudh. A good parallel to the pagoda under discussion may be seen just south of Pagān in the Shwesandaw, built by King Anuruddha in the eleventh century.

There are other interesting features about the temple of Mahā-Tāt, and not the least among them is the entrance gateway (Fig. 98) which leads eastwards from the main *stūpa*. This gateway is formed of three enormous, round, equidistant laterite blocks, surmounted by two more enormous blocks joined together and laid horizontally, with pointed gable ends, and rising from the centre is a pinnacle showing a four-faced figure of either Brahmā or Çiva (or Avalokiteçvara) on the analogy of the tower at the famous Bayon in Angkor T'om. At one end the gable has now disappeared. There is an exactly similar entrance gate on the western side of the main *stūpa*.

The temple grounds are enclosed within a long, low wall of laterite blocks (copies in laterite of trunks of trees), which Claeys likens to the famous wall at Sānchī in Bhopal, and the main buildings are on a lower level than the one just described. The steps leading down to this lower level from the entrance gateway are themselves formed of circular blocks of laterite placed side by side, and the entrance passage is now so low that it seems as if the ground level in the second enclosure must at one time have been lower than it is to-day. The low wall is seen in Fig. 99, as is also an interesting stone pillar, the only one of a series still intact, ornamented with grotesque figures in stucco round the capital.

In front of this pillar, in the north-eastern corner of the second or main enclosure, is a small shrine containing a beautiful image of the Buddha seated on the Nāga king (Fig. 100). The proportions are excellent and the Nāga hood may be rightly called magnificent. The features of the image are Siamese or Tai, but, considering the fondness of the Khmer for this particular type, one wonders whether the same process has not been at work as at Lopburi, and a perfectly genuine Khmer figure transformed into a Siamese one. When I examined it, I was not then aware of the alterations made to Khmer images at Lopburi: hence my suspicions were not aroused, and I did not make a close inspection of it. It would be interesting to examine it again.

[1] H.M. King Rama VI (Vajiravudh), *A Visit to the Country of P'ra Rūang* [in Siamese]. Bangkok, 1908.
[2] Ch. Duroiselle, *A.S.I.A.R.* 1928–9, pp. 107–8.

# Chapter VII

## THE ORIGINS OF THE TAI AND RELATIONS WITH BURMA

THE coming of the Tai, or Siamese as they are called by Europeans, and the cultural influences which they brought with them offer a problem, the solution of which is still by no means clear.

The Tai are a Mongoloid race with a tonal speech akin to Chinese (though much influenced later by Sanskrit), and their original habitat is believed to have been in Southern China, south of the Yangtsze-Kiang; but what religion, if any, they held when they first came to Siam is not clearly established, nor yet what cultural influences had been affecting them during their journeys southward.

According to Credner, the Tai were always a people who preferred rice cultivation in a tropical climate to living on hill-tops, and concludes therefrom that their home must be sought in the tropical lowlands of the river plains and coastal regions of Southern China, in the provinces of Kwang-Si and Kwang-Tung.[1]

This theory is opposed to all previous ones and has not yet found general acceptance, but, wherever the Tai came from originally, it is certain that at the time of the rise of the T'ang Dynasty of China (A.D. 618–906), the Province of Yunnan was divided into six Tai principalities, and that about A.D. 650 Mêng Hua became the chief of these principalities under a Prince called Hsi-Nu-Lo.

This prince's great grandson, P'i-Lo-Ko, who reigned from A.D. 729 to 748, made himself master of the whole of Western Yunnan and set up his capital at T'ai-Ho (Tali-Fu) at the south-west corner of the great Lake Erh-Hai. His kingdom was called Nan-Chao by the Chinese. Credner has recently explored the site of this ancient city and found the remains of a fortress, as well as portions of brick and earth-built walls. P'i-Lo-Ko had cordial relations with the Chinese Emperor, who honoured him with a grand title, but his son, Ko-Lo-Fêng, who succeeded him, allied himself with Tibet and waged war against China, the former's mortal enemy, on account of alleged insulting treatment which he had received from the Chinese Governors of the bordering provinces. In T'ai-Ho may still be seen the *stela* which Ko-Lo-Fêng set up in A.D. 766 to commemorate

[1] W. Credner, *Cultural and Geographical Observations made in the Tali (Yunnan) region*, p. 11. (Trans. by E. Seidenfaden.) Siam Society, 1935.

his victories over China, for which he was given the title of "Emperor of the East" by the Tibetans. This *stela*, which is in Chinese, has been translated by Chavannes.[1]

Ko-Lo-Fêng is stated, in the annals of the T'ang Dynasty, to have conquered P'iao, i.e. the land of the Pyu, an extinct race that once occupied a great part of Burma, and also Sian-Chuan, which I am told lay between Myitkina on the Northern Burmese border and Southern Szechuan.[2] The conquest of Lower Burma was evidently only temporary as, according to Harvey, the Shan or Tai Yai did not take possession of the plains until the twelfth century.

Chavannes quotes the T'ang annals as saying that "the barbarians (i.e. the Tai) worship the spirits, and those who preside at the sacrifices offered to them are called 'sorcerers'".[3] This would tend to show that in early T'ang times the Tai were still animists, pure and simple, and that Buddhism had not yet reached them. On the other hand, the *stela* records that Ko-Lo-Fêng opened the door to all three religions of China—Confucianism, Taoism and Buddhism.[4] This is the first mention of Buddhism in the kingdom of Nan-Chao, and it must be borne in mind that the Buddhism here referred to means the *Mahāyāna* or Greater Vehicle, and not the *Hīnayāna* or Lesser Vehicle adopted by their Tai descendants both in Burma and Siam.

It is certain that Nan-Chao had a profound affinity with China, to whom she owed all her intellectual culture. The inscription on the *stela* is in Chinese; the native tongue, probably an idiom of Tai, had no script, and Chinese was the only language written, as in Corea, Japan, and Annam. A Chinese, named Chêng Hui, composed the text of the *stela*, and an old Chinese family of Tuan presided at its erection as Counsellors of State. Indeed, at a later date, a descendant of Chêng Hui destroyed the last of the Nan-Chao Tai royal family about A.D. 900, and in A.D. 938 a member of the Tuan family founded the realm of Tali on the ruins of Nan-Chao.[5]

Rocher has written an account of Nan-Chao under the title of "Histoire des Princes du Yunnan" and describes how in A.D. 903 the last Tai king of Nan-Chao died, leaving only an infant son who was promptly murdered by the Chinese

[1] E. Chavannes, "Une Inscription du Royaume de Nan-Tchao", *J.A.* vol. XVI (Nov. Dec. 1900), pp. 381–450.

[2] Private information from G. H. Luce. Cf. E. Chavannes, "Une Inscription", *J.A.* vol. XVI, p. 430 n.

[3] E. Chavannes, "Une Inscription", *J.A.* vol. XVI, p. 407, footnote 6.

[4] According to Perceval Yetts, the most probable date of the introduction of Buddhism into China is 2 B.C., in which case it must surely have reached Nan-Chao by the seventh century A.D.

[5] E. Chavannes, "Une Inscription", *J.A.* vol. XVI, p. 390.

Minister at the Court, who then seized the royal power. In 908, to expiate his crime, he built a huge temple and placed in it ten thousand bronze statues of the Buddha.[1] In the tenth century Buddhism apparently enjoyed much favour in Nan-Chao, and magnificent temples, which Rocher visited, were built at a place called San-T'a-T'zŭ. The Mahāyānist form of Buddhism was evidently being practised, as Rocher found a bronze headless statue of Kuan-Yin two metres in height.

Wood states that the Tai Kingdom of Nan-Chao was a highly organised State and that the Tai, although labelled as such by the Chinese, were no more "barbarians" than the Chinese themselves. There were Ministers of State, Censors, Generals, Record Officers, Chamberlains, Judges, Treasurers and so forth, while the administration was divided among different departments called *Shwang* which, as Wood suggests, may be the same word as the modern Siamese word, *Krasūang*, for a "Ministry". Military service was compulsory, as in modern Siam, for all able-bodied men, lots being drawn for each levy; while land was apportioned to each family according to rank, a system still surviving in Siam in the nominal *sakdina* grade conferred upon officials.[2]

With regard to the religion of the Tai, Wood gives it as his opinion that, while Northern Buddhism was probably known to the Tai of Nan-Chao for several centuries before many of them migrated south and some of the inhabitants may have been Buddhists, the bulk of the people were almost certainly animists and those coming to Siam did not adopt Buddhism until their arrival there, since these have always been adherents of the Southern or Hīnayāna School of Buddhism, which has flourished in Siam from the earliest times.[3]

While one may agree with Wood's opinion as a general statement, I feel that, before coming to a definite conclusion, more light needs to be shed upon the cultural environment of the Tai who, according to the *Pongsāwadān Yōnaka* and Prince Damrong, set up the first Tai principality in the north of Siam in the second half of the ninth century A.D.

Prince Damrong states that, at a time when the Tai were still powerful in Nan-Chao, members of this race had set up an independent State in the valley of the Salwin river and that, owing to the pressure of population, a number of them migrated farther westward and settled in Burma, while others went east

[1] E. Rocher, "Histoire des Princes du Yunnan", *Toung Pao*, vol. x, 1st series (1899), pp. 126–35.

[2] W. A. R. Wood, *A History of Siam*, p. 37. T. Fisher Unwin Ltd., London, 1926. *Sakdina* represents a degree of dignity (*sakdi*) originally expressed by the number of fields or lands (*na*) granted to the noble.

[3] *Ibid.* p. 38.

and south to Tonkin, the *Sipsong Panna* and Lūang Prabāng. From that time they continued to found colonies in the south until about A.D. 860 a Tai prince called Brahma crossed the Mekōng river and founded the first Tai settlement in what is now Siam at Chai Prakā in the district of Chiengrai.[1] Those who settled in Burma and the valley of the Salwin became known as Tai Yai (Great Tai), now called Shan, and those who settled in the Lao states and Siam were called Tai Noi (Little Tai), now the Siamese.

Wood ascribes to Brahma the feat of conquering the territory of the Cambodian empire down as far as Sawank'alōk and of founding a city there (at that time called Jalieng).[2] That an earlier Tai settlement was founded on the site of old Khmer Sawank'alōk is almost certain, from the pottery discovered there, but I doubt if it was by right of conquest or as early as the ninth century. In any case the territory conquered could not have been Cambodian, since the latter did not arrive at Sawank'alōk until the twelfth century at the earliest.

Accepting Prince Damrong's views as having most weight, it seems that the Tai first made their appearance in Siam at a time when the Tai kingdom of Nan-Chao was within sight of its close. The question, then, which requires an answer is, What relations, if any, had the Tai who came south with their kinsmen whom they had left behind in Nan-Chao? I myself incline to the view that, although they were of the same original stock, the intimate links which had bound the two branches together had weakened to a considerable extent and that, having long been subjected to foreign influences from the west and south, the emigrants to Siam brought influences much more closely connected with India (through Burma) than with China.

To-day even the two branches of emigrants, the Shan and the Siamese, are easily distinguishable, both physically as to features and dress and culturally as to language; which shows that the process of differentiation from the parent stock must have begun many centuries ago.

In Northern Siam it is difficult to find traces of an *early* Chinese influence (except in the use of the cyclical calendar of years) either in customs, dress, literature, art or religion; and the many quasi-Chinese tribes, such as the Yao and Miao, who inhabit the hilly regions of Northern Siam, keep themselves strictly apart and do not mix with the native population.

The only obvious relationship between China and Siam to-day lies in the

[1] H.R.H. Prince Damrong Rajanubhab, "Preface to History of Siam during the Ayudhya period" [in Siamese]. Trans. by (Sir) J. Crosby, *J.S.S.* vol. XIII, pt. 2, p. 28.

[2] W. A. R. Wood, *A History of Siam*, p. 50.

temple architecture, where the tiers of roofs so commonly seen in Siamese temples are certainly akin to Chinese forms. It is not yet known when this style of roofing was first introduced into Siam, or by whom, but it must have been some time after the arrival of the Tai, since even their early temples in Siam are in the form of Pagān buildings. The accompanying illustrations of temple and other buildings standing to-day in Southern Yunnan and the Shan States are included for comparison with those seen in Siam.[1]

Fig. 101 shows a temple in the district of Müang Hai in the Chinese Province of Yunnan (lat. 22·2° N., long. 100·2° E.), which has certain obvious affinities with the architecture of Northern Siam as seen in Fig. 102, which is the well-known Wat P'ra Sing at Chiengmai. In the Chinese temple there is a kind of Yamên entrance court, which is lacking in the Siamese building, and the eaves come down rather closer to the ground, though similar low eaves are also to be found in Northern Siam, especially where there are no side-walls. The serpent gable-ends seen on the roofs of Wat P'ra Sing are a distinctive feature of Siamese architecture, though I understand they are also to be found in Norway. They are not seen in China, or, I believe, in Burma. Fig. 103 shows an attractive type, slightly south-west of Müang Hai, which is not found in Siam but may well be compared with Fig. 104 (illustrating a temple in Chiengtung in the Southern Shan States, lat. 21·25° N., long. 99·75° E.); this in a debased form has now been used as a model throughout Upper Burma. Fig. 105 shows a type of *Sālā*, or resting-place for travellers, at Müang Yong in the Shan States (lat. 21·2° N., long. 100·3° E.), which has become common throughout Siam.

We must now turn to consider the cultural and religious conditions as they existed in the north of Siam at the time of the arrival of the Tai. The indigenous inhabitants, the Lawā, were apparently animists, pure and simple, and their culture was of a very primitive form. The only Lawā remains known to me (and these are conjectural) are the mud walls of an ancient town lying between the present city of Chiengmai and Doi Sut'ep, the mountain which rises to its north-west. We still know very little of their customs or habits or methods of government, though attempts have been, and are being, made by Kerr, Hutchinson and Seidenfaden to recapture their language from remnants of Lawā tribes still living in the hills to the west of Chiengmai.

The earliest cultural centre of which we have any certain knowledge was Haripūnjaya, the ancient name for the modern Lamp'ūn, 17 miles south-east

[1] I am indebted for these photographs to the courtesy of the Rev. Kenneth E. Wells, through the intermediary of Mr E. W. Hutchinson, both of Chiengmai.

of Chiengmai, on the Me K'ūang, a tributary of the Me Ping. I have already mentioned that there has always been a strong Siamese tradition that this town was founded and the district around it (including Nakon Lampāng (ancient K'elāng) 40 miles south-east from Lamp'ūn on the Me Wang) colonised by a Khmer Princess, Chām T'ewī (Chāma Devī) who came north from the Khmer city of Lavō (Lopburi) in the second half of the seventh century, with a large following including 500 priests learned in the Scriptures. This theory has now been exploded, and Cœdès has shown conclusively that the culture and religion which was brought to the north by Chām T'ewī was Môn in origin. Strong natural confirmation of this lies in the fact that there are no signs of Khmer dominion anywhere in the north of Siam, while the Môn tradition is still very strong in certain parts of the country, especially in the districts round Lamp'ūn, Lampāng and P'rê, which latter town lies 60 miles east of Lampāng. This influence is still often seen to-day in the use of the *hamsa* bird, the emblem of Môn sovereignty, to adorn the summits of the "flag"-poles of monasteries.

The earliest epigraphical evidence so far discovered only takes us back to the beginning of the thirteenth century, but the seven inscriptions found at different temples in Lamp'ūn are all in the Môn language, and the script is identical with that of the Môn inscriptions of Pagān.[1] Three of these inscriptions are dated A.D. 1213, 1217 and 1219 respectively, and Cœdès says that their palaeography is of a later date than that of Kyanzittha of Pagān (A.D. 1084–1112). But, in addition to these, much further evidence has been obtained from two Chronicles, recently translated and annotated by Cœdès, namely the *Camadevivamsa* (The History of Chāma Devī) written by the monk Bodhiramsi about the beginning of the fifteenth century either at Chiengmai or Lamp'ūn,[2] and the *Jinakalamālini* (The Garland of the Times of the Buddha) by the monk Rattanapanna of the Rattavana Mahāvihāra monastery at Chiengmai in A.D. 1516. Both are translations from Pāli manuscripts in the National Library at Bangkok.[3]

Rattanapanna was a monk of the Hīnayāna sect which, having been established in the Lao country about 1375, received a fresh impetus from Ceylon in the fifteenth century and expanded its influence under the name of Sihalagana. His narrative, as relating to history, is concise, even dry, but he gives the essential

[1] G. Cœdès, "Documents", *B.E.F.E.O.* vol. xxv, p. 17.

[2] The same author wrote the history of the famous "P'ra Sihing" Buddha image.

[3] Where abbreviated forms are used hereafter, *Camadevivamsa* is expressed by CDV, and *Jinakalamālini* by JKM.

facts in a form which is worthy of every credence.[1] Bodhiramsi is more discursive in his style, and much of his narrative is legendary, but he is of considerable use as a check on the *Jinakalamālini*.

According to the latter, Chām T'ewī was a daughter of the King of Lavō who married the King of Ramannanagara (i.e. the Môn country of Lower Burma), but left her husband in A.D. 663 to lead the missionary expedition to the north of Siam. She was already pregnant at the time and, soon after her arrival at Lamp'ūn, gave birth to two sons, one of whom became King of Lamp'ūn, and the other King of a new city, Lampāng (K'elāng).

The statuary of the Dvāravatī kingdom, the finding of the Môn-inscribed pillar of the seventh century at Lopburi,[2] and Chām T'ewī's alliance with a Môn King of Ramanna point clearly to the conclusion that the ruling class in the south was of Môn descent, and that the people who went with Chām T'ewī to the north of Siam, if not pure Môn themselves, were probably Môn-speaking and imbued with Môn customs and religion. The CDV says that Chām T'ewī founded five monasteries in Lamp'ūn, among others, the Mahāvana to the west of the city. There is still a temple of that name near the west gate of Lamp'ūn, and one of the Môn inscriptions was found there.[3] Chām T'ewī is also credited with the foundation of another city at Alambanganapuri (Lampāng Lūang), 10 miles south-west of Lampāng, where she built a temple and retired after her second son became King of K'elāng (Lampāng); though she went back to Haripūnjaya to die. The memory of Chām T'ewī is still preserved at Lampāng Lūang, especially in connection with a well which gave forth water at the Queen's entreaty.[4] To the temple at Lampāng Lūang, which is one of the most beautiful in all Siam, I will refer again later in chapter x.

Cœdès is inclined to put the arrival of Chām T'ewī in the eighth and not the seventh century, but this is of minor importance, as there is no vestige of remains in the north to-day, either architectural or sculptural, which can be attributed to her period, and in both chronicles we have from that time nothing but a list of names of kings until we reach the end of the tenth century. The only possible relics of the first millennium are certain coins resembling bracelets or crescents from the north of Siam which appear to be allied to coinage types of the Pyu of

[1] G. Cœdès, "Documents", *B.E.F.E.O.* vol. xxv, pp. 11–12.

[2] G. E. Harvey, in his *History of Burma*, says that the script on this pillar is based on a Pallava script of Conjeeveram, of the time of Dhammapāla (fifth century A.D.). He adds that this is the earliest Môn inscription known: p. 7 and Appendix, p. 307.

[3] G. Cœdès, "Documents", *B.E.F.E.O.* vol. xxv, p. 77, footnote 1.

[4] *Ibid.* p. 78, footnote 3.

Lower Burma.[1] The CDV affirms that a certain King of Lamp'ūn, Rundhayya, the great-grandson of Chām T'ewī, reverted to the ancient faith, i.e. animism, and proved himself an enemy of Buddhism.[2] The JKM records that in the reign of Trabaka, which Cœdès places towards the end of the tenth century, this King of Lamp'ūn made an attack by river on the King of Lavō, whose name is given as Ucchitta-Cakkavatti. When the latter went forth to meet his rival, another king, Jivaka of Siridhammanagara (Ligor in the Malay Peninsula), seized the opportunity to capture Lavō: whereupon both the other kings fled towards Lamp'ūn, but the King of Lavō arriving before Trabaka, the latter was forced to return to his original attack on Lavō.[3] From the evidence of subsequent history, it is clear that this assault was in vain, and he vanishes from the picture. The JKM further records that, after this event, the King of Lavō came north to attack Lamp'ūn but was heavily repulsed. From the fact that Ucchitta was welcomed in Lamp'ūn and reigned there as king, it would seem probable that the dynasties of Lavō and Lamp'ūn were still of the same race, which supports once more the theory of Môn dominion over Siam. This is again re-inforced by a passage from the CDV which records that in the middle of the eleventh century the people of Lamp'ūn fled "en masse" from the city and district to escape a severe epidemic of cholera. They went first to Thatôn, north-west of Moulmein, but being harassed by the King of Pagān, went on to Hongsāwadi (Pegu), where they were welcomed by their brethren, because "their speech was identical, without showing the least difference".[4] There is no reason to doubt the accuracy of this record, and it is perhaps the most conclusive evidence of the identity of the settlers in northern Siam with the Môn people of their homeland. The CDV, indeed, in recounting the fights that took place between the realms of Lamp'ūn and Lavō always refers to the people of Lamp'ūn as Ramanna, the name given to Lower Burma, and when it refers to a village of Tai boatmen, it calls it Deyya-gama (i.e. the Pāli for Tai).

From the point of view of our present study, this flight of the people of Lamp'ūn to Burma is of the first importance. The reference to the King of Pagān harassing them at Thatôn is to King Anuruddha (or Anawratā, as he is called in Burma), the first Burmese King of Pagān, who attacked Manuha, the Môn King of Thatôn, in A.D. 1057, sacked the city and carried off the king and all the monks and sacred scriptures to Pagān.[5]

[1] Reginald le May, *The Coinage of Siam*, Pl. III. Siam Society, Bangkok, 1932.

[2] Cœdès, "Documents", *B.E.F.E.O.* vol. xxv, p. 30.

[3] *Ibid.* p. 23.

[4] *Ibid.* pp. 17, 80.

[5] G. E. Harvey, *History of Burma*, pp. 27–8.

For a clear understanding of the intricate problem involved in the introduction from India of a new form of Buddhist art into Northern Siam, it is essential now to put before the reader a brief description of the cultural history of Burma up to the reign of King Anuruddha.

The earliest evidence available brings us into contact with two races in the lower half of Burma, the Môn (or Talaing) with their capital at Thatôn just north of Moulmein, and the Pyu, a Tibeto-Burman tribe, with their capital at Prome (old Hmawza) on the Irawadi river (lat. 18·75° N., long. 95·25° E.). The Talaing came, it is thought, from the region of Telingāna on the eastern seaboard of India and began to colonise Lower Burma at a very early date. They were probably Hīnayāna Buddhists. Unfortunately, little is known about the early period of their establishment at Thatôn except that at one time it was a sea-port, and the whole of this district still awaits a thorough investigation. The city of Pegu, about 50 miles north-east of Rangoon, which was apparently a distinct Môn kingdom, later became the principal centre of Môn influence. As the Pyu are now extinct as a race, and only scraps of their written language have yet become available for students, their origin and history is still very obscure, but the Chronicles of the T'ang Dynasty of China tell us that the people were Buddhist with a hundred monasteries in Prome itself. They used gold and silver for money, the shape of which was crescent-like. At seven years of age the children cut their hair (i.e. performed the top-knot ceremony) and entered a monastery, and the women, who knotted their hair on top of their heads and ornamented it with strings of pearls, wore a natural-tinted skirt of cotton and threw pieces of delicate silk over the upper part of their bodies.[1] This is clearly a description of the *lunggyi* and bodice still worn by the women of Burma, and of the *pā-sin* and *pā-hom* still worn by the women of Northern Siam: in both countries, too, the women have always worn their hair knotted on the top of their heads, while the peasant women of Central and Lower Siam keep theirs cut short.

How far north the authority of the Pyu extended is not yet clear, but their remains have been discovered as far up as Haling'yi in the Shwebo district (lat. 22·5° N., long. 95·75° E.),[2] and I have already referred to the conquest of P'iao (or the land of the Pyu) by Ko-Lo-Fêng of Nan-Chao between A.D. 760–70. It is recounted that in A.D. 808 the Prince of Nan-Chao took to himself the title of P'iao-Hsin, which Pelliot thinks might be construed as "Lord of the Pyu".[3]

[1] G. E. Harvey, *History of Burma*, pp. 12–13.
[2] G. H. Luce, private letter.
[3] P. Pelliot, "Deux Itinéraires de Chine en Inde", *B.E.F.E.O.* vol. IV, p. 165.

If this is correct, it would tend to show that the land of the Pyu must have bordered upon Nan-Chao, and how at an early date the Tai of the north and the Pyu of the south came into close contact with one another. The Pyu were also tributary to China, and in A.D. 802 the king's brother was sent to the Chinese Court to escort a party of musicians to the Emperor.[1]

Recent excavations at old Prome, especially the unearthing of Khin Ba's mound, have made it probable that both forms of Buddhism, Hīnayāna and Mahāyāna, as well as Viṣnuism and Çaivism, were all practised together at one and the same time. Duroiselle was fortunate enough to find the relic-chamber of a *stūpa* intact and containing a number of most important objects. Chief of these was a silver-gilt miniature *stūpa*, 26 inches high and 16 inches round at the base, with four Buddhas and four attendants repoussé in high relief. It was inscribed with two lines in Pyu and Pāli in an early Telugu-Canarese script of Southern India, very closely allied to the Kadambas of Vanavasi and the Pallavas of Kānchīpuram (Conjeeveram), in fact, practically the same script as that on the Maunggan plates already described from Ranjan Ray's work.[2] Two names were mentioned in it, both ending in Varman. The figures of the Buddha were of the Hīnayāna School, and may be of the time when the Hīnayāna School of Buddhism at Conjeeveram was flourishing in the fifth and sixth centuries under Pallava rule. Ancient Talaing writings make frequent mention of Dhammapala, the great commentator who founded the School at Conjeeveram.[3] At other places near by were found remains of a Linga, 14 inches high, showing that Çaivism existed side by side with Buddhism and Viṣnuism; and also partial statues of Bodhisattvas, analogous (from the description given) to those which I have already described in chapter IV from Buddh Gayā, but these are probably rather later in period.

At a subsequent date Duroiselle found a stone statue of the Buddha of local make; the head was missing, but the figure showed undeniable Gupta influence in the treatment of the body and robes. It bore a long inscription on the pedestal in Sanskrit and Pyu, which is said to be the earliest and longest Pyu inscription so far discovered. The Pyu is in the character of the early South-Indian script, while the Sanskrit is in a Gupta-like script of the seventh or eighth century. In addition, he also found at old Prome clay votive tablets of the Nālandā type with inscriptions in Nagarī of the ninth to tenth centuries.[4]

It seems probable then that, while the Pyu were Hīnayāna Buddhists for a

[1] P. Pelliot, *loc. cit.* p. 173.
G. E. Harvey, *History of Burma*, p. 7.

[2] *A.S.I.A.R.* (1926–7), pp. 171 *et seq.*

[4] *A.S.I.A.R.* (1927–8), pp. 128–31.

considerable period of time, there were also colonists from India among them practising Viṣnuism and Çaivism, very much as still obtains to-day, both in Burma and Siam. There are large colonies of Hindus in both countries, and they naturally have special Hindu temples for their own worship.

Up to the ninth century the Chinese always referred to Burma as P'iao (i.e. Pyu), but not long after A.D. 800 the kingdom of Prome broke up owing to internal dissensions, and from that time we can date the gradual rise of Pagān to pre-eminence.[1]

Of Pegu before the ninth century as little is known as of Thatôn, but, if the local tradition has any credit, it would appear that the people were of Talaing or Môn race, and that the kingdom was separate from that of Thatôn. The old name for Pegu was Ussa, which is the same as Orissa, and Harvey says that Pegu was colonised from Orissa.[2]

After the fall of Prome, the Pyu were merged with other local tribes and became Burmese. Pagān was originally a cluster of villages near the confluence of the Chindwin and Irawadi rivers and, though now in the dry zone, was formerly fertile, since mediaeval inscriptions dedicate extensive rice-fields in Pagān where now no rice will grow.[3]

An early chief of Pagān, Popa Sawrahan (A.D. 613–40), is said to be the originator of the Burmese era beginning in March 638, which era was much later introduced into Siam and was still in official use up to 1889. It was known in Siam as the *Chula-Sakarāt* or "Little Era", as opposed to the *Mahā-Sakarāt* or "Great Era" of A.D. 78. The Burmese chronicles also state that a later King of Pagān, Nyaung-U (A.D. 931–64), sent to Thatôn and Prome for plans of temples and, as a result, erected five such temples at or near Pagān, but none of these have as yet been identified.[4]

Pagān was naturally in early days a backward hinterland, but, according to Harvey, it seems that Indian influences came into Burma, not only via the coast of Arakan, as witness the Mahāmuni shrine at Akyab, but also overland through Assam, bringing with them Mahāyānism as early as the fifth century, as witness the lower structure of the Kyaukku Onhmin near Pagān. The great stone vault is much admired, and Harvey regrets the supersession of this fine stonework by the Talaing "brick and shoddy", which swamped Burma after the eleventh century.[5]

[1] G. E. Harvey, *History of Burma*, pp. 11–12.
[2] *Ibid.* pp. 5–6.
[3] *Ibid.* pp. 15–16.
[4] *A.S.I.A.R.* (1927–8), p. 133.
[5] G. E. Harvey, *History of Burma*, p. 17. I personally do not feel confident about influences coming into Burma overland through Assam.

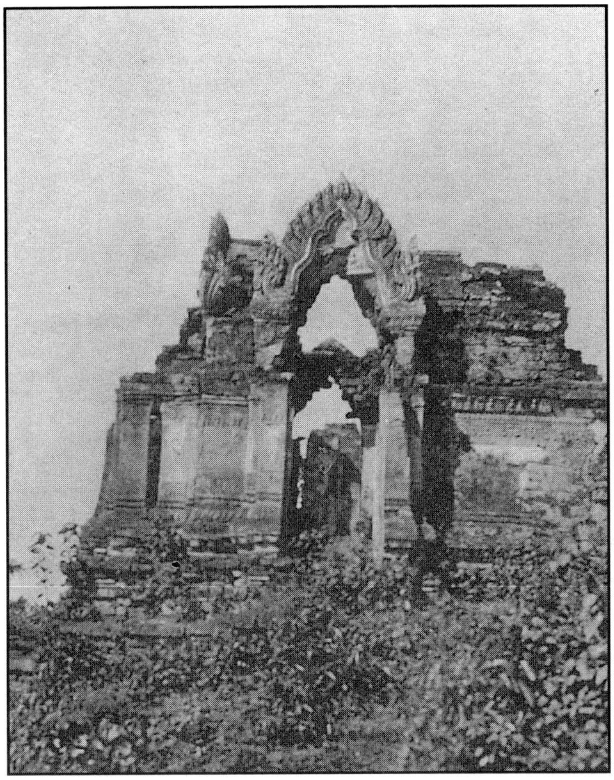

93. Khmer Temple of Çulamāni, Pitsanulōk. Southern Entrance.

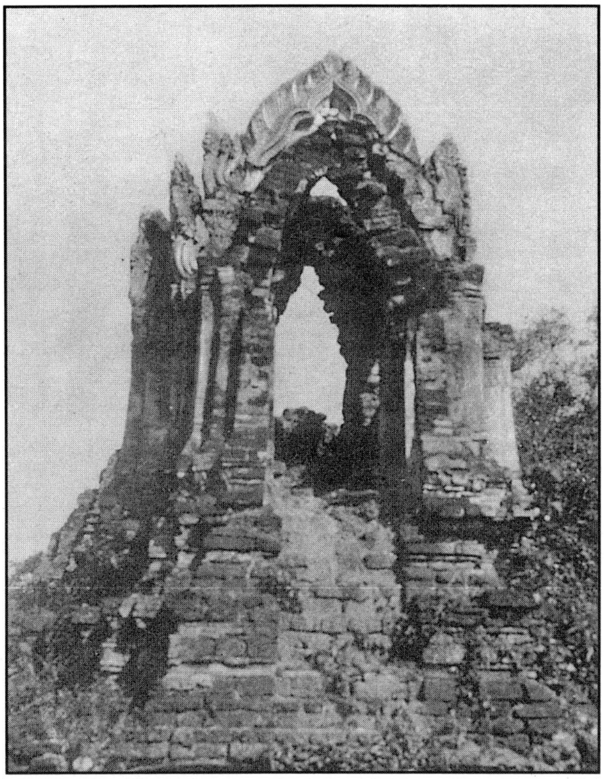

94. Temple of Çulamāni. Eastern Entrance.

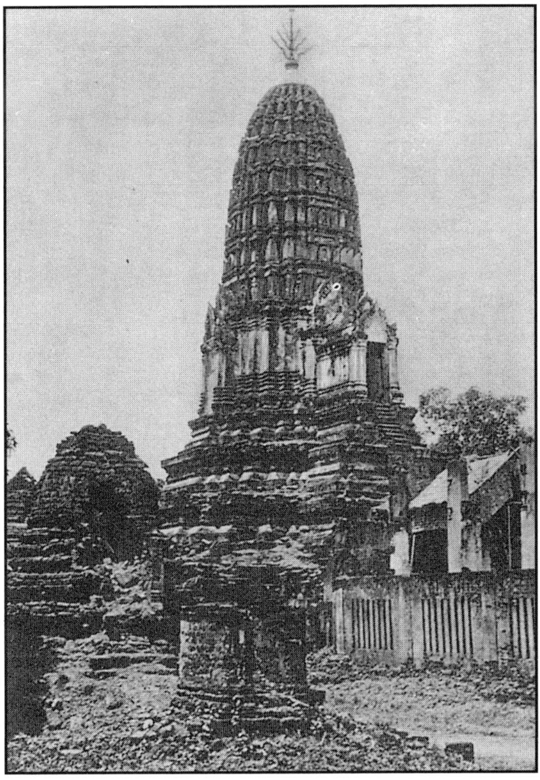

95. Tai-Khmer Temple of Mahā-Tāt, Sawank'alōk. Sanctuary Tower.

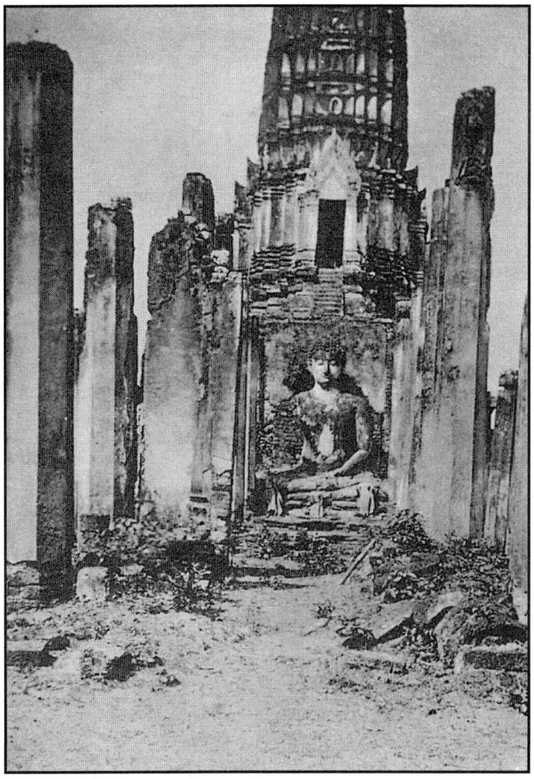

96. Temple of Mahā-Tāt, Sawank'alōk. Ruins of *Vihāra,* with Buddha on Altar.

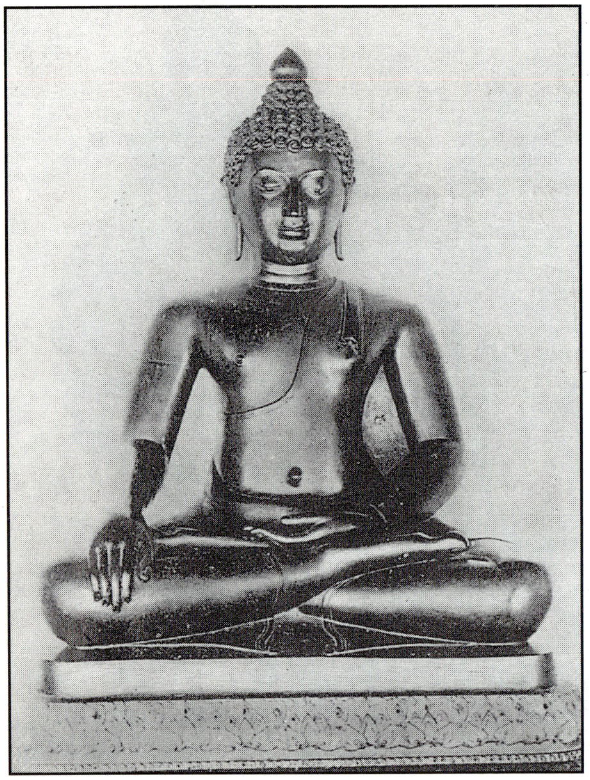

117. Bronze Buddha, Tai. Pāla style, from North Siam. Temple of Benchamabopit, Bangkok.

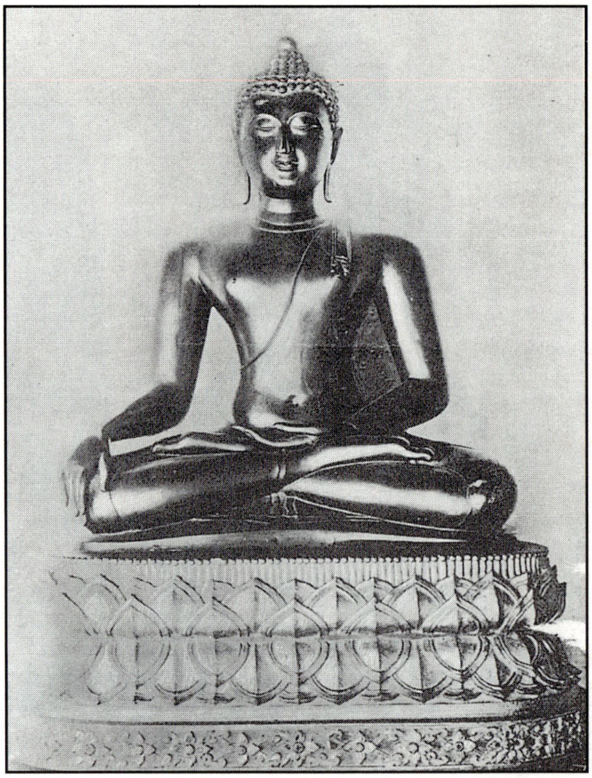

118. Bronze Buddha, Tai. Pāla style, from North Siam. Temple of Benchamabopit, Bangkok.

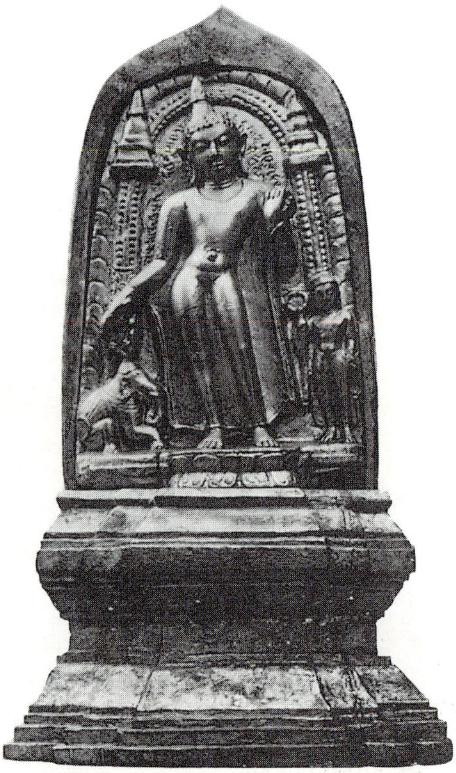

119. Stone Buddha, with Elephant Nālagiri and Ānanda. Pāla type, from Buddh Gayā. Now at Chiengmai.

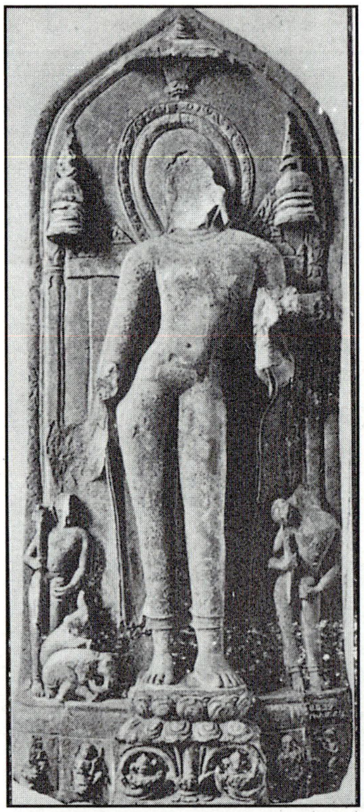

120. Bronze Buddha, with Elephants and Disciples. Pāla type, from Buddh Gayā.

In the same way one may well regret the passing of the Khmer dominion over Siam, with its stately stone edifices, but all the same there is much of a "homely charm" about many of the later Burmese and Siamese temples —they breathe a very friendly, almost an intimate air. I found this atmosphere of intimate peace particularly strong in the North of Siam.

The Mahāyānism brought into Burma from India was of a low order, and the *Arī* cult which held sway in Upper Burma till the eleventh century was distinctly a development of Tibetan Buddhism. The *Arī* were centred at Thamahti village a few miles south-east of Pagān and fostered a Nāga cult in which a Buddha and his Çakti wives figured. The *Arī* were bearded, grew hair four fingers long, wore robes dyed blue-black, rode horses, boxed, went into battle, drank intoxicants and, last but not least, practised the *droit de seigneur*. They had books of magic and a Mahāyāna Canon of the Scriptures in Sanskrit. It is known that Nyaung-U, the Cucumber King (A.D. 931–64), followed the *Arī* teachers and put up a figure of the Nāga king instead of an image of the Buddha.[1]

Pagān itself first became of importance as a city when in A.D. 849 its Chief, Pyinbya, enclosed it with a wall, of which remains still exist at the Sarabha gate, but it does not take on the pre-eminence that it was to hold during the next 250 years until the arrival of the famous King Anuruddha in A.D. 1044.

Up to this time, then, we have a very debased form of Mahāyānism in Upper Burma, while in Lower Burma, in the Pyu kingdom of Prome, and the Môn or Talaing kingdoms of Pegu and Thatôn the Hīnayāna creed flourishes, with Hinduism of both schools living quietly and peacefully alongside it, and a possible outcrop of Mahāyānism at varying periods.

There was another rather mysterious centre of Indian culture in Burma—at Tagaung (lat. 23½° N., long. 96° E.), on the Irawadi, just north of the Ruby Mine district. It became at one time prominent when Führer, the archaeologist from India, stated (in 1894) that he had found a stone slab there dated A.D. 416 with a Sanskrit inscription relating how Tagaung was founded by immigrant princes from Hastināpura (Old Delhi). This was accepted in some places at the time, but the stone has never been produced and, in view of Führer's subsequent record, this evidence cannot be accepted.[2] Luce states that the earliest *dated* inscription from Tagaung is of the year A.D. 1354, but he adds that, according to the Hmannan Yazawin (the chief Burmese Chronicle), the city was founded by Anuruddha; which he considers as very probable, seeing that clay votive tablets in Pāli-Sanskrit have been found there with his name upon them. He

[1] G. E. Harvey, *History of Burma*, pp. 17–18.

[2] *Ibid.* p. 310 (Appendix).

adds that anything earlier about Tagaung is gravely suspect.[1] Until further evidence is forthcoming, Tagaung cannot therefore be considered of any special importance as an early centre of culture in Burma.

In 1056 King Anuruddha of Pagān, being presumably determined to drive out the debased *Arī* from his capital, sent a courteous request to King Manuha, the Môn King of Thatôn, for a supply of priests and scriptures to teach his people the Hīnayāna form of Buddhism. It is not yet clear whence Thatôn had derived its Buddhism of this particular period, whether from Ceylon or India, but I am inclined to think it must have come from the Pāla kingdom in Bihar and Bengal. Anuruddha's request was rejected with contumely and the king, enraged at this insult, at once gathered an army, attacked Thatôn, seized the king and carried him off to Pagān with all his priests and scriptures. Strange to tell, the temple of Nan Paya which King Manuha built for himself just south of Pagān city is full of Brāhmanic sculptures, and Harvey says that his form of religion was clearly more Hindu than Buddhist.[2] The fact of the Brāhmanic temple sculptures is rather hard to explain, but, from subsequent events, it seems reasonably clear that Thatôn Buddhism was *not* Hinduistic nor even Mahāyānist in type.

Anuruddha's request to Thatôn was probably based on a meeting which he had with a young Môn monk from Thatôn of the Theravāda (reformed or primitive) school of Hīnayāna Buddhism, Shin Arahan by name, who had come to Pagān in 1056 as a missionary of the Faith and who attracted his attention. When he had captured Thatôn, Anuruddha then proceeded to raze the walls of Prome and finally stripped the pagodas of their relics, which he took to Pagān to enshrine in pagodas and temples of his own building. Thatôn never recovered the prosperity which it had formerly enjoyed through sea-trade, because the receding coast-line left it high and dry.

The results of the capture of Thatôn were of prime importance for religion and art in Burma. First and foremost, Hīnayāna Buddhism succeeded Mahāyānism as the principal form of religion in Upper Burma, and Pāli superseded Sanskrit as the language of the Scriptures. Secondly, the Burmese adopted the Talaing (Môn) alphabet and wrote their own language for the first time, the earliest Burmese inscription known being dated 1058. Thirdly, there was a great influx of craftsmen from Thatôn into Pagān, and Anuruddha inaugurated the great era of temple-building which lasted for more than two centuries.[3]

[1] G. H. Luce, private letter.

[2] G. E. Harvey, *History of Burma*, p. 28.

[3] *Ibid.* pp. 28–9.

According to Harvey, in Anuruddha's time the kingdom of Burma was enclosed within an area 200 miles long from north to south, and only about 80 miles broad from east to west. The northern boundary ran with Nan-Chao, to the east were a host of small Shan (Tai) principalities, on the far west were the Arakanese, and on the south, after the extinction of the Pyu kingdom, were the Môn of Pegu. Anuruddha did receive the homage of the nearer Tai chiefs, though this was purely nominal, and he had to establish outposts all along the eastern hills to prevent their raids and encroachments.[1] But here we have a definite contact between the Burmese in the west and the Tai in the east and north, and, with the growth and spread of Hīnayāna Buddhism in Burma, it is most probably from the middle of the eleventh century that the Tai of Northern Siam and the intervening region began to be influenced by the forms of religion introduced at this time into Upper Burma.

It is related that Anuruddha also attacked Nan-Chao (Tali-Fu), but the result was inconclusive and ended in an exchange of gifts. On his return to Pagān, Anuruddha visited the Shan States, and the Chief of the principal State, Maw, presented his daughter in marriage.

On the evidence of a statement by Sir George Scott that there were no indications of many ancient *stūpas* and *vihāras* at Thatôn, Prince Damrong has made the interesting suggestion that the city of Thatôn, which Anuruddha is said to have conquered, was none other than the ancient city of P'rapatom in South-central Siam, and that Anuruddha extended his territory as far as the valley of the Menam Chao P'ya, thereby bringing the Khmer into subjection under him.[2] This does not accord, however, with Burmese history, which is explicit, nor with the evidence of the flight of the people from Lamp'ūn back to Thatôn in 1057. One of the chief difficulties, from the point of view of this study, which the identification of Thatôn with P'rapatom creates is that, if Anuruddha actually conquered Central Siam, we ought to find the same type of Buddha image there as was introduced into Northern Siam during this period, but the Chiengsen school, with which I am about to deal, does not occur in the lower valley of the Menam.

In Anuruddha's time the centre of culture in Northern Siam was still at Haripūnjaya (Lamp'ūn), and the *Pongsāwadān Yōnaka* records that, when the people came back from Pegu after the epidemic of cholera had run its course,

[1] G. E. Harvey, *History of Burma*, p. 29.

[2] H.R.H. Prince Damrong Rajanubhab, "History of Siam prior to the Ayudhya period", *J.S.S.* vol. XIII, pt. 2, pp. 30–1.

many of their Burma brethren came with them and introduced the Môn style of writing. This may well be true as the modern Lao form of script is very similar to the Môn and Burmese (and not at all like modern Siamese), and the Môn inscriptions of the early thirteenth century found at Lamp'ūn are almost identical with Môn inscriptions from Burma of the same period.[1] It is also suggested that the Lamp'ūn people taught the Môn of Pegu, and thence the people of Pagān, the art of lacquer-work when the former migrated to Burma in 1057.

[1] G. Cœdès, "Documents", *B.E.F.E.O.* vol. xxv, p. 80, footnote 6.

## Chapter VIII

### FURTHER RELATIONS WITH BURMA AND INDIA, AND THE RISE OF THE CHIENGSEN SCHOOL

THE earliest temple building standing at Lamp'ūn is Wat Kŭkŭt in the village of Sān Mahāpol, about half a mile west-north-west from the west gate of the city. It is said to have been erected by the Môn king, Dittarāja (A.D. 1120–50), to commemorate his victory over the army of Lavō which came north to attack him.[1] It is a square monument in brick with five storeys rising from a plinth and surmounted by a ringed, or terraced, pinnacle (Fig. 108). There is a smaller leaning *stūpa* beside it. On each side of the main *stūpa* are fifteen niches in five rows of three, with a standing image of the Buddha in each, making sixty images in all. It is very similar to the Sat Mahal Prāsāda at Polonnāruwa in Ceylon, which dates from the end of the twelfth century,[2] and there is also an analogous temple, of later date, called Wat Sī Liem (the Square Temple) near the site of Wieng Kŭm-Kām, Nang Hoi, on the Lamp'ūn road, which was the actual site of the first city built by Meng Rai, the Tai conqueror of the north in the second half of the thirteenth century (Fig. 106). At the temple of Kŭkŭt Cœdès found two Môn inscriptions of the early thirteenth century, and Dupont, in an interesting article recently published, has concluded from them that this temple was built by the then Môn king, Sabadhisiddhi, about the year A.D. 1218; but actually the inscriptions refer to *restorations* by this king, and consequently the *stūpa* itself must be earlier.[3] But Dupont has done a service in drawing attention to the figures of the Buddha in the niches, in which he sees a distinct affinity, if of later date, to the art of Dvāravatī (Fig. 109). With this I agree, and, indeed, it is not in any way surprising when we consider that the city was still in the hands of the Môn who were responsible for the art of Dvāravatī at an earlier period in the south.

The origin of this type of structure has still to be determined. In Ceylon itself it is of a most exceptional style and was pronounced by Bell to be of Cambodian origin; but, without further ocular demonstration, I cannot accept this attribution,

[1] G. Cœdès, "Documents", *B.E.F.E.O.* vol. xxv, p. 83, footnote 2.

[2] Vincent A. Smith, *History of Fine Arts in India and Ceylon*, p. 55; J. E. Mitton, *Lost Cities of Ceylon*, p. 208.

[3] Pierre Dupont, "Art de Dvāravatī et Art Khmer", *Revue des Arts Asiatiques*, p. 72. Paris, 1935.

and if, as seems likely, the temple of Kŭkŭt is anterior in date to that at Polonnaruwa, one is inclined to think that it was the result of an original conception on the part of the Môn King of Lamp'ūn, from which the Ceylon temple was copied, unless, indeed, we have here the one remaining example in Siam of the architectural style of Dvāravatī, a possibility which is not by any means without the bounds of reason.

The Môn King of Lamp'ūn who followed Dittarāja is known as Adittarāja, and is famed in history as the builder of the Great *Stūpa* at Lamp'ūn between the years A.D. 1150–75 (Fig. 107). The present *stūpa* is not the original one, but as it appeared after its restoration and enlargement in the Tai style in 1447 by Tilōkarāja, the valiant King of Lānnātai, as the northern kingdom was then called.[1] The original temple is said to have been connected with the miraculous appearance of a golden casket of Açoka's reign containing a relic of the Buddha. The relic emitted six different colours and, having been duly worshipped, then disappeared into the ground. Adittarāja promptly built a *stūpa* over the spot to mark the celebrated occasion. This took place about A.D. 1163.[2] In the north-west corner of the temple enceinte may still be seen a *stūpa* in the form of Wat Kŭkŭt, which is said to be a model of the original *stūpa* now encased in the present *stūpa*.

In the eleventh and twelfth centuries wars with the Khmer kings of Lavō were frequent owing, no doubt, to the Khmer desire to incorporate the north within their empire, but, although their attacks came to nothing, a relic of the contact with Lopburi is still to be seen at the Great *Stūpa* in the shape of an image of the Buddha which is called "P'ra Lavō". The present image is of fairly recent date but is doubtless a copy of an ancient image.

Evidence of the actual relations between the north of Siam and Pagān during the great period of that kingdom, between 1050 and 1250, is at present scanty in the extreme. Harvey relates that in Anuruddha's reign a party of Lao Shans (Tai) from the Chiengmai district raided Pegu, and that Kyanzitthа, a reputed son of his by a princess from Vesali, who afterwards became King of Pagān (1084–1112), drove them off and by his feat became a hero to the Môn of Pegu.[3] The Lao Chronicles make no mention of this raid, and one is left wondering whether it has any connection with the exodus of Lamp'ūn people to Pegu already related—in which case the raiders would have been Môn and not Tai—

[1] *Lānnātai* may mean either (i) the million (*lān*) Tai fields (*nā*), or (ii) the Tai threshing-floor (*Lānnā*).

[2] G. Cœdès, "Documents", *B.E.F.E.O.* vol. xxv, p. 85.

[3] G. E. Harvey, *History of Burma*, p. 31.

but perhaps it was another event altogether. Harvey also records that, when he became king, Kyanzittha called in a wizard of Hti Laing, by name Shin Popa, who had studied at Chiengmai and was probably an *Arī*.[1] At the end of the eleventh century Chiengmai had not yet been built, but if the term is merely used to refer to the north of Siam generally, it opens up a problem of the introduction of *Arī* Mahāyānism which requires further investigation. Possibly the small Tai principalities of the far north of Siam were not sufficiently important to warrant any Court relations between the two countries, and the connection was formed by the natural coming and going of wandering priests and travelling traders.

But, whatever the relations may have been, it is now clear that during the early part of the Pagān period a new form of the Buddha image was introduced into Burma from India, and passed on by the Burmese to the Tai of Northern Siam, who were gradually rising to power in that region. I hope to show conclusively that this new form was closely connected with the Pāla art of Bihar and Bengal, as already suggested by Cœdès.[2]

The latter half of the eleventh century was witnessing the closing stages of Buddhism in India, and Ceylon was being subjected to attacks as well. It is recorded that the King of Ceylon, Vijaya Bāhu I (A.D. 1065–1120), sent for assistance to King Anuruddha against the Cholas of Southern India, and in A.D. 1071 asked for and obtained a deputation of monks with scriptures to strengthen the religion which had fallen on evil times.[3] It is also recorded that in Kyanzittha's time large numbers of devout Buddhists, fleeing from persecution in Northern India, migrated to Burma and even as far as Siam. Many came to Pagān, and the construction of the wonderful Ānanda temple by Kyanzittha is said to be directly due to the inspiration he received from eight Indian Buddhist monks who told him of the great cave temple of Ananta in the Udayagiri hills of Orissa. This temple of Ānanda, which was built in 1090, is the first of the great temples of Pagān called "Caves", consisting, as they do, "of masses of brick in which aisles, pillars and mysteriously lit recesses are, as it were, hewn out of some deep hillside".[4] It is, indeed, the Westminster Abbey of Burma. At this time Pagān became an important religious centre and pilgrims came from far and wide, even from India itself, to worship at its magnificent shrines.

Kyanzittha finished the great Shwezigon *stūpa* which Anuruddha had begun—a *stūpa* which became the prototype of all cylindrical structures in Burma (and

[1] G. E. Harvey, *History of Burma*, p. 37.

[2] G. Cœdès, "Le Musée National de Bangkok", *Ars Asiatica*, vol. XII, p. 31. Paris, 1928.

[3] G. E. Harvey, *History of Burma*, p. 32.

[4] *Ibid.* p. 40.

Northern Siam) and commemorates the triumph of the Southern School over Northern Buddhism,[1] and also the restoration of the holy Buddhist temple at Buddh Gayā in Bihar. This is confirmed by Cunningham, who found a Burmese inscription carved on black stone, which was fixed in the wall of the Mahant's house at Buddh Gayā, recording that the work was begun in C.S. 441 (A.D. 1079) and finished in C.S. 448 (A.D. 1086). The Burmese work extended to a complete restoration of the whole temple, and included the rebuilding of the pinnacle.[2] This act shows clearly that there was a close connection between Buddh Gayā and Pagān during the reign of Anuruddha and his successor, and this period coincides with the fame of Nālandā in Bihar as a University and Mission-training centre, as well as a School of Art.

In the eleventh century the sovereignty of the Pāla kings, who had ruled in Bihar and parts of Bengal since the time of Gopāla I (about A.D. 750), was drawing to a close, and early in the twelfth century they were ousted from their dominions by the Senas. But the three hundred and more years of their rule had seen the rise and flowering of a prolific Buddhist as well as Brāhman art. Stella Kramrisch says that "this school grew up in an age agitated by political disturbances.... During a relatively consolidated and more successful period it enjoyed the possession of the art-form it had built up....Later it was seized by a slight stagnation but coming generations finally stirred it up with a baroque luxuriousness until it was suffocated by Islam."[3]

In the ninth century, when Pāla art seems to have reached its apogee, the images were mainly Buddhist, and Brāhmanic figures were few. In the tenth century Brāhmanic images tended to increase and by the twelfth century Viṣnu images were so abundant that they could scarcely be counted.[4] In the case of Buddhist sculptures, it is clear that there was a gradual turning from the Hīnayāna to the Mahāyāna School, if we may judge from the images of the Buddha and Bodhisattvas still extant. To quote Stella Kramrisch once more: "A religion of faith and devotion towards divine mediators who had voluntarily renounced their own salvation, replaced a philosophy of the ideal of personal nihilism. This deviation was reinforced in Pāla times, and more and more directed towards Tara and Sakti."[5] Finally, Buddhism disappeared and its place was taken by Brāhmanism, where it was not choked by Islam. Indeed, the Mahāyāna Buddhism

[1] *Ancient Monuments in Burma* (Amended List). Govt. Printing Press, Rangoon, 1921.

[2] Sir A. Cunningham, *Maha-Bodhi, or the Great Buddhist Stupa at Buddhagaya*, pp. 75–7. Allen and Co., London, 1892.

[3] Stella Kramrisch, "Pala and Sena Sculpture", *Rūpam*, no. 40 (Oct. 1929), p. 109.

[4] *Ibid.* p. 110. [5] *Ibid.* p. 112.

of Pāla times was hardly to be distinguished from Brāhmanism in anything but names and forms. The people were always Hindu in spirit, and when the doctrine of personal nihilism, as taught by the Buddha, had ceased to influence them, the change over to Brāhmanism was easy. It was merely a change of habit, not of real faith.

E. J. Thomas gives his interpretation of this change in a passage which is of striking value when we consider the religion of Bihar and Bengal on the one hand and that of Burma and Siam on the other:

> "The great difference of organisation between Hinduism and Buddhism lay in the fact that the Brahmin priests were not an ascetic body apart from the laity. They were part of the social structure and an essential part in carrying out the rites and sacraments for the laity. In this function they were essential even for the Buddhist laity. While the Order [of Buddhist monks] continued, there was a body in existence in open opposition to Brahminism and the disappearance of the Order meant the end of Buddhism. The Buddhist layman, who was all along a member of a Hindu caste, worshipped deities differing little from the Hindu gods. If the educated monk and his community disappeared, there was no essential principle to distinguish the Buddhist layman from the Hindu. Mr N. Vasu has shown how in Orissa a form of Buddhism survived which became disguised as a form of Hinduism. With the disappearance of the monks and the absence of any definite teaching the god Dharma became another of the numberless gods of India."[1]

This change of feeling in Northern India is expressed in the images. Stella Kramrisch is right in saying that the figure of the Buddha, as sculptured in the ninth century, generally exhibits a satisfied and insipid smile, and a plump smoothness of stiff limbs, but that a novel and manifold grace is infused into the Bodhisattva figures: Buddhism becomes permeated with the Tantric view of life. But the Buddhist art of the Pālas was never the art of the people, of whom the majority remained within Brāhmanism, but rather of the monks, and this would certainly account for its introduction into Burma by the monkish missionaries from Nālandā who resorted to Pagān in the eleventh century. The interesting feature from our point of view is that, though Mahāyānism was, of the two forms of Buddhism, apparently in the ascendant in Bihar at this period, Bodhisattvas of Pāla style are almost completely absent in Pagān, while the figure of the Buddha himself was accepted with eagerness and adopted as the national expression of faith. E. J. Thomas again explains this by saying that the simple peoples of Burma (and Siam), having no Brāhmanic teaching behind them, showed no interest whatever in the Mahāyānist form of Buddhism or in any of the Tantric

[1] E. J. Thomas, *History of Buddhist Thought*, p. 247. Kegan Paul, London, 1933.

systems of life, but found in the simpler Hīnayāna form a more suitable vehicle for their devotional religion. It must not be forgotten that to the vast majority of Siamese (and Burmese) peasants Buddhism is, and always has been, what I call "The Decoration of Life", and the people themselves have remained at heart animists. Their lives fall into two parts. They pay their devotions and give their offerings to the Lord Buddha, so that their merit may increase and their Karma may enrich them in future lives, but in the present life there are a host of *p'ī*, or spirits, to be propitiated if evil is not to befall them, and the latter are, therefore, continually courted and feasted to this end.[1]

The particular type of the Buddha image which found most favour in Pagān, and in Siam before the rise of Suk'ōt'ai, is well illustrated by Fig. 110, which shows an image from Buddh Gayā, dated about the tenth century and now in the British Museum. It is carved out of a black stone called *kasti pathar*, quarried in the Rajmahal hills in the Santāl Parganas of Bengal.[2] There are certain characteristics about this seated image by which we can definitely trace its affinity with the type of image which appeared shortly afterwards both in Pagān and the North of Siam. It is, indeed, very seldom that one can show such a clear relationship between the parent and the colonial art.

The above figure shows the Buddha seated with the right hand raised in the attitude of Dispelling Fear, and the left hand lying in the lap. The face is long and oval, with a small sharply-defined mouth and a highly sensitive nose, and the arched eyebrows spring from the bridge in two long upward curves. The eyes are half-closed, looking downwards. The robe is only lightly defined, leaving the right nipple bare, and one of the peculiar features of this type is seen in the short upper fold of cloth which comes down over the left shoulder and ends above the left nipple in a sharp-pointed fork. The hair is composed of pronounced spiral curls, and the *uṣnīṣa*, which rises knob-like from the centre of the head, is covered with similar curls. The other two especial features of this type of image are (*a*) that the throne on which the Buddha is seated is always an expanded and stylised lotus-flower (in the figure shown with lion supports beneath), and (*b*) that the legs are crossed, with both soles of the feet uppermost.[3]

Let us first compare this figure with a seated bronze figure of the Buddha from Pagān of the eleventh or early twelfth century, as shown in Fig. 111. The form

[1] Reginald le May, *An Asian Arcady*, p. 135. Heffer, Cambridge, 1926.

[2] Stella Kramrisch, "Pala and Sena Sculpture", *Rūpam*, no. 40 (Oct. 1929), p. 115.

[3] This attitude, to a European, has often seemed an impossible one, but I have seen it adopted, simply and naturally, by a Siamese youth.

may, of course, be localised in execution, but the conception and treatment are almost identical. We have the legs crossed, with both soles of the feet uppermost, a feature which is almost entirely peculiar to the three schools which I am now discussing; the *uṣnīṣa* is covered with knob-like curls ending in a full lotus-bud; the eyebrows spring from the bridge of the nose in arched curves; the body is smooth and plump above, but with a rather slender waist, the mouth is small and well defined, and again we see the short fold of the robe falling over the left shoulder and ending in a sharp fork above the nipple. When we then look at the lotus-throne, we feel there can be no doubt as to the origin of this type of Buddha image being in the sculpture of the Pāla empire of the tenth and eleventh centuries.[1]

Now look at this third image, this time a bronze figure from Northern Siam, Fig. 112. It is a representative image of what is called the Chiengsen or pre-Suk'ōt'ai period, and is probably the earliest form of Tai Buddha image to be found in Siam.[2] There is a subtle change in the physiognomy as rendered by the Tai artist. The face is more oval in shape; the nose is more pronounced, but the mouth is even smaller, and the eyebrows are more rounded and do not meet at the top of the bridge. Were it not for this definitely local expression of racial form, this image would be hardly distinguishable from the images just described, so closely has the artist adhered to the formula laid down for throne, body, legs, clothfold and *uṣnīṣa*.

With this evidence before me, I feel on safe ground in agreeing with the suggestion thrown out by Cœdès that the origin of the Northern School of Tai art must be sought among the Pālas of Bihar. If the reader wishes to see further examples of that school bearing out this type which came to Burma and Siam, he will find them in Banerji's book on Eastern Indian Sculpture—two particularly clear and happy examples[3]—and also in Stella Kramrisch's work on "Pala and Sena Sculpture".[4] Figs. 113, 114 and 115 are all bronze images, representative of the same school. Fig. 113, which is 15½ inches high, is nearest, indeed very near, to the Indian prototype, as it has a rounder face, and the eyebrows spring from the

1 An interesting feature in this image is the introduction of the YALI, an Indian fabulous animal with a goat-like beard, a motive which, I am told by Perceval Yetts, also appears in Chinese art.

2 Chiengsen, which is on the Mekōng in the farthest north of Siam, was one of the earliest Tai capital cities in that country, and it is in this region that the type of image now under discussion is chiefly found.

3 R. D. Banerji, *The Eastern Indian School of Mediaeval Sculpture*, Pls. XVIII C and LXVI C. A.S.I. Delhi, 1933.

4 Stella Kramrisch, "Pala and Sena Sculpture", *Rūpam*, no. 40 (Oct. 1929), fig. 43.

bridge of the nose. Fig. 114, $5\frac{1}{4}$ inches high, is still closely allied, but Fig. 115, 15 inches high, is already taking on a more local Tai expression of feeling, and is perhaps the most beautiful example of the Chiengsen School known. There are also some fine life-size images of this early period at Wat Benchamabopit in Bangkok (Figs. 117 and 118).

There is another type of Buddha image found in Burma of the same period, which I wish to illustrate, Fig. 116, taken from the *Annual Report of the Archaeological Survey of India* for 1926–7.[1] It is obviously allied to Fig. 111 but in a sense, although showing strong Indian influence, it is fast becoming Burmese. Indeed, the interest in this figure (and in one illustrated by Banerji[2]) is that it seems to be the forerunner of the modern Burmese type of Buddha image, and to show how the differentiation between the Burmese and Siamese Schools began already in the twelfth century, although both drew their inspiration from a common source. In the figure illustrated the details of the formula are true to type, but note that the head is just beginning to droop forward and to sink on to the shoulders, perhaps the most conspicuous feature of the modern Burmese image.

Having thus shown the affinity between the Pāla style of image and that introduced into the Chiengsen area of the north of Siam through the intermediary of Burma, it will be of interest to record that one direct connection, at least, can be traced between the north of Siam and the Pāla School of Sculpture. At Wat Chiengmān in Chiengmai is still preserved a much venerated image of the Buddha known as *P'ra Sīla* (which simply means "the Stone Buddha"), Fig. 119. To show how local traditions are formed, this image is said by the legendary histories to have been made by Ajātaçatru at Rājagriha after the death of the Lord Buddha and to contain relics of him: to have been taken to Ceylon by three monks and thence brought to Chiengmai via Suk'ōt'ai and Lampāng. It is now firmly connected with "prayers for rain", and it is confidently believed that, if water is poured upon the image with due ceremony and ritual, rain will certainly fall and the crops be assured. As with so many legends, there *may be* some truth in the latter half of the story, and it is possible that the image came to Siam via Ceylon with the band of Buddhist monks who visited Ceylon in A.D. 1423 and, after a stay there of some years, came back to Chiengmai, bringing with them a reinforcement of the Sinhalese form of Buddhism. But this is mere conjecture, and the more obvious solution is that it was brought to the north of Siam from India through Burma.

[1] *A.S.I.A.R.* (1926–7), Pl. XXXIX C.

[2] R. D. Banerji, *The Eastern Indian School of Mediaeval Sculpture*, Pl. XVI A.

The image itself, which is in a blackish stone (later gilded over) with a wooden stand and frame, is a representative example of a type which seems to have been a favourite one at Buddh Gayā in the ninth and tenth centuries (cf. Fig. 120).[1] The scene, which is common to both schools of Buddhism, is that of the Buddha taming the fierce elephant, Nalagiri, which was sent to kill him by Ajātaçatru, and the small figure to his right, holding the fan, is his chief disciple, Ānanda. The treatment of the torso and drapery still carries on the Gupta tradition, with the diaphanous robes and suggestion of a sexless nude, but there is already a much more sensuous feeling creeping into the artist's conception, foreign to Gupta art, in the swaying hips and rhythmic movement of the arms and hands.

In the Buddh Gayā image (Fig. 120) there are two attendants and two elephants, and also small figures of devotees with scroll-work below the lotus-pedestal on which the Buddha is standing, but otherwise the main conception and even the execution is almost identical in the two figures.

Banerji also illustrates another example of the same scene,[2] but, although the treatment of the torso and robes is similar to the last, the sensuous, rhythmic feeling is lacking and the image is nearer to the Gupta form and conception. Stella Kramrisch gives two representations of the scene, both of which appear to be earlier in style than the two illustrated here.[3] One is inscribed in the third year of the reign of Vigrahapāla (or Surapāla I) and may be dated between A.D. 820–30, and the other is ascribed to the end of the ninth century. In both the figure of the Buddha is much nearer to the Gupta tradition. Perhaps the most striking analogy to the Chiengmai image, from the affinity standpoint, is seen in another of Banerji's illustrations.[4] This is a *stela* from Shibbati, in the Khulna district, where the Buddha is seated cross-legged on a lotus-throne between two pillars under a canopy, with multitudinous figures and images of Buddha all round him, but the robe fits tightly and smoothly round the body and shoulders, just leaving the neck bare, the ears are long and wide, and the *uṣṇīṣa* which protrudes more than usual ends in a lotus-bud, just as in the Chiengmai figure. There is a distinct community of feeling between the two.

Another style of image which has found favour in the north of Siam is seen in Fig. 121, now in the British Museum, which represents a Bodhisattva seated in the earth-touching attitude. The image, which is in the same grey-black stone as

[1] R. D. Banerji, *The Eastern Indian School of Mediaeval Sculpture*, Pl. XXVI A.

[2] *Ibid.* Pl. XXVI C.

[3] Stella Kramrisch, "Pala and Sena Sculpture", *Rūpam*, no. 40 (Oct. 1929), figs. 10 and 20.

[4] R. D. Banerji, *The Eastern Indian School of Mediaeval Sculpture*, Pl. XIX C.

Fig. 110, is of about the tenth century and the three peculiarities of the Pāla school are again seen, namely the lotus-throne, the short fold of the robe over the left shoulder, and the crossed legs with both soles uppermost. But the presence of the crown and diadem, the neck-collar, the bracelets on the arms and the elaborate ear decorations stamp this figure clearly as belonging to the Mahāyāna school. Similar images are illustrated by Stella Kramrisch[1] and R. D. Banerji.[2]

We may compare the above with the illustration, Fig. 122, which depicts a type very popular in Northern Siam, especially among the Lü tribe, where it is known as *P'ra Song Krüang*, or "the Decorated Buddha". In Burma it is apparently not common. This particular image, which is in bronze, may be as late as the sixteenth century, but if so, it has retained very faithfully the chief peculiarities of its prototype. Especially noticeable are the ear decorations. The attitude in this case is that of *Samādhi* or Meditation. I do not think that it is necessary to assume from this form of image that Mahāyānism was prevalent among a certain sect of Northern Tai or Lü, but rather that the type appealed to them as being beautiful, and consequently they rejoiced in fashioning it. In much the same way we find bronze statues of Viṣnu, Çiva, and Lakṣmi made by the Tai in the fifteenth and sixteenth centuries, but we must not conclude from this that the Tai nobility were turning from Buddhism to Brāhmanism. A typical Tai example of this style of Bodhisattva is seen in Fig. 123, now set up in Wat Kao Tü at Chiengmai. It is said to be composed of earth, lime, flowers and lacquer, and is coloured red and gold. Emeralds and rubies are depicted on the robe in their natural colours in mica. I doubt if it is of any great age, but it is a good representative of the style as seen in Northern Siam.

A third type, which has always enjoyed great favour in the north of Siam, indeed, throughout Siam, is seen in Fig. 124, also in the British Museum, which represents the *Mahā-Parinirvāna* of Gautama, the Lord Buddha, with disciples mourning below. A novel and amusing feature is introduced into the *stela* in the heavenly hands and arms beating the drum and clashing the cymbals seen above. The relief is in blackish basalt, identical with the other two figures shown: and here again we see the fidelity to type in the treatment of the *uṣnīṣa* and the short fold of the robe. I know of no reclining images of the Buddha in the north of Siam early enough in period to be strictly analogous to the Pāḷa style, but the scene depicted in this type of image is so common in Siam that there seems little doubt as to its origin, if we take it in conjunction with the other styles introduced.

[1] Stella Kramrisch, "Pala and Sena Sculpture", *Rūpam*, no. 40 (Oct. 1929), Figs. 14, 15 and 17.

[2] R. D. Banerji, *The Eastern Indian School of Mediaeval Sculpture*, Pls. XXII B–XXVI D.

R. D. Banerji, who also gives illustrations of the *Mahā-Parinirvāna* from examples of Pāla sculpture,[1] remarks: "In the Bengal school we find a class of image bas-reliefs, representing the death of Buddha, which are very rare in Indian sculpture." This statement is a strong confirmation of the theory of a Pāla derivation for the type found in Siam.

Before leaving the subject of the origin of the Chiengsen School, I must refer to an interesting suggestion made by Dupont in this regard. In his monograph on Siamese Art he remarks that "the curious stylisation of the arcaded eyebrows in particular, which already appears in Indo-Greek Buddhas from Afghanistan, must come from China of the Wei period (Tien Lung Shan) after passing through Central Asia".[2] He then quotes me as indicating the existence from the ninth century onwards of images in the style of Chiengsen but adds "he has not published these, nor has he given any reasons for proposing this date".[3]

I must admit that for a long time I was inclined to Dupont's theory myself, although I could never find any support for it among other savants, and even now there is still a kind of lingering belief in my mind that the Tai must have brought with them some small portion of the Chinese spirit which would appear in their earliest images. But the Wei period is much too far removed in point of time, and the evidence here produced (especially Fig. 110) is, I fear, too strong to allow me to retain the theory of conscious adaptation any longer, and, except that the local Tai expression of the Pāla School may instinctively show some affinity with China from which the Tai came, one must definitely attribute the origin of the style to India. It may be that Dupont has been influenced to some extent by my indication of a Chiengsen style from the ninth century onwards: if so, I hasten to correct it. In the Table of Schools of Sculpture in Siam, annexed to my article in *Indian Art and Letters*,[4] the print is so faint that possibly the question-mark preceding the words "Ninth to Twelfth century A.D., ChiengRai" was not noticed by him. The fact is that I was for a long time puzzled by the find of a stone image of a saint fast embedded in a limestone cave some distance from Chiengrai, of which I was able to recover the head, as it had been broken off and was lying on the floor of the cave (Fig. 125). This head presents unusual features, since in profile it has not only a sharply ridged, straight, sensitive nose, but an exceptionally firm mouth and chin, almost Graeco-Roman in type; and I

[1] R. D. Banerji, *The Eastern Indian School of Mediaeval Sculpture*, Pls. XIV D, and XXXI C, D.

[2] P. Dupont, *Catalogue des Collections Indo-Chinoises du Musée Guimet*, pp. 54–5. Paris, 1934.

[3] Reginald le May, "Sculpture in Siam", *I.A.L.* vol. IV, no. 2 (1930), p. 102.

[4] *Ibid.* p. 102.

wondered if this might not be an early expression of Tai art in the north of Siam. I am, however, satisfied now that it must be, as pronounced by Prince Damrong, an example, though an unusual one, of Ayudhyan art of the fifteenth century. I must therefore withdraw my suggestion of the possibility of an early Tai School of stone sculpture in Northern Siam.

I do, however, subscribe to Dupont's suggestion that the artistic development of the Tai did not necessarily correspond with the period of their independence. It is quite possible, in fact probable, that the earliest examples of the Chiengsen School in the north of Siam date from the twelfth century. What is likely to have happened is that, after the Tai had settled in Siam, they first found contact with Buddhism of the Môn type, which by this time was artistically decadent, and that, when the new impulse of the Nālandā School was introduced into Burma and thence into Siam, they eagerly adopted it.

# Chapter IX

## THE RISE OF THE TAI IN SIAM AND THE ORIGIN OF THE SUK'ŌT'AI SCHOOL

WE have seen that during the eleventh and twelfth centuries the Tai were, in ever greater numbers, penetrating Northern and North-Central Siam and gradually consolidating their position there. At the end of the twelfth century the Khmer empire was definitely on the wane and the Môn element in Siam, since the conquest of their parent kingdom of Thatôn by Anuruddha, had gradually lost their source of power and were being assimilated with the Tai, with whom they had more spiritual if not more racial affinity than with the Khmer. The time was becoming ripe for a revolution in political, religious and artistic thought, and about the middle of the thirteenth century certain events happened which brought this revolution to a head. Once again the old saying proved true that "the hour produces the man"—in this case, "the men".

First of all, the kingdom of Nan-Chao in Southern China was conquered by the all-powerful Kublai Khan, thereby causing a further pressure of Tai southwards into the Shan States, Burma proper and the no-man's land bordering Siam, and, though I do not think that this event exercised any artistic influence, still it probably played its part in the rise of the Tai to power in Siam. Also about the same time two male children were born, Meng Rai and Rām K'amheng, who were each destined to bring part of the territory of Siam under Tai sovereignty for the first time, the one in the north and the other in the centre and south. Let us deal with the northerner, Meng Rai, first.

Meng Rai, who was born in A.D. 1239, is always regarded by the Tai as a Tai, but I doubt if it is strictly true that he was of pure Tai descent. The "History of the North", after recounting the legendary history of twenty-three Lawā Chiefs of Chiengsen, states that Lao Meng, the last of them, married the daughter of the Tai Chief of Chiengrung in south-western Yunnan (a place to which I have already referred) and that Meng Rai was their son. If this is correct, then Meng Rai was only Tai on the distaff side.[1] However this may be, Meng Rai succeeded his father as Chief of Chiengsen in 1259, founded Chiengrai (to which city he

[1] G. Cœdès, "Documents", *B.E.F.E.O.* vol. xxv, p. 87, footnote 4.

gave his name) in 1262, seized Chiengkong in 1269, founded Müang Fang in 1273, captured Nān in 1274, attacked P'ayao in 1276 and made a treaty with its chief, and finally in 1292 captured Lamp'ūn, the Môn capital, thereby making himself master of practically the whole of the north of Siam. In 1290 he is said to have undertaken a campaign against Pagān itself, but seeing that Pagān is 350 miles from Chiengsen and 300 miles from Lamp'ūn across very hilly country, I feel on this occasion more inclined to agree with Lefèvre-Pontalis who says that in 1290 Meng Rai paid a visit to Pagān, which was then under nominal Chinese suzerainty but in reality in the hands of Shan (Tai) chiefs, and brought back with him artists and artisans.[1] In 1296, with the help and guidance of his brother chief, Rām K'amheng, and also of the Chief of P'ayao, he founded his new capital city, Chiengmai, which he called Nabbisi and which from that time onwards became the most important town in Northern Siam. In the meantime another Tai Shan, Makato or Wareru, had founded a new kingdom of Martaban, which included Thatôn and Pegu, and Meng Rai came to blows with him in 1287 over the frontiers of their respective realms. In the end Wareru presented one of his daughters to Meng Rai together with a town on the Me Niam as dowry, and peace was concluded.

Meng Rai was evidently a devout Buddhist and, as a result of his visit to Pagān, had already founded in 1292 the temple of Chiengmān, whose remains still stand in the most northern part of the old Palace-fort of the city of Chiengmai, though the present *stūpa* is probably not the original one but as restored by Tilōkarāja in 1471 (Fig. 126). This is the oldest foundation inside the city of Chiengmai, and is clearly in the Pagān style, though in the original construction there were possibly none of the stucco elephants which now surround and adorn the base. In 1288 Meng Rai had already founded one city at Kŭm-Kām, between Chiengmai and Lamp'ūn, built a temple there exactly similar to Wat Kŭkŭt at Lamp'ūn with sixty images of the Buddha, and dedicated two bronze statues of the Buddha, of which one is said to be that now standing in Wat Kalakot in Chiengmai.[2] All that remains of Kŭm-Kām is a series of earth-mounds at Pā Yāng in Amp'ur Sarap'i, but, as already related in the last chapter, there is still a temple, Wat Sī Liem (Fig. 106), near this site in the form of Wat Kŭkŭt, which may be on the site of that built by Meng Rai. As for the image at Wat Kalakot, I cannot attribute this to Meng Rai: it is a standing image of the Buddha, with the right hand raised in the attitude of Dispelling Fear, and with the walking

[1] P. Lefèvre-Pontalis, "L'Invasion Thaie en Indo-Chine", *Toung Pao* (1910), p. 110.

[2] G. Cœdès, "Documents", *B.E.F.E.O.* vol. xxv, p. 90, footnote 5.

movement of the feet. It is clearly in the Suk'ōt'ai style, and the *uṣnīṣa* is adorned with the flame-top, which is closely connected with the new style of image introduced into Suk'ōt'ai from Ceylon. If Meng Rai was actually its originator, then the Suk'ōt'ai style of image must have been introduced into the north of Siam at a much earlier date than the evidence warrants at present, and I personally doubt it. Indeed, from the photograph, the image appears to be late, rather than early Suk'ōt'ai in style.[1]

There is, however, another temple on the outskirts of Chiengmai near the Chang Kien stream of Doi Sut'ep which may well be attributed to Meng Rai, namely Wat Chet Yôt, or the Seven-spired Temple. This temple is obviously a copy of the Mahābodhi temple at Pagān, which was built early in the thirteenth century by Htilo-Minlo, the last of the Burmese Builder-Kings, and which itself is an imitation of the famous temple at Buddh Gayā in Bihar (Fig. 127). Meng Rai is the only King of Northern Siam known to have visited Pagān, and, although there is no record of its foundation, it was already considered an ancient monument when discovered by Tilōkarāja in 1453. The latter founded an *ārām* there and planted a sacred *ficus*. Later he built a *vihāra* and in 1487 his successor rebuilt the *stūpa*; and it is probably from his time that the seated figures adorning the outer walls date, as they are typically Tai in style (Fig. 128).

When Kublai Khan's grandson conquered Pagān in 1287 and put an end to the Burmese line that had ruled there since the days of Anuruddha, Meng Rai seems to have escaped his attentions and to have preserved his independence, possibly because he had already acknowledged the Mongol Emperor as overlord and had agreed to pay tribute, like all the other princelings and chiefs of Eastern Asia, but, according to Lefèvre-Pontalis, in 1303 he rebelled and refused to send the tribute, and once again in 1312. On both occasions expeditions were sent against him, but they appear to have been only half-hearted and peace was eventually restored.[2] The JKM gives the date of Meng Rai's death as 1311, at the age of seventy-two, but the "History of the North" is probably more correct in its statement that he died (was struck dead by lightning) in 1317, having reigned as Chief of Chiengsen and Chiengrai from 1261 to 1292, and as king of practically the whole of the north from 1292 to 1317.[3]

And now to turn to his brother king, Rām K'amheng, who may justly be called the first Tai king of Siam. In the middle of the thirteenth century

[1] Cf. J. Y. Claeys, "L'Archéologie du Siam", *B.E.F.E.O.* vol. XXXI, p. 440, Pl. XCIII A.

[2] P. Lefèvre-Pontalis, "L'Invasion Thaie en Indo-Chine", *Toung Pao* (1910), p. 113.

[3] G. Cœdès, "Documents", *B.E.F.E.O.* vol. XXV, p. 91, footnote 1.

Suk'ōt'ai and Sawank'alōk were under the control of a Khmer governor, while somewhere in the vicinity were two unidentified petty states, Müang Rat and Müang Bang Yang, ruled over by two Tai chiefs, P'a Müang and Bang Klang Tao respectively, under Khmer sovereignty. P'a Müang had received a Cambodian title and had married a Cambodian princess. The origin of the rising is still obscure, but suddenly P'a Müang and Bang Klang Tao, having joined forces, simultaneously attacked both Suk'ōt'ai and Çri Sachanalai (the name formerly given to old Sawank'alōk). But little resistance was offered, and, Suk'ōt'ai once occupied, Bang Klang Tao was crowned king by his friend and ally, P'a Müang, under the title of Çri Indrapat-indraditya. In Rām K'amheng's famous *stela* this name is shortened to Indraditya, but the later Pāli works, such as JKM, refer to him as Rōcarāja or Suranga.[1] Thus was founded the Tai state of Suk'ōt'ai, which was destined, within fifty years, to achieve sovereignty over practically the whole of Siam except the north, but which, within a hundred years, was to give way to the new Tai dynasty that established its capital at Ayudhya, 150 miles farther south. Indraditya has, however, since been immortalised by the Tai under the name of P'ra Rūang, their national hero.

Indraditya had three sons, of whom Rām K'amheng was the youngest. The eldest died young, while the second only reigned for a few years; and about the year 1275 we find Rām K'amheng ruling over his father's State. He had already when a lad given proof of his mettle in a pitched battle with the Chief of Müang Chôt (Mesôt) on the Burma frontier, and it is clear from the deeds modestly recorded in the inscription of 1292 that he has more real claim, in spite of his father's successful rebellion against the Khmer, to be considered the national hero of Siam. Before his death he claimed to have established dominion over the country as far to the north-east as Lūang Prabāng on the Mekōng (now a French Lao state), as far south as Nakon Srītammarāt (Ligor) on the east side and Tenasserim and Mergui on the west side of the Malay Peninsula, and as far west as Raheng and Mesôt on the Burma border. Even Pegu and Martaban, under a Tai usurper, acknowledged him as overlord. The north, under Meng Rai, remained independent, and there was always a strong bond of friendship between the two kings, so strong that, when Rām K'amheng became involved in an intrigue with the wife of a neighbouring chief (of P'ayao), Meng Rai was called in as arbitrator to settle their differences. Wood claims that there were already by this time Tai chiefs of U-T'ong in the south-west and of Ayudhya in the south,

[1] G. Cœdès, *Recueil des Inscriptions du Siam*, Part I (1924), pp. 7–8 and pp. 49–75 (French). National Library, Bangkok. In Siamese and French.

either independent or under the sovereignty of the Khmer king,[1] but, whether this is correct or not, there were undoubtedly strong Tai elements all over the country who were glad to acknowledge a Tai overlord.

Relations between Suk'ōt'ai and the Court of China were of a cordial nature, and the annals record that Rām K'amheng paid two visits to the Emperor, the first in 1294 while Kublai Khan was still alive, and the second in 1300. On the latter occasion he is said to have married a Chinese princess, and to have brought back with him a number of Chinese potters, who established the kilns of Suk'ōt'ai, where a coarse type of Tz'ŭ-Chou black and white ware was produced, and later took over the Tai kilns at Sawank'alōk, where they introduced the traditional Celadon and most of the other Sung-like wares of the period.[2] Those visits were probably the result of the arrival of Chinese embassies at the court of Rām K'amheng in 1293 and 1295 (or 1296) to announce Imperial orders. In 1299 the King of Hsien (as the kingdom of Suk'ōt'ai was called by the Chinese in contradistinction to Lohu, the name for Lopburi or Lavō) petitioned the Emperor for white horses with saddles and bridles and gold-thread garments, as given to his father. But the Emperor was advised not to accede to this request (as Hsien was only a small kingdom) and in the end only gold-thread garments were given.[3] But although Rām K'amheng maintained such excellent relations with the Imperial court and sent tribute regularly up to the time of his death, there is no indication that he was ever influenced by the Chinese form of Buddhism or introduced any Chinese form of the Buddha. On the contrary, he himself, in his famous *stela*, gives the clue to the problem of how the great change which now occurred in the iconography of Siam came about. In North-Central Siam, in the regions of Suk'ōt'ai, Sawank'alōk, Pitsanulōk, and Kampengp'et the Khmer style of Buddha image disappears entirely, and its place is taken by a totally different conception of the Founder of the Faith; in other words, there is an artistic revolution, a complete break with Khmer art. Instead of the square, strong, ruthless man's head and face we find an idealised conception of a Higher Being almost feminine in feeling. Indeed, Europeans often mistake this form for one of a feminine divinity, so fully developed is the upper part of the body. The face becomes long and oval, the eyebrows highly arched, the nose long and hooked; the lips are pressed tightly together and the mouth is small, while the

1 W. A. R. Wood, *A History of Siam*, p. 53. T. Fisher Unwin, London.

2 Reginald le May, "The Ceramic Wares of North-Central Siam", *Burlington Magazine*, vol. LXIII, nos. 367–8 (Oct. Nov. 1933).

3 P. Pelliot, "Deux Itinéraires de Chine en Inde", *B.E.F.E.O.* vol. IV, pp. 242–3.

chin is represented by a single incised curve. The eyes look downwards with a half-closed mystic expression, and the eyelids are formed of wavy lines rising upwards towards the outer corners. The treatment of the hair is entirely different from the Khmer style, being composed of large shell-like, spiral knobs circling from left to right, and a long, pointed flame-like emblem (which the Siamese call *ketumāla*) rises erect from the *uṣṇīṣa.* In seated figures the legs are never crossed but rest one above the other, and the fold of the robe-cloth comes down as far as the hips. The hands sometimes rest together in the lap in the attitude of Meditation, or one hand rests on the right knee in that of the Conquest of Mara or Earth-touching, while the other rests in the lap (Fig. 129). The standing figures are more often than not depicted in the act of walking, with the right (or sometimes the left) hand raised in the attitude of Preaching, where the thumb and forefinger are seen to be touching. In the earlier forms the body is represented as particularly lissome and supple and the movement is very free (Fig. 130), but in later images the treatment becomes stiffer and more conventional, while still maintaining all the traditional features.

Now where did this new conception of an idealised Super-Being in the minds of the Suk'ōt'ai folk originate? No single, direct answer can be given to this question, but it seems clear that Burma, through its intermediary, Chiengsen, played a certain part, while the new impetus of Hīnayāna Buddhism from Ceylon, which at this time penetrated the heart of Siam, duly left its impress on the new forms now to be modelled. It is only reasonable to suppose that the Chiengsen type of Buddha image had been well known among the Tai of the Suk'ōt'ai region for many years past, and I feel satisfied that in the main the Suk'ōt'ai style is a natural evolution from the former school. Pierre Dupont inclines to think that the chief influences that went to form the Chiengsen School came from China, but, though for a long time I held the same opinion myself and should still like to think so, I cannot now sustain that conclusion.[1] Still, accepting the Chiengsen type as the base of the Suk'ōt'ai School, there are obviously other influences at work, and there is no doubt that the origin of these must be sought in Ceylon. The true Suk'ōt'ai type is thus a blend of Chiengsen and Ceylon.

That island, after undergoing many vicissitudes in the realm of religion, in the eleventh century, under Vijaya Bāhu I, witnessed a revival of Hīnayāna Buddhism, and Parākrama Bāhu (1164–97), who deserves his title of "Great" and who is called "The incomparable Champion of the Faith", brought about a reunion of the Church and the triumph of the Hīnayānist School. Sanskrit inscriptions are

[1] P. Dupont, *Catalogues des Collections Indo-Chinoises du Musée Guimet*, p. 54. Paris, 1934.

found in Ceylon throughout the first millennium of the Christian era, but in the twelfth and thirteenth centuries the inscriptions are almost always in Pāli, the language of the Hīnayāna School.[1] From this time onwards up to the beginning of the sixteenth century it is true to say that Ceylon was regarded by its brother Buddhist countries, Siam, Burma and Cambodia, with almost as much veneration as the Holy Places of Buddhism in India itself, as the fountain-head of the pure Theravāda doctrines.[2]

Burma was the first of the three countries to feel the influence of the new impulse from Ceylon. Panthagu, the Primate, after quarrelling with the King of Pagān, retired to Ceylon in 1167, but returned to Burma after the latter's death in 1173 and took up his office once again. He was followed by Uttarajiva, who went to Ceylon in 1180 and became known as the "First Pilgrim to Ceylon". His companion, Chapata, who was called the "Second Pilgrim", stayed in Ceylon for ten years and, returning in 1190, brought with him four other monks including Ananda of Conjeeveram and a Prince of Cambodia. All five settled at Nyaung-U, north of Pagān, and built a pagoda in the Sinhalese style. By this time Conjeeveram had become entirely Hindu or Brāhman and was no longer a source of Buddhist doctrine; and henceforth Ceylon Buddhism was the chief influence on the religion in Burma. Chapata, indeed, set up a schism in the Church, in opposition to the disciples of Shin Arahan and the Thatôn School (who followed the Môn (or Former) Order), and his sect became eventually known as the Sinhalese (or Latter) Order.[3]

It is not absolutely certain when Sinhalese Buddhism first came to the Malay Peninsula, but it was probably at the close of the twelfth or the beginning of the thirteenth century. The Ceylon Chronicles record that during the reign of Parākrama Bāhu II a king called Chandrabhanu of Jāvaka or Tambralinga (i.e. of Nakon Srītammarāt) twice unsuccessfully invaded Ceylon, in 1230 and 1256,[4] and it has been suggested with some plausibility that these attacks were primarily made to gain possession of a miraculous image of the Buddha, the famous

[1] A. K. Coomaraswamy, *History of Indian and Indonesian Art*, p. 162. E. Goldston, London.

[2] S. Paranavitana, "Religious Intercourse between Ceylon and Siam in the thirteenth to fifteenth centuries", *J.R.A.S.* (Ceylon), vol. XXXII, no. 85, p. 190.

[3] G. E. Harvey, *History of Burma*, pp. 55–6. Longmans, Green and Co., London. It is true that these events are drawn from the Burmese chronicles (Glass Palace and Kalyani), but they certainly bear witness to a new religious movement from Ceylon, even if there is as yet no indisputable evidence to support the detailed facts.

[4] It is doubtful whether the second attack took place. The Chronicles probably refer to the mission sent from Siam to request the gift of a famous image of the Buddha.

P'ra Sihing, whose renown had reached Siam.[1] This fact in itself is strong evidence that Peninsular Siam was by this time throwing off its allegiance to the Mahāyāna School and was ready to receive the new, purified Hīnayāna doctrine from Ceylon.

The history of the P'ra Sihing[2] is important, as it is closely bound up with the new style of image which appeared in Siam, and was the cause of many struggles for its possession in that country. According to the JKM this image was fashioned in the second century A.D. at the command of a king of Ceylon in the style of a likeness of the Buddha created miraculously by the king of the Nāgas. When polished, the image appeared bright and resplendent as the living Buddha himself. In the middle of the thirteenth century (it is said, in the year A.D. 1256) Rōcarāja, the Tai King of Suk'ōt'ai, was paying a visit to the King of Nakon Srītammarāt (presumably Chandrabhanu) and heard glowing accounts from the latter of the wonderful Sinhalese image of the Buddha. He at once desired its possession, but was dissuaded from going himself to secure it by Chandrabhanu, who told him that Ceylon was protected by four powerful divinities.[3] Thereupon the two kings sent an envoy to the King of Ceylon earnestly entreating that the image might be presented to them, and the Sinhalese king, after worshipping the image for seven days and nights, was pleased to accede to this request and solemnly handed it over to the envoy for safe conveyance to Nakon Srītammarāt. On the way back the envoy's ship was unfortunately wrecked on a reef, and the image went floating away to sea resting on a ship's plank. Through the power of the Nāga king, however, it was borne in the direction of Nakon Srītammarāt, and the king of this city, having been apprised of its arrival in a dream, recovered it from the sea and brought it home in triumph and paid due homage to it. But it was not to remain with him for long, for, as soon as Rōcarāja heard of its arrival, he came south post-haste, and, claiming it as his own, carried it off to Suk'ōt'ai, where it was set up and duly worshipped with appropriate rites and ceremonies. To provide it with a suitable setting, Rōcarāja built at Çrī Sachanalai (Sawank'alōk) a magnificent *stūpa* in brick and stone, covered with white stucco, and a *mandapa* of gilded copper.[4] The image remained at Sawank'alōk for a hundred years, but it would take too much space to recount its adventures during the succeeding fifty years, between 1350 and 1400, when it became the "sport" of all the local chiefs and kings to try and gain its possession. Suffice it to say

[1] S. Paranavitana, "Religious Intercourse", *J.R.A.S.* (Ceylon), p. 195.

[2] "Sihing" is a corrupt form of Sihala, and "P'ra Sihing" simply means "the Sinhalese Buddha".

[3] This evidently refers to his own unsuccessful attack in 1230.

[4] G. Cœdès, "Documents", *B.E.F.E.O.* vol. xxv, pp. 97–9.

that it was taken successively to Chaināt, Ayudhya, Kampengp'et, then to Tāk (Raheng), thence to Chiengmai, Chiengrai, Chiengsen, back to Chiengrai, and finally came to rest at the end of the fourteenth century at Chiengmai in the temple named after it, Wat P'ra Sihing (or Sing),[1] where it remained in peace until the capture of the town in 1662 by King Naraiyana, who carried it off to Ayudhya. When Ayudhya fell and was sacked by the Burmese in 1767, the image was restored to Chiengmai, but in 1795 was brought to Bangkok where it has been ever since. It is now in the Chapel of the erstwhile Second King's Palace, which forms part of the National Museum. There are, however, two other images of the Buddha in Siam which claim to be the image of the legend, one at Nakon Srītammarāt and another at Chiengmai, which, according to Cœdès, exhibits all the normal characteristics of the School of Chiengsen. Cœdès thinks that the image now in Bangkok has the best claim to be considered the genuine image for which the Tai principalities fought in the fourteenth century, as it possesses all the qualities which distinguish the School of Suk'ōt'ai from that of Chiengsen, and presents a fair example of what must have been the first type of image made at Suk'ōt'ai in the middle of the thirteenth century. He adds: "Without any doubt it is the one which reproduces most faithfully the features of the renowned P'ra Sihing, the Sihalapatimā, that is, the Sinhalese image of the legend".[2]

Wherever the image, now so much venerated in Siam, was made, one thing is clear: it was not made in Ceylon, as will be apparent from a comparison of the renowned statue itself with a typical Sinhalese image of the thirteenth century (Figs. 131 and 132). And yet this comparison is interesting, for it shows a close connection between the two. The P'ra Sihing image of Siam, which is 26 inches high, is seated on a lotus-throne, the head is lifted more off the shoulders, the hair is formed of more pointed and sharply-defined spirals, and the lyre-like emblem on the top of the head has taken on a more flame-like form, but the position of the hands and legs, the wide-spreading knees, and the whole conception of the body are so akin in both images that there can be no doubt whence the P'ra Sihing derived its inspiration. Cœdès says that it is rather difficult to decide whether the position of the legs and the treatment of the scarf are borrowed from the technique of the Khmer School of Lopburi or are due to influence from Ceylon, but a comparison of the above two figures should, I think, resolve all doubts on this point.[3]

[1] G. Cœdès, "Documents", *B.E.F.E.O.* vol. XXV, pp. 100–3.

[2] G. Cœdès, "Le Musée National de Bangkok", *Ars Asiatica*, vol. XII, p. 33

[3] *Ibid.* p. 32.

Its attachment to the Chiengsen School is, however, still shown both by the lotus-throne and by the face, which is round and has not yet assumed the oval form which later became so characteristic of the Suk'ōt'ai School. As for the statue now at Chiengmai, it may well be the copy referred to in the JKM as having been made by the Chief of Chiengrai of an alloy of gold, silver, copper and tin, while the famous image remained in his possession.[1]

The use of the *ketumāla*, or flame-like emblem, raises an interesting problem as to its symbolic meaning. The word itself is both Sanskrit and Pāli, of which *ketu* means "sign" or "mark", and *māla* "a garland". This does not help us very much, but Childers in his *Dictionary of Sinhalese Pāli* says that it is an emblem of the Buddha equivalent to the halo of Christianity; and a former well-known missionary in Ceylon has supplemented this to me with the interesting suggestion that it represents the "aura", or emanation of light, which proceeds from the Buddha.[2]

In Ceylon the emblem takes the form of a lyre-like instrument, but in Siam it assumes much more the likeness of a flame, and I have noticed that in many Siamese images the central portion has the form of the *ūrnā*, which is a definite mark of the Buddha. In Sanskrit the *ūrnā* is the tuft of hair growing between the eyebrows from which emanate rays of the six colours of the Buddhist Faith lighting up the world. Thus the *ūrnā* may well be said to be the "aura" of the Buddha, and it is indeed sometimes, though not often, actually seen on the forehead of a Siamese image of the Buddha. It seems possible, then, that the Siamese took hold of the *ketumāla* from Ceylon in order to work into it the symbol of the *ūrnā* which, in their case, has rather the form of an inverted question-mark with a spiral tail.

It is not yet definitely decided when this emblem was first used in Ceylon. According to Paranavitana[3] the development of sculpture in Ceylon is as yet very imperfectly understood, for there are very few sculptures which can be definitely dated. It is, therefore, quite possible that some of the known works of art are really older than the dates to which they have been assigned in books on Indian art and *vice versa*. Vincent Smith ascribes his Fig. 179, a seated Buddha from Polonnāruwa, to the twelfth century because it was found in a twelfth-century shrine, but it is quite possible that the image is older than the shrine

[1] G. Cœdès, "Documents", *B.E.F.E.O.* vol. xxv, p. 102.

[2] Sir John Marshall states that the *ketumāla* represents the *tejas* of the Buddha, the divine heat which still burns with the struggle leading to his enlightenment (cf. the front face of the south pillar of the Western Gateway at Sānchī).

[3] S. Paranavitana, private letter.

itself. Conversely, there is a tradition that his Fig. 180, the great Buddha at Aukana, which has the flame-top, dates from the fifth century, but this may be too early for it. I may add that Vincent Smith assigns this image to the late twelfth century. The great Buddha images at the Galvihāra at Polonnāruwa, which are definitely known to have been the work of Parākrama Bāhu the Great in the twelfth century, do not have the flame-like top to the *uṣnīṣa*.[1] Some bronze images which exhibit this development of the *uṣnīṣa* have recently been found, which in other respects should be attributed to a date earlier than the eleventh century.

Now the two most important periods of Ceylon history are: (i) the Anurādhapura period, which dates from (?) 457 B.C. to A.D. 750, and (ii) the Polonnāruwa period, which ranges from A.D. 750–1240. Figs. 133 and 134 are typical examples of these two periods. Fig. 133 shows an enormous and beautiful stone Buddha at Toluvila, Anurādhapura, assigned to *c.* the sixth century A.D., and, as is clearly discernible, there is no sign of a flame-like instrument on the *uṣnīṣa*. If this figure is compared with Fig. 134 it will be seen how the portrayal of the form of the Buddha, in the set of the arms and legs, persisted right down to the thirteenth century. Fig. 134 depicts one of the rock-cut images at Galvihāra, dating from the second half of the twelfth century and showing exactly the same form of the Buddha; and, as far as can be seen from the photograph, there is similarly no sign of any instrument or device arising from the head. We cannot, therefore, come to any conclusion as to the actual date of the introduction of the flame-like instrument, but I think it is safe to say that it must have occurred sometime during the Polonnāruwa period and more probably in the latter rather than in the earlier half.

There is in the British Museum a large and striking image of a standing female figure called Pattinī Devī from Ceylon. It is ascribed to possibly the tenth century and its form and the shape of its countenance appear to me to have a strong affinity with the style developed in Suk'ōt'ai. It might indeed almost be a Tai figure of that period, were it not for other details.

[1] Dr Andreas Nell informs me, however, that these images originally did have flame-like instruments, but that the latter have been broken off.

# Chapter X

## THE SUK'ŌT'AI SCHOOL

It is possible that Rōcarāja (or Indraditya) did no more than introduce the new style of Buddha image into Suk'ōt'ai, but it is on record that his son, Rām K'amheng, invited the famous priest, Sangharāja, who was preaching the Sinhalese Theravāda doctrine at Nakon Srītammarāt, to take up his abode at Suk'ōt'ai,[1] that the invitation was accepted, and that Rām K'amheng built a special monastery for him, Wat Arannika, to the west of the city.[2]

The ancient cities of Suk'ōt'ai and Sawank'alōk (Çrī Sachanalai), as known to Rām K'amheng, are to-day nothing but deserted ruins, and the modern cities bearing these honoured names are in both cases some miles away from their former sites, the removal being due to a change in course of the Me Yōm. I have visited both the old and the new cities on several occasions, chiefly for the purpose of examining the kiln-sites, but at the same time I paid some attention to the ancient temples now, alas, in ruins.

The modern city of Suk'ōt'ai is called T'ani and here at the temples of Rājat'ani and P'rachum P'on may be seen rather remarkable collections of standing Buddha images in bronze of several periods, chiefly Suk'ōt'ai, U-T'ong and Ayudhya. Claeys illustrates a number of them in his "Archéologie du Siam".[3]

It is not possible to give a full description here of old Suk'ōt'ai, which is reached by a road some miles long, called P'ra Rūang's road, made of laterite blocks leading from the river bank. Claeys says that there were three concentric walls encircling the city, the inner one built of laterite and the two outer of earth, and that there was an entrance gateway in the centre of each wall.[4] To-day most of these walls and of the buildings which they enclosed are lost in the invading jungle, but, in order to give the reader some idea of the type of architecture employed and an aspect of the ruins as they stand at the present time, I have chosen two temples for illustration, those of Mahā-Tāt and Çrī Chŭm.

[1] G. Cœdès, *Recueil des Inscriptions du Siam*, Part I (1924), p. 55 (Siamese), and pp. 41, 46 (French).

[2] The ruins of this monastery, now called Wat Tapān Hin (The Stone Bridge Temple), are still to be seen.

[3] J. Y. Claeys, "L'Archéologie du Siam", *B.E.F.E.O.* vol. XXXI, Pls. LXXIII, LXXIV LXXV.

[4] *Ibid.* p. 416.

The temple of Mahā-Tāt, according to Claeys, originally comprised no less than one hundred and eighty-nine different structures, in the centre being a Tai *p'rajedi* or *stūpa* with annexes in Khmer style, and to the east of this building a huge Assembly Hall (*vihāra*) 50 metres (160 feet) long.[1] In the illustration (Fig. 135) is seen this *vihāra*, of which only the lower halves of the columns which supported the roof remain, with the *p'ra-jedi* and an enormous standing Buddha in the background. The columns are made of cylindrical laterite blocks encased in cement. Also to be seen at Wat Mahā-Tāt is a Buddhist scene in stucco on laterite, which is probably somewhat later in style (Fig. 136). Khmer elements, if in a debased form, are still visible in the decoration of the pediment ending in *makara* heads, but the Death-scene of the Buddha with mourners underneath is typically Tai. Below this scene, in a niche, is a standing figure of the Buddha with an aureole, of a singularly captivating beauty. The poise of the head, the expression on the clear-cut features, and the slender form of the body exercise a subtle fascination which it is hard to convey, but which will be readily appreciated by the sensitive mind.

It was on the site of the palace near this temple that King (then Prince) Mongkut discovered in 1833 the famous inscribed obelisk of Rām K'amheng as well as the stone throne which a few years ago was placed by King Vajiravudh (Rama VI) in the Throne Hall at Bangkok and now, like our own famous stone which Edward I brought from Scotland, serves as the Coronation stone of Siam.[2] It was near by here, too, that I picked up a beautiful fragment of a Sung celadon dish showing the raised fish in the centre.

The temple of Çrī Chŭm (Fig. 137), being in brick and stucco, is almost certainly later in date and may be ascribed to the reign of Dharmarāja I of Suk'ōt'ai, the grandson of Rām K'amheng, in the middle of the fourteenth century. As will be seen from the accompanying illustration (Fig. 138) the sanctuary containing a gigantic sitting image of the Buddha still stands, but only the columns remain of the former *vihāra*. The sanctuary, which is rectangular, is peculiar in style, with its high, narrow, vaulted entrance, through which the figure of the Buddha can be dimly seen; but it appears to have been copied at Ayudhya, when the great bronze image of the Buddha was set up there about a hundred years later. Otherwise I know of no other temple to compare with it in Siam. Except for a little moulding in stucco high up on the walls, like a fringe on a cloth, there is no decoration visible, and the chief interest lies, not in the

[1] J. Y. Claeys, "L'Archéologie du Siam", *B.E.F.E.O.* vol. XXXI, p. 417.

[2] G. Cœdès, *Recueil des Inscriptions du Siam*, Part I (1924), p. 37 (French).

Buddha image which in any case is now horribly disfigured, but in the series of sculptures discovered there, illustrating scenes from the *Jātakas*. One such scene is shown here (Fig. 139), and though the execution is undoubtedly Tai in spirit,[1] it is clear that the influence inspiring it came from Ceylon, if one compares it with the Apsaras and attendant from Sīgiriya of the fifth century (Fig. 140), and with the later twelfth-century figures from Polonnāruwa in that island. It is also conceivable that the sanctuary of Çrī Chŭm itself was based on some influence from Ceylon. All these frescoes may even be linked up with those in Caves I and XVII at Ajantā, dating from A.D. 500–650, of which illustrations are given in Codrington's revised edition of Vincent Smith's *History of Fine Art in India and Ceylon*, Plates 180 and 181. These sculptured scenes are now practically hidden in a dark corridor high up in the sanctuary, but it is believed that they were originally set up in the temple of Mahā-Tāt just described, and were later removed to the temple of Çrī Chŭm, when the former fell into disrepair or, possibly, when some disaster such as fire overtook it.

Sawank'alōk (Çrī Sachanalai), the sister-city of Suk'ōt'ai, is now, alas, also buried deep in the jungle, and but little remains of its former state. It lies about 12 miles north of the new town on the west bank of the Me Yōm, near some rapids, and many a time have I trod its ancient secret-holding soil in search of fragments of pottery. Portions of the city wall are met with near the banks of the river, and the main temple of Mahā-Tāt stands outside the old town, on a peninsula formed by a sharp bend of the river. I have already shown illustrations of this temple with the Khmer and other ruins attached to it (Figs. 95–100), and I have also described it in detail in the *Journal of the Siam Society*.[2] Inside the old city itself I have chosen the best known monument, of which the ruins still exist, to illustrate the type of architecture built by the early Tai sovereigns of Siam. The temple of Chāng Lôm, which is attributed to Rām K'amheng, shows clearly its affinity to the Sinhalese style, with its bell-shaped *dagoba* and its elephant terrace. I was fortunate enough to visit this temple on one occasion shortly after the passage of Royalty, and so was able to obtain a photograph of it cleared of the jungle (Fig. 141). The fact that it is built of laterite covered with stucco places it near to the Khmer period of domination, before the use of laterite gave way to that of brick; so here we have an interesting meeting between Cambodia and

[1] A. K. Coomaraswamy, in *History of Indian and Indonesian Art*, p. 177 (Fig. 320), says that the script on the picture is identical with that on inscriptions of A.D. 1357 and 1361 of the King of Suk'ōt'ai, to which I refer later.

[2] Reginald le May, "A Visit to Sawankalōk", *J.S.S.* vol. XIX, part 2 (1925), pp. 65–72.

Ceylon in the heart of Siam. It was on one of the terraces of Chāng Lôm that I once picked up two small bronze heads of the Buddha, the one typical of the Suk'ōt'ai style, but the other, which is 4 inches high, showing definite traces of Khmer influence in the square face, straight forehead, broad nose and long mouth with thick lips (Fig. 143). There is great power and nobility of character in this face.

Another temple, that of P'rajedi Chet Teo (The Seven Rows of *Stūpas*), is probably rather later in date, though still of laterite construction, if we may judge from a beautiful Tai Buddha image seated on the Nāga king after the Khmer fashion, as at Wat Mahā-Tāt, which has withstood all the ravages of six hundred years and still remains in its niched alcove oblivious of time and serenely imperturbable (Fig. 142). The folds of the Nāga king have been damaged, possibly by thieves in their search for buried treasure, but the image and the magnificent hood are intact and it is certain that in this case a Khmer image has not been subsequently transformed into a Tai one. The wide-spreading knees and the hands folded in the lap in the attitude of *Samādhi* (Meditation) show the Sinhalese influence, while the features are unmistakably of the Suk'ōt'ai School, in its settled and well-defined form of the early fourteenth century.

The first occasion on which I visited the old city of Çrī Sachanalai I examined certain other remains of temples, such as Suan Keo Utayān, which stood in a very picturesque setting, and also Somdet Nāng P'ya (Her Majesty the Queen), which had almost disappeared beneath the vegetation but still possessed some mural decoration in stucco in good preservation. I saw, too, the monument called the Lăk Müang which was always set up at the foundation of a city with (so the ancient story goes) a human sacrifice buried beneath it to propitiate the *p'ī*, or spirits, and to bring good fortune to the inhabitants.

Apart from the ruins and objects still standing, our chief source of knowledge of all that pertains to the dynasty of Suk'ōt'ai, the first Tai dynasty of Siam, lies in the stone inscriptions of which more than twenty have been found since the days of King Mongkut. These have now been set up in the National Museum, and fifteen of them have been deciphered and translated into French by Cœdès in the volume so often referred to in this work. For a study of the evolution of the Siamese script alone they are invaluable, but, in addition, the earlier ones are so full of details of the customs and religion of the princes and their people that a tolerably clear idea can be obtained of the life in Central Siam in those early days.

I have already spoken of the famous *stela* of Rām K'amheng, the obelisk which dates from A.D. 1292 and forms the Magna Carta of Siam. In this inscription, which is in the earliest form of Tai script, the king records how both he and all his people, high and low, men and women, "without distinction of rank or sex", practise the religion of the Buddha with devoutness and always faithfully observe his precepts during the rainy season. At the close of this season there is the grand ceremony of *Kat'in,* or "presenting robes to the priests", such as still obtains to-day, and everyone gives himself over to music and laughter. "Whoever wishes to play, plays: he who wishes to laugh, laughs; he who wishes to sing, sings." In the midst of Suk'ōt'ai there were temples and statues of the Buddha both great and small, some of the latter measuring 30 feet in height (as seen in Fig. 135). Rām K'amheng then records how he built the monastery of Arannika specially for the Patriarch, who had come from Nakon Srītammarāt and who had completely studied the Three Baskets (*Tripitaka*). This monastery also contained an image of the Buddha 30 feet high.

The facts so strikingly given in this inscription are supplemented to an unusual degree by another long inscription, also in Tai script, found in Wat Çrī Chŭm but probably belonging to Wat Mahā-Tāt, on which no precise date is discoverable, but which may be ascribed to the reign of Dharmarāja I, the grandson of Rām K'amheng, about the period A.D. 1350–70. After a graphic description of how the Tai dynasty of Suk'ōt'ai came into being (which I have already related), the story told is chiefly concerned with a prince who, in imitation of Sakya Muni himself, laid aside his royal robes and way of living and entered a monastery, fully determined to become a future Buddha himself. The great interest from the point of view of this study lies in the many references to Ceylon. For instance, the prince "loved to wander in the forest, straying here and there and neglecting his food (living on fruit and roots), behaving in every respect after the manner of the monks of Sinhala" (Ceylon). Further, the prince restored the Temple of the Great Relic at Suk'ōt'ai (Wat Mahā-Tāt), and the inscription adds that "when the Somdet P'ra Mahāsami [i.e. the priest Sumana who will be discussed later] came from Sihala [Ceylon] he brought a body of laymen with him and, in his faith, brought also two precious relics of the Buddha". These relics performed innumerable miracles, which were seen by the laymen of Sihala who threw themselves on the ground in adoration, and the reason for them was to urge all the folk to go to Lankadvīpa (Ceylon) to help in furthering the cause of their religion and thereby gain much merit.[1]

It is thus clear that by the middle of the fourteenth century the Hīnayāna (Theravāda) doctrine of Sinhalese Buddhism was firmly established in the heart

[1] G. Cœdès, *Recueil des Inscriptions du Siam,* Part I (1924), pp. 61–79 (Siamese), and pp. 49–75 (French).

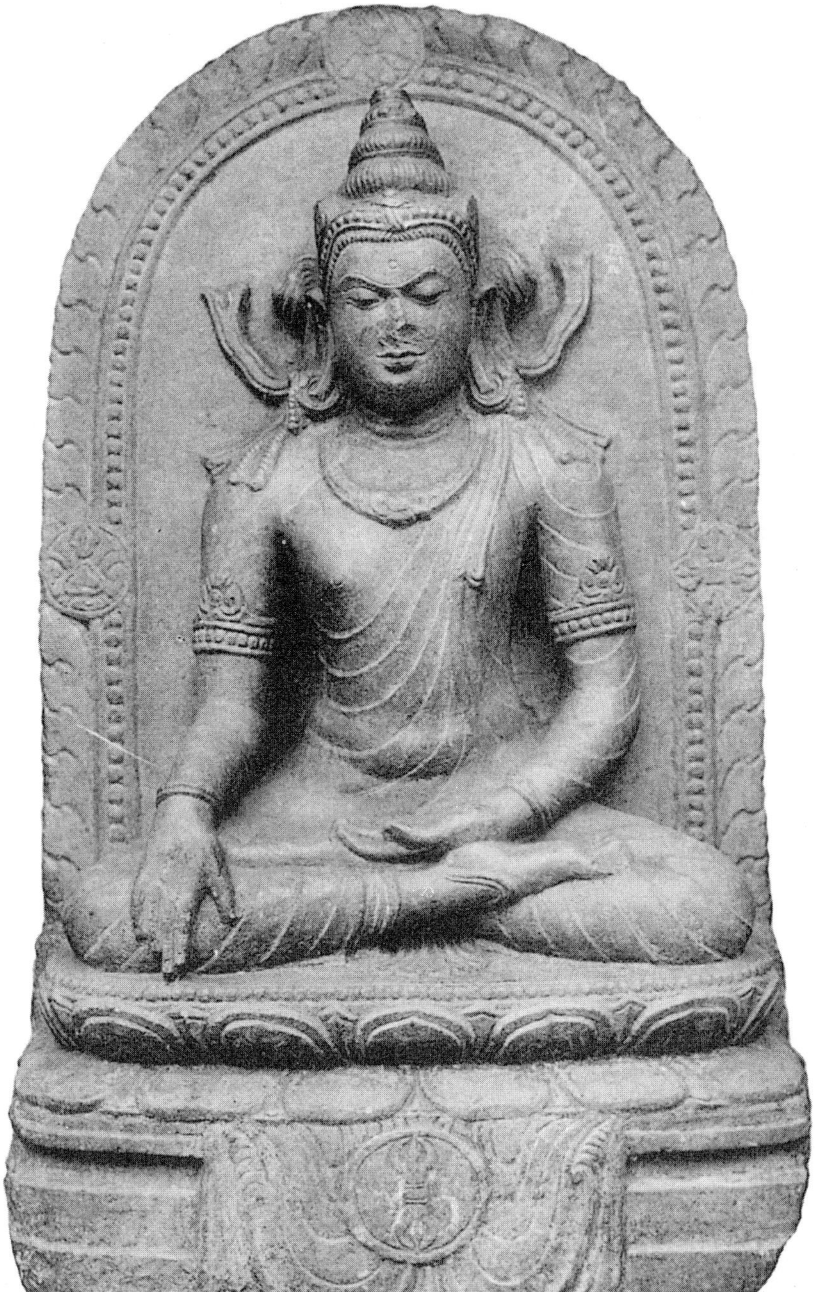

121. Stone Buddha. Pāla decorated type, from Buddh Gayā.

122. Bronze Buddha. Tai-Lü decorated type, from North Siam.

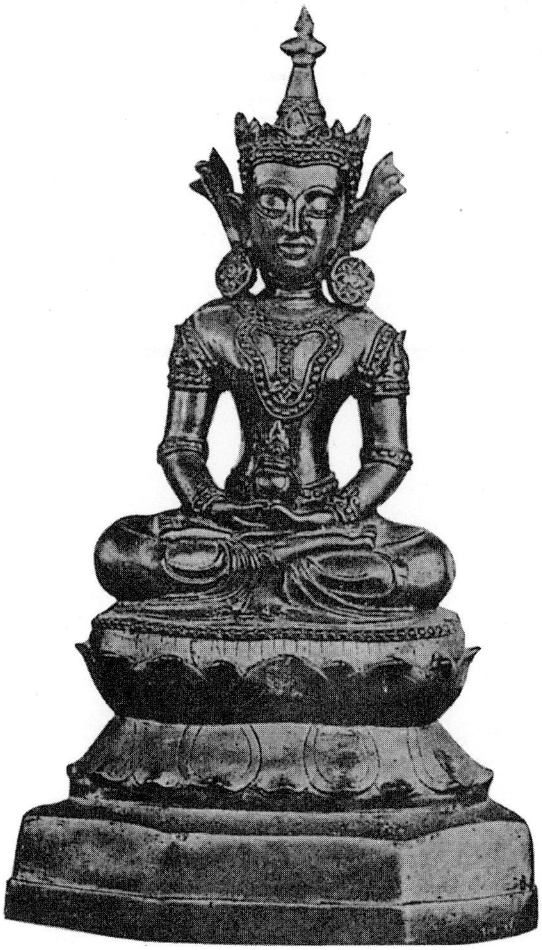

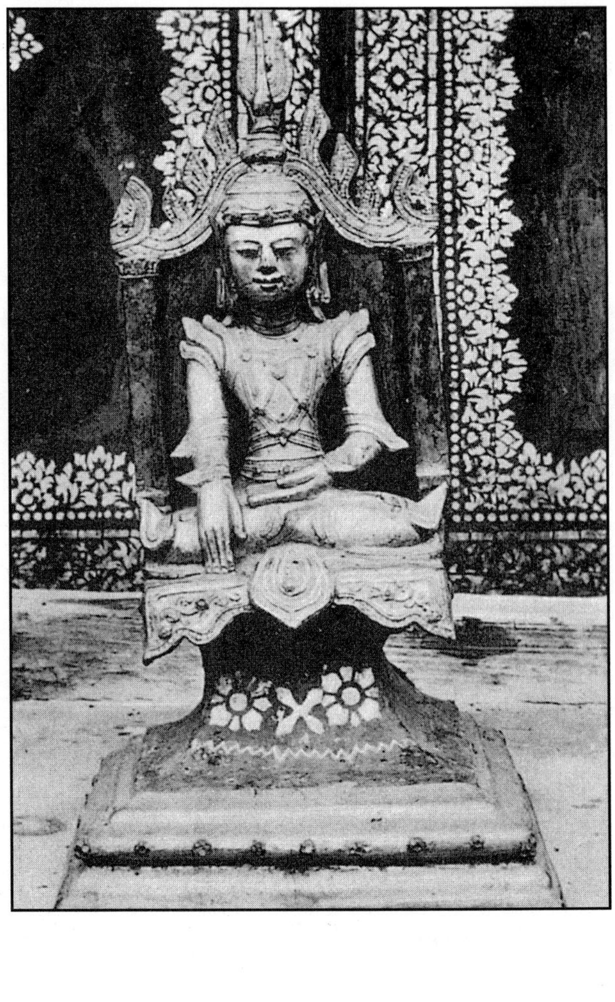

123. Lacquered Earthen Buddha. Tai decorated type.
Temple of Kao Tü, Chiengmai.

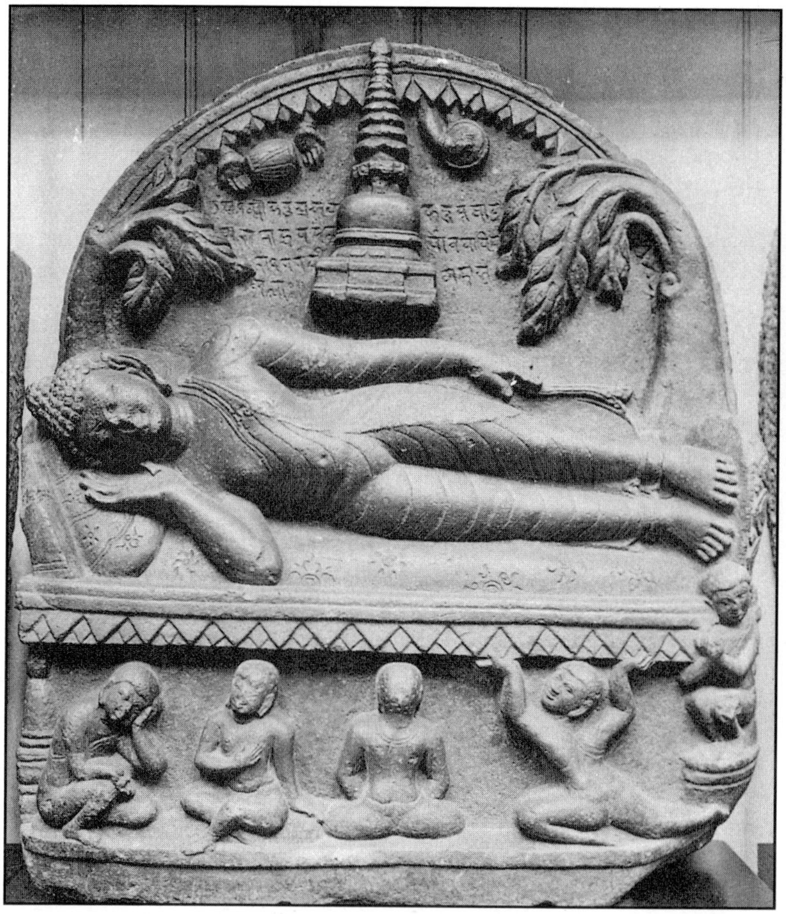

124. Stone Stela representing Mahā-parinirvāna of Buddha. Pāla type, from Buddh Gayā.

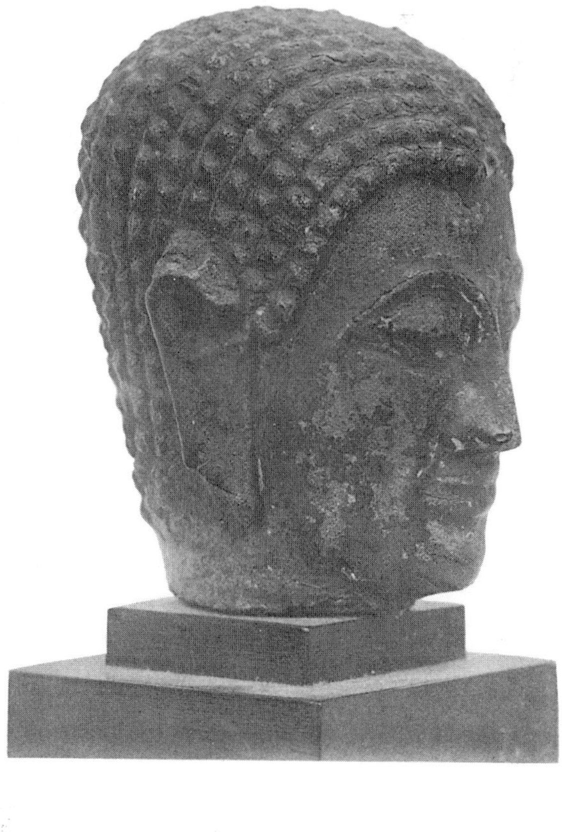

125. Lacquered Stone Head of Buddhist Saint. Tai (Ayudhya) type. Found in Cave near Chiengrai.

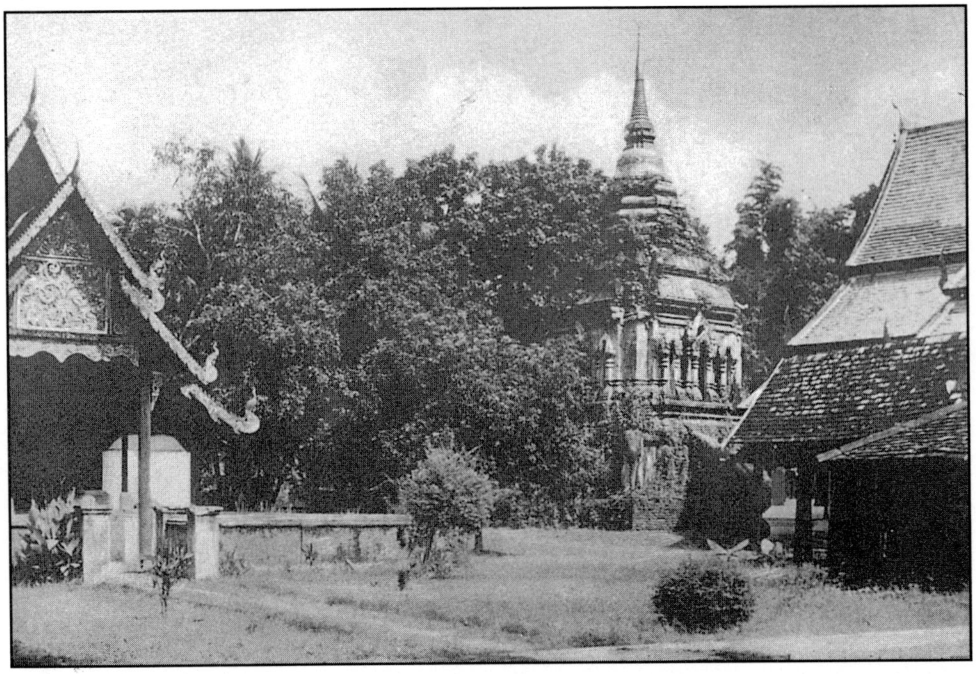

126. Temple of Chiengmān. Pagān style, in Chiengmai.

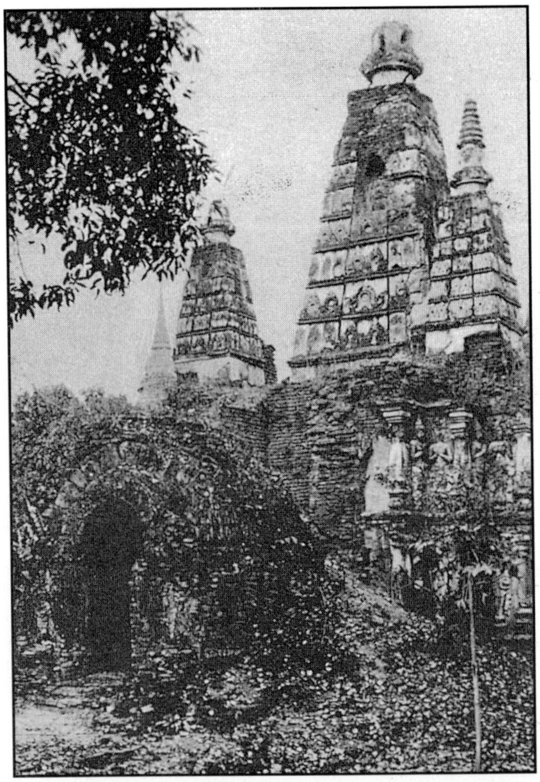

127. Temple of Chet Yôt. Pagān style, near Chiengmai.

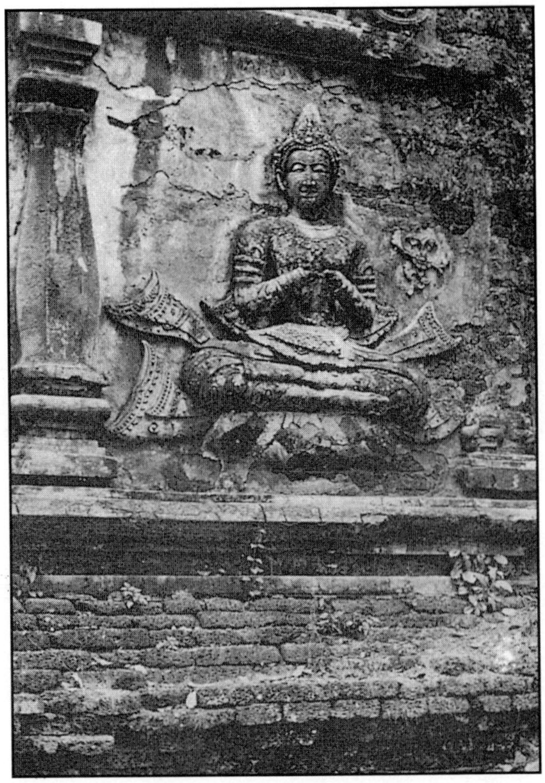

128. Brick and Stucco Buddha on exterior of Temple of Chet Yôt. Tai type.

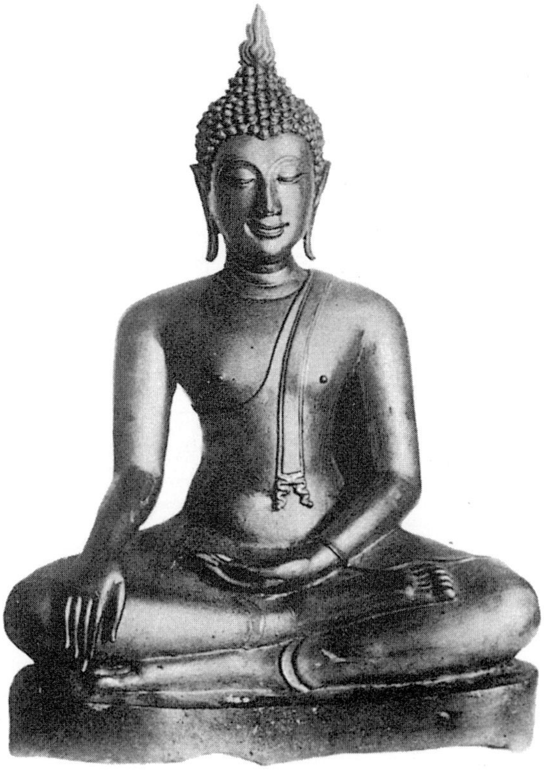

129. Bronze Buddha. Tai (Suk'ōt'ai) type.

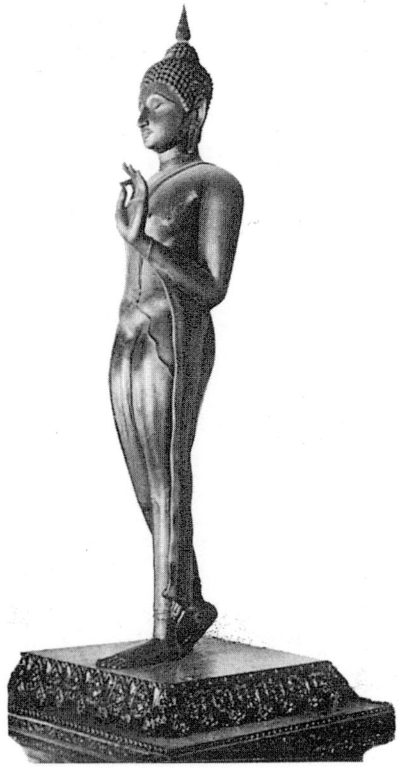

130. Bronze Buddha, Tai (Suk'ōt'ai) type. Temple of Benchamabopit.

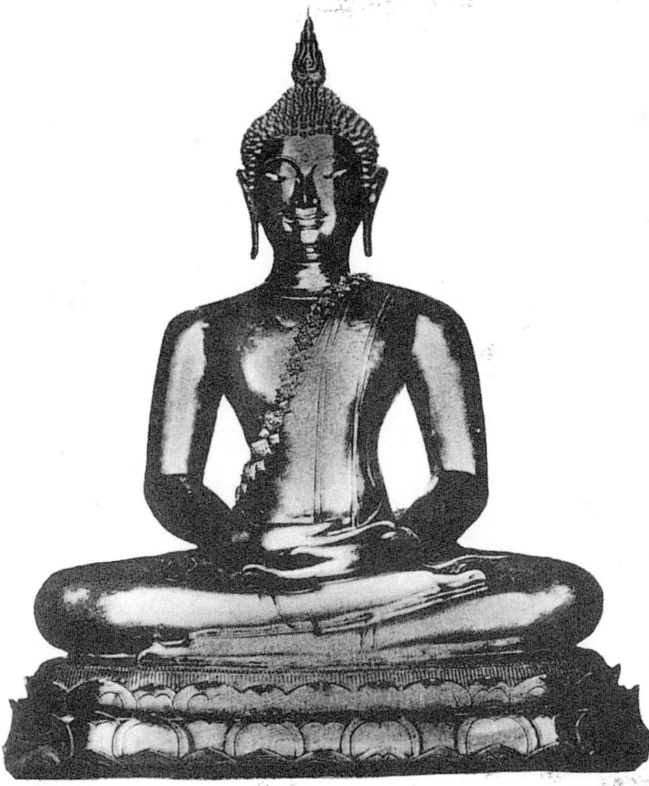

131. Bronze Buddha (P'ra Sihing). Tai (Suk'ōt'ai) type.

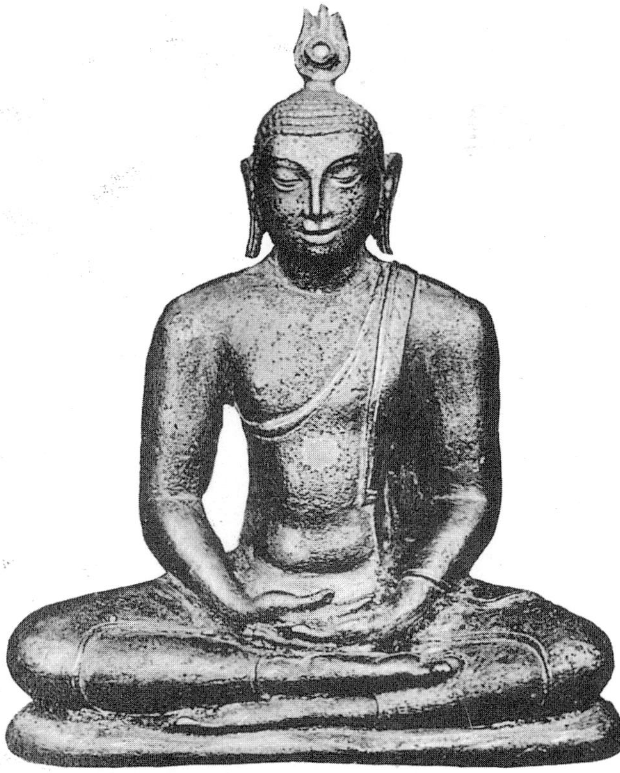

132. Bronze Buddha. Sinhalese.

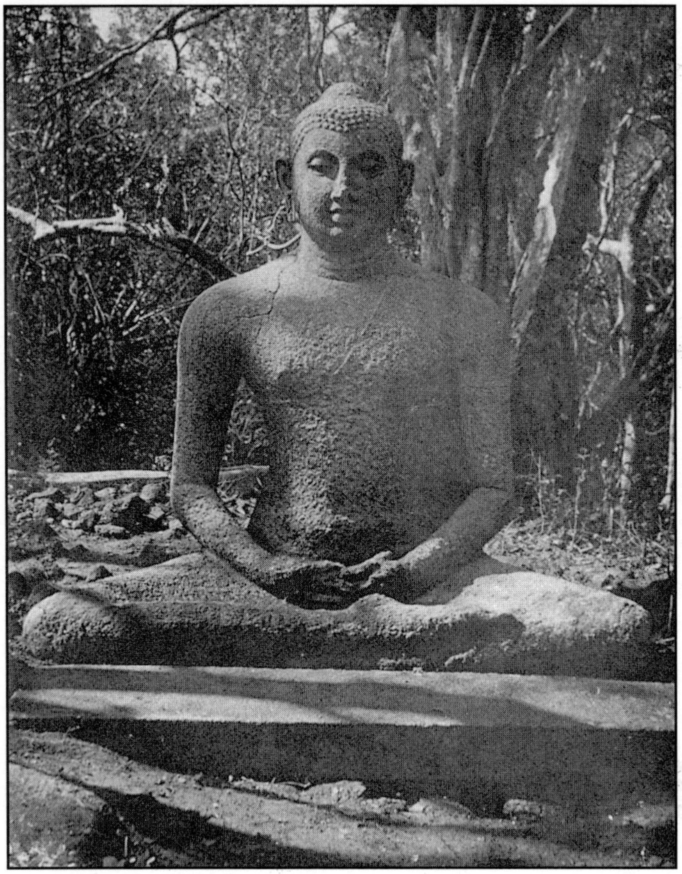

133. Stone Buddha. Sinhalese, at Anurādhapura, Ceylon.

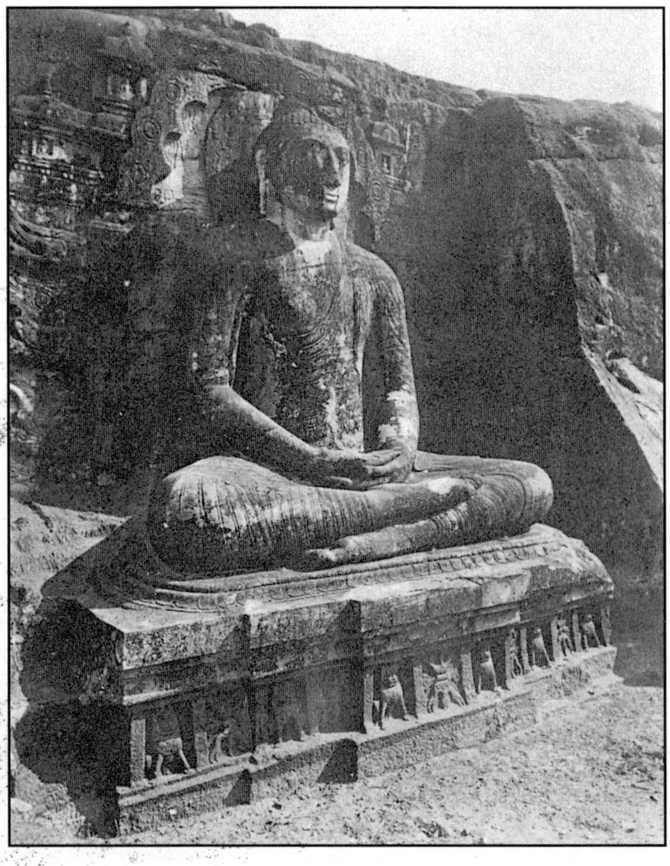

134. Rock-hewn Buddha. Sinhalese, at Galvihāra, Polonnāruwa, Ceylon.

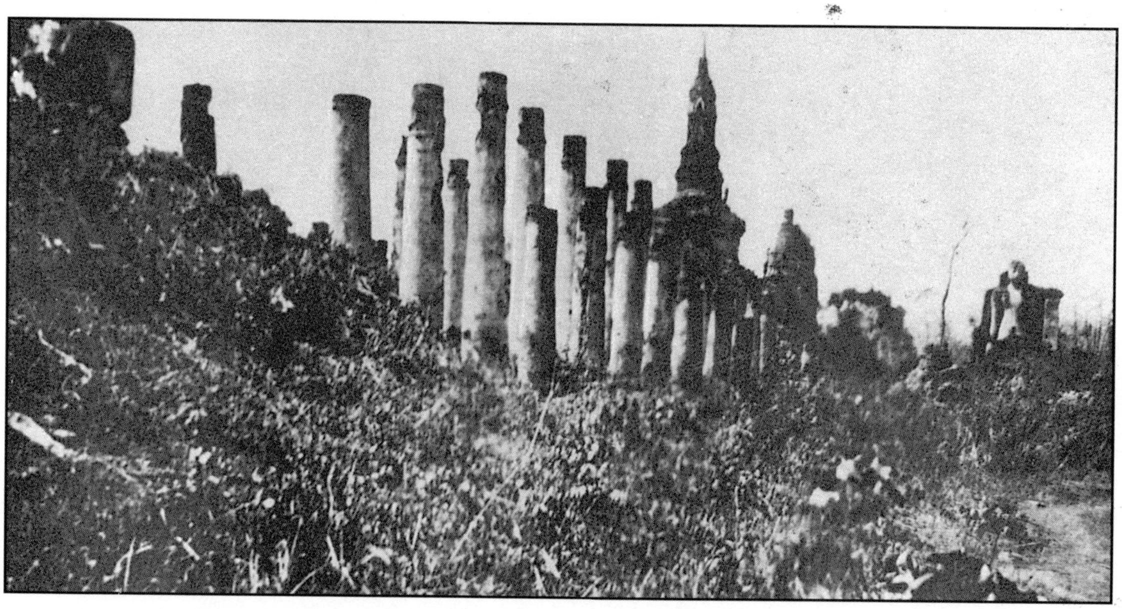

135. Ruins of Temple of Mahā-Tāt at old Suk'ōt'ai, with standing Buddha.

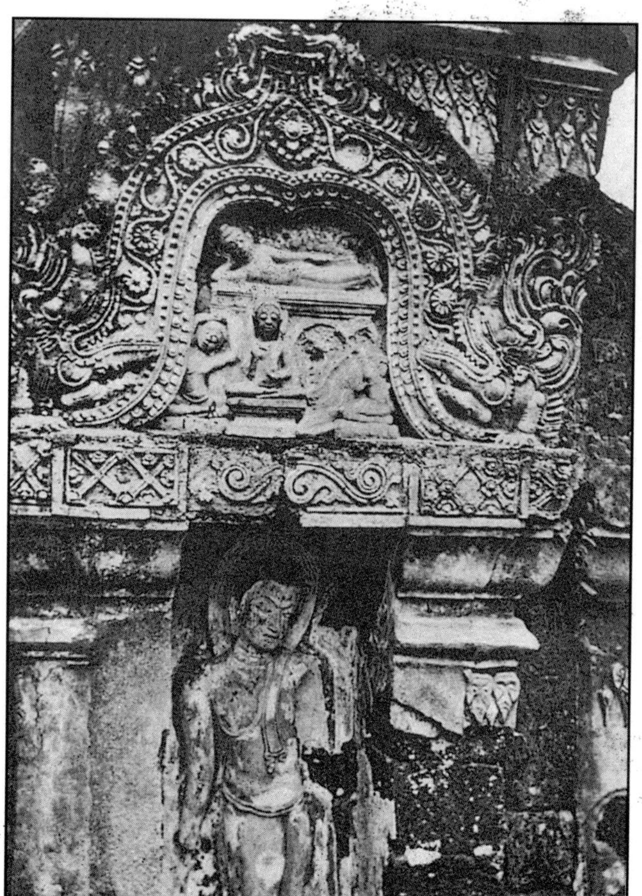

136. Laterite and Stucco Buddha (with Mahā-parinirvāna of Buddha above) at Temple of Mahā-Tāt, old Suk'ōt'ai.

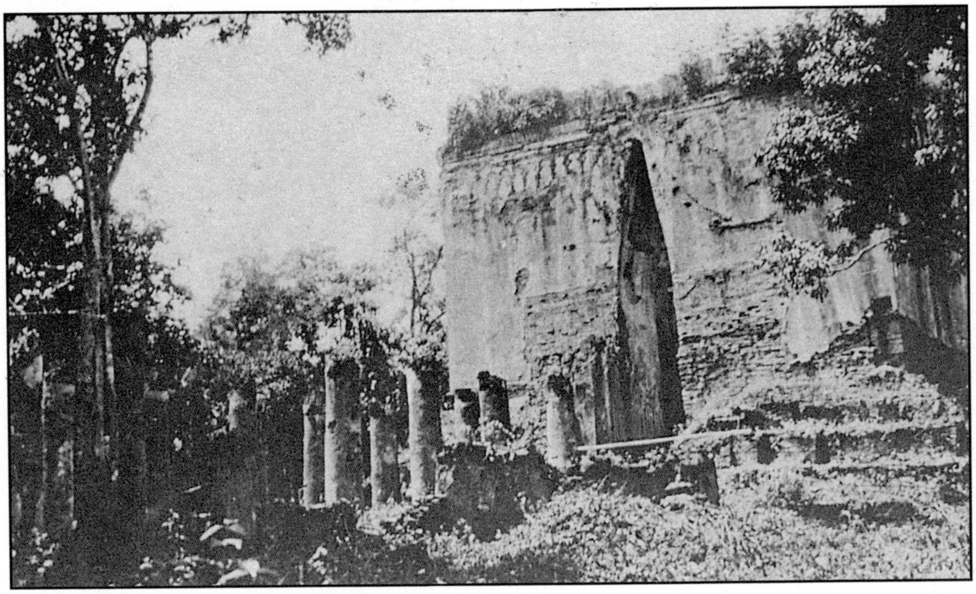

137. Ruins of Temple of Çrī Chŭm at old Suk'ōt'ai.

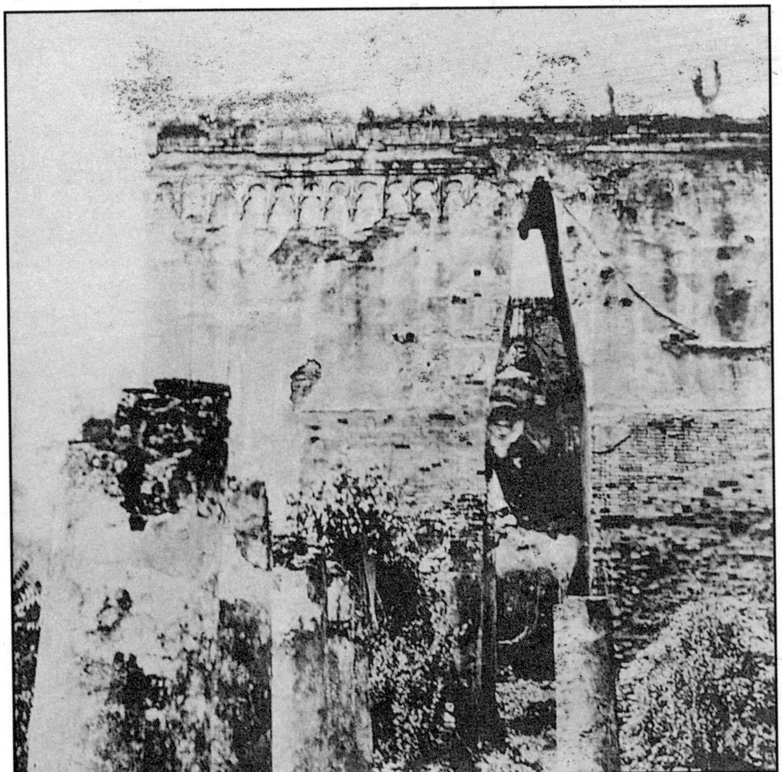

138. Façade of Temple of Çrī Chŭm showing ruined Buddha inside.

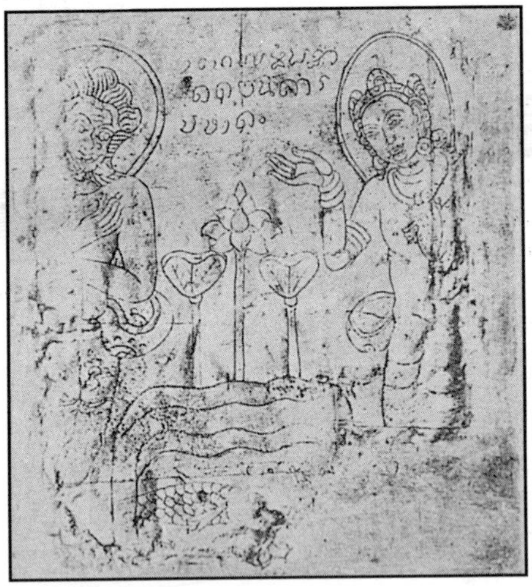

139. Engraving on Stone at Temple of Çrī Chŭm.

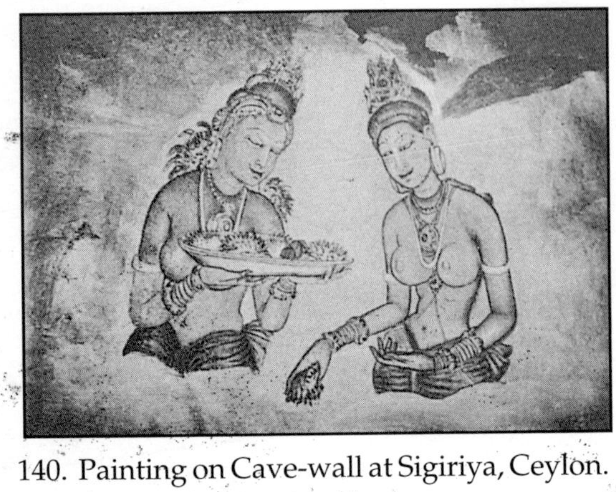

140. Painting on Cave-wall at Sigiriya, Ceylon.

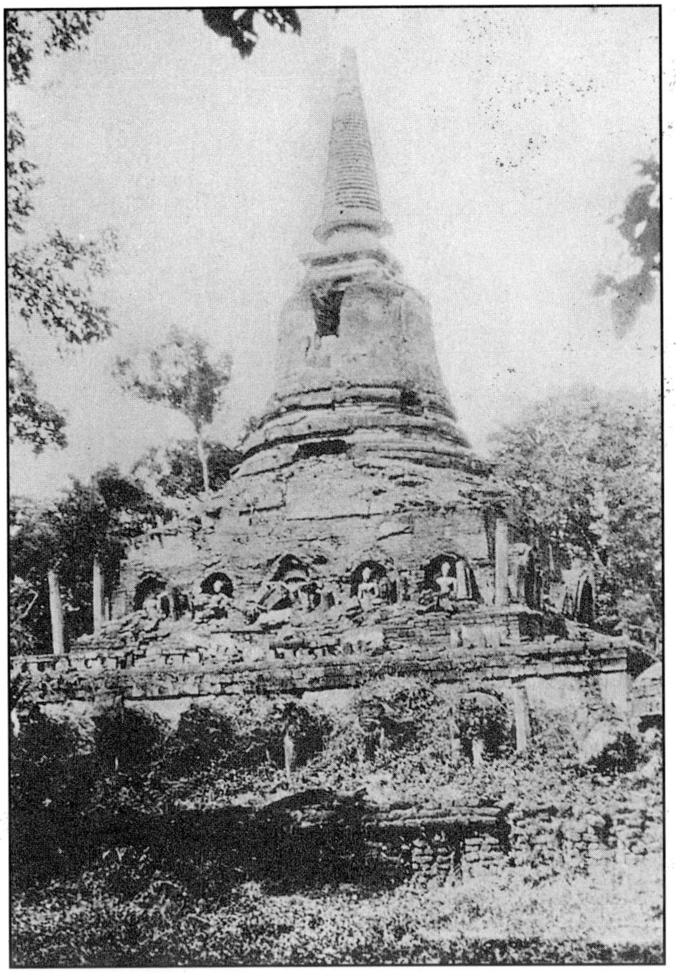

141. *Stūpa* of Tai Temple of Chāng Lôm at old Sawank'alōk.

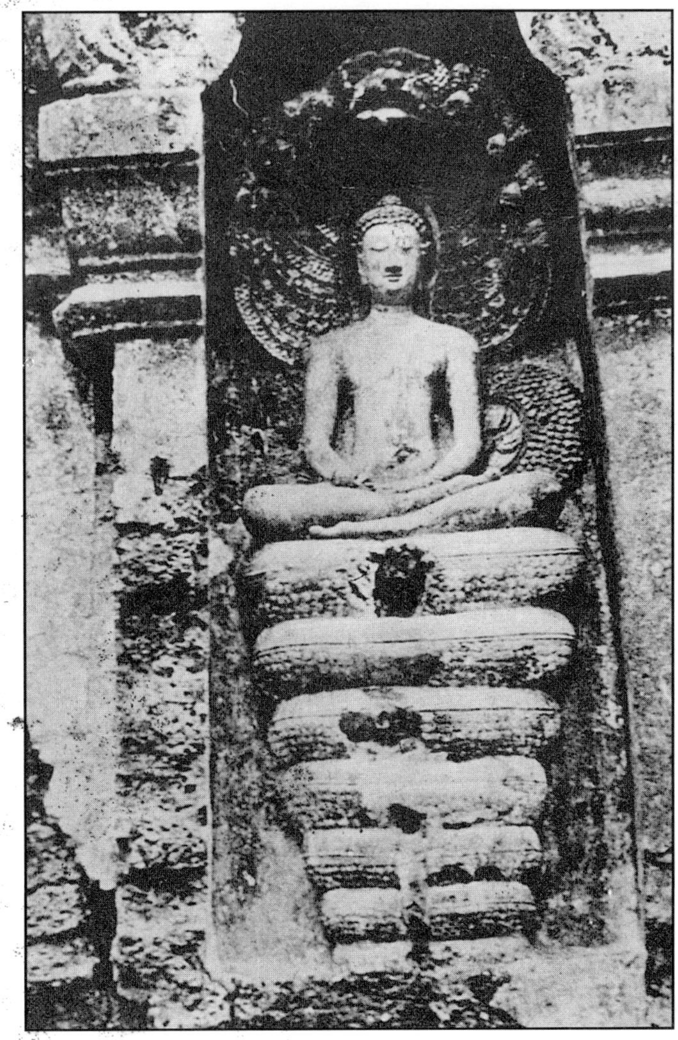

142. Stone Buddha on Nāga King. Tai, in niche at Temple of P'rajedi Chet Taeo, old Sawank'alōk.

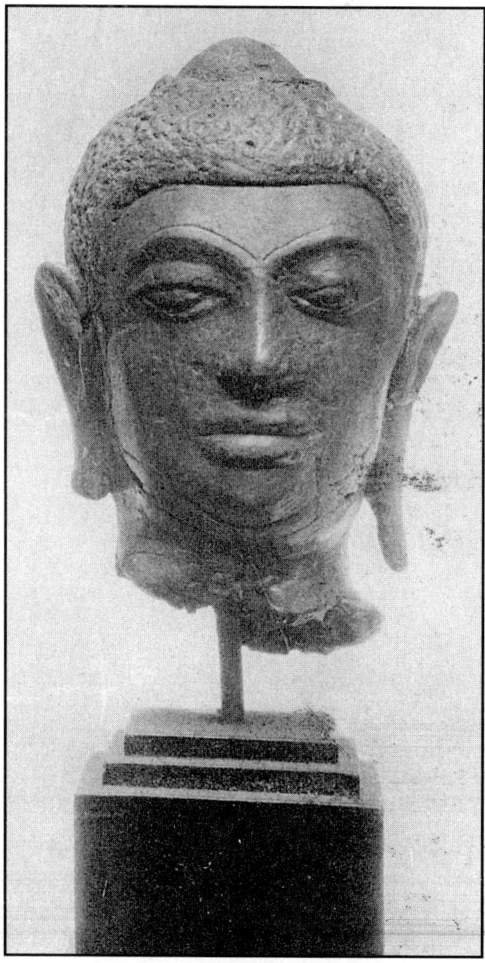

143. Bronze Head of Buddha. Tai-Khmer, from ruins of Temple of Chāng Lôm, old Sawank'alōk.

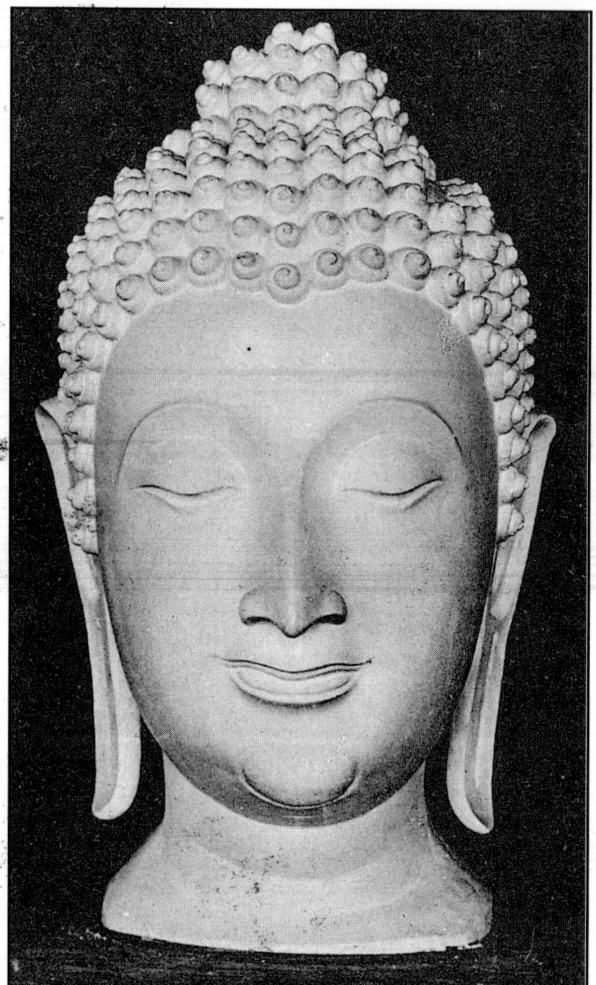

145. Bronze Head of Buddha. Tai (Suk'ōt'ai) type.

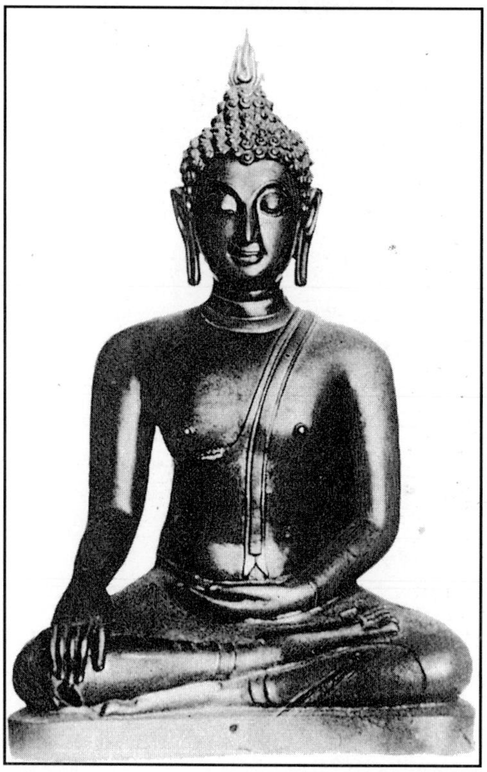

144. Bronze Buddha. Tai (Suk'ōt'ai) type.

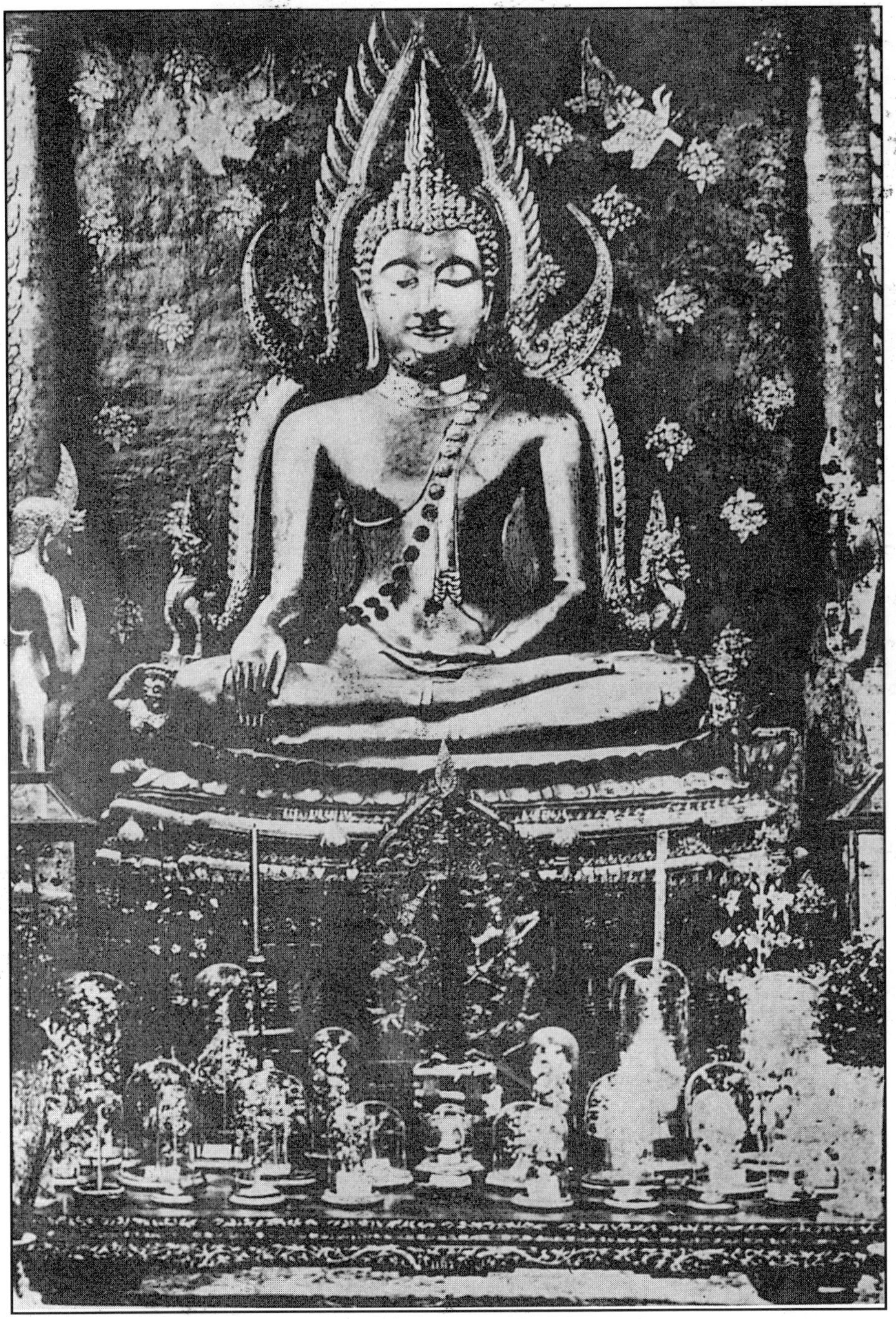

146. Bronze Buddha. Tai (Suk'ōt'ai) type, in the great Temple at Pitsanulōk.

147. Bronze Head of Buddha. Tai (Suk'ōt'ai) type.

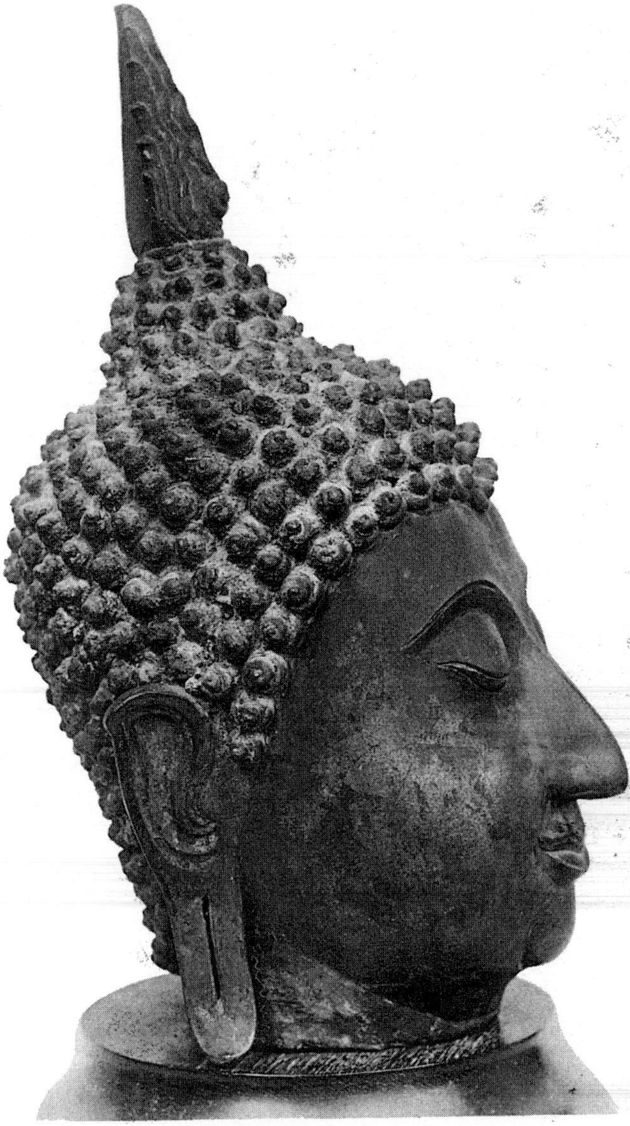

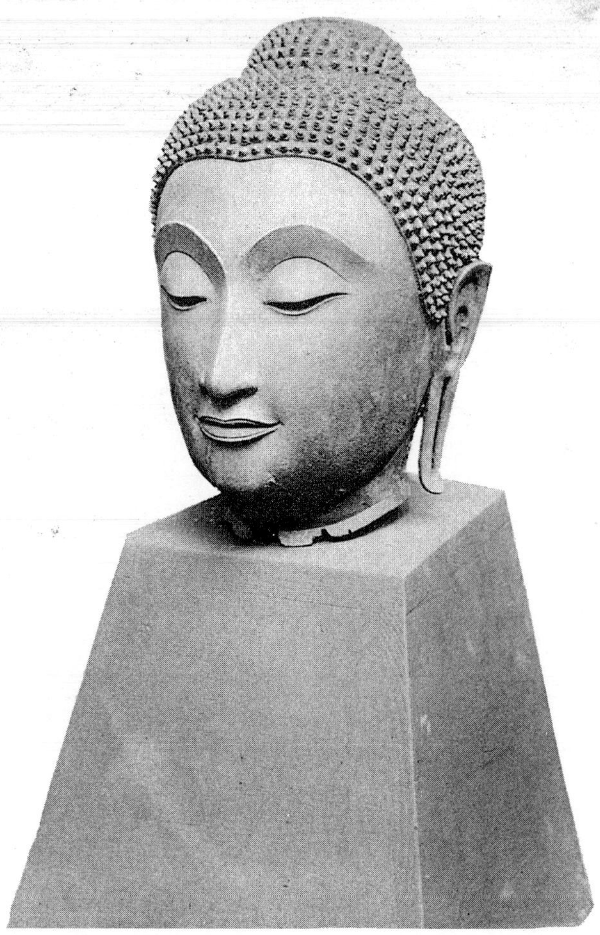

148. Bronze Head of Buddha. Tai (Suk'ōt'ai) type modified.

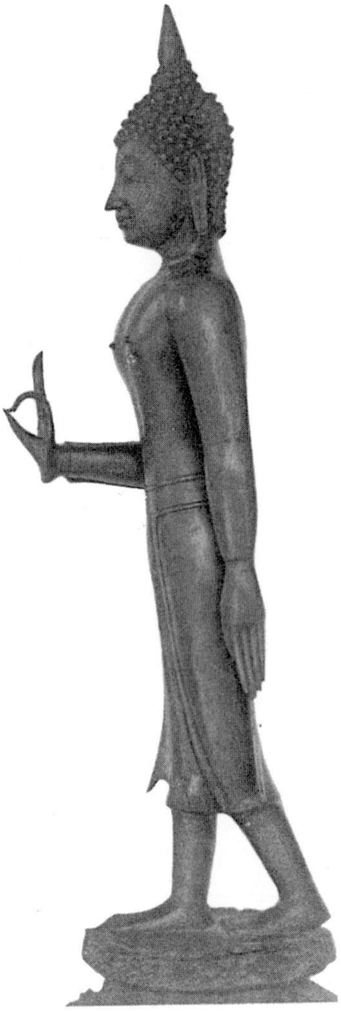

149. Bronze Buddha. Tai (Suk'ōt'ai) type.

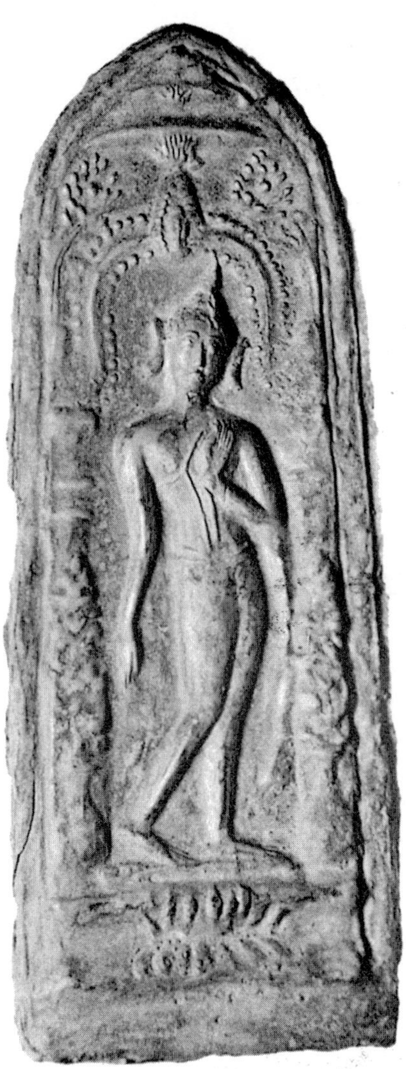

150. Tin Votive Tablet. Tai (Suk'ō̃t'ai) type.

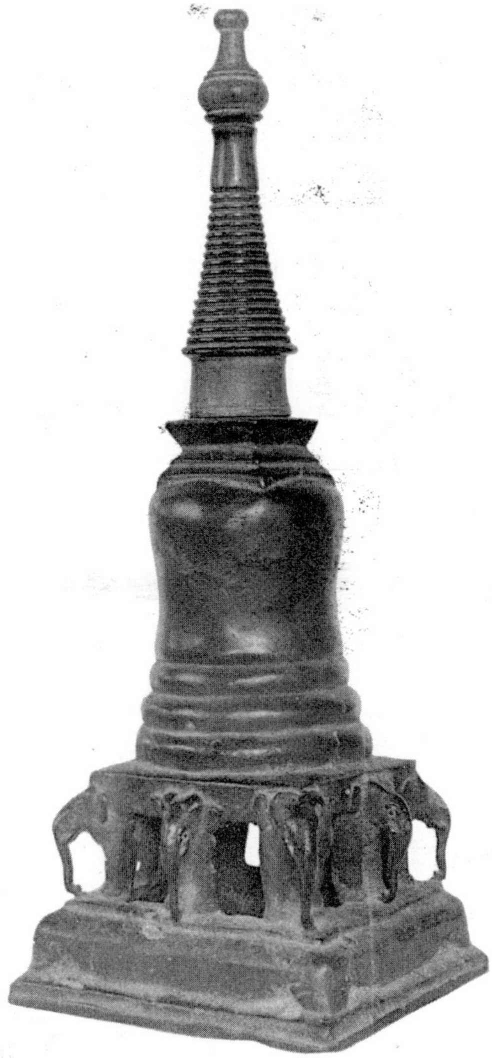

151. Bronze model of *Stūpa* with Ivory pinnacle. Tai (Suk'ōt'ai) type.

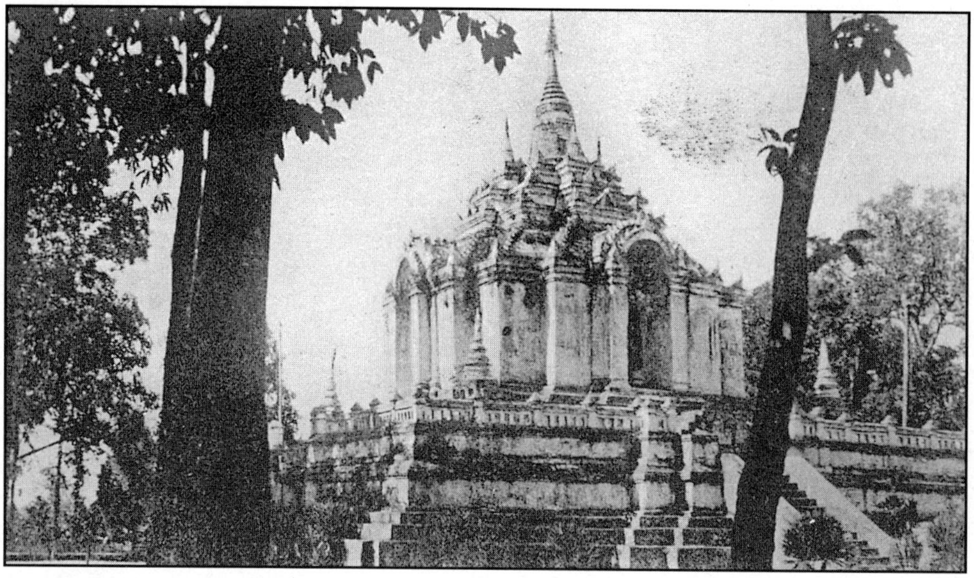

152. Tai Temple of P'ra Yün at Lamp'ūn.

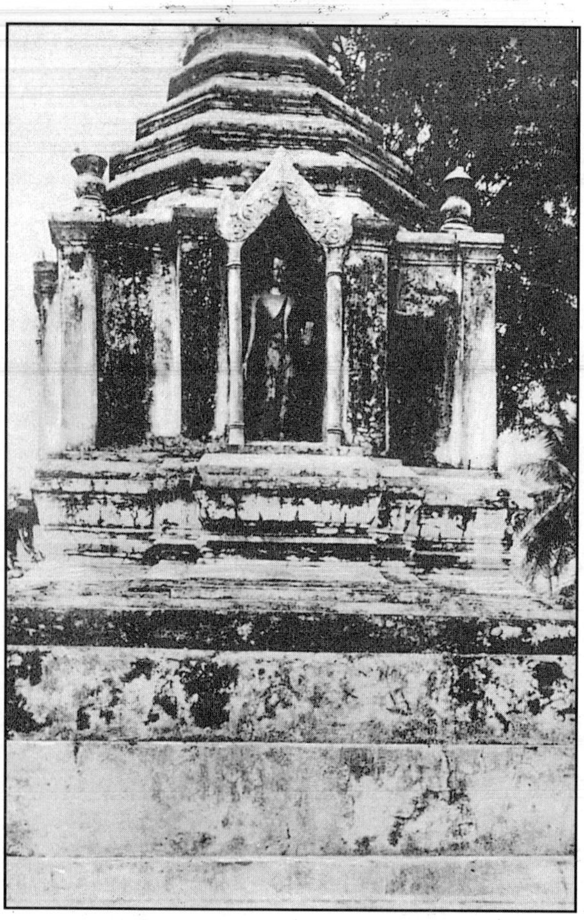

153. *Stūpa* of Tai Temple of Siriküt near Chiengmai.

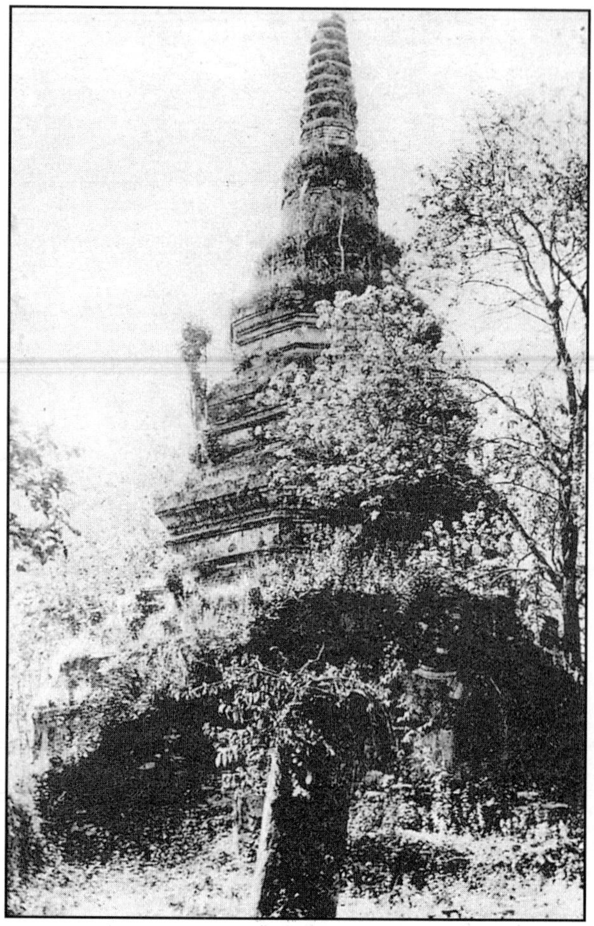

154. Ruined *Stūpa* of Tai Temple at old Chiengsen, with Buddha image.

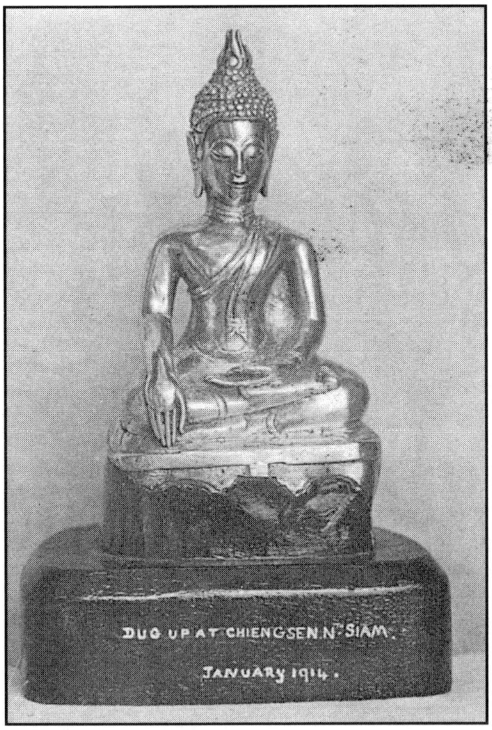


155. Silver Buddha. Tai (Chiengsen) type.

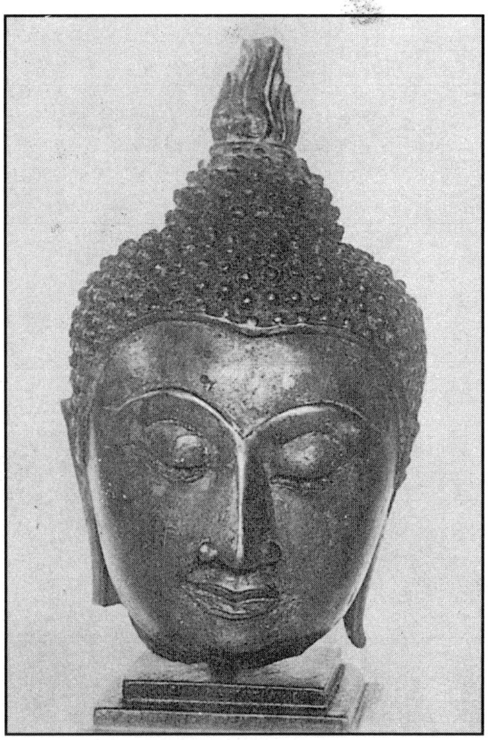

156. Bronze Head of Buddha. Tai (Chiengsen) type.

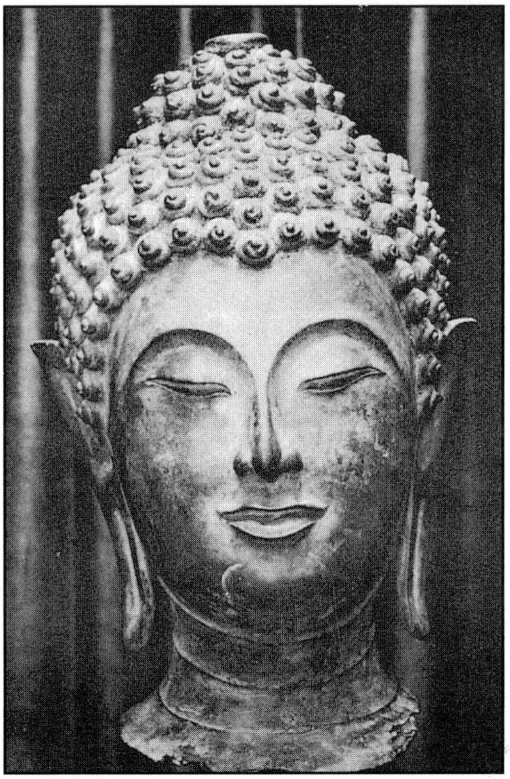

157. Bronze Head of Buddha. Tai (Chiengsen) type.

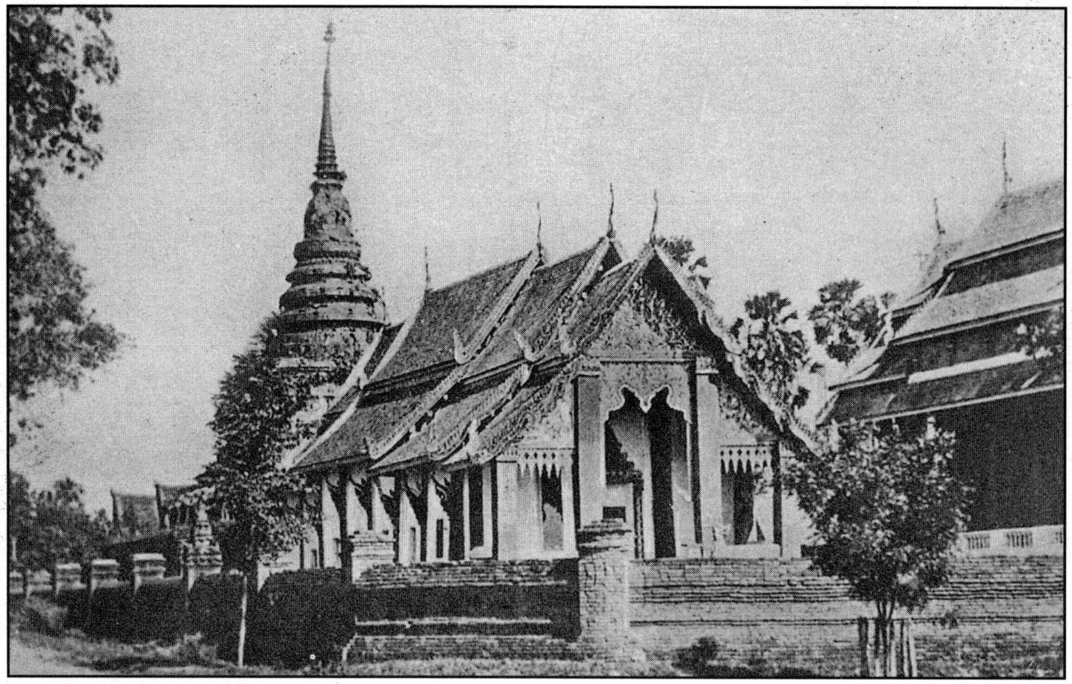
158. Tai Temple at Nān.

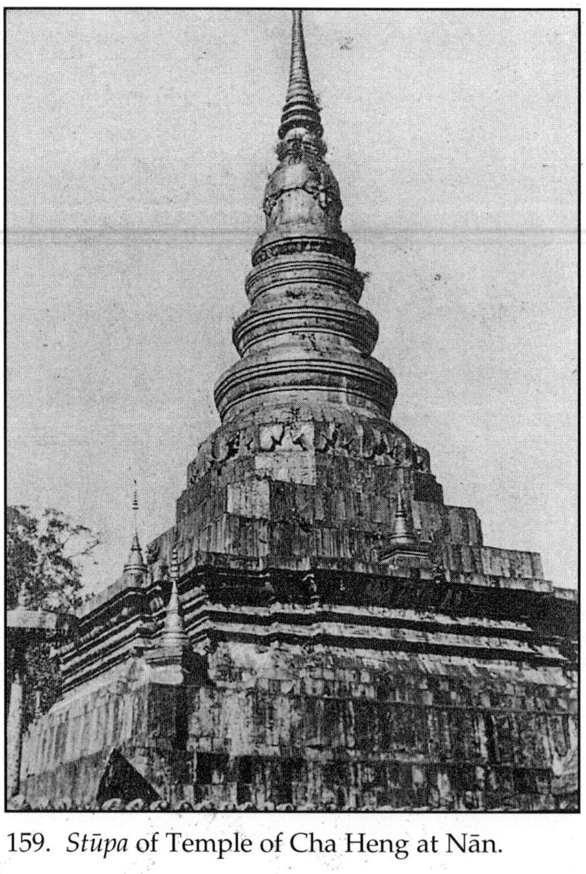
159. *Stūpa* of Temple of Cha Heng at Nān.

of Siam, and, as will be seen later, it received a number of new impulses direct from Ceylon up to the sixteenth century.

I cannot leave the subject of this second inscription without reference to a very singular passage contained in it which is so remarkable that I reproduce it in full. It runs as follows:[1]

> When the great brick sanctuary [of Wat Mahā-Tāt] was finished and solemnly opened, a search was made for ancient *stone* images of the Buddha. Homage was paid to them and they were collected together in the Great Sanctuary. In one place a neck or a bust had been found; in another place the hair or an arm or a breast; sometimes the head had fallen and was far from the body and it needed *four men* to carry it; sometimes a leg or a thigh had been found, sometimes a hand or a foot. All these stone statues of the Buddha were of large size. They had to be placed on a barrow or a cart to be transported to the Great Sanctuary where they were joined together with lime [cement]. Some of these statues were magnificent and beautifully decorated, just as if Indra had made them himself. Once restored, they became large, durable and extremely fine statues of the Buddha. The Great Sanctuary was filled with them and they were placed together in groups or ranged along the galleries.

Were it not that there could be no motive in relating such a story, if fictitious, the whole account would appear to be incredible; but it undoubtedly has a ring of truth about it, and it is hard to know which quality to admire the most in our Royal Priest, the pietist, the art-lover or the archaeologist, for he seems to have been all three combined in one, and must surely be one of the earliest of whom the record is so clear, at any rate in the East. And the puzzling question remains—what type of ancient stone Buddha image was he likely to find lying about in quantities in deserted ruins in the region of Suk'ōt'ai? As far as one may hazard a guess, they must have been of Khmer origin and workmanship. There had scarcely been time by 1350 for the creation of *ancient* Tai images, and, besides, the Tai of Suk'ōt'ai and the north seldom worked in *stone*; nor are there any traces of Môn-Indian (Dvāravatī) sculpture in this region. There remain, therefore, only the Khmer; and yet, judging from the evidence available, the Khmer themselves did not penetrate so far north as Sawank'alōk and Suk'ōt'ai until the latter half of the twelfth century, so that even their images would scarcely deserve the epithet of "ancient". Moreover, the size and plentifulness of these images is so difficult to understand—heads and bodies requiring four men to carry them and enough images to fill the Great Sanctuary and the galleries of Wat Mahā-Tāt at Suk'ōt'ai. Where are they now—what has become of this galaxy of beautiful large stone

[1] G. Cœdès, *Recueil des Inscriptions du Siam*, Part I (1924), p. 70 (French). Author's translation. The italics are mine.

images? There is no sign of them to-day among the desolate ruins of the temple, and one can only imagine that Indra, seeing the courts and temples forsaken, must have spirited them away.

Two other well-known inscriptions of this period must be mentioned. The first is called the *stela* of Nagara Jum. This is dated 1279 of the *Mahā-Sakarāt* (A.D. 1357) and was formerly set up at Wat Parama Tāt near the old city of Kampeng-p'et on the Me Ping, between Nakon Sawan and Tāk (Raheng). It records the installation by Dharmarāja I of Suk'ōt'ai of a precious and authentic relic of the Buddha obtained from Ceylon, and also of the planting of a branch of the original sacred Fig-tree under which the Buddha sat and conquered the army of Māra, the Prince of Evil.

The second is an inscription in the Khmer language set up by the same King of Suk'ōt'ai in the Monastery of the Mango Grove, to the west of Suk'ōt'ai and outside its walls, and was specially made to commemorate the arrival of a venerable monk from Ceylon in 1362,[1] his installation at the Monastery of the Mango Grove and the ordaining of King Dharmarāja I as a priest. There is also a duplicate (or almost a duplicate) of this inscription in Tai script, which was found some years ago in a temple to the north of Ayudhya.

Thus we have two more clearly defined instances of the influence played by Sinhalese Buddhism in Siam at this time, and I shall have occasion to refer again to the venerable monk of the inscription, since he was destined to play a great part in the spread of Sinhalese Buddhism, and indirectly its artistic influence, throughout the whole country.

Claeys strikes a true note when he says that "Suk'ōt'ai was in reality the centre where Khmer architecture and the Tai contribution brought from the north met and fused together,[2] the crucible from which emerged the true Tai architecture, which still awaits analysis, and the true Tai sculpture, which is more clearly defined".[3] Dupont admits that the Chiengsen style must be anterior, and therefore contributory to the Suk'ōt'ai style of sculpture, but is strongly of the opinion that certain details owe their origin to China. This I have already dealt with. He goes on to establish two distinct forms of the Suk'ōt'ai style (and here I feel he is on firm ground), one of which is distinguishable by the extremely soft rendering of the eyebrows and eyes and by a still relatively large mouth, while in

[1] This is Sumana, the Primate referred to in the undated inscription, who brought the laymen with him. Apparently he came directly from Burma, but had resided for many years in Ceylon.

[2] Together with the Sinhalese influence (author's note).

[3] J. Y. Claeys, "L'Archéologie du Siam", *B.E.F.E.O.* vol. XXXI, pp. 414–15.

the other the features are more sharply defined and hence take on a more conventionalised form, especially seen in the sharp ridge formed by the eyebrows.[1] Figs. 144 and 145 demonstrate this difference, and, judging from later developments in Siam, the seated figure (Fig. 144) is probably the earlier of the two. Both these examples are in the National Museum, and Fig. 145, about 24 inches high, may perhaps be considered without prejudice the most beautiful example of the Suk'ōt'ai style known in any collection. It makes an intensely spiritual appeal. Dupont, however, goes further and suggests that, although owing to the use of bronze as opposed to stone there is an almost complete difference between Tai and Khmer art in Siam, yet the half-closed eyes, the gentle smile, and the calm, meditative expression of the Suk'ōt'ai figures bring clearly to mind certain Khmer images of the Bayon style, especially certain Bodhisattvas and Taras. He admits that it is too early as yet to do anything but point out certain analogies, but he wonders if there were not actually a rather complex transitional period in which the final examples of the Môn and Khmer periods were linked up with the beginnings of Southern Tai art.[2] This is a very interesting suggestion, as are most of those put forward by Dupont, and, as I have already shown in Fig. 143 which I found myself in old Sawank'alōk, we may undoubtedly look for transitional links between the Tai and the Khmer even in North-Central Siam. At the same time, if the influence from Ceylon began to come in about the middle of the thirteenth century, this transitional Tai-Khmer period could not have been of long duration.

The most venerated image of the Buddha of the Suk'ōt'ai period still *in situ* is the larger than life-size figure to be seen in the temple of Mahā-Tāt at Pitsanulōk. In Siamese eyes this is considered the most beautiful image known, and is the object of a yearly pilgrimage by large numbers of the people (Fig. 146). An exact replica of this image, which is called P'ra Chinnarāt, was made in the reign of King Chulalongkorn and set up by him in his new temple of Benchamabopit in Bangkok early in this century. The original brother image, P'ra Chinna-Çrī, was brought to Bangkok many years ago and is now to be seen in the temple of Bavaranivēs.

Figs. 147 and 149, from my own collection, are also illustrative of the Suk'ōt'ai type. Fig. 147, 17 inches high, is very typical and shows the arched eyebrows and the long nose, which became such a marked characteristic. Fig. 149, 26 inches high, belongs, I should say, to the second or later type, as it is more conventional

[1] P. Dupont, *Catalogue des Collections Indo-Chinoises du Musée Guimet*, pp. 55–6. Paris, 1934.
[2] *Ibid.* p. 56.

in its treatment. But this type of walking figure, with the left arm raised and the fingers touching (in Exposition), is not often seen in figures of this size. Notice the full development of the breast, which is also a marked feature of the later Suk'ōt'ai figures.

Fig. 148, 14 inches high, also in my possession, shows a modified form of the style, and may perhaps be the product of Pitsanulōk or Kampengp'et as derived from Suk'ōt'ai. It has a most benign and spiritual expression and the modelling of the features is particularly pleasing, while the bronze in this instance has taken on a beautiful patina.

Associated with the School of Suk'ōt'ai is a type of *P'ra P'im* or Votive Tablet, which is of considerable interest and is almost large enough to be classed as sculpture. Fig. 150 shows such a tablet, 12 inches long and $4\frac{1}{2}$ inches wide, made probably of tin, which displays all the features of a walking figure of the Suk'ōt'ai School. There is an actual figure of colossal size, made of masonry and almost identical with the illustration, still to be seen *in situ* at the temple of Mahā-Tāt at Sawank'alōk.[1] Curiously enough, this type of votive tablet is popularly said to be found more often in the region of Supanburi than at Suk'ōt'ai, but I am unable either to deny or to affirm this statement as I have never visited Supanburi.

My last illustration of the Suk'ōt'ai period, Fig. 151, is an exceptional one. It is the model of a *stūpa* in bronze, 12 inches high (with an ivory pinnacle), in my possession and is undoubtedly intended to represent the temple of Chāng Lôm at Sawank'alōk seen in Fig. 141. It is the only such model known to me that can be confidently ascribed to the Suk'ōt'ai period and, as such, deserves a place in this work.

The Suk'ōt'ai period is undoubtedly the most important from the Tai standpoint in Siam, and the form created represents the "ideal" in Siamese eyes. To Europeans the Khmer forms are generally considered more pleasing, but that is because the European generally prefers the individualistic or human rather than the symbolic form in art. Each is entitled to its share in our appreciation of beauty, but the more we live with and strive to understand the symbolic form, the more we shall tend to enrich our spirit as opposed to our senses. It has taken me personally a long time to realise this truth, but my own experience has been such that I cannot doubt it now.

In Siam itself the importance of the new school of doctrine and art combined was made manifest at once, and within a hundred years practically the whole

[1] J. Y. Claeys, "L'Archéologie du Siam", *B.E.F.E.O.* vol. XXXI, Pl. LXXI A.

country had accepted it and adapted the Suk'ōt'ai ideal to its own immediate needs. As we have seen, Rām K'amheng had taken the first step by inviting the renowned teacher of Sinhalese Buddhism from Nakon Srītammarāt. In 1362, at the request of Dharmarāja I, a second high priest, who had studied in Ceylon, arrived at Suk'ōt'ai and was provided with a monastery especially built for the purpose. The accounts are rather conflicting as to where this priest came from originally, but I think it may be accepted that he came directly to Suk'ōt'ai from Pegu (where another famous teacher-priest named Udumbara Mahāsami resided), and that his name was Sumana. The title Sami, or Mahāsami, is one that was given by the King of Ceylon to foreign priests who came to the island to study the Sinhalese form of Buddhism. The JKM says that Sumana was a native of Suk'ōt'ai who went to Pegu to be ordained, but the inscription of Dharmarāja I makes no mention of this.

After Sumana had resided at Suk'ōt'ai for five or six years his renown reached the ears of the King of Chiengmai, who at that time was Kü Na (or Kilāna), and, after repeated requests from the latter, he finally agreed to accept a mission to that country to preach the new form of Buddhism.[1] He set out in 1369 and was received by the king himself at Lamp'ūn, which was probably still the most important religious centre in the north, and installed there at the temple of P'ra Yün (the Standing Buddhas). This temple (Fig. 152) is situated about a mile to the east of the city of Lamp'ūn and is so called because of four standing images of the Buddha which have been set up in niches on the four sides of the building. An inscription in Pāli and Tai (Suk'ōt'ai script), describing the foundation in detail, was found some years ago *in situ*, and has been translated by Cœdès.[2] The style of the Buddha image is based on that of Suk'ōt'ai though, curiously enough, the arms and hands hang down on both sides of the body, but the style of the temple itself is undoubtedly Burmese, and resembles that of the temple of That-Byin-Nyu at Pagān. One may reasonably conclude from this that it was Sumana himself who superintended the erection of the building, and that he based his plans on a temple he had seen in Burma. There is another small temple at Chiengmai in somewhat the same style, Wat Sirikūt, which may be included for comparison (Fig. 153), and here the figure of the Buddha bears a very close resemblance to the Suk'ōt'ai School, both in the general style and the particular pose. There is a singular charm about both these temples.

From this time the Suk'ōt'ai style of *stūpa* architecture and Buddha image

[1] Reginald le May, *An Asian Arcady*, pp. 130–4. Heffer, Cambridge.
[2] G. Cœdès, "Documents", *B.E.F.E.O.* vol. xxv, pt. 1, pp. 32, 95–7.

spread rapidly throughout the north of Siam, and the countryside is covered with *stūpas* in the Burmo-Sinhalese form, though the other temple buildings in the true Tai style appear to owe nothing to Ceylon. The old city of Chiengsen on the Mekōng in the far north was re-founded by Sên P'u, the grandson of Meng Rai, in 1328 when he made it his capital city, but it is now almost completely deserted and, when I first visited it over twenty years ago, one had to cut one's way through the jungle *inside* the city walls; and the District Officer told me that he had recently fired at a rhinoceros almost at his office door. Fig. 154 gives a good impression of the present state of one of the principal temple sites, though it is only fair to say that the Archaeological Department has in places cleared a great deal of the jungle-growth away. The *stūpa* is more Burmese than Sinhalese in style, as is witnessed by the successive tiers and angular corners, but the Buddha image is post-Suk'ōt'ai and is probably of the late fourteenth or even fifteenth century. I have described this temple and its surroundings in *An Asian Arcady*.[1] It was in Chiengsen, too, that, bursting through some thick bushes, I suddenly came upon a truly remarkable collection, or "Council", of Buddha images both of bronze and stone, headless, armless and legless, lying in their dozens here, there and everywhere. And near by, while digging under the floor of a small sanctuary chapel, I unearthed the only ancient Buddha image cast in silver that I know of (Fig. 155). It is 7 inches high and late in style, and, artistically, of no particular quality, but it is a treasured possession all the same. Fig. 156 shows, on the other hand, a bronze head, 4¼ inches high, of great artistic merit in the early style after the Suk'ōt'ai influence had passed through the north. The treatment of the eyebrows, nose and mouth is most sensitive, and the eyes give the features that half-mournful, half-peaceful unearthly look that expresses all that is best in Buddhism. This is quite a small head, but Fig. 157 shows one of gigantic size, 18 inches high, which is a fine example of the middle period, say in the mid-fifteenth century, before the general debasement began. Both are from my own collection. One of the best examples of the large seated figures of this later style is to be seen in the temple of Sūan Dôk (Flower-Garden) on the outskirts of Chiengmai (Fig. 160), which can be definitely ascribed to the year 1505.

As regards the temples themselves, the north of Siam is so full of beautiful examples that it is quite impossible to do them full justice here. Indeed, the temple architecture of the Tai needs further careful study and, although Döhring has published an interesting work on this subject, his treatment is more descriptive and purely technical than analytical or artistic. For my present purpose I do not

[1] Reginald le May, *An Asian Arcady*, p. 216. Heffer, Cambridge.

think I can do better than illustrate three of the most beautiful out of all those that I visited in the north. The first two of these are at Nān, while the third is at Lampāng Lūang, a hallowed spot of which I have already spoken in a previous chapter. The first (Fig. 158) is quite a small ensemble, but it shows unusually well the type of pillar, pediment, roof-tier, nāga-tip and eaves so characteristic of the Tai style. I forget its name. The second (Fig. 159) is the *stūpa* of the temple of Cha Heng lying outside the city, across the river and padi-fields. It is approached up a slope guarded by two enormous Nāgas, each a hundred yards long, which rear their serpent heads 30 feet high in the air, and is flanked by two magnificent banyan trees, one on either side. When I saw it, the copper casing of the *stūpa* shone like gold, and its slender pinnacle soared majestically to heaven against a background of deep blue. All the earth around was swept and clean, and I breathed an air of indefinable peace. There is also at Nān an interesting temple with four images of Buddha back to back in the interior (Fig. 161) and opposite each image a beautifully carved teak double door. One of these is shown here (Fig. 162), while another is illustrated in *An Asian Arcady*. If these four images are a relic of Brāhmanism, it is the only such instance in the North known to me.

The third is the temple at Lampāng Lūang about ten miles south of Lampāng. The original temple is said to have been built by Chām T'ewi herself, but the present buildings were erected in 1501 in the reign of P'ra Müang Keo of Chiengmai.[1] When I visited them last in 1920 they were being kept in perfect order by the then Chief (Chao) of Lampāng, as will be seen from the illustrations which were taken at the time: but I am told that since his death some years ago they have been allowed to fall into disrepair (Figs. 163, 164 and 165). A more beautiful setting could scarcely be imagined. The giant trees all around speak of its age, and I was reminded at every step of some well-ordered college at Oxford or Cambridge. The buildings themselves are splendid examples of the architecture of the period, especially the massive, solid *stūpa*, the beautiful façade of the *vihāra* which is of wood, the pinnacled entrance gateway gleaming white in the sun, and the long eaves of the roof which come down low and lend an air of mystery to the interior. It will be seen that there are no side-walls to the *vihāra*: this is a feature of many temples in the north of Siam.

The fifteenth century was an age of great devotional activity in Siam, and witnessed another strong influx of Sinhalese Buddhism. In 1423 a body of twenty-five priests from Chiengmai, together with eight from Cambodia, went

[1] G. Cœdès, "Documents", *B.E.F.E.O.* vol. xxv, Pl. I c.

to Ceylon to receive ordination anew, and were there joined by six Môn priests from Burma. They returned in 1425, stopped awhile at Ayudhya, Suk'ōt'ai and Sawank'alōk on their way home, and finally reached Chiengmai again in 1430. Strangely enough, the King of Chiengmai at this time, Sām Făng Ken, was a heretic without faith, who adored demons and spirits, and it is possible that it was this deplorable fact that sent the priests to Ceylon to try and revive the people's waning enthusiasm for the true Faith.[1] They established themselves at the temple of Pā Deng two miles west of Chiengmai, and soon after their return the priests embarked on a mission throughout the north, visiting Lamp'ūn, Lampāng, Chiengrai and even Chiengsen, where they consecrated a monastery at the foot of the hill Chom Kitti.

Thus was founded the sect of Sihala Bhikkus to whom Rattanapanna, the author of the JKM, belonged, and who, by implanting the purest form of Sinhalese Buddhism, gave rise to a great revival of Pāli literature and learning in Siam. In 1442 Sām Făng Ken was deposed by his successor Tilōkarāja (after Meng Rai the most renowned King of Chiengmai), who was his sixth son, and sent to the Shan States where he died a few years later. In this year took place a great ordination of five hundred "sons of family" (i.e. of important families) on the banks of the Me Ping, and the revival of Pāli Buddhism had taken root. In 1452 Tilōkarājā had the hallowed limits for the future ordination of priests consecrated at the temple of Pā Deng, and in 1475 a great council was held at Chiengmai for the revision of the Pāli Scriptures. This revival of Pāli literature produced such works as the *Mangaladīpani* which, together with the *Dhammapadatthakatha*, forms the basis of the religious system in Siam, north and south, and also in Cambodia. Similar events took place in Burma about the same time, according to the Kalyani inscriptions which were engraved in 1476 on stone tablets by order of the King of Pegu.[2]

To complete this brief history of Northern Siam, in 1558 the kingdom of Chiengmai was attacked and conquered by the King of Pegu, and remained, with intermissions, a vassal state of Burma until near the end of the eighteenth century, when the Burmese were finally driven out with the help of the King of Bangkok, to whom Chiengmai then became vassal in turn.

The town of Chiengmai possesses a singular beauty. I was stationed there in 1913, and again in 1915, and completely succumbed to its charms; and, when I visited it afresh in 1927, after twelve years' absence, I found it more enchanting than ever, with its brick-red palace-fort surrounded by a lotus-filled moat dating

[1] G. Cœdès, "Documents", *B.E.F.E.O.* vol. xxv, pp. 32, 104–8. [2] *Ibid.* pp. 32–3.

from about 1350,[1] its shady avenues, its broad flowing river, and its innumerable temples each within its leafy garden, where the tiled roofs and stately *stūpas*, the swept courtyards, the green mango-trees and the heavenly blue sky above all combined to induce a feeling of such peace and happiness as it would be hard to match elsewhere. And then, standing sentinel over all, the forest-clad Doi Sut'ep, rising to a height of 5000 feet at a distance of only a few miles and giving courage to all who "will look unto the hills". I saw it from my bedroom window every morning as I opened my eyes.

Most of the important temples in Chiengmai were built during the fourteenth and fifteenth centuries. The temple of P'ra Sing was founded about 1350 and a crypt added later by King Kilāna (Kü Na) to contain the famous Buddha image of that name. The temple of Sūan Dôk was founded in 1371, and in 1373 the relic of the Buddha brought to Laoland by Sumana was solemnly installed there. The temple of P'rajedi Lūang (The Royal Pagoda) was begun in 1401 but not completed until 1478 by Tilōkarāja. It was to this temple that the latter brought the most famous image of all, the Emerald Buddha (now in the Royal Temple at Bangkok), and built a special resting-place for it in 1481. The origin of the Emerald Buddha is obscure, but what is known of its history and cult has been ably set down by Lingat, who ascribes it to the Chiengsen School of the late fourteenth century.[2] King Mongkut stated in a declaration that the statue was made of jade and concluded from this that the stone had been brought from China. Lingat suggests that it may have been hewn out of a stone found in the Nān region, which has been analysed as a variety of quartz. The legendary chronicles record that the image was "born" in India in Açoka's time, was taken thence to Ceylon and later found its way to Angkor. From there it was brought to Ayudhya and finally to Lampāng and Chiengmai. It is not possible to examine this renowned image at close quarters but, judging from the photograph (Fig. 167), it seems to be clearly of local manufacture and probably belongs, as Lingat suggests, to the second period of the Northern School. It appears to be about 2 feet high. I know well the greenish stone produced in the Nān region and consider Lingat's suggestion a feasible one. Were this the proper place, I could tell an amusing story of the old lady of Nān and the green stone Buddha which she produced for my inspection and admiration, with an eye to its eventual sale.

As a pendant to this survey of Buddhist art and architecture in Northern Siam, it will, I think, interest the reader to see the kind of folk who still uphold the

[1] Cf. Frontispiece to *An Asian Arcady*.

[2] R. Lingat, "Le Culte du Bouddha d'Émeraude", *J.S.S.* vol. XXVII, pt. 1, pp. 9–38.

Buddha, the Law and the Order in that region. Here in this photograph (Fig. 166) you may see for yourself a group of priests, acolytes, and children too young as yet to wear the yellow robe. Remark how their features, both of old and young, recall the Tai type of Buddha features we have been looking at so often—how serious and thoughtful, and yet how calm. But I think I like the Boy-scout best of all.

# Chapter XI

## THE SCHOOLS OF U-T'ONG, LOPBURI (TAI) AND AYUDHYA

WHILE epigraphical evidence is abundant as to the eclipse of the Khmer at the hands of the Tai in the Sawank'alōk region in North-Central Siam in the second half of the thirteenth century, the course of events in the lower valley of the Menam, especially at Lopburi, during this period is not so clearly defined. Pelliot discusses the question—what happened to Lopburi after the Khmer had been driven out by Indraditya?—and seems to arrive at the conclusion that Lo (as the Chinese called Lavō or Lopburi) first of all became a vassal state to Hsien (or Sawank'alōk-Suk'ōt'ai).[1] This would be the more easily acceptable were it not that, in his *stela* of A.D. 1292 recounting the extent of his dominions, Rām K'amheng, although he includes Nakōn Sawan, Supanburi, Rājaburi, and Petchaburi, expressly omits all mention of Lopburi; and, seeing that Lopburi was the centre of Khmer sovereignty in Siam, it seems hardly possible to account for such an omission if he had actually absorbed it as well.[2]

Wood remarks: "It must not be assumed that King Rām K'amheng exercised effective control over all these regions [i.e. those mentioned in the above *stela*]. For instance, the Prince of Supan had by this time already attained to a powerful position, and the Tai rulers of Lopburi and the ancient city of Ayodhia (both related to King Rām K'amheng) were either independent or subject to the King of Cambodia".[3] And again: "In Siam itself, moreover, a rival power [i.e. rival to Suk'ōt'ai] had sprung up which was destined to obtain, in time, dominion over the whole kingdom. This was the Principality of Suwanp'umi [i.e. Supanburi] or Ut'ong, ruled over by an energetic Prince who was descended from the Chiengsen Princes and was probably a distant relative of King Mengrai. Before the end of King Loet'ai's reign [King of Suk'ōt'ai, *c.* 1317–47], the Prince of Ut'ong had annexed a large portion of the dominions of the Suk'ōt'ai Kingdom. Parts of the Cambodian Empire, moreover, which had never been conquered,

[1] P. Pelliot, "Deux Itinéraires de Chine en Inde", *B.E.F.E.O.* vol. IV, pp. 253–6.

[2] G. Cœdès, *Recueil des Inscriptions du Siam*, Part I (1924), pp. 57–8 (Siamese), and pp. 42, 48 (French).

[3] W. A. R. Wood, *A History of Siam*, p. 53.

even by King Rām K'amheng, were annexed by the Prince of Ut'ong, including Lopburi, the old city of Ayodhya and Chantabun."[1]

Wood cites no references or authorities for his statements that there were at this time *Tai* rulers of Lopburi and old Ayudhya, or that the Prince of U-T'ong had annexed these cities by the middle of the fourteenth century. But it seems reasonable to suppose, from subsequent events, that there were large settlements of Tai in the south who were gradually gathering power and who would not be slow to take advantage of the revolution successfully carried out by Indraditya in the north. Unfortunately no Tai or Khmer inscriptions have yet been discovered dealing with this eventful period of Siamese history.

The Prince of U-T'ong, to whom Wood refers, is well known to history as Rāma T'ibodi I, who set up the capital of Siam at Ayudhya in 1350 near the site of the old city of Dvāravatī and thus established the Ayudhyan Dynasty of Tai Kings of Siam which endured until the sack of the city by the Burmese and the downfall of the kingdom in 1767. The city of U-T'ong, the ruins of which lie to the west of the modern city of Supanburi, is of very ancient date, judging from the fragments of sculpture discovered there which resemble those of Dvāravatī, but hitherto it has not been scientifically excavated. The reason for its final abandonment in favour of Ayudhya is said to have been a serious epidemic, but of what disease is not known.

Prince Damrong has been at some pains to discuss the origins of this Prince of U-T'ong and to try and extract the probable truth from the many legends in which his history is wrapped. As a result, he believes that a Tai descendant of King Brahma of Chiengsen named Jaya Çiri, fleeing from the Peguans who had attacked his kingdom in the far north about the year 1188, came southwards and established himself in the region of P'rapatom. This ruler eventually extended his kingdom to Supanburi (or U-T'ong) which is close at hand and became the founder of the Prince of U-T'ong's line. As for the Prince of U-T'ong himself, he is thought to have been the son-in-law of his predecessor and not of royal birth himself. The name, U-T'ong, is popularly supposed to denote "a golden cradle" because the prince was given a cradle of gold by his father, but Prince Damrong is much more likely to be right in his opinion that U-T'ong is simply the Siamese equivalent of *Suvarnabhūmi* (Supan) which in Pāli means the "land" or "source" of gold.[2] If these conclusions are correct, then one must assume that during the

[1] W. A. R. Wood, *A History of Siam*, p. 58.

[2] H.R.H. Prince Damrong Rajanubhab, "History of Siam prior to the Ayudhya period", *J.S.S.* vol. XIII, pt. 2, pp. 35–40.

Khmer rule in South-Central Siam Tai chiefs were allowed to spring up, who held their principalities in fief to the King of Cambodia at Angkor and that, when the Khmer were driven from Sawank'alōk, the latter soon lost their control over Lopburi as well. But they had been masters there for two and a half centuries and the influence of their culture and race is clearly seen in the sculpture of the transition period which has been classed by Cœdès under the style of "School of U-T'ong". His reasons for adopting this name are given in his own words:

> This name of U-T'ong has been chosen to designate the period to which certain images appear to belong which show a strong Khmer influence allied with various features of a true Siamese art. The greater number of images of this type so far found come from Ayudhya and Lopburi, but they have also been found at Supanburi and as far north as Muang San,[1] in short, throughout the territory which formed the nucleus of the Kingdom of Ayudhya. If one were sure that these images were all *posterior* to the foundation of this Kingdom in 1350, they might be naturally classed under the title 'School of Ayudhya, early style'. But it is quite possible that those which came from Supanburi and its neighbourhood are *anterior* to the foundation of Ayudhya, and it seemed that the name of U-T'ong, corresponding to the name of the capital of the principality which was the cradle of the realm of Ayudhya, would be a suitable one for this mixed or transition style which doubtless reflected the political vicissitudes of the country.[2]

In the absence of inscribed and dated images it is difficult to come to a definite conclusion as to when this transition period of sculpture between Khmer and Tai began in the south, but I have been at some trouble to bring together a considerable number of examples of the period, and these show such an extraordinary variety of features, ranging from almost pure Khmer to entirely pure Tai, that I feel the transition must have occupied a long interval of time, and I should not be surprised if it were eventually shown to have had its beginnings early in the thirteenth, or even in the twelfth century.

Cœdès says that "of the features of the 'School of Lopburi' the sculpture of U-T'ong preserved the form of the face, the band enclosing the hair on the forehead and the male appearance of the torso. One may even perhaps find a far-removed trace of the style of Dvāravatī in the treatment of the arcading of the eyebrows and the lines of the mouth, but on the other hand the use of the flame-pointed *uṣṇīsa* shows that the influence of Ceylon had already arrived, probably during the period of annexation to the realm of Suk'ōt'ai."[3]

[1] I cannot trace Muang San on the map, but it probably lies between Supanburi and Chaināt to the north. U-T'ong images can also be seen now in temples at new Suk'ōt'ai (T'ani).

[2] G. Cœdès, "Le Musée National de Bangkok", *Ars Asiatica*, vol. XII, p. 34. Paris, 1928. Author's translation.

[3] *Ibid*. p. 34.

Cœdès then develops his views by dividing the sculpture of U-T'ong into two principal groups. The first is represented by a type of image whose elongated oval face is analogous to the style of Suk'ōt'ai: this type becomes the direct ancestor of the modern statuary of the School of Ayudhya. The second type shows, on the other hand, a reaction against the style of Suk'ōt'ai and exaggerates, sometimes in rather a clumsy fashion, the chief Khmer characteristics. He adds: "It would seem as if these images were the work of Siamese artists who have tried to copy the Khmer and who, fearing to fall into the style of Suk'ōt'ai, have exceeded all reasonable bounds in their imitation of the Khmer style. The face is even shorter than the Khmer, the projecting chin is marked by a dimple, and the shin-bones are marked by a sharp outline."[1] (Fig. 168.) This image, which is life-size, is now in Wat Benchamabopit in Bangkok, where Prince Damrong has rendered a notable service in assembling such a fine collection of Buddha images. A similar statue, made in Chiengmai in 1483 to resemble a Khmer image, still bears to-day the name of "P'rachao Keng Kom" or "the Buddha with the sharp[-edged] legs".

Dupont also divides the sculpture of U-T'ong into two groups but regards the question from rather a different angle. According to him the first group is a normal derivative of Khmer art and especially of the Bayon style. The face is broad, the expression soft, and certain details are repeated such as the band describing a curve on the forehead, and the divided chin. The second group, on the other hand, has obvious affinities with the Tai schools of art. The face is thinner, and the expression is more "nuancée"; of Khmer influence there only remains the band on the forehead. Dupont finds it difficult to establish priority between these groups and rather pertinently asks—At what stage of development of the Tai schools have we arrived when the art of U-T'ong appears?[2]

Of the two classifications Dupont's appears to me to be the more satisfactory if regarded in a broad sense. For my own part I feel that, taken as a whole, the School of U-T'ong represents a normal development from the Khmer to the Tai throughout Lower-Central Siam, and that, before a true Tai type was evolved, Tai or Tai-Khmer sculptors were giving such a free rein to their individual tastes and fancies in the delineation of the features such as never occurred before or since in the country. As the Bayon style of Khmer art is now attributed to the end of the twelfth century, it would naturally play an important part in influencing the work of the Tai artists; yet I do not think the latter were bound by any one

[1] G. Cœdès, "Le Musée National de Bangkok", *Ars Asiatica*, vol. XII, p. 35. Paris, 1928.

[2] P. Dupont, *Catalogue des Collections Indo-Chinoises du Musée Guimet*, p. 57. Paris, 1934.

style, but that they fashioned their images in their own localities entirely independent of one another, until the School of Suk'ōt'ai had had time to penetrate this region and cast its all-pervading influence over them.

For the actual type of image produced in this period two figures will suffice. Fig. 169 shows a large image in stone in a temple on the hill of T'ammamūn in the Supanburi district, which is almost identical with the bronze image shown in Fig. 168. It is undoubtedly Tai-Khmer in style, but is probably late in date as the *uṣṇīṣa* carries the flame-top derived from Suk'ōt'ai. Prince Damrong calls the bronze image (Fig. 168) "Ayudhya period, early style", which he confines within the period A.D. 1350–1490.[1] In this case both images would represent examples of Cœdès' first type, in which he considers that the Tai were consciously imitating the Khmer, rather than natural derivatives from the true Khmer image. Fig. 170, on the other hand, shows a bronze image, 20 inches high, which is a good representative example of the transition from Khmer to Tai. The band confining the hair on the forehead, the broad mouth, the arcading of the eyebrows and the shape of the face all bespeak the influence of the earlier periods, but the treatment of the hair (in tiny round knobs), of the torso, and of the legs, has now become wholly Tai. The set of the arms and hands, however, is still as seen in small Khmer bronze figures from Siam (cf. Fig. 87). The flame-top is missing in this image.

Stone images of this period are comparatively rare and the sculptors, being Tai, modelled mostly in bronze. A noticeable feature is the quality of the bronze composition, possibly due to the presence of gold, which has a smooth texture and nearly always takes on a beautiful patina, thereby giving a most pleasing effect from a purely artistic point of view.

So much for the characteristic types of image of the U-T'ong period. What I propose to do now is to put before the reader a series of heads which will show how great a diversity of face-types appears at this time, and at the same time illustrate the change from features which some might consider purely Khmer to those which are entirely Tai in feeling and which, as Cœdès says, form the parent stock from which the national school of Ayudhya was derived. Gradually we leave the realm of concrete personalities and enter that of abstract idealism which governed the Tai so strongly in their representation of the Buddha during their early formative years. How long this period of transition lasted cannot be definitely stated. Dupont thinks that it may have lasted until the fifteenth century,[2] and this may

[1] H.R.H. Prince Damrong Rajanubhab, *History of Buddhist Stupas in Siam* (in Siamese), p. 114. Bangkok, 1926.

[2] P. Dupont, *Catalogue des Collections Indo-Chinoises du Musée Guimet*, p. 57. Paris, 1934.

well be true, even if we exclude the conscious imitations referred to by Prince Damrong and Cœdès.

Fig. 171 shows a head, 4½ inches high, which approximates most nearly to the true Khmer type. The rectangular face, the almost straight forehead, the long, thick-lipped mouth, and the *uṣṇīṣa* without a flame-top are pure Khmer. But the nose, the eyebrows and the treatment of the hair indicate a new influence which has crept in and add a touch of feeling which is Tai. There is no dimple in the chin. The modelling is excellent; there is a poise and a dignity in the head, and a strength in the features which betoken an originality of conception far removed from any conventionalised form. I feel certain that this head must ante-date any influence from Suk'ōt'ai, and that it is *anterior* to Ayudhya.

Fig. 172, 4½ inches high, appears to be also of this same period. The face is square, the forehead is straight, the mouth is long, and the *uṣṇīṣa* still lacks the flame-top. But the Tai feeling is growing, and the features are losing that strength and ruthlessness which are characteristic of the Khmer. There is a small dimple in the chin. This type persists among the Siamese of to-day.

In Fig. 173, 4½ inches high, the features are still close to the Khmer. But the flame-top now appears and the Tai feeling which pervades the face betrays the influence from Suk'ōt'ai. Fig. 174, 9 inches high, however, though some of the details such as the flame-top and the treatment of the hair are wholly Tai, shows a much stronger resemblance to the Khmer type in spirit. The square face and jaw and the long mouth curling up at the ends lead one to the belief that the artist must have been strongly imbued with Khmer feeling. The modelling is superb, and I consider this head a great work of art. A well-known art critic has declared it to be as fine a work of art as ever came out of Egypt. Could praise be higher?

Fig. 175, 6 inches high, which I think has lost its flame-top, shows a most original type of countenance. The face, though still rectangular, has become much longer, and the mouth, though it still has a thick lower lip, is shorter. The most noticeable feature about it is the distance between the nose and the upper lip. This is perhaps exaggerated, but the type is a true Tai-Khmer one and still persists among the Siamese of to-day: it is in fact a portrait. The bronze in this figure is of a particularly smooth and beautiful texture.

Fig. 176, 5 inches high, depicts another original type, in which the features are very deeply cut. Here the face is more ovoid in shape, and the eyebrows form almost a straight line across the brow. The open, thick lips are remarkable and, were it not for these, the face might almost be a European one. I have not met another example of the U-T'ong period resembling this in any way.

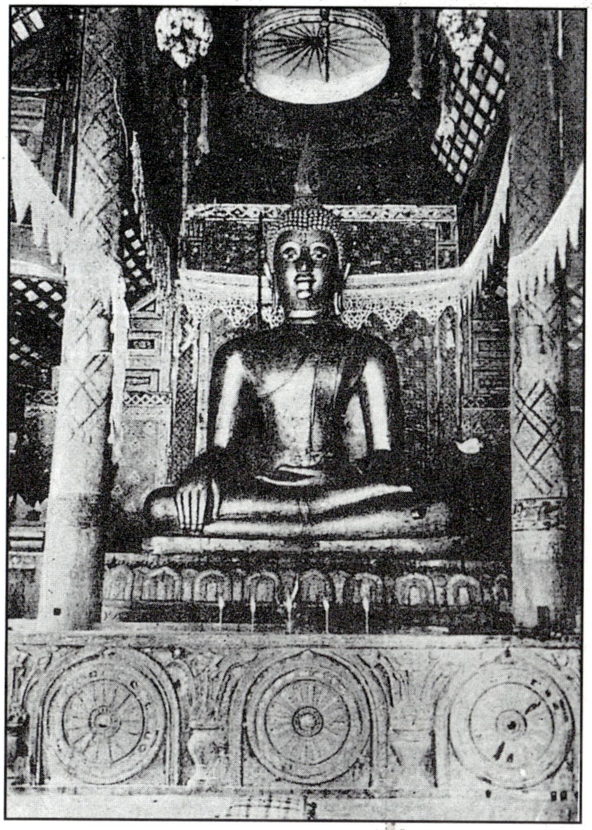

160. Bronze Buddha. Tai (Chiengsen) type. In Temple at Chiengmai.

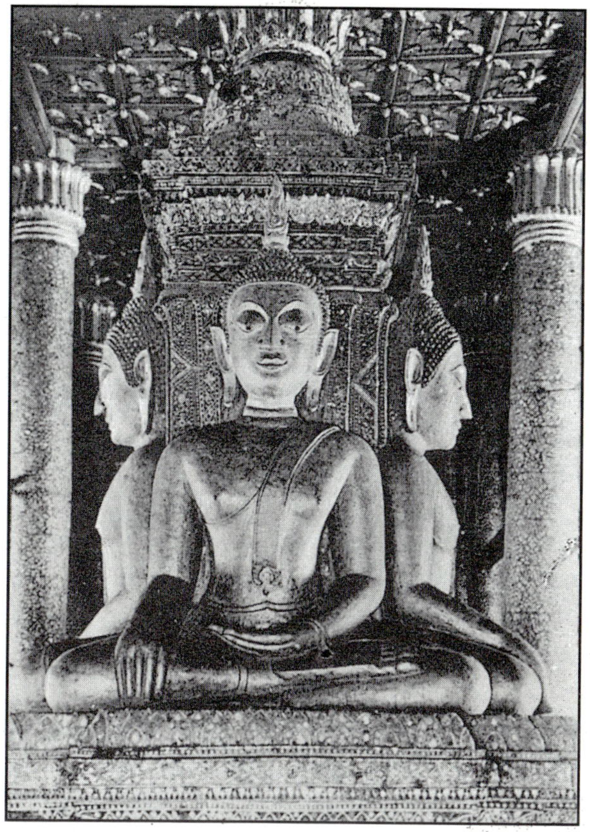

161. Four Images of Buddha, back to back, Tai type. In Temple at Nān.

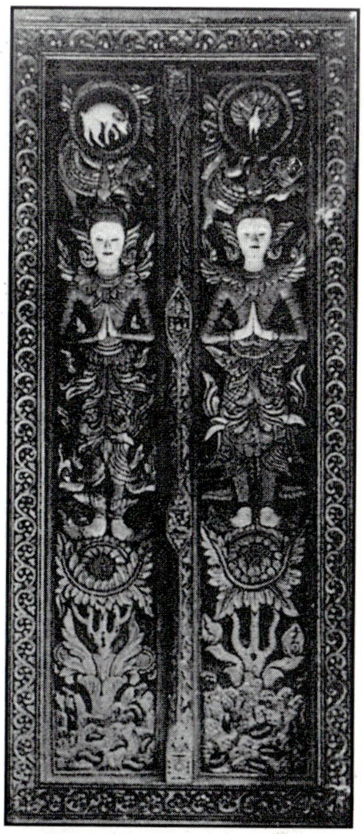

162. Carved Teak Door facing one of four images of Buddha (of Fig. 161).

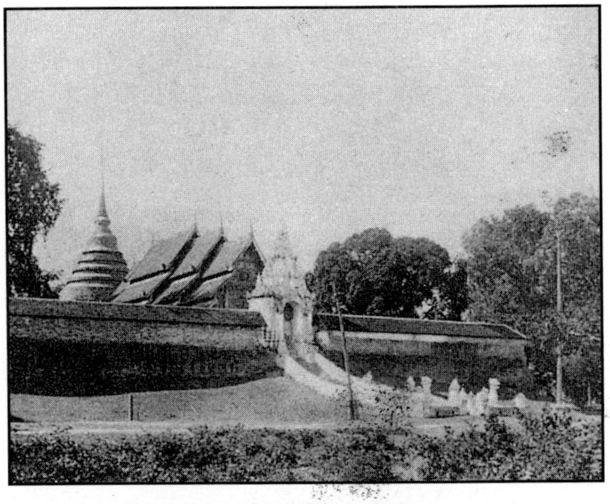

163. Tai Temple at Lampāng Lūang.

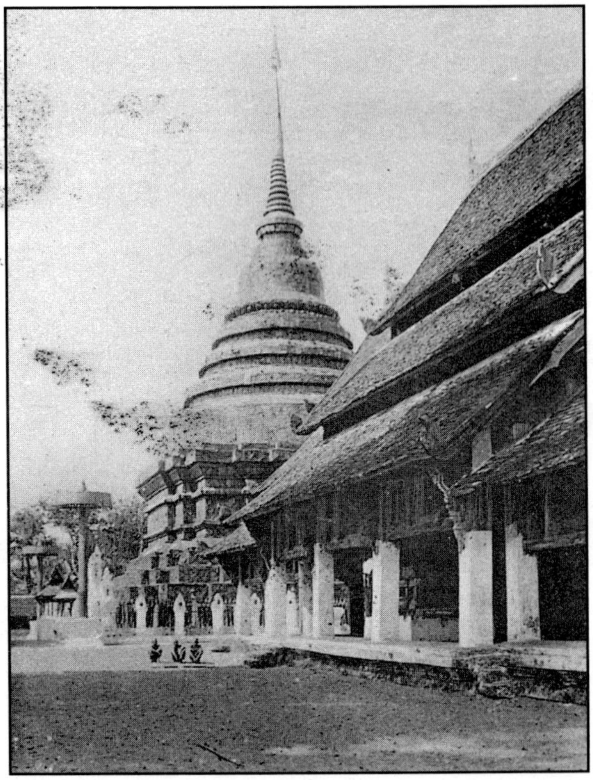

165. The *Stūpa* at Lampāng Lūang, behind the *Vihāra.*

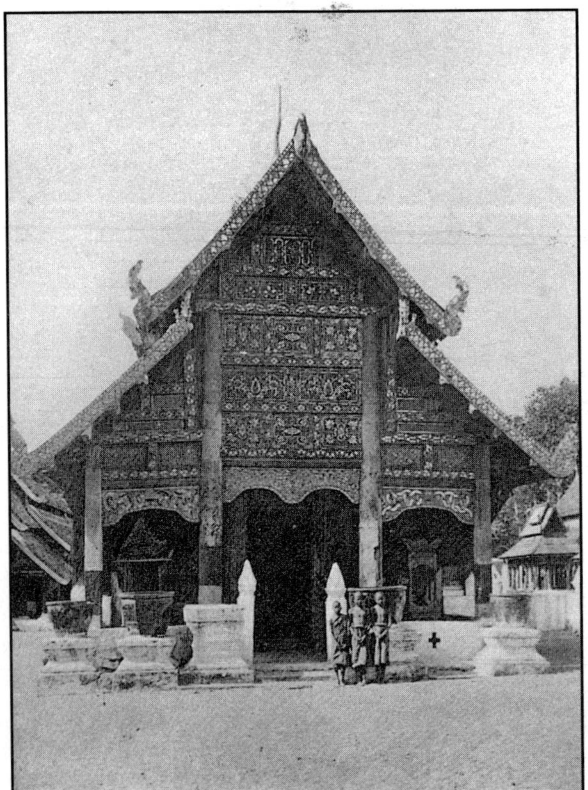

164. The *Vihāra* at Lampāng Lūang. Front View.

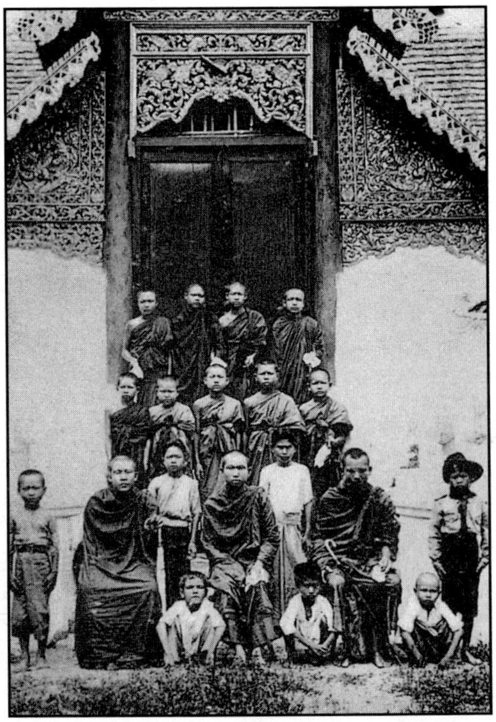

166. Group of Buddhist Priests and Acolytes in Northern Siam.

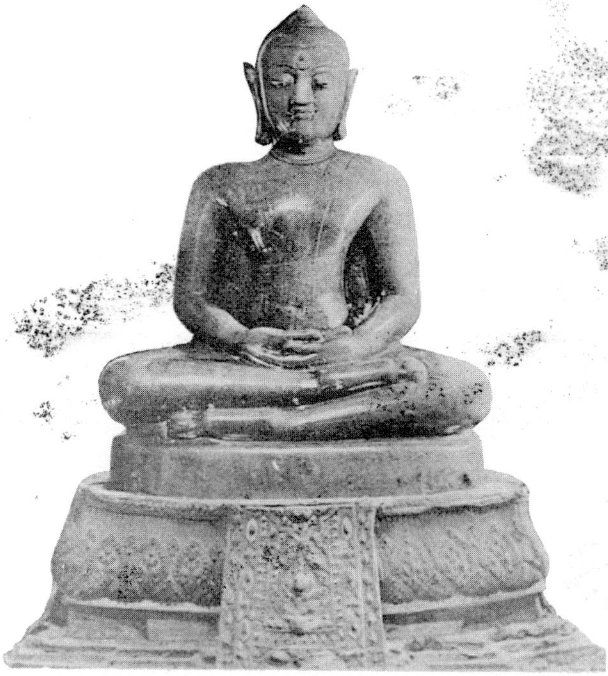

167. The "Emerald" Buddha in the Royal Temple at Bangkok. Tai (Chiengsen) type.

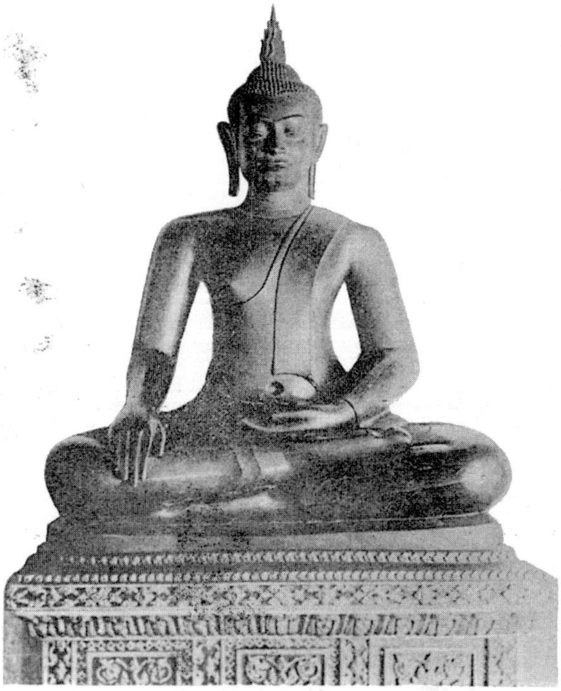

168. Bronze Buddha. Tai (early Ayudhya) type. Temple of Benchamabopit, Bangkok.

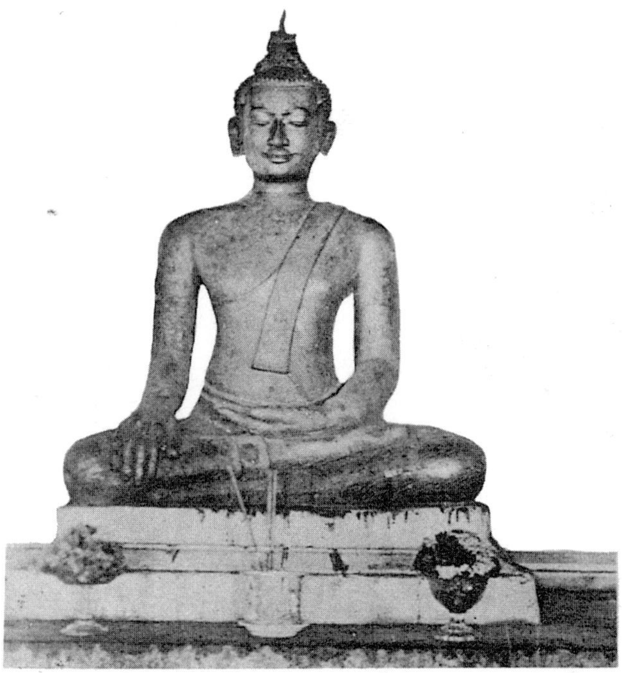

169. Stone Buddha. Tai (early Ayudhya) type. Temple in Supanburi district.

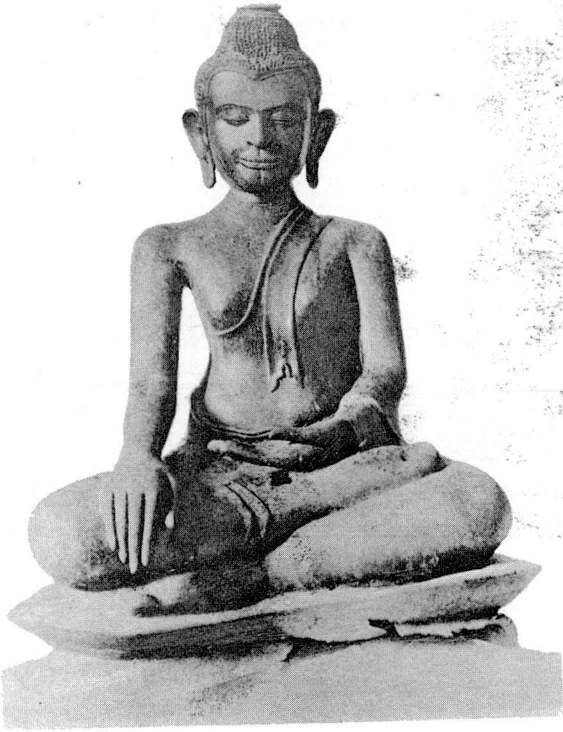

170. Bronze Buddha. Tai (U-T'ong) type.

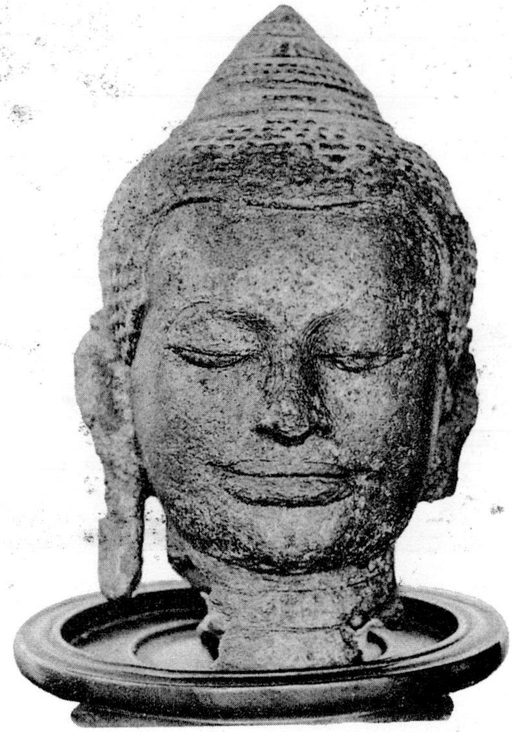

171. Bronze Head of Buddha. Khmer-Tai. First U-T'ong type.

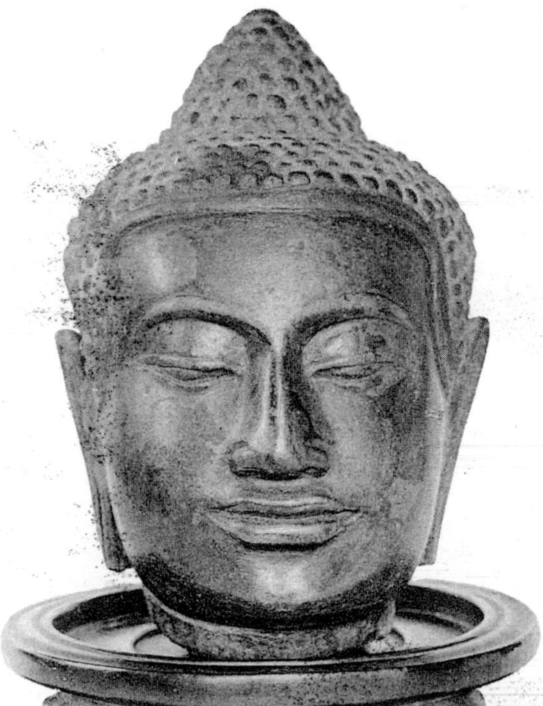

172. Bronze Head of Buddha. Khmer-Tai. First U-T'ong type.

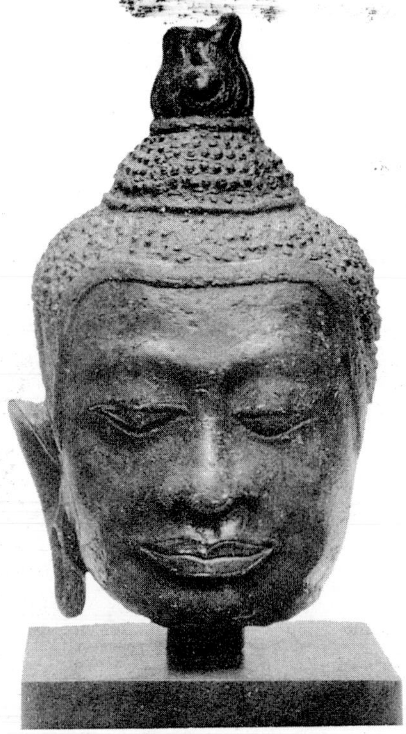

173. Bronze Head of Buddha. Khmer-Tai, with Flame-top. Second U-T'ong type.

186. Sandstone Head of Buddha. Tai (Lopburi) type, showing Khmer influence.

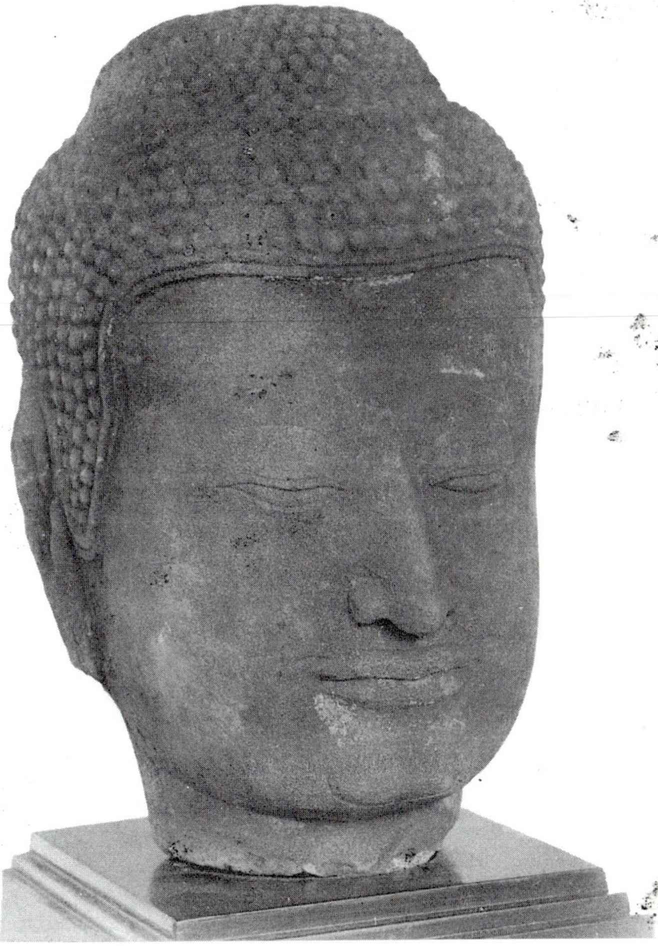

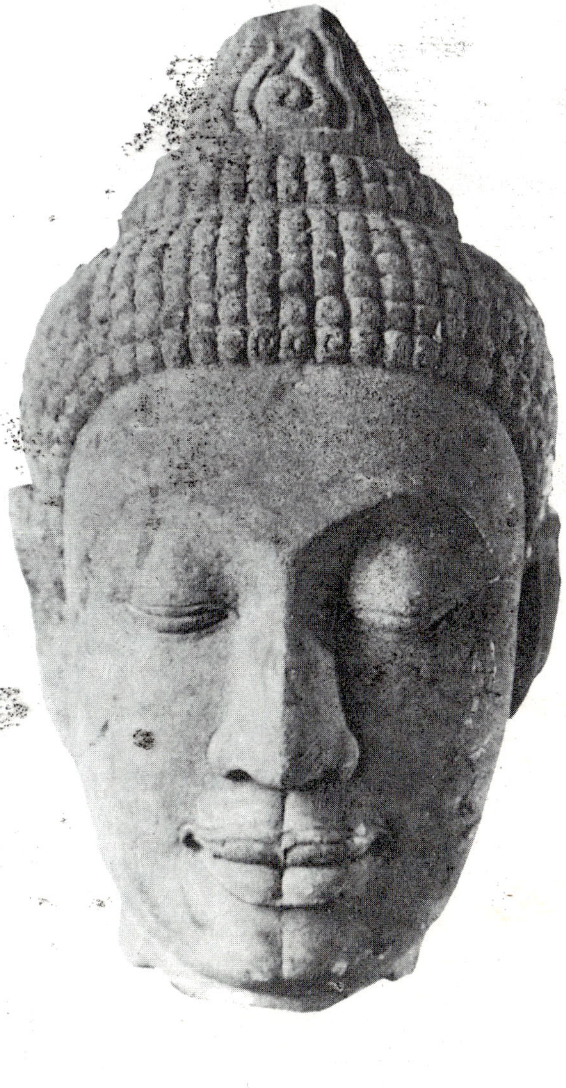

187. Sandstone Head of Buddha. Tai (Lopburi) type, showing Suk'ōt'ai influence.

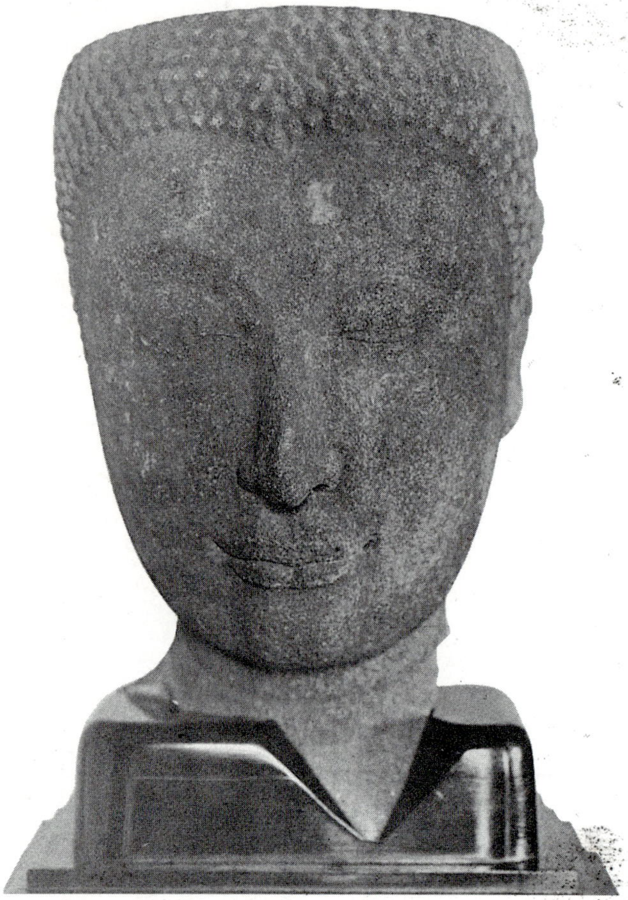

188. Sandstone Head of Buddha. Tai (Lopburi) type. Later style.

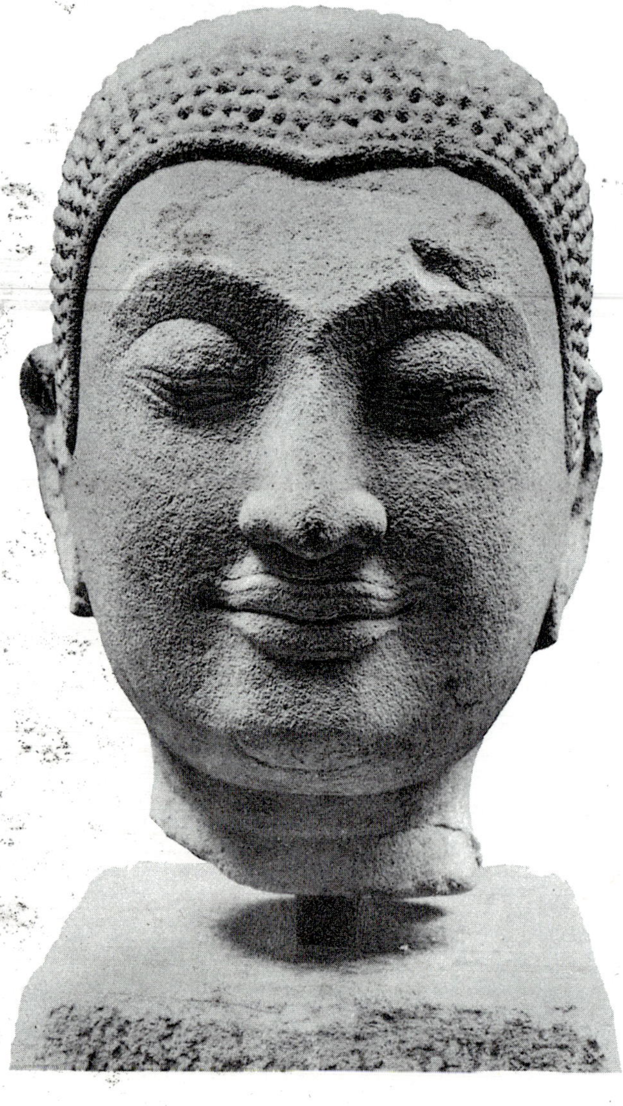

189. Sandstone Head of Buddha. Tai (Lopburi) type. Final style.

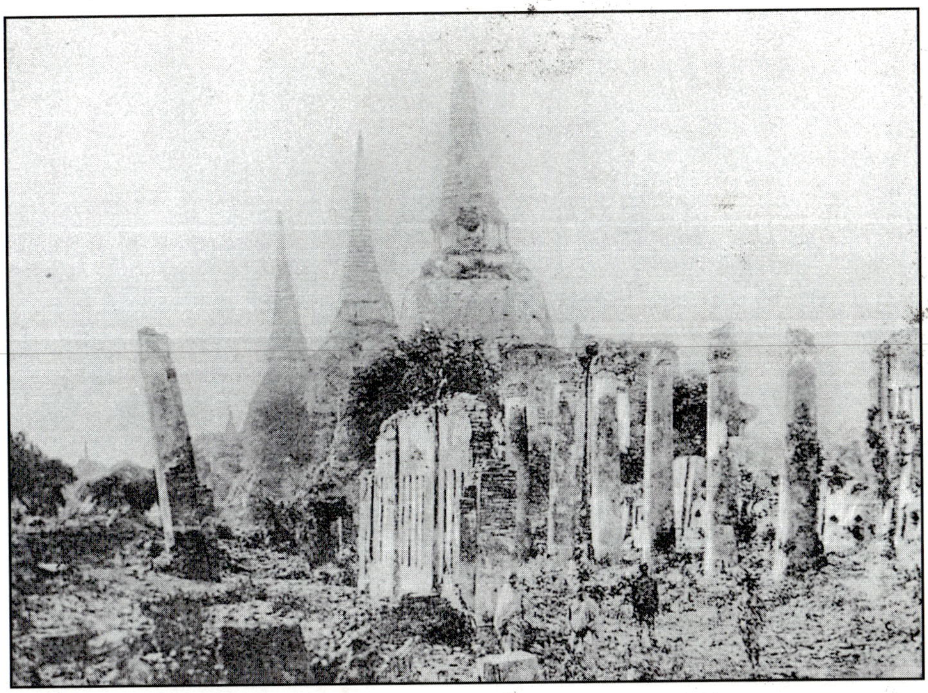

190. Ruins of Temple of Çrī Sarap'et at Ayudhya.

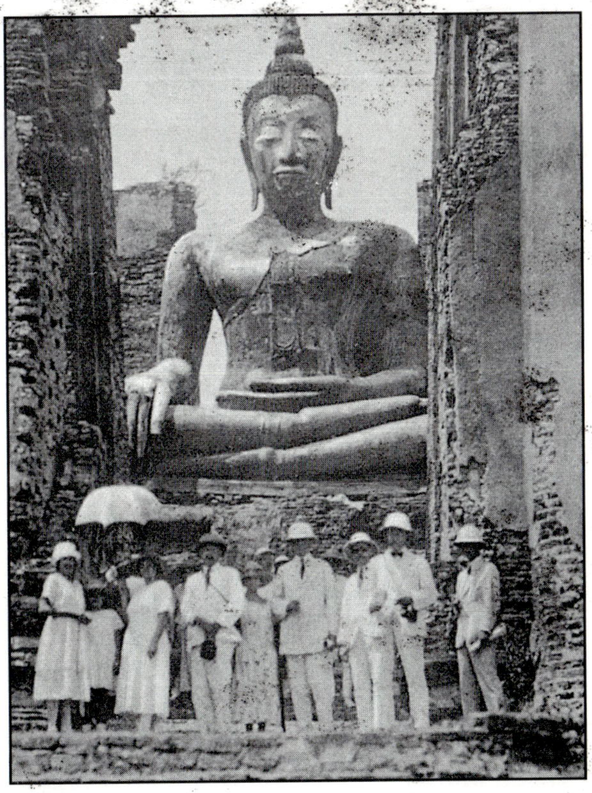

191. Great Bronze Buddha. Tai (Ayudhya) type.
Near Temple of Çrī Sarap'et, Ayudhya.

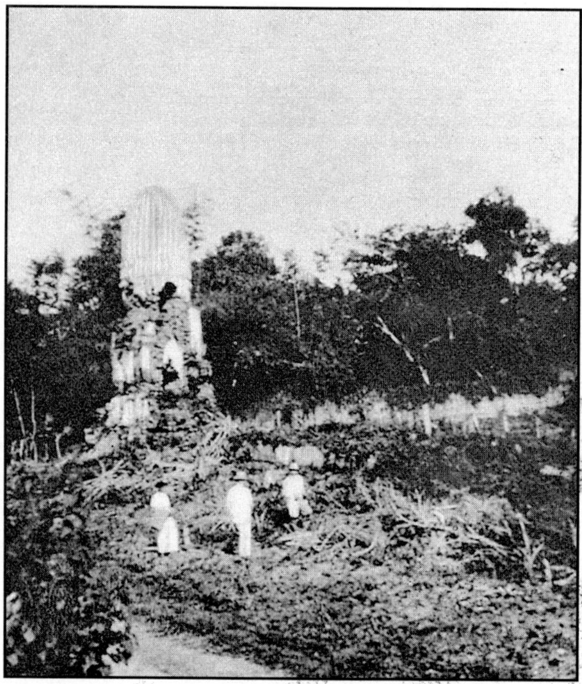

192. Ruined Brick and Stucco *Stūpa.* Tai (Ayudhya) type, at Lopburi.

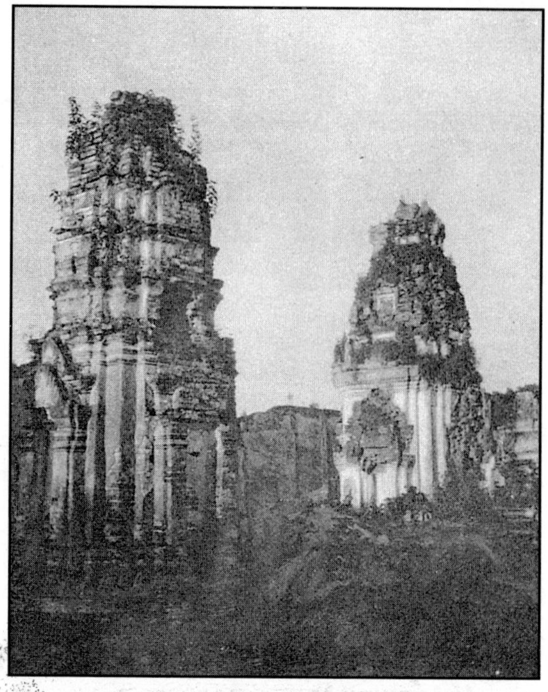

193. Ruined Brick and Stucco *Stūpas.* Tai (imitation Khmer) type, at Lopburi.

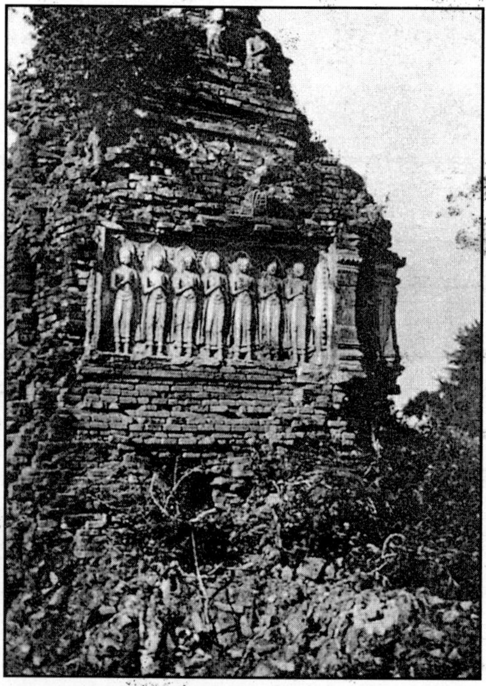

194. Row of Disciples in Stucco. Tai (Ayudhya) type, at Lopburi.

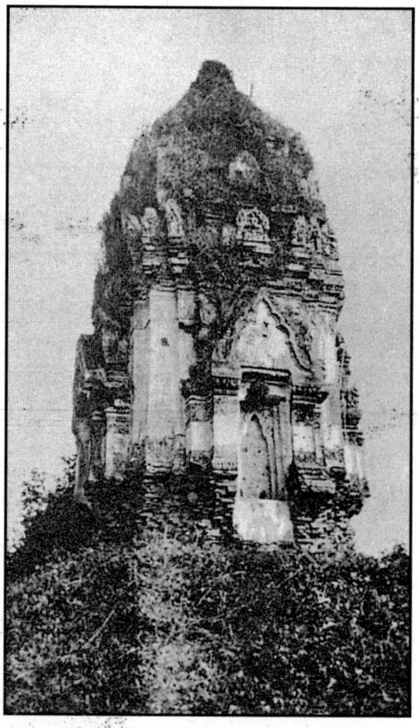

195. Ruined *Stūpa.* Tai (imitation Khmer) type, at Lopburi.

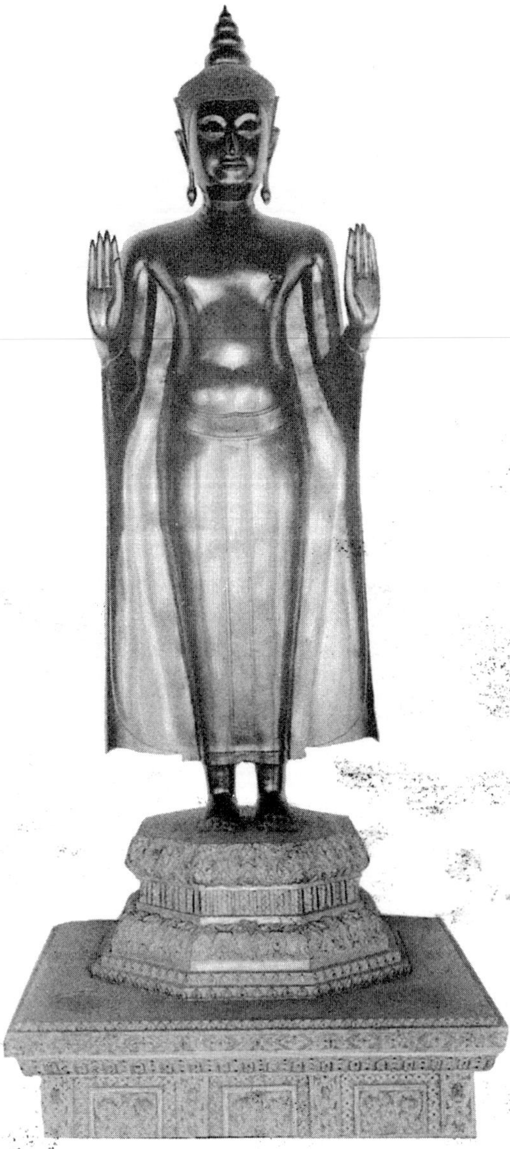

196. Bronze Buddha, standing. Tai (Ayudhya) type. Temple of Benchamabopit, Bangkok.

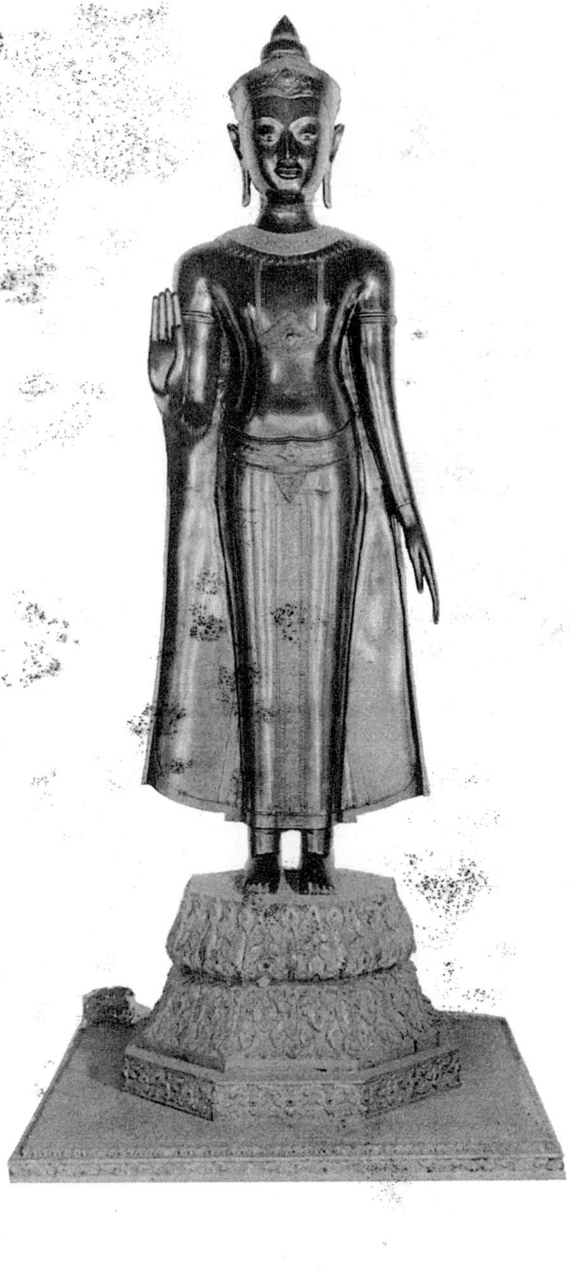

197. Bronze Buddha, standing. Tai (Ayudhya) type. Temple of Benchamabopit, Bangkok.

199. Gilt-bronze Head of Buddha. Tai (Ayudhya) type.

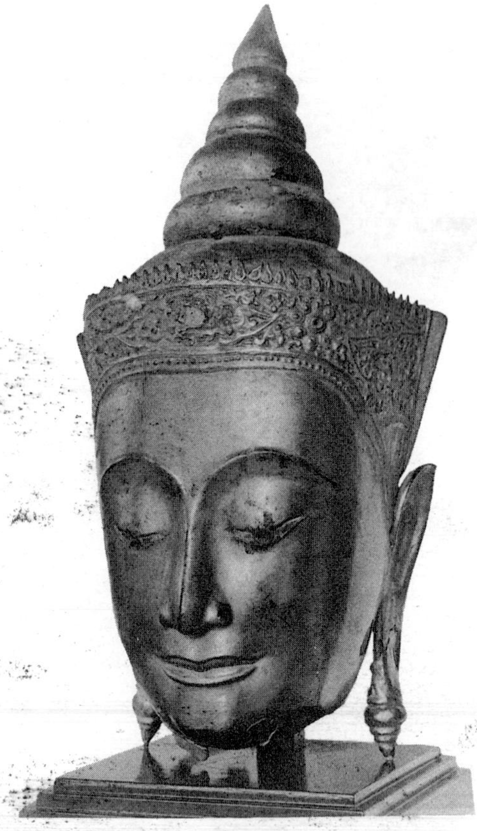

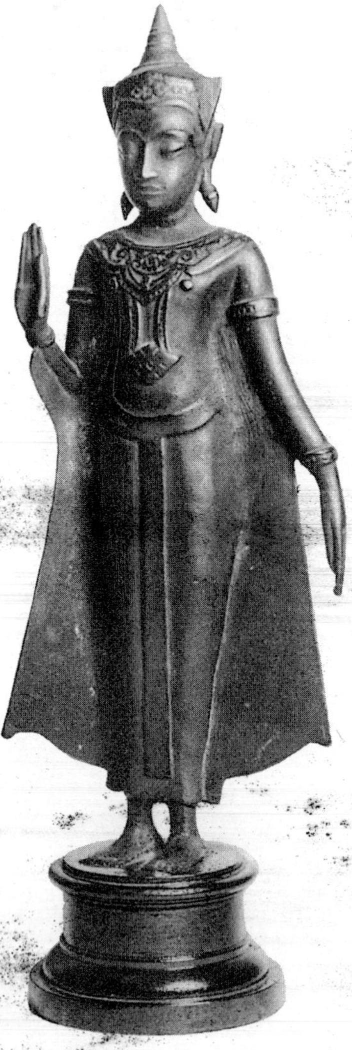

198. Bronze Buddha, standing. Tai (Ayudhya) type.

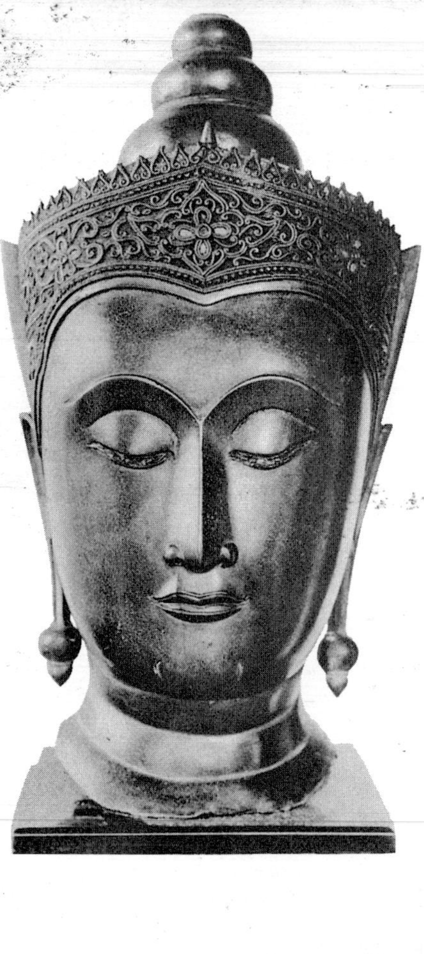

200. Bronze Head of Buddha. Tai (Ayudhya) type.

201. Bronze Head of Buddha. Tai (Ayudhya) later type.

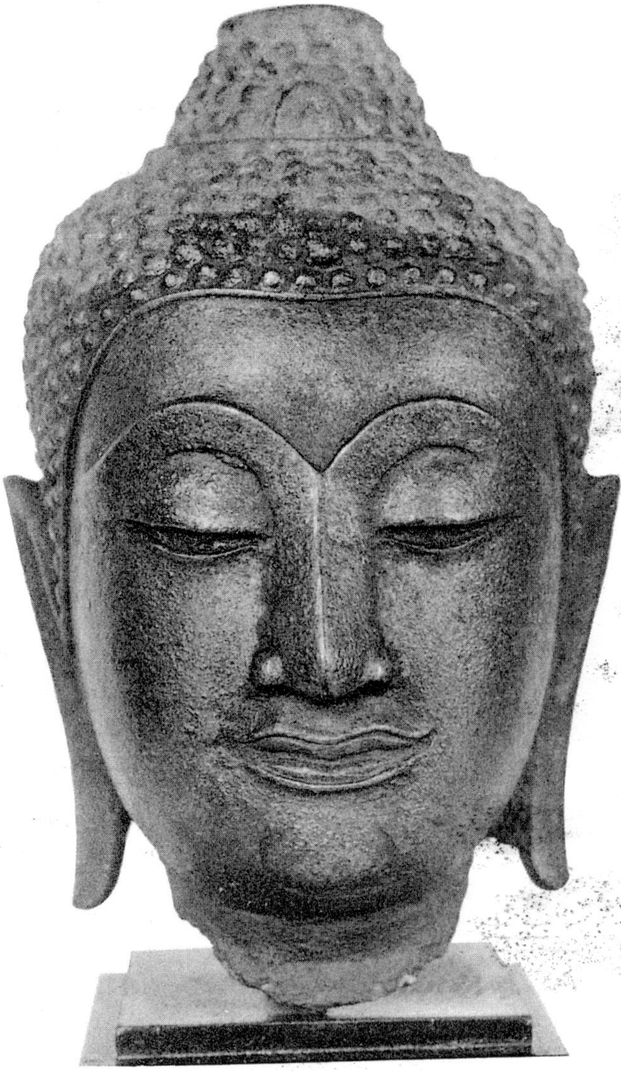

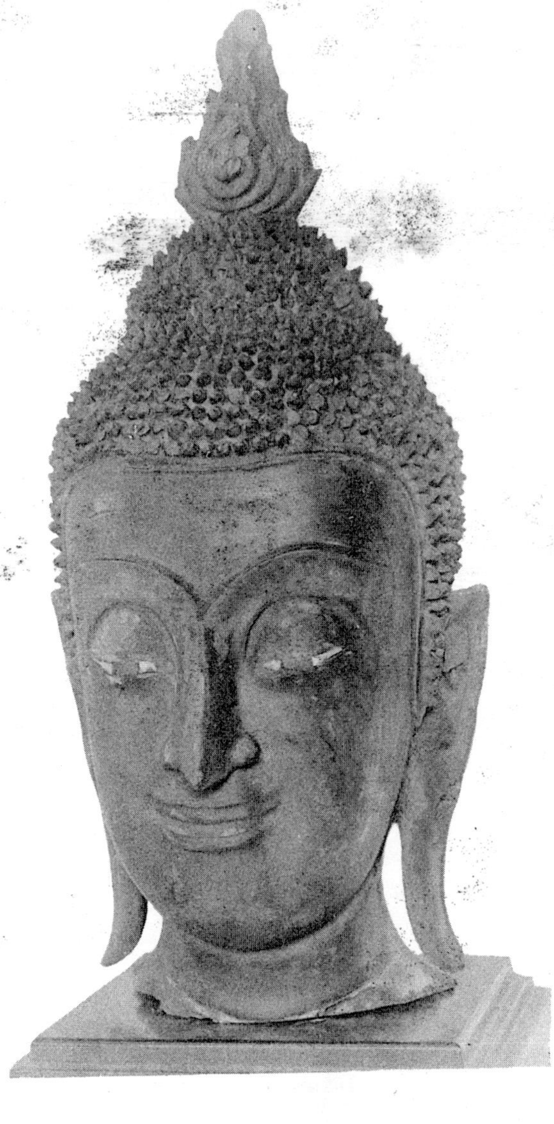

202. Wooden Head of Buddha (lacquered). Tai (late Ayudhya) type.

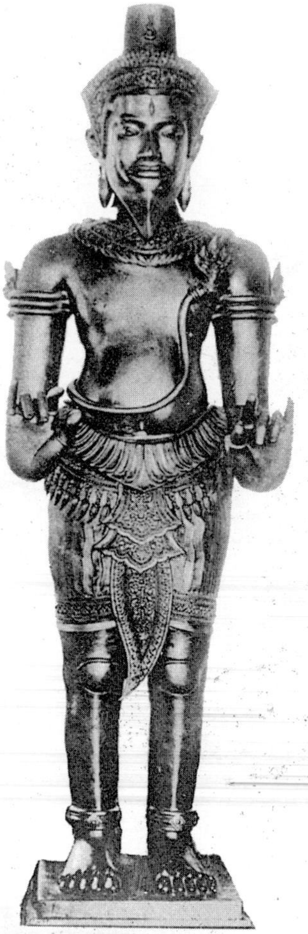

203. Bronze Çiva, standing. Tai (Ayudhya) type.

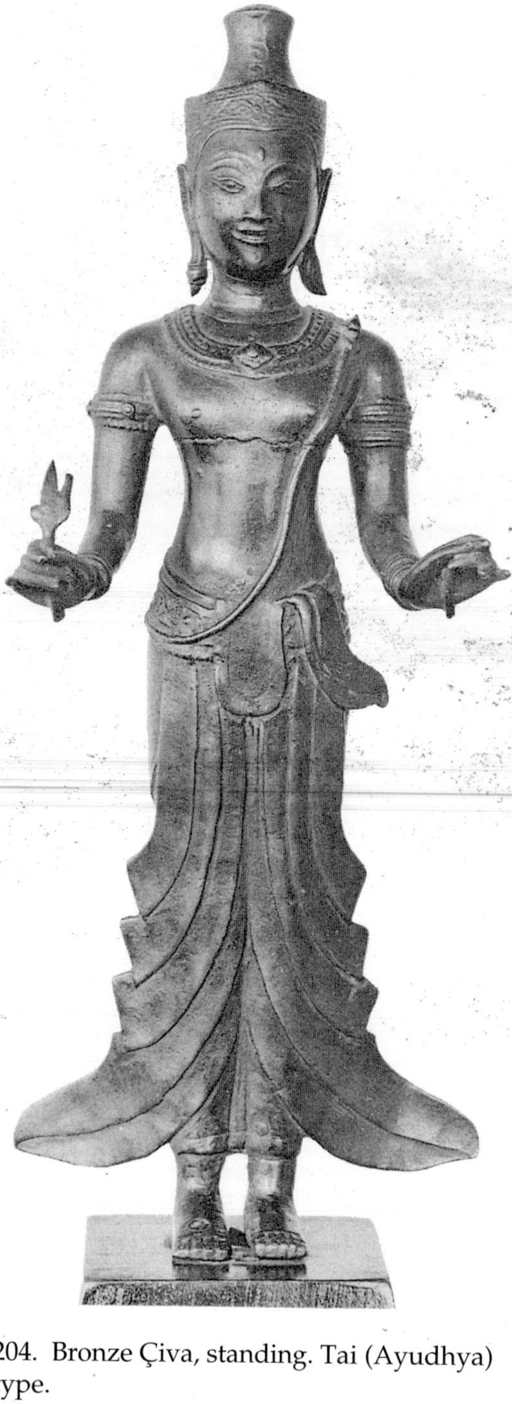

204. Bronze Çiva, standing. Tai (Ayudhya) type.

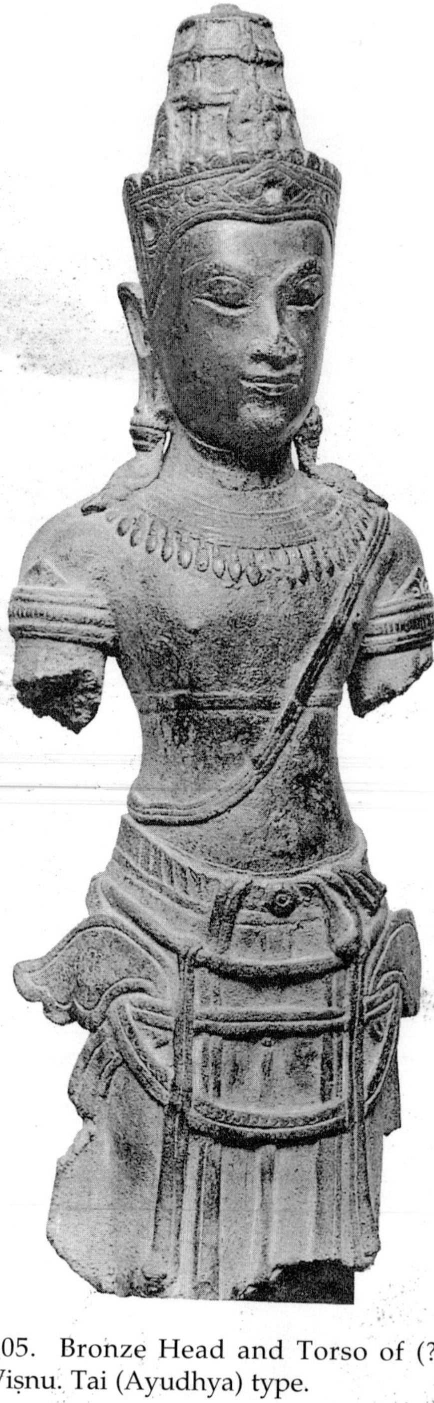

205. Bronze Head and Torso of (?) Viṣnu. Tai (Ayudhya) type.

Fig. 177, 7 inches high, is a fine piece of modelling and has a very original flame-top, while Fig. 178, $5\frac{1}{2}$ inches high, shows a most sensitive response to the artist's feeling. In both one sees clearly how the Tai element is growing stronger as the Khmer influence weakens.

Fig. 179, 8 inches high, is a gilded bronze head which has taken on a beautiful red and green patina, where the gilt has worn off. Its sharply cut outline still shows its affinity with its Khmer ancestry, but all the same it is the work of a Tai artist. The delicate nose, the firm mouth and chin, the noble forehead, the half-closed eyes, and the poise of the head all combine to produce a form full of intense feeling, at once regal and yet meditative, mystic and serene.

Fig. 180, 5 inches high, shows a form which is creeping one stage nearer to the true Tai type. The face is now becoming oval, the mouth is growing smaller, the forehead is lower and the nose has the nostrils clearly indicated. All that remains of the Khmer is the band across the forehead and the lightly indicated eyebrows. Portraiture and independence of outlook are disappearing, and symbolism is beginning to emerge.

In Fig. 181, $8\frac{1}{2}$ inches high, the process is carried one stage further. Here the band takes an inward curve on the forehead and the eyebrows, now arched, are sharply marked with incised lines. Finally, in Fig. 182, 5 inches high, the transition is complete, and we have arrived at the point when it may be said that the Khmer influence has disappeared entirely and that the form portrays a true Tai ideal. This is undoubtedly the parent of the national School of Ayudhya and, though one cannot say for certain how long this particular type persisted, it is quite possible that it was still being produced in Lower-Central Siam up to 1450.

Before we leave the U-T'ong School, I would like to show two more heads which come from the Lopburi-Supanburi region and which, I feel, deserve a place here.

Fig. 183, $11\frac{1}{4}$ inches high, is obviously related to the two preceding figures, but still has a character all its own. It shows the idealistic spirit underlying the Tai conception of the Buddha more, perhaps, than any other image that I know. This gentle, beautiful, sorrowful face is fully cognisant of the sufferings of this world, and there is a quality of expression about the eyes which it is impossible to describe.

Fig. 184, $4\frac{1}{2}$ inches high, must also be classed with the School of U-T'ong but is frankly nothing short of a "freak". The slanting slits of eyes, which are so close together, give a strange cast to the features and one cannot help thinking that the sculptor had some particular face in his mind; but the modelling is so good that I have thought it worthy of reproduction.

Finally, I must include a walking figure of the Buddha of singular charm in the *Abhaya-mudrā* (Dispelling Fear), 11 inches high, which I cannot attribute to any other school than that of U-T'ong (Fig. 185). In South-Central Siam this type of figure is extremely rare, but the form of the *uṣṇīṣa*, the girdle round the waist and the fold of cloth falling from the centre are obvious links with Khmer statuary, though the features are entirely Tai. The robe hangs closely to the body as if it were wet, and such images are known in Siam as *P'ra piak nam* or the "Water-soaked Buddha". Though this image has a certain obvious analogy with the walking figures from Suk'ōt'ai, the features are not at all similar to those of that school, and I think we must ascribe it to a period anterior to 1350.

Although the rise of the Tai and the disappearance of the Khmer meant in general the forsaking of stone for bronze, still at Lopburi itself the old tradition lingered for a long while, and stone images continued to be made even, it is said, until the reign of King Narai in the seventeenth century. This would cover a period of almost four hundred years—which it is rather difficult to credit unless there were a sudden recrudescence of stone sculpture after a longish interval—but there is no doubt that stone sculpture was executed at Lopburi for some centuries after the Khmer had vanished, and the local museum at Lopburi contains a large series of Tai heads which have all been found in the neighbourhood. These heads, which are of life-size or larger in many cases, vary to a great extent in artistic merit, but about the best there is a certain delicacy of feeling and a sensitiveness for form which admirably express the Buddhist spirit.

The earliest of these heads show a distinct Khmer influence, as is seen in Fig. 186, 11 inches high. Here we still see the straight band across the forehead, the rectangular, if slightly elongated face, and the long mouth with a suspicion of a moustache: but the eyebrows are now taking on a sharply defined curve, and the eyes themselves and nose are clearly Tai, as is the treatment of the hair. This may belong to the early fourteenth century, but Fig. 187, 21½ inches high, is certainly later and already shows the influence of Suk'ōt'ai. The spiral curls of the hair and the flame-top itself are directly borrowed. The band across the forehead has gone, the face is now long and oval, the mouth is smaller, the chin is rounded with a dimple, the nose has a sharp ridge, and the eyebrows are rising in an arched curve. This head must be attributed to the late fourteenth or early fifteenth century. Fig. 188, 15 inches high, shows a still further development of the Tai ideal, and, although the form is becoming conventionalised, there is still an original beauty and nobility of expression combined in this image. Eventually the type becomes stylised to a degree and Fig. 189, 11½ inches high, shows the last stage of the evolution. This particular head is not altogether without merit, but there is a certain smugness of expression, the face is too moon-like in shape, and the features are becoming insignificant. The seeds of decay are clearly shown, and with this type, whether of the sixteenth or seventeenth century, the thousand-year old School of Lopburi comes to an end. During this long period it has of necessity experienced many vicissitudes of race and character, but, taken all in all, it may well compare with any other school of sculpture in the world.

And now we have reached the last phase of Tai or Siamese art of which I propose to treat, namely:

## THE SCHOOL OF AYUDHYA

All writers on Siamese sculpture are agreed that, once the Tai had firmly established their dominion over the country from Sawank'alōk in the north to Nakon Srītammarāt in the south, the national art which was formed out of a coalescence of all the earlier forces and currents quickly blossomed and as quickly faded, just as we see the brilliant, scarlet blooms of the Flamboyant tree suddenly burst upon us in April in all their glory and then, within one short month, fall to the ground and wither away. It would seem as if, stability once attained, all impulse to create died, and a dead conventional form was soon evolved which has lasted till the present day.

Of the early history of Ayudhya and its kings something must be said. The former capital of Siam, which lies 45 miles north of Bangkok, was built on an island having a circumference of about 14 miles and formed by the confluence of three rivers, the Pā Săk and two tributaries of the Menam Chao P'ya. It is said to be on or near the site of the ancient city of Dvāravatī, and the full title of Ayudhya still contains that name. It remained the capital of Siam until 1767 when it was sacked and almost completely destroyed by the Burmese; and, although a new administrative provincial capital has sprung up on the island within modern times, yet the centre of it to-day is filled with nothing but picturesque ruins, but faintly recalling the glories of the past, when Ayudhya was said by seventeenth-century writers to be as fine and as large a city as London. Kaempfer, the German physician, writing in 1690, is not quite so enthusiastic, but gives on the whole a graphic and, what reads to the writer as, an exact description of the city in those days.[1] He says that "the streets run in a straight line along the canals; some of them are tolerably large, but the greater part very

[1] E. Kaempfer, *History of Japan* (1690–2), vol. 1, pp. 41 *et seq.* Glasgow, 1906.

narrow and all, generally speaking, foul and dirty. Some also are overflow'd at high water. Considering the bigness of the city, it is not very populous and in some parts but thinly inhabited, particularly on the West side on account of its remoteness, and towards the south by reason of the morassy ground, over which people make shift to get upon planks or paltry bridges....There are abundance of empty spaces and large gardens behind the streets wherein they let Nature work, so that they are full of grass, Herbs, Shrubs and Trees that grow wild."

After describing the three Royal Palaces, he takes notice of the temples. "They are in great number, for as the whole country is stocked with Priests and monks, this city abounds in all parts with Temples, the courts of which keep a regular proportion with the streets and are full of pyramids and columns of divers shapes and gilt over. They do not equal our churches in bigness, but far exceed them in outward beauty by reason of the many bended roofs, gilt frontispieces, advanced steps, columns, pillars and other ornaments. Within they are adorned with many images as big as the life and bigger, skilfully formed of a mixture of plaister, rosin, oyl and hair, the outside of which is first varnished over black then gilt." He then adds: "In a Peguan temple out of the city there sits on an eminence such an Idol strongly gilt, the proportion of which is such that it would be of 120 foot in length if standing."

I have no space for more, but this seems to me to give a picture of Siam of all times—as it was in 1350, in 1690, and as may still be seen to-day—magnificence, beauty and squalor all happily and naturally mingled together. But it is not without significance that, in the making of large Buddha images for the temple, stone gives way first to brick and stucco and finally to "plaister, rosin, oyl and hair"!

Wood says that at the time of Rāma T'ibodi I, in the second half of the fourteenth century, Ayudhya was a very small city, with a wall of mud and that the buildings, including the Royal Palace, were constructed of timber.[1] The brick wall, of which parts may still be seen, was built by King Chakrap'at (1549–65) and the Palace, of which only the foundations now remain, dates from the time of King Trailōkanāth (1448–88). The principal ruins to be seen to-day are those of the vast temple of Çrī Sarap'et, which also dates from the second half of the fifteenth century (Fig. 190). The two largest *stūpas* in this temple, both in the Sinhalese style, were built of brick and stucco by King Rāma T'ibodi II in 1491 to receive the ashes of his father, Trailōkanāth, and of his elder brother, Boromorāja III, who died after a reign of only three years. Near by may also

[1] W. A. R. Wood, *History of Siam*, p. 64.

be seen one of the largest bronze images of the Buddha in the world (Fig. 191), known as P'ra Mangala Pabitra. It is said to be about 50 feet high including the base, and is made of sheets of copper-bronze fastened on to a core of brick. From the purely conventional style portrayed, it is clearly of late date, possibly sixteenth-century, and is not of great artistic value. There is, however, still a sense of dignity and proportion about the image which makes it sufficiently imposing, and any comparison with that at Kamakura in Japan will not be to its disadvantage. The right arm, the fingers of the left hand, and the point of the flame-top have been restored within recent years. This image is a good representative example of the conventional style into which the School of Ayudhya eventually developed.

There had at one time been another gigantic image of the Buddha, ordered in 1499 for the temple of Çrī Sarap'et by Rāma T'ibodi II. This image was also about 50 feet high, and the pedestal was 24 feet long. It was covered with gold plates weighing nearly 800 lb., and took more than three years to complete. It was destroyed by the Burmese in 1767 and, when the first King of the Bangkok dynasty found it impossible to restore the broken fragments, he had them buried beneath a pagoda in Wat Jetup'on in Bangkok.[1]

When he first assumed the throne, Rāma T'ibodi I was probably only acknowledged as King or Overlord from Lopburi southwards to Singora, but it was not long before he attacked Cambodia and, in spite of an initial reverse, succeeded in capturing its capital, Angkor, in 1352; whereupon its puppet king became vassal to Ayudhya.[2] His successor, Boromorāja I, carried the work of consolidation still further by invading the realm of Suk'ōt'ai in 1371, and finally in 1378 capturing all its principal cities from Kampengp'et northwards to Pitsanulōk and Sawank'alōk.[3] This was the end of the independent kingdom of Suk'ōt'ai, and the succeeding chiefs became vassal to Ayudhya, until in 1438 this territory was incorporated in the kingdom of Siam. In 1393 the vassal King of Cambodia endeavoured to break his bonds and attacked Siam, but was routed and deposed in favour of a grandson who was placed under the tutelage of a Siamese general and garrison.[4] Again, in the reign of Boromorāja II (1424–48), war broke out with Cambodia, and this was the final act of the drama. Angkor was captured and sacked after a siege of seven months in 1431, its vassal king died, and the King of Siam set up his own son as King of Cambodia. A large quantity of bronze images of animals were brought back to Siam by the king and may still

[1] W. A. R. Wood, *History of Siam*, p. 96.
[2] *Ibid.* p. 65.
[3] *Ibid.* pp. 71–2.
[4] *Ibid.* p. 76.

be seen at P'rabāt. The capital of Cambodia was later removed to Pnompenh and thence to Lōvek, and the great Khmer empire sank into insignificance and ruin.[1] Much mystery is often made to-day over the disappearance of Angkor. There is no mystery. Thus by the time of the accession of Trailōkanāth in 1448 the kingdom of Siam had absorbed its neighbour, Suk'ōt'ai, had broken the power of Cambodia and had set up its dominion over most of modern Siam. There only remained the northern State of Chiengmai to be brought to heel, but, although Trailōkanāth spent most of his long reign in attempts to conquer it, the task proved beyond his powers, and it was left to the Burmese king, Bureng Naung, in the middle of the following century to put his iron hand on Chiengmai and to bring the line of Meng Rai to an inglorious end. The northern region was, in fact, not finally incorporated in the kingdom of Siam until 1874, when a Siamese High Commissioner was sent to reside at Chiengmai for the first time. An interesting fact referred to by Wood is that in 1463, owing to the constant attacks by Chiengmai, Trailōkanāth removed his capital northwards to Pitsanulōk and appointed his elder son to be Governor of Ayudhya. Pitsanulōk remained the capital until his death in 1488.[2]

Ayudhyan remains in brick and stucco of the fifteenth and sixteenth century are still to be seen at Lopburi in juxtaposition to the older Khmer temples, of which they are mostly conscious imitations. Their extremely dilapidated state is probably due as much to the depredations of robbers seeking the supposed treasures buried in their hearts as to the hand of time. This effect of spoliation is clearly seen in Fig. 192, which represents an attempt to produce a Khmer *prāng*. It stands in a field just outside the temple of Mahā-Tāt, as do also the two towers seen in Fig. 193. In spite of their debased style there is still something monumental about these structures, though their chief attraction is perhaps due to their crumbling condition. Near by is the *p'rajedi* seen in Fig. 194 which was originally built in the pointed Sinhalese style, but which is now chiefly remarkable for the stucco panel of seven Buddhist disciples preserved on one of its sides. Above them can be seen the mutilated figure of the Buddha with one disciple on either side. Considering the limitations of the materials used, the artist has achieved a delightful rhythm and harmony in working out his conception. This is the finest fragment of Ayudhyan decorative sculpture still in existence. Farther away, near the railway line, can also be seen the *prāng* of a temple (Fig. 195) which is called Wat Nakon Kosā T'ibodi, as it was said to have been erected by Chao P'ya Kosā T'ibodi in King Narai's reign (1656–88) in imitation of a Khmer tower. I cannot

[1] W. A. R. Wood, *History of Siam*, p. 81.

[2] *Ibid.* p. 88.

gainsay this, but it looks to me to be older, and on constructional grounds I should class it with the others in the late fifteenth or early sixteenth century.

Of the sculpture of the Ayudhyan period not much to its credit has hitherto been written. Cœdès goes so far as to say that the mediocrity of the School of Ayudhya has caused him to exclude it altogether from his work on the National Museum,[1] while Dupont gives it very little space in his essay on Siamese Art. According to him, "all attempts at classification are impossible, chiefly because the general decadence of Tai art does not entice one to further study of it."[2] These are hard sayings which are possibly justified if we regard Tai art from 1600 onwards. But the earlier manifestations are not without their artistic value, and even if the first joy of creative genius has subsided, there is still much to appreciate in the earlier products of the National School. From our brief historical survey it is easy to see how Suk'ōt'ai and Cambodia met at Ayudhya to form the basis of that school. The part played by Suk'ōt'ai, being of Tai origin itself, was a natural evolution, to which was added, as in the buildings of the period, a conscious imitation of the Khmer style which was clearly much admired by the Tai kings. The reader will be able to judge for himself how far the combination of these two elements succeeded in producing a work of art from the illustrations which follow. Figs. 196 and 197 show two bronze statues greater than life-size now preserved, through the care of Prince Damrong, in Wat Benchamabopit in Bangkok. They may be taken as typical of the period, and the characteristics mentioned above are clearly marked. The features, which are unmistakably Tai, represent an abstract ideal and show a softness and a roundness of expression altogether foreign to Khmer traditions. The modelling of the head is good and still shows careful handling, but the lower part of the torso and the legs and feet are stiffly conventional and the broad flowing robe seems, as it were, stuck on to the body. The diadem with its crowning point, the large necklace with its hanging pendant, the ear ornaments, the bracelets on the upper part of the arms, the girdle round the waist and the broad fold of cloth running down from its centre are all copied directly from the Khmer. Fig. 196, which wears no jewels and in which the face is much squarer, is probably the earlier of the two. Dupont is in some doubt whether the crown and diadem are derived from the art of the Bayon period in Cambodia, or from the more ancient crowns of the temple of Angkor.[3] But this type of crown is known to me in certain examples of Khmer art from Siam itself,

[1] G. Cœdès, "Le Musée National de Bangkok", *Ars Asiatica*, vol. XII, p. 35. Paris, 1928.

[2] P. Dupont, *Catalogue des Collections Indo-Chinoises du Musée Guimet*, p. 58. Paris, 1934.

[3] *Ibid.* p. 57.

and I do not think it necessary to look any further for the origin of the Tai inspiration. Dupont states, further, that the clothing reproduces exactly that found on Buddha images from Prah Khan (a temple adjoining the city of Angkor) and that the ornaments equally point to a Khmer influence. There can be no doubt of this, and I would even say that the Tai artist probably had a Khmer model in his mind when the first examples of this type were evolved. As I have said already, it is not in my opinion a question of Khmer influence, but of conscious and direct imitation whether from Siam or Cambodia itself. Fig. 198, 12 inches high, shows a similar bronze figure, for household use, from my own collection. Here the robe and the lower part of the body are stiff and conventional to a degree, but there is a charm about the features which are well modelled and still express a living ideal. Coupled with these I show two heads in my possession, Figs. 199 and 200, which show how the type developed. Fig. 199 shows a gilt, bronze head, 20 inches high, which is the finest of its kind, artistically, known to me. The soft lines of the eyebrows, the delicate nose, the sensitive mouth, and the downcast eyes, set in a face of perfect proportions, represent the totality of the Siamese conception of their ideal Being. There is a majesty as well as beneficence about this head which cannot be denied and which demands respect from any beholder. Here the gilt has overlaid the details of the work in the diadem of the crown, but it will be seen in the next illustration (Fig. 200) to what heights the Siamese craftsman could rise in his manipulation of the bronze. This head, which is 13 inches high, must be a later production. The band across the forehead is no longer straight, the ear ornaments have diminished in size, the features have become insignificant, and are sharply outlined, having lost that softness of line seen in the preceding figure. But the bronze itself is of fine quality and the detail of the decoration is worthy of a jeweller. The general style of the head, though not the features in detail, always reminds me of an early portrait of Queen Victoria.

At a later date, probably in the sixteenth century, the crown, diadem, and ornaments were abandoned and the type shown in the gigantic image at Ayudhya (Fig. 191) became the national style. It speaks for itself, and one can understand why students find no inclination to push their researches further. Fig. 201, 5 inches high, which belongs to this period, does, however, show that all is not yet lost even at this late date. The treatment is strictly conventional and symbolic in the sharp lines of the forehead, eyebrows, nose and mouth, but the eyes give the face that mysterious, subtle expression so often seen in the best Buddhist sculpture. Knowledge and sorrow are its chief ingredients.

My last illustration of the School of Ayudhya is of some interest as it shows a large head of the Buddha, 17½ inches high, made of a sweet-scented wood (*mai chan hôm*) found in the eastern district of Siam (Fig. 202). The face is covered with lacquer and the hair is formed of lacquer knobs; the eyes are filled with mother-of-pearl, a decoration, in itself witness of decadence, which came into fashion in the seventeenth century to which this head probably belongs. Small wooden images of the Buddha are to be found everywhere throughout the country, sometimes coated with silver, but figures of such size carved out of wood are uncommon.

In the Bronze Hall of the National Museum at Bangkok are ranged, one on either side, two rows of Brāhmanic statues of life-size, or greater in some cases, of Tai workmanship, which date from the Ayudhyan period. One of these is illustrated here, Fig. 203. It is a bronze image of Çiva in his aspect of Teacher, 6 feet 8 inches high, which was cast and set up by a prince, who called himself Çrī Dharmaçokarāja, at Kampengp'et in the year 1510. It shows how, even at that late date, Khmer influence still exercised a fascination over the Tai, and the other statues in the Museum, of Viṣnu and other male and female deities, all bear witness to this same fact. The statue shown here is of special interest as it bears a long inscription in Siamese on the top of the pedestal, running round the feet, recounting how the prince made this statue for the protection of all human beings, and how he had repaired the temples, roads and canals in his territory. For all the work he has carried out he offers the merit acquired to their Majesties, the two Kings, i.e. King Boromorāja of Ayudhya, and his son, Prince Jetta (afterwards King Rāma T'ibodi II), who was then Crown Prince, ruling at Pitsanulōk.[1] The prince, who ordered the image, must have been a local chief, probably descended from the once Royal House of Suk'ōt'ai.

In the Victoria and Albert Museum are two small statues which are said to have come from the Shan States but which are indisputably Tai Brāhmanic figures of the same period. Both are reproduced here, Figs. 204 and 205. In both the features are clearly Tai, and the headdress in Fig. 204, which is also an image of Çiva, 11½ inches high, is exactly similar to that of figures in the Bangkok Museum. The god is recognised by the third eye in the centre of the forehead and by the trident in the right hand. Fig. 205, 9½ inches high, is possibly Viṣnu. All three have the sacred thread of the "twice-born" round the torso.

The presence of these figures in the heart of Siam does not mean that there was a sudden outburst of Brāhmanism at the beginning of the sixteenth century

[1] G. Cœdès, *Recueil des Inscriptions du Siam*, Part I (1924), pp. 157–9. But, according to Wood, Boromorāja died in 1491, and Prince Jetta reigned as King Rāma T'ibodi II until 1529.

consequent on a decadence of Buddhism. On the contrary, the creator of the Çiva image hopes that it will exalt both the Buddhist and Brāhman religions and cult of the gods, so that they may not fall into obscurity and darkness. Throughout the history of Siam the religion of the Buddha has been no hindrance to the worship of the Brāhmanic gods, and still to-day P'ra In (the god Indra) is the Protector of the Buddha, and watches over all his works. Buddhism is, indeed, the most tolerant of all religions and it is only a few years ago that I heard King Prajadhipok pay a moving tribute to a Christian Mission in his country and say that, as long as they contributed to the happiness of his people and the maintenance of good government, so long would he welcome their presence in Siam.

I have now reached the end of this survey of Buddhist Art in Siam. As I said in my Introductory Chapter, I do not pretend to have solved all the intricate problems involved in tracing the development of sculpture and architecture in Siam: few countries, indeed, offer so rich a field for research. But in the space at my command I have endeavoured to fit together all the fragments so far discovered into the pattern of my mosaic picture, and to indicate the lines of any future search for those pieces still missing.

I have undertaken this task, which has been a labour of love, because I have an intense desire to introduce and interpret this little known realm of Eastern art to all those English-speaking people who appreciate beautiful sculpture. I have also the hope that it may help the Siamese people to realise the richness of their inheritance, and the Government its responsibility for maintaining and furthering the cause of archaeological and artistic research.

In conclusion, may I express the hope that one day, in the far distant future, our descendants will recognise that our present histories are all wrong. The true greatness of a people does not lie in the recounting of victories won on the battlefield and in the so-called "glory" of heroic deeds of arms. Such vauntings of human physical force only serve to feed our national pride and lust for conquest. The deeds themselves have their little day and vanish, leaving ashes and ruins in their train. No, the real greatness of a people lies in its contribution to that expression of the human spirit which is called by the name of "art", and there can be no doubt that, in the last, by that contribution will the people be judged. The question will be asked—not, whom have you conquered and how many have you killed in battle, but, what have you done to enrich and develop the *spirit* of mankind? If only the will to create were greater than the will to destroy, no height of glory would be unattainable and man would cease to be a savage.

# BIBLIOGRAPHY

## A. GENERAL

Containing a list of selected works dealing with Indian and allied Art and History recommended as a groundwork for the study of Buddhist Art in Siam.


ADAM, L. *Buddha-Statuen.* Stuttgart, 1925.

BACHHOFER, L. *Early Indian Sculpture.* 2 vols. The Pegasus Press, Paris, 1929.

BHATTACHARYYA, B. *Indian Images I. The Brahmanic Iconography.* Calcutta and Simla, 1921.

—— *The Indian Buddhist Iconography.* London, 1924.

BINYON, L. *Examples of Indian Sculpture at the British Museum.* London, 1910.

BOSE, P. N. *The Indian Colony of Champa.* Madras, 1925.

BURGESS, J. *The Buddhist Stupas of Amarāvati and Jaggayyapeta.* London, 1887.

—— *The ancient Monuments, Temples and Sculptures of India.* 2 vols. London, 1897.

*Cambridge History of India*, vol. I. Cambridge, 1922.

CHANDA, R. P. "Beginning of the Sikhara of the Nagara (Indo-Aryan) Temple." *Rūpam*, no. 17, 1924.

—— "Mediaeval Sculpture in East India." *Calcutta Univ., Journ. Dept. Letters*, III, 1920.

CODRINGTON, K. DE B. *Ancient India (to the Guptas).* Ernest Benn, London, 1926.

—— V. A. Smith's *History of Fine Arts in India and Ceylon* (Revised). Clarendon Press, Oxford, 1930.

COHN, W. *Buddha in der Kunst des Ostens.* Leipzig, 1925.

—— *Asiatische Plastik* (Sammlung Baron Eduard von der Heydt). Berlin, 1932.

COOMARASWAMY, A. K. Bronzes from Ceylon. Memo. Colombo Museum I. Colombo, 1914.

—— *The Aims of Indian Art.* Essex House Press, Broad-Campden, 1908.

—— "The Indian Origin of the Buddha Image." *Art Bulletin*, New York Univ., vol. IX, 1927 (and *J.A.O.S.* vol. XLVI, 1926).

—— "The Buddha's Hair, Cuda, Uṣṇiṣa and Crown." *J.R.A.S.* 1928.

COUSENS, H. "The Ancient Temples of Aihole and Pattadakal." *A.S.I.A.R.* 1907–10.

—— "Buddhist Stupas at Mirpūr Khas, Sind." *A.S.I.A.R.* 1909–10.

CUNNINGHAM, Sir A. *A.S.I.A.R.* vols. I to XXIII (1862–87), especially vol. XI (pp. 40–6) and vol. XVII (pp. 25–9). Calcutta.

ELLIOTT, Sir H. M. *Hinduism and Buddhism.* 3 vols. London, 1922.

FERGUSSON, J. *Tree and Serpent Worship.* London, 1893.

—— *A History of Indian and Eastern Architecture.* London, 1910.

FOUCHER, A. *The Beginnings of Buddhist Art.* London, 1918.

—— *L'art Gréco-bouddhique du Gandhara.* Paris, 1900–18–23.

—— *L'Iconographie Bouddhique de l'Inde.* Paris, 1900–5.

—— "Matériaux pour servir à l'étude de l'art Khmère." *B.C.A.I.* Paris, 1912–13.

—— *The influence of Indian Art on Cambodia and Java* (Sir A. Mookerjee Memorial), vol. III. Calcutta, 1922.

—— "Le Grand Miracle de Sravasti." *J.A.* Paris, 1909.

GANGULY, M. *Orissa and her remains, Ancient and Mediaeval.* Calcutta, 1912.

GETTY, A. *The Gods of Northern Buddhism.* Oxford, 1914.

GOLOUBEV, V. "Peintures Bouddhiques aux Indes." *Ann. Musée Guimet.* Paris, 1914.
—— "Le Temple de la Dent à Kandy." *B.E.F.E.O.* vol. XXXII (2). Hanoi, 1932.
GRÜNWEDEL, A. *Buddhist Art in India* (English edition). London, 1901.
—— *Buddhistische Kunst in Indien* (2nd edition with Waldschmidt). Berlin, 1919.
HAVELL, E. B. *Indian Sculpture and Painting.* London, 1908.
—— *Handbook of Indian Art.* John Murray, London, 1920.
HOCART, A. M. *Ceylon Journal of Science* (G), Archaeological Summary. Colombo, 1924–7.
JOUVEAU-DUBREUIL, G. *Archéologie du Sud de l'Inde.* 2 vols. P. Geuthner, Paris, 1914.
—— *Pallava Antiquities.* Probsthain and Co., London, 1916.
—— *Ancient History of the Deccan.* Pondicherry, 1920.
KRAMRISCH, STELLA. *Indian Sculpture.* Heritage of India series. Calcutta, 1933.
KROM, N. J. *Hindoe-Javaansche Geschiednis.* (K.I. Voor de Taal. . .en Volkenkunde van Ned-Indie.) The Hague, 1931.
—— "L'Art Javanais dans les Musées de Hollande et de Java." *Ars Asiatica*, vol. VIII. Paris, 1926.
— *Borobodur, Archaeological Description.* 2 vols. The Hague, 1927.
LONGHURST, A. H. "Ancient Brick Temples in the Central Provinces." *A.S.I.A.R.* 1909–10.
MARSHALL, Sir J. H. *Guide to Sanchi.* Calcutta, 1918.
—— *Guide to Taxila.* Calcutta, 1918.
—— "Monuments of Ancient India" (in *Cambridge History of India*, vol. I). Cambridge, 1922.
MENDIS, G. C. *Early History of Ceylon.* Y.M.C.A. Publishing House, Calcutta, 1935.
MITTON, J. E. *Lost Cities of Ceylon.* John Murray, London, 1916.
MOOKERJI, N. B. *A history of Indian Shipping and maritime activity.* London, 1912.
MUS, P. "Barabudur, Les origines du Stupa et la transmigration." *B.E.F.E.O.* vol. XXXII (1). Hanoi, 1932.
PARKER, H. *Ancient Ceylon.* London, 1909.
PARKER, J. H. *A Concise Glossary of Architecture.* Parker and Co. Oxford, 1913.
REA, A. "Pallava Architecture." *A.S.I.* Madras, 1909.
REINACH, S. *La Représentation du Galop dans l'art ancien et moderne.* Leroux, Paris, 1925.
RHYS DAVIDS, T. W. *Buddhism.* S.P.C.K. London, 1925.
—— *Buddhist India.* T. Fisher Unwin, London, 1917.
SMITH, VINCENT A. *History of Fine Arts in India and Ceylon.* Oxford, 1911.
THOMAS, E. J. *Life of Buddha.* Kegan Paul, London, 1927.
—— *History of Buddhist Thought.* Kegan Paul, London, 1933.
VOGEL, J. PH. "The Mathurā School of Sculpture." *A.S.I.A.R.* Calcutta, 1906–7, 1909–10.
—— "Buddhist Sculptures from Benares." *A.S.I.A.R.* Calcutta, 1903–4.

## B. SPECIAL

Containing a list of works dealing with Art and History, which have a direct bearing on the forms of Art found in Siam.

*Ancient Monuments in Burma* (Amended List). Govt. Printing Press, Rangoon, 1921.
AYMONIER, E. *Le Cambodge.* 3 vols. E. Leroux, Paris, 1900–4.
BANERJI, R. D. *The Eastern Indian School of Mediaeval Sculpture.* A.S.I. Delhi, 1933.
BEGLAR, J. D. "Report on a Tour in the Central Provinces in 1873–4." *A.S.I.A.R.* vol. VII, 1878.

BEYLIÉ, L. DE. *L'Architecture Hindoue en Extrême-Orient.* Paris, 1907.

BORIBAL, LUANG. *Ancient Monuments in Siam,* Part I (in Siamese). Bangkok, 1933.

BRADLEY, C. B. "On Tai Script." *J.S.S.* vol. VI (1), 1909, and vol. X (1), 1913.

BURNAY, J. (and CŒDÈS, G.). "On Tai Script." *J.S.S.* vol. XXI (2), 1927.

CHAVANNES, E. "Une Inscription du Royaume de Nan-Tchao." *J.A.* (vol. XVI). Paris, 1900.

CLAEYS, J. Y. "L'Archéologie du Siam." *B.E.F.E.O.* vol. XXXI. Hanoi, 1931.

CŒDÈS, G. "Le Royaume de Çrivijaya." *B.E.F.E.O.* vol. XVIII (6). Hanoi, 1918.

—— "Tablettes Votives Bouddhiques du Siam." *Études Asiatiques.* Paris, 1925 and *J.S.S.* vol. XX (1), 1926.

—— *Recueil des Inscriptions du Siam,* Part I (1924) and Part II (1929). National Library (Part I) and Royal Institute (Part II), Bangkok.

—— "Documents sur l'Histoire Politique et Religieuse du Laos Occidental." *B.E.F.E.O.* vol. XXV (1). Hanoi, 1925.

—— "Le Musée National de Bangkok." *Ars Asiatica* (G. Van Oest), vol. XII. Paris, 1928.

—— "Les Inscriptions Malaises de Çrivijaya." *B.E.F.E.O.* vol. XXX. Hanoi, 1930.

—— "Documents sur la Dynastie de Sukhodaya." *B.E.F.E.O.* vol. XVII (2). Hanoi, 1917.

—— "Bronzes Khmer." *Ars Asiatica* (G. Van Oest), vol. V. Paris, 1923.

—— "Études Cambodgiennes." *B.E.F.E.O.* vol. XXXII. Hanoi, 1932.

—— "Excavations at Pong Tük." *J.S.S.* vol. XXI (3). Bangkok, 1928.

——"On the origin of the Sailendras of Indonesia." *J.G.I.S.* vol. I (2). Calcutta, 1934.

—— (with BURNAY, J.). "On Tai Script." *J.S.S.* vol. XXI (2). Bangkok, 1927.

—— "Notes sur quelques sculptures provenant de Çrideb (Siam)." *Mélanges Linossier,* Musée Guimet, Paris.

—— "New Archaeological Discoveries in Siam." *I.A.L.* vol. II (1). London, 1928.

—— "Indian Influences in Siamese Art." *I.A.L.* vol. IV (1). London, 1930.

COOMARASWAMY, A. K. *History of Indian and Indonesian Art.* E. Goldston, London, 1927.

CREDNER, W. *Cultural and Geographical Observations made in the Tali (Yunnan) region.* Siam Society, Bangkok, 1935. (Translated by Erik Seidenfaden.)

CUNNINGHAM, Sir A. *Maha-Bodhi, or the Great Buddhist Stupa at Buddhagaya.* Allen and Co. London, 1892.

DAMRONG RAJANUBHAB, H.R.H. Prince. "History of Siam prior to the Ayudhya period." *J.S.S.* vol. XIII (2). Bangkok, 1920. (Translated by (Sir) J. Crosby, K.B.E., C.I.E.)

—— *History of Buddhist Stupas in Siam* (in Siamese). Bangkok, 1926.

DÖHRING, K. *Buddhistische Tempelanlagen in Siam.* 3 vols. W. de Gruyter and Co. Berlin, 1920.

—— *Kunst und Kunstgewerbe in Siam (Lackarbeiten).* Berlin, 1925.

DUPONT, P. "Art de Dvāravatī et Art Khmer." *Revue des Arts Asiatiques.* Paris, 1935.

—— *Catalogue des Collections Indo-Chinoises du Musée Guimet.* Paris, 1934.

DUROISELLE, CH. "Stone Sculptures of the Ananda Temple, Pagān." *A.S.I.A.R.* 1913–14.

—— "The Ari of Burma and Tantric Buddhism." *A.S.I.A.R.* 1915–16.

—— "Explorations at Pagān and Hmawza (old Prome)." *A.S.I.A.R.* 1924–9.

FERRAND, G. *L'Empire Sumatranais de Srivijaya.* Paris, 1922.

FINOT, L. "Dharmaçalas au Cambodge." *B.E.F.E.O.* vol. XXV. Hanoi, 1925.

—— "On Tai Script." *B.E.F.E.O.* vol. XVII (5). Hanoi, 1917.

—— "L'Inscription de Prah Khan." *B.E.F.E.O.* vol. IV. Hanoi, 1904.

—— "Les Origines de la Colonisation Indienne en Indo-Chine." *B.E.F.E.O.* vol. XII (8). Hanoi, 1912.

FOURNEREAU, L. *Le Siam Ancien.* Paris, 1908.

FRENCH, J. C. *Art of the Pal Empire.* Oxford Univ. Press, London, 1928.

GANGOLY, O. C. "A Group of Buddhist Sculpture from Siam." *Rūpam*, nos. 38, 39. Calcutta, 1929.

GERINI, G. E. "Siamese Archaeology, a Synoptic Sketch." *J.R.A.S.* London, 1904.

GRAHAM, W. A. *Siam.* 2 vols. De la More Press (A. Moring Ltd.), London, 1924.

GROSLIER, G. "Note sur la Sculpture Khmère ancienne." *Études Asiatiques.* Paris, 1925.

—— *Recherches sur les Cambodgiens.* Paris, 1921.

—— *La Sculpture Khmère.* Paris, 1925.

HALLIDAY, R. (and C. O. BLAGDEN). "Les Inscriptions Môn du Siam." *B.E.F.E.O.* vol. XXX. Hanoi, 1930.

HARVEY, G. E. *History of Burma.* Longmans, Green and Co. London, 1925.

HONG NAVANUGRAHA, NAI. *Bronze Images of the Buddha.* Bangkok, 1927.

KAEMPFER, E. *History of Japan (and Kingdom of Siam)*, vol. I. Univ. Press, Glasgow, 1906.

KRAMRISCH, STELLA. "Pala and Sena Sculpture." *Rūpam*, no. 40. Calcutta, 1929.

LAJONQUIÈRE, LUNET DE. "Essai d'Inventaire archéologique du Siam." *B.C.A.I.* Paris, 1912.

—— *Inventaire Descriptif des Monuments du Cambodge.* 3 vols. Paris, 1902–7–11.

LE MAY, REGINALD. "Introduction to study of Sculpture in Siam." *Burlington Magazine.* London, 1929 (and in *I.A.L.* vol. IV (2), 1930).

—— "A Visit to Sawankalōk." *J.S.S.* vol. XIX (2). Bangkok, 1925.

—— "Pra Vihara, a Khmer Hill-Temple." *I.A.L.* vol. VIII (2). London, 1935.

—— *An Asian Arcady.* Heffer, Cambridge, 1926.

—— *Siamese Tales, Old and New.* Noel Douglas, London, 1930.

—— "The Legends and Folklore of Northern Siam." *J.S.S.* vol. XVIII (1). Bangkok, 1924.

—— *The Coinage of Siam.* Siam Society, Bangkok, 1932.

—— "The Ceramic Wares of North-Central Siam." *Burlington Magazine.* London, 1933.

LEFÈVRE-PONTALIS, P. "L'Invasion Thaie en Indo-Chine." *Toung Pao*, Paris, 1910.

LINGAT, R. "Le Culte du Bouddha d'Émeraude." *J.S.S.* vol. XXVII (1). Bangkok, 1934.

MAJUMDAR, R. C. "The Sailendra Empire." *J.G.I.S.* vol. I (1). Calcutta, 1934.

—— "Les Rois Sailendra de Suvarnadvipa." *B.E.F.E.O.* vol. XXXIII (1). Hanoi, 1933.

—— "The Decline and Fall of the Sailendra Empire." *J.G.I.S.* vol. II (1). Calcutta, 1935.

MUS, P. "Le Buddha Paré." *B.E.F.E.O.* vol. XXVIII. Hanoi, 1928.

PARANAVITANA, S. "Religious Intercourse between Ceylon and Siam in the thirteenth to fifteenth centuries." *J.R.A.S.* (Ceylon), vol. XXXII. Colombo, 1932.

PARMENTIER, H. "L'Art Khmer Primitif." *B.E.F.E.O.* vols. XI and XXII. Hanoi, 1911, 1922. Also *Eastern Art* (Philadelphia), vol. III, translated by L. J. Robbins, 1931.

—— "Cartes de l'Empire Khmer." *B.E.F.E.O.* vol. XVI (3). Hanoi, 1916–17.

—— *Études Asiatiques*, vol. II. Paris, 1925.

—— "The Common Origin of Hindu Architecture in India and the Far East." *Rūpam*, no. 37. Calcutta, 1929.

PELLIOT, P. "Le Founan." *B.E.F.E.O.* vol. III. Hanoi, 1903.

—— "Deux Itinéraires de Chine en Inde." *B.E.F.E.O.* vol. IV. Hanoi, 1904.

PETITHUGUENIN, P. "Notes Critiques pour servir à l'Histoire du Siam." *B.E.F.E.O.* vol. XVI (3). Hanoi, 1916.

P'YA PRAJAKICH KORACHAKR. *Pongsāwădān Yōnaka* (in Siamese). Bangkok, 1907.

PRZYLUSKI, J. "The Sailendravamsa." *J.G.I.S.* vol. II (1). Calcutta, 1935.

RAMA VI (King of Siam). *A visit to the country of P'ra Ruang* (in Siamese). Bangkok, 1908.

RAY, NIHAR RANJAN. *Brahminical Gods in Burma.* Univ. Calcutta, 1932.

ROCHER, E. "Histoire des Princes du Yunnan." *Toung Pao*, vol. X (1st series). Paris, 1899.

SAINSON, C. *Histoire particulier du Nan Tchao*. Leroux, Paris, 1904.

SALMONY, A. *Sculpture in Siam*. Ernest Benn, London, 1925.

SCHMITT, M. In *Mission Pavie*. Paris, 1898.

SEIDENFADEN, E. "Complément à l'Inventaire des monuments du Cambodge pour les quatre provinces du Siam Oriental." *B.E.F.E.O.* vol. XXII. Hanoi, 1922.

—— "An Excursion to Pimai." *J.S.S.* vol. XVII (1). Bangkok, 1923.

—— "The Temple of Khao Panom Rung." *J.S.S.* vol. XXV (1). Bangkok, 1932.

—— *Guide to Nakon Patom*. Siam State Railways. Bangkok, 1929.

—— *Guide to Ayudhya*. Siam State Railways. Bangkok, 1931.

—— *Guide to Petchaburi*. Siam State Railways. Bangkok, 1931.

THOMANN, T. H. *Pagān, ein Jahrtausend Buddhistischer Tempelkunst*. Heilbronn, 1923.

VORETZSCH, E. A. "Über altbuddhistische Kunst in Siam." *O.Z.* vols. V and VI. 1916–17.

—— "Indian Art in Siam." *Rupām*, no. 3. Calcutta, 1920.

WALES, H. G. QUARITCH. "A newly-explored Route of Ancient Indian Cultural Expansion." *I.A.L.* vol. IX (1). London, 1935.

WOOD, W. A. R. *A History of Siam*. T. Fisher Unwin, London, 1926.

## C. JOURNALS

American Oriental Society (*J.A.O.S.*).

Archaeological Survey of Ceylon, *Annual Report* (*A.S.C.A.R.*).

Archaeological Survey of India, *Annual Report* (*A.S.I.A.R.*).

Burma Research Society, Rangoon (*J.B.R.S.*).

Commission Archéologique de l'Indo-Chine, Paris (*B.C.A.I.*).

École Française d'Extrême-Orient, Hanoi (*B.E.F.E.O.*).

*Études Asiatiques*, Paris.

Greater India Society, Calcutta (*J.G.I.S.*).

India Society, London, *Indian Art and Letters* (*I.A.L.*).

*Journal Asiatique*, Paris (*J.A.*).

*Musée Guimet, Annales du*, Paris.

*Orientalische Literatur-Zeitung*, Berlin (*O.L.Z.*).

*Ostasiatische Zeitschrift*, Berlin (*O.Z.*).

*Revue des Arts Asiatiques*, Paris.

Royal Asiatic Society (*J.R.A.S.*).

Royal Asiatic Society, Ceylon Branch.

Royal Asiatic Society, Malayan Branch.

*Rūpam*, Calcutta (ceased publication).

Siam Society, Bangkok (*J.S.S.*).

*Toung Pao*, Paris.

# Index


Açoka, 18, 27, 98
Adittarāja, 98
Aihole, 66
Ajantā, 22, 23, 122
Ajātaçatru, 104, 105
Akyab, 92
Amarāvatī, 13, 18, 45
Ānanda, 105
Ānanda temple (Pagān), 99
Ananta temple (Orissa), 99
Angkor, 21, 48, 50, 54, 55, 61, 69, 145; (Angkor T'om), 55, 81; sack of, by Tai, 58, 145
Angkor Borei, 56
Animism, 102
Anurādhapura, 16, 119
Anuruddha, King, 81, 89, 93, 94, 99
*Apsaras*, 62
Ardhanari, image of, 51
*Arī* cult of Buddhism, 93, 94, 99
Aukana, 119
Aymonier, 7, 35 f., 60, 71
Ayudhya, 23, 25, 51, 58, 112, 117, 121, 136; early history, 143 f.; school of sculpture, 135, 141, 143 ff.

Bādāmi, 66
"ball-flower," 72
Bān Hin K'on, 69
Banerji, R. D., 43, 103, 105, 106, 107
Bang Klang Tao, 112
Bangkok, National Museum, 6, 149
Banka inscription, 36
Banteai Srei, 62
Bassac, 55
Bastian, 7
Battambang, 57
Bavaranives, Temple of, 127
Bayab, Circle of, 13
Bayang tower, 66
Beglar, J. D., 64 ff.
Bharhut, 70
Bhavavarman, 57
Bhitargaon, 65
Bo Ika, 69
Bock, Carl, 7
Bodhiramsi, 87 f.
Borobudur, 80
Boromorāja I, 145; II, 145; III, 144
Brahma, Tai prince, 10, 136
Brāhmanic sculpture, 41 f., 44, 51, 56, 73, 94; Pāla, 100; statues at Bangkok, 149
Buddha, images: early, 5; pre-Khmer, 22 ff. (standing, 22 f., seated, 23, date, 24); Khmer, 50 ff.; at Tāt Panom, 60, others, 67; Mōn images at Lopburi, 73; Tai image, 74; Nan-Chao, 84; "P'ra Lavō," 98; Burmese, from India, 99, 104; rise of Tai style, 113 f.; the P'ra Sihing, 116 f.; images at Mahā-Tāt (Suk'ōt'ai), 125 f.; the Emerald, 133; "P'rachao Keng Kom," 138; *Abhayamudrā*, 142; *P'ra piak nam*, 142; P'ra Mangala Pabitra, 145
Buddha-Gupta, 24
Buddh Gayā, 43, 91, 100, 102, 105, 111
Buddhism and Hinduism, 101
Buddhist customs of the Pyu, 90
Buddhist symbols: the Deer, 26; Wheel of the Law, 26, 60, 74
Bureng Naung, 146
Burma, relation with Siamese art, 82 ff.; cultural history of, 90 ff.; earliest Burmese inscription, 94; inscriptions, 100

Çaivism, in Funan, 53 f.; at Prome, 91 f.
*Camadevivamsa*, 87
Cambodian language, 50
Celadon ware, 113
Ceylon, decline of Buddhism in, 99; mission to Siam, 104; revival of Buddhism and its influence, 114; art periods, 119; relics from, 126; second mission to Siam, 131 f.
Chaisiri, 27
Chakrap'at, 144
Chalukya empire, 46 f.; influence on Brahmin art in Siam, 52
Cham art, 63
Chām T'ewī, 12, 87, 88, 131
Champā, 53, 56
Chan Nakon, 55
Chandrabhanu, 40, 115, 116
Chandragupta, 66
Chantaburi, 55
Chao-ju-kua, 48

Chao P'ya Kosā T'ibodi, 146
Chapata, 115
Chaudoc, 56
Chavannes, 83
Chêng Hui, 83
Chiengmai, 19, 53, 86, 104, 106, 110, 117, 146
Chiengrai, 85, 107, 109 f., 132
Chiengrung, 109
Chiengsen, 47; sculpture, 95, 103, 107, 109, 114, 126
Chiengtung, 86
Ch'ih-t'u, 55 f.
Chinese art, 3; trade with India, 19; account of Funan, 53; influence on Tai race in Siam, 84 ff., 107 f.; relations with Suk'-ōt'ai, 113, 121 f.
Chitrasena, 53, 57, 69 f.
Chola period, art of, 52
Chulalongkorn, King, 22, 27, 48, 127
*Chula-Sakarāt*, 29, 92
*çikhara*, 7, 27, 63, 66
Çiva as Teacher, image of, 149, 150
Çivagupta, 66
Çiva-Umā, combined image, 51
Claeys, 7, 79, 80, 81, 120 f., 126
Codrington quoted, 65
Cœdès, Georges, 7, 8, 34, 36, 51, 67, 99, 103, 139, 147; quoted, 44, 47, 52, 68, 117, 125, 137 f.; work on inscriptions of Siam, 21, 37, 38, 87, 97, 123 f., 125
Conjeeveram, 19, 29, 45, 91
Coomaraswamy quoted, 4; references, 8, 25
Credner, 82
Çresthapura, 57
Çrīdeb, 50, 51
Çrī Dharmaçokarāja, 149
Çrī Sachanalai, 116, 120, 122 f.
Çrīvijaya, 19, 35 ff., 54
Çrutavarman, 57
Çulamāni-Varman, 37
Cunningham, 42 f., 66, 100

*dagoba*, 41
Damrong, H.R.H. Prince, 6, 31, 34, 42, 61, 76, 84 f., 95, 108, 136, 138, 139, 147
Deer, the, 26
*Devas*, 62
*Dhammapadatthakatha*, 132
Dhammapala, 91
Dharmarāja I, 121, 124, 126, 129
*dhoviti*, 51
Dittarāja, 97, 98

Döhring, 7, 130
Dong Dūang, 16
*droit de seigneur*, 93
Dudhadhari Math, 64
Dupont, 97, 107, 114, 126 f., 138, 139, 147, 148
Duroiselle, 81, 91
Dvāravatī, meaning, 24 and n.; kingdom, 25, 26; city, 136, 143
Dvāravatī school of sculpture, 22, 48 f., 97 f., 137

Eastern and Western art, contrasting characteristics, 2 ff.
economy of line, 2 ff.
Elgin Marbles, 3
Erh-Hai (Lake), 82

Fa Hsien, 19
Finot quoted, 52, 69
Flying gallop, the, 61 and n.
Foucher, 25
Fournereau, 7
French archaeologists' work in Siam, 58 f.
French Colonial Exhibition, 62
Führer, 93
Funan, kingdom of, 13 f., 25, 50 ff.; Chinese account of, 53

Galvihāra, 119
Ganga dynasty, 45
Gangoly, O. C., 8
Garnier, Francis, 7
Gautama, the *Mahā-Parinirvāna* of, 106 f.
Gerini, Col., 7
Gopāla of Bengal, 46, 100
Graeco-Roman lamp, 16
Graham, W. A., 7
Grahi, 48, 49
"Greco-Khmer" art, 25
Greek art, 2 f.
Gupta type, statues of, 22, 24, 36, 41, 52, 91; architecture, 66; basis of Môn-Indian art, 76

Hacchimalligudi temple, 66
Haling'yi, 90
*hamsa* bird, 87
Hari-Hara, images of, 51
Haripūnjaya, 11, 88, 95; foundation, 12, 86 f. *See also* Lamp'ūn
Harshagupta, 66
Harvey, 83, 92, 95, 98

Hīnayāna Buddhism, 19, 29, 30, 41, 53, 83, 87 f., 90, 91, 95, 100; appeal to Siamese, 102, 114, 124 f.; sculpture, 34
Hmannan Yazawin, the, 93
Hsi-Nu-Lo, 82
Hsüan-Tsang, 24
Htilo-Minlo, 111

Içanapura, 53
Içanasena, 53
Içanavarman, 57
I-Ching, 24, 36
India, cultural influence on neighbours, 1 ff.; Dvāravatī school of sculpture in Siam, 21 ff.; in Burma, 99
Indraditya, 112, 120
Inscriptions, 21, 37, 38, 49, 50 n., 53, 54, 55, 57, 59, 66, 69, 70, 78, 82 f., 87, 91, 92, 93, 114 f., 123 f., 125 f., 132, 149
Isān, 59

Javabhūmi, 40, 46
Jāvaka, 40, 115
Jaya, centre of Indian culture, 19, 38 ff., 44
Jaya Çiri, 136
Jayavarman (early Khmer), 57
Jayavarman II, 55, 69 f., 72; IV, 55; V, 62, 70
*Jinakalamālini*, the, 11, 53, 87, 88
Jivaka, 89

Kaempfer, 143 f.
Kalinga, 45
Kalyani inscriptions, 132
Kamakura (Japan), image of Buddha at, 145
Kāmārnava, 45
Kampeng Sen, 27 f.
Kampengp'et, 53, 78, 117, 126, 128, 149
Kānburi, 16, 74
Kānchī, 19, 45
Kānchīpuram, 91
K'ao Panom Rung, 69
*kasti pathar*, 102
Katāha, 37
*Kat'in*, 124
Kaundinya Jayavarman, 32, 56
K'elāng, 88
*ketumāla*, 114, 118
Kharod, 64, 65
Khin Ba's mound, 91
Khmer period in Siam, 50 ff.; history, 53; inscriptions, 58, 59, 69, 126
Khmer race, rise of, 10 f.; art in Funan, 50 ff.; ousted by Tai, 58; transition from Môn art, 67 ff.; contrast with Tai art, 113 f.; influence on U-T'ong school, 136 f.; transition to Tai art, 139 ff.
Kilāna, 129, 133
Koh Ker, 52, 55
Ko-Lo-Fêng, 82 f., 90
Korāt, 16, 55, 59, 69, 72, 74
Kramrisch, Stella, 43, 100, 101, 103, 105, 106
Kublai Khan, 109, 113
Kŭm Kām, 110
Kü Na, 129, 133
Kwang-Si, 82
Kwang-Tung, 82
Kyanzittha, 98, 99
Kyaukku Onhmin, the, 92

Lacquer-work, 96
Lajonquière, Lunet de, 7, 51, 59, 60, 71 f.
Lăk Müang, the, 123
Lakṣmana temple (Sirpur), 64, 65, 66
Lam Chi river, 59
Lampāng Lūang, 88, 131
Lamp'ūn, 9, 30, 86 ff.; flight of people to Burma, 89; Wat Kŭkŭt, 97 f.; the great *Stūpa*, 98; captured by Meng Rai, 110; P'ra Yün, 129
Lang-Ya-Hsiu, 35
Lānnātai, 98
Lao, modern script, 96
Lao states, the, 53
Lavō, 11, 87, 89
Lawā, the, 10, 78, 86, 109
Lefèvre-Pontalis, 7 f., 110, 111
Liang, 35, 36
Lingat, R., 133
Loet'ai, 135
Lohan pottery figure, 4
Lopburi, 11, 21, 48, 50, 53, 58, 65, 67 f., 70, 72 f., 78, 87; school of sculpture, 135 ff.; stone images, 142
Lōvek, 58, 146
Lūang Prabāng, 112
Luce, G. H., 93
*lunggyi*, 90
Lü Tai, 80 f.

Mahā-Bodhi, 42 f.
*Mahā-Sakarāt*, the, 10, 29, 48, 92
Mahā-Tāt, *see* Temples
Mahāyāna Buddhism, 23, 36, 53, 83, 91, 92 f., 100, 116; sculpture, 42, 72

Mahendravarman, 57, 69
*mai chan hôm*, 149
Majumdar, 39 f., 45 f.
Malay Peninsula, Indian and Chinese immigration, 35
Mālegitti temple, 66
*Mangaladīpani*, 132
Manuha, 94
Maravi-jayottunga-Varman, 37
Martaban, 16, 18, 30, 110
Maspero, 59
Mathurā, 70
Maunggan, 29, 91
Mekōng, the, 14, 53, 55, 57, 59, 85, 112
Me K'üang, the, 87
Menam valley, the, 13, 50 ff., 95
Mendis, G. C., quoted, 19
Mêng Hua, 82
Meng Rai, 97, 109 ff., 112, 146
Me Ping, the, 78, 87, 126, 132
Me Yōm, the, 120, 122
*Mission Pavie*, 7
Môn people: in N. Siam, 13; in Central Siam, 21 ff.; inscriptions, 21 f., 87, 88, 97; sculptural influence, 48 f.; transition to Khmer, 67 ff.; origin of Môn-Indian art, 76; influence on Khmer art, 77; in Burma, 90
Mongkut, King, 27, 121, 123
Mouhot, Henri, 7
Mraten Çrī Nano, 48, 49
Müang Bang Yang, 112
Müang Hai, 86
Müang Rat, 112
Muang San, 137
Müang Tam, 70
Müang Yong, 86
Mukdahān, 59
Mūn river, the, 55, 57, 59

Nāga king, the, 32, 47 f., 93; Khmer form, 54, 73, 76 f., 81; Tai form, 123
Nagara Jum, *stela* of, 126
Nagarī script, 45, 91
Nāgasena, 32
Nai Hong Navanagruha, 17, 77
Nakon Lampāng, 87
Nakon Panom, 59
Nakon Sawan, 135
Nakon Srītammarāt, 11, 41, 54, 112, 115, 117, 120
Nālandā, 100, 108
Nān, temples at, 131, 133
Nan-Chao, 82, 83 f., 90 f., 109
Narai, King, 142, 146
Naraiyana (Narai), 117
Narasinhavarman, 19
National Library, Bangkok, 87
National Museum, Bangkok, 6
Nihar Ranjan Ray quoted, 29
Nyaung-U, 92, 93, 115

Pagān, 89, 92; Ānanda temple, 99; bronze Buddha, 102 f.; Meng Rai at, 110, 111; That-Byin-Nyu, 129
*pā-hom*, 90
Pāk Hin Būn, 59
Pāk Mūn, 69
Pāk Tung Chại, 69
Pālas, the, and Malaya, 46 f.; Burma, 99; art, 100 ff.
Pāli literature, revival in Siam, 132
Pallavas, the, 19, 91; sculpture, 44 f., 51; influence on art in Siam, 52, 63
Paloura, 45
P'amniep, 55
P'a Müang, 112
Pandiyas, the, 52
Panom Rung, 58, 69, 70, 71
Panom Wan, 58, 70
P'an-P'an, 36, 40
Panthagu, 115
Parākrama Bāhu I, 114, 119; II, 115
Paranavitana, 118
Parmentier, 7, 40, 52, 55, 63, 70
*Paryankānasa*, 79
Pā-săk river, 50, 52, 56, 143
*pā-sin*, 90
Pātaliputra, 18
Pattadakal, 66
Pattinī Devī, 119
Pegu, 81, 90, 92
Pelliot, 7, 50, 55, 57, 90, 135
Petchabūn, 52
Petchaburi, 14, 135
P'iao (Pyu), 83
P'i-Lo-Ko, 82
Pimai, 67 f., 70, 72
Pitsanulōk, 72, 77, 78 f., 127 f., 146, 149
Pnompenh, 25, 51, 56, 58, 75, 77, 146
Polonnāruwa, 97, 118, 119, 122
*Pongsāwadān Yōnaka*, 10, 84, 95 f.
Pong Tük, 15 ff., 34
Popa Sawrahan, 92
Prabāt, 72, 146
Prachinburi, 32

P'ra Chinnarāt, 127
P'rachum P'on, 120
Prah K'an, 54
Prajadhipok, King, 6, 150
*p'ra-jedī*, 7, 27, 121, 146
P'ra Müang Keo, 131
P'rapatom, 16, 22, 27, 34, 95
*p'ra P'im* (Votive Tablet), 128
*p'ra-prāng*, 7
P'ra Rūang (Suk'ōt'ai), 79, 112, 120
P'ra Sihing, the, 116 f., 133
*P'ra Sīla*, 104
*P'ra Song Krüang*, 106
P'ra Vihāra, 54, 55, 70
P'rê, 87
Prome, 81, 90, 91, 94
Pulakesin II (Chalukya), 46
Pyinbya, 93
Pyu, the, in Burma, 90

Quaritch Wales quoted, 19, 38
quartz, Buddha image in, 28 f.

Rahmanadeça, 29
Rāhu, 31
Raipur, 64
Rājaburi, Hermit's Cave at, 22, 23; bluish limestone, 74
Rāja-rāja I, 37
Rājat'ani, 120
Rajendra-Chola, 37
Rama VI (Vajiravudh), King, 6
Rāma T'ibodi I, 136, 144, 145; II, 149
Rām K'amheng, 28, 49, 50 n., 53, 80, 109, 110, 111 ff., 120, 129, 135; inscribed obelisk, 121, 123 f.
Rangoon, 81
Ranjan Ray (Nihar), 91
Rattanapanna, 87 f., 132
Rōcarāja, 112, 116, 120
Rocher, 83 f.
Rūdravarman, 56
Rundhayya, 89

Sabadhisiddhi, 97
Sailendra empire in Sumatra, 38 f.; Indian origin, 45 ff.; origin of name, 46
Sakon Nakon, 57 f.
Sakya Muni, 124
Salmony, 7, 8 ff.
*samādhi*, 32, 76 f., 106, 123
Sām Făng Ken, 132
Sānchī, 70, 81
*sanghārāma*, 63
Sangharāja, 120
Sān Mahāpol, 97
Sanskrit inscriptions, 69, 91, 93, 114 f.
San-T'a-T'zŭ, 84
Sārnāth, 22, 23, 26
Sat Mahal Prāsāda, 97
Savannaket, 59
Sawank'alōk, meaning, 9; references, 28, 77 f., 80, 85, 116, 122 f.
Say Fon, 59
Sculpture, various materials, 74 f.
Seidenfaden, 59, 69, 71
Sên P'u, 130
Shans, the, 10
Shibbati, 105
Shin Arahan, 94, 115
Shin Popa, 99
Shwe Dagon, 27
Shwezigon, 99 f.
Siam: aboriginal race, 10; fusion of races in, 10; early immigration from India, 18
Siamese architecture, eclecticism of, 6 f.
Siamese art, French and German interest in, 7 f.; different schools, 13 ff. (table, 15; pure Indian, 15 ff.)
Sian-Chuan, 83
Sihala Bhikkus, founding of the, 132
Sirichai, 27
Siridhammanagara, 89
Sirpur, 64
Sona and Uttara, 27
Srāvastī, 23, 30 f.
Srisaket, 70
Stung Treng, 57
*stūpa*, of two kinds, 7
Suk'ōt'ai, meaning, 9; stone inscription, 49, 50 n., 53; Khmer temple ruins, 77 ff.; origin of school, 109 ff.; Tai state founded, 112; end of independence, 145
Sule Pagoda, 81
Sumana, 124, 126 n., 129, 133
Sung Nern, 69
Supanburi, 18, 128, 135
Suranga, 112
Surapāla I, 43, 105
Surāshtradhāni, 51
Surin, 55, 69
Sūryavarman I, 11, 48, 70; inscriptions, 53, 54, 58
Suvarnadvīpa, 40, 46
Suvarnapuri, 18

Tagaung, 93 f.
Tai art, contrast with Khmer, 113 f.
Tai race: origin, 9 f., 13, 82 ff.; conquest of Khmer race, 58, 78; first settlement in Siam, 85
Tai sculpture, Salmony's theory, 9 ff.
T'ai-Ho, 82
Tāk'ek, 59
Takuapā, 51
Talaing, derivation, 45 f.; in Burma, 90
T'am Pet T'ong, 69
T'am Prasāt, 69
Tāmralipti, 18, 24, 30, 45
T'ang Dynasty, Chronicles of, 90
T'ani, 120
T'an Pao, 56
Tāt Panom, 59
Temples:
  Ajantā, 22, 23
  Angkor, 61 f.
  Bādāmi, 66
  Banteai Srei, 62
  Benchamabopit, 22, 48, 76, 104, 127, 138, 147
  Chāng Lôm, 122 f., 128
  Çrī Chŭm (Suk'ōt'ai), 121 f., 124
  Çrī Sarap'et, 144, 145
  Çulamāni, 72, 78 f.
  Dudhadhari Math, 64
  Hacchimalligudi, 66
  K'ao Panom Rung, 69, 71
  Lakṣmana (Sirpur), 64
  Mahā-Tāt (Lopburi), 21, 65, 67, 73, 75, 78
  Mahā-Tāt (N. Srītammarāt), 41
  Mahā-Tāt (Pitsanulōk), 127
  Mahā-Tāt (Sawank'alōk), 72, 80 f., 128
  Mahā-Tāt (Suk'ōt'ai), 120 f., 124
  Maheyang (N. Srītammarāt), 41
  Nan Paya, 94
  Na P'ra Tāt, 40 f.
  Pā Deng, 132
  Panom Wan, 70
  P'ra Meru, 23
  P'ra Pai Lūang, 79
  P'ra Prāng Sām Yôt, 73, 80
  P'ra Sing, 86, 117, 133
  P'ra Vihāra, 54, 55, 70
  P'ra Yūn (Lamp'ūn), 129
  P'rah Khan, 148
  P'rajedi Chet Teo, 123
  P'rajedi Lūang, 133
  P'rapatom, 22, 23, 26, 27
  P'rakeo (Royal Temple), 133
  Sisawai, 80
  Somdet Nāng P'ya, 123
  Sūan Dôk, 130, 133
  Tāt Panom, 59, 60 f.
  That-Byin-Nyu (Pagān), 129
  Virupaksa, 66
Thatôn, 18, 30, 90, 94, 95
Thomas, E. J., quoted, 46, 101 f.
Tibetan Buddhism, 93
*Tillottamā*, 62
Tilōkarāja, 98, 110, 111, 132
Ting ware, 2
Tiruttani, 45
T'o-lo-po-ti, 24, 56
Trabaka, 89
Trailōkanāth, King, 78 f., 144, 146
Treang, 57
Tz'ŭ-Chou ware, 113

Ucchitta-Cakkavatti, 11, 89
Udayadityavarman, 70
Udorn, 33, 59
Udumbara Mahāsami, 129
Umā, combined with Çiva, 51
universal appeal, absent in European art, 3 f.; present in Eastern, 4
*ūrnā*, 118
*uṣnīṣa*, 29, 30, 47, 67, 75, 102, 103, 105, 111, 114, 119, 139, 140
U-T'ong, 18, 112, 135 f.; school of sculpture, transitional, 138 f.; meaning of name, 136
Uttarajiva, 115

Vajiravudh (Rama VI), King, 28, 81, 121
Vat Prei Vier, 56
Vat P'ū, 55
Victoria and Albert Museum, 75 f.
Vieng Sra, 36, 37, 44, 51
Vigrahapāla, 105
Vijaya Bāhu I, of Ceylon, 99, 114
Vincent Smith, 2, 118
Viravarman, 57
Viṣnuism at Prome, 91 f.
Voretzsch, E. A., 7, 8
Vyadhapura, 56

Wareru, 110
Wat Arannika, 120, 124
Wat Benchamabopit, 22, 104
Wat Chet Yôt, 111
Wat Chiengmān, 104, 110
Wat Çulamāni, 72
Wat Hua Wiang, 47

Wat Jetup'on, 145
Wat Kŭkŭt, 97 f., 110
Wat Mahā-Tāt, 23, 67, 73, 75
Wat Nakon Kosā T'ibodi, 146
Wat Parama Tāt, 126
Wat P'ra Meru, 23
Wat P'ra Sing, 117
Wat P'ra Tāt, 38
Wat Sī Liem, 97, 110
Wat Siriküt, 129
Wheel of the Law, 26, 60
Wood, W. A. R., 84, 135 f., 144

Yaçovarman, 55, 70
Yakṣi, images of, 51 f.
Yali, the, 103 n.
Yun Pao, 56
Yunnan, Tai principalities of, 82

Zābag, 38, 39

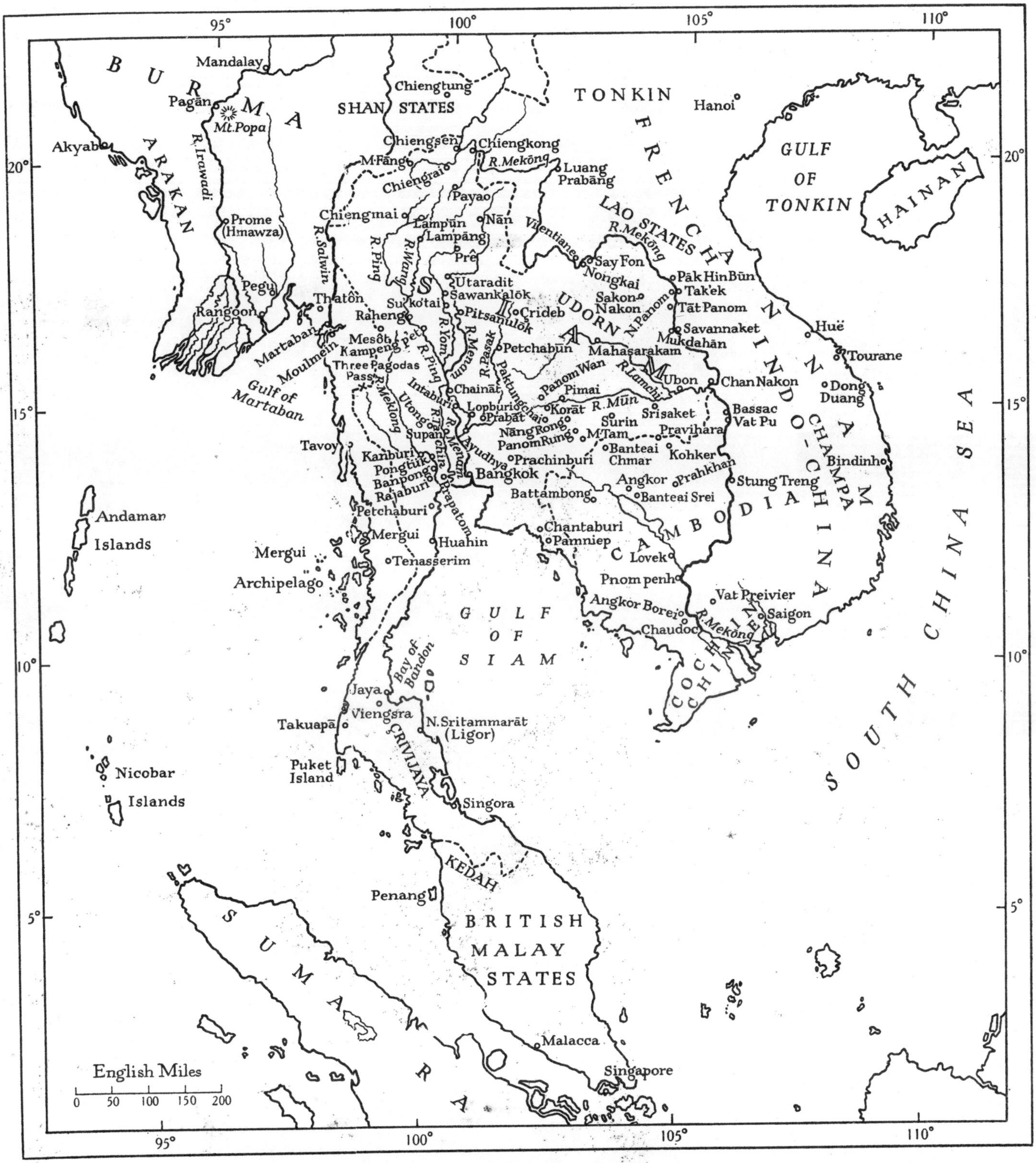


Siam and the adjoining Countries